R00341 51910

HAR   R

D0202574

THEATRE FOR YOUNG PEOPLE

cover photograph:

Honolulu Theatre for Youth: *Folktales of the Philippines.* Created and directed by Wallace Chappell. Touring set and costumes designed by Joseph Dodd. Honolulu Theatre for Youth tours each year to all six islands of the state of Hawaii through grants from the State Foundation on Culture and the Arts and the National Endowment for the Arts. This performance is in Naalehu gym on the Big Island of Hawaii.

Photo by Karen Yamamoto

THEATRE FOR YOUNG PEOPLE

A SENSE OF OCCASION

HELANE S. ROSENBERG
RUTGERS UNIVERSITY

CHRISTINE PRENDERGAST
PERFORMING ARTS REPERTORY THEATRE

HOLT, RINEHART AND WINSTON

NEW YORK   CHICAGO   SAN FRANCISCO   PHILADELPHIA
MONTREAL   TORONTO   LONDON   SYDNEY
TOKYO   MEXICO CITY   RIO DE JANEIRO   MADRID

Publisher Robert Rainier
Editor Anne Boynton-Trigg
Special Projects Editor Pamela Forcey
Production Manager Nancy Myers
Design Supervisor Renée Davis
Text Design Scott Chelius
Cover Design Fred Charles
Drawings John Traversa

Acknowledgments 19: From "Why I Write for Children" from *Nobel Lecture* by Isaac Bashevis Singer. Copyright © 1979 by Farrar, Straus and Giroux, Inc. Reprinted by permission of Farrar, Straus and Giroux, Inc. **75:** "If I Were King of the Forest" from *The Wizard of Oz.* Lyric by E. Y. Harburg, music by Harold Arlen. © 1938, 1968 Metro-Goldwyn-Mayer Inc.; © renewed 1966 Metro-Goldwyn-Mayer Inc.; rights throughout the world controlled by Leo Feist, Inc.; international copyright secured; all rights reserved; used by permission. **112–113:** The Actor's Warmup Exercises from Evangeline Machlin, *Speech for the Stage.* Copyright © 1966 by Evangeline Machlin. Used by permission of the publisher, Theatre Arts Books. **118:** James M. Barrie, from *Peter Pan.* Copyright 1928 James M. Barrie; copyright renewed 1956 Lady Cynthia Asquith and Peter Llewelyn Davies. Reprinted with the permission of Charles Scribner's Sons. **148:** Quotations from Jeffrey Sweet, *Something Wonderful Right Away.* Published by Avon Books, 1978. Reprinted by permission of the author. **256–257:** Three Don'ts from Stephen Langley, *Theatre Management in America,* revised edition, Drama Book Specialists/Publishers, New York, 1980. Reprinted by permission of the author.

Library of Congress Cataloging in Publication Data

Rosenberg, Helane S.
    Theatre for young people.

    Bibliography: p.
    Includes index.
    1. Children's plays—Presentation, etc.
I. Prendergast, Christine. II. Title.
PN3157.R66   1983   792'.0226   82–15873

ISBN 0-03-039911-4

Copyright © 1983 by Helane S. Rosenberg and Christine Prendergast

Address correspondence to:
383 Madison Avenue
New York, NY 10017

All rights reserved
Printed in the United States of America
Published simultaneously in Canada

3 4 5 6 7   039   9 8 7 6 5 4 3 2 1
CBS COLLEGE PUBLISHING
Holt, Rinehart and Winston
The Dryden Press
Saunders College Publishing

ART SECTION
FINE ARTS DIVISION

For Freddie

H.S.R.

This work is for the artist and the child who live within us all. It is especially for my nieces Katherine, Anne, Heather, Caroline, and Mary and my godchild Karun, who have given the gift of love freely and consistently, creating over and over again in my life a sense of occasion.

C.P.

ART SECTION
FINE ARTS DIVISION

FOREWORD

The subject of *Theatre for Young People* is of great importance. Live theatre, like all worthwhile pleasures in life, to be fully enjoyed and fully effective, demands a variety of skills and the development of discernment and taste. Young people's theatre can lay the foundations for an informed, intelligent, aware, participating, and thus *fully human* audience.

The authors of this book must be congratulated on tackling this all-important task with a seriousness and thoroughness that refuse to make concessions: young people's theatre to them is not a reduced or lesser form of theatre; it is, above all, *theatre,* and must be made to become theatre at its very best. That is why their emphasis, again and again, on the basic principles of good theatre, acting, playwrighting, and design is of the utmost value.

The work of actors, playwright, designers, and technicians is co-ordinated and integrated by the director. The authors' emphasis on the central role of the director, their taking the director's work as the unifying principle of their theory and practice, thus is only logical and should greatly enhance the practical usefulness of this book. In young people's theatre the director's role is, if anything, even more responsible than in theatre for adults. In addition to all the other necessary qualifications the director, here, must be a psychologist and educationist as well as a theatrical artist.

The director's role—and this is frequently overlooked even by otherwise expert critics—begins at the earliest of all stages in the process of theatrical creation: the choice of the play. It is here that "children's theatre" tends to sin most grievously; how often material is chosen that in literary quality and intelligence would offend even the most infantile audience! The younger the audience the more excellent the material that is offered to them must be: theirs, after all, is a taste that is still to be formed; the earlier they are confronted with works of the highest standard the higher will be their standards of taste in later life. The best fairy tales, the best children's books—*Robinson Crusoe, Gulliver's Travels, Alice in Wonderland*—are among the greatest masterpieces of world literature.

To achieve such high standards cannot—and will not—be easy. American theatre, even at its best, labors under the heavy handicap of a severely restricted, narrowly circumscribed style of acting. Dare I say it without unleashing a storm of protests at such blasphemy? The admirable training in the so-called "method" has greatly impoverished the range of American acting in any other style than "naturalistic." This is true at least as far as the non-musical theatre is concerned. The American musical, of course, the chief glory of American theatre in the rest of the world, has remained immune from this impoverishment: tap-dancing, singing, broad comedy are anything but naturalistic; they are "externalized," *presentational*.

I regard it as one of the main achievements of this book that its authors recognize the fact that theatre for young people must be presentational, must be able to confront its audiences with the full range and vocabulary of styles, from *commedia dell'arte* to classical verse drama, burlesque comedy, Brechtian alienation, or grotesque expressionistic acting. The subject matter of the domestic drama and comedy for which the naturalistic style is best suited is simply too uninteresting, too drab for children, with their vivid imagination, their capacity for fantasy and romance. Perhaps, if the pleas of the authors of this book are heeded, the young people's theatre may lay the foundation for a more comprehensive and artistically more varied adult theatre in this country.

This book is more than a mere theoretical treatise. It is a tool, an instrument for practical work. As such I find it admirably well conceived: it is clear, proceeds by realistically graduated steps, and is highly readable and therefore readily assimilated. It should thus be a major aid in furthering the cause to which it is dedicated— a task of major importance in the struggle to create a more humane—a more *human*—youth in the difficult, crisis-laden years ahead of them.

Martin Esslin

Professor of Drama, Stanford University
Head of BBC Radio Drama, 1963–1977
Author of *The Theatre of the Absurd; Brecht: The Man
    and His Work; Mediations; Pinter the Playwright*

PREFACE

Theatre for Young People: A Sense of Occasion is, fundamentally, about theatre for audiences aged five through fifteen; the book was written as a comprehensive textbook for university students seeking a firm introduction to the field. It is also intended to be of value to school teachers, parents, community leaders, actors, education majors, and anyone interested in devoting their efforts to creating or presenting good theatre for our children.

Readers will explore the fundamentals of young people's theatre through the comprehensive eyes of the director. We chose this particular viewpoint for realistic and practical reasons: *realistic* because often in theatre for young people the director is the only professional hired and is the central figure who should be knowledgeable in most of the topics described in this book; *practical* in that this viewpoint creates a certain focus to unify the vast scope of the book.

Each of the chapters builds on the previous one. Following an overview of the field of young people's theatre in Chapter 1, Chapters 2–7 take the reader through the creative processes and into the production phases of children's theatre. Chapters 8 and 9—management and sponsorship—cover the practical and business aspects so necessary to bring theatre successfully to the young audience. The final chapter, more research-oriented, explores the unique educational requirements and potential of the field.

Although we cannot give the gift of talent to our readers, we can try to teach the basic fundamentals and provide a body of principles that govern everyday procedures and facilitate setting sound objectives. Talent without awareness of these fundamentals and principles is valueless.

We have structured each chapter to begin with the general and proceed to the particular. The first part (usually about one-third) of each chapter reviews the basic principles pertaining to theatre in general; the second (major) part of the chapter outlines those principles that apply specifically to young people's theatre. We chose to include *general* theatre principles as a necessary, not merely useful, way to improve the current state of the art of theatre for young people. We feel that too much emphasis has been placed on the child audience and not enough on the craft.

We believe that at the core of all good children's theatre is the presentational style. The emphasis on the established principles of this style is probably the major philosophic statement in this text. Readers will become familiar with presentational aspects of the craft as these come up in each chapter.

We have chosen to use many examples from the works of such fine playwrights as James M. Barrie, Arthur Fauquez, Aurand Harris, Jonathan Levy, and Suzan Zeder. Many of the discussions center around Barrie's *Peter Pan* and Fauquez' *Reynard the Fox,* which we hope will stimulate students' curiosity enough to read these fine representative works.

Each chapter (except the first) is followed by an edited transcript of an interview with an expert in the subject matter covered in that chapter. The outstanding professionals whom we have chosen discuss their unique philosophies and experiences, offering advice to students and teachers, as well as to working practitioners. These talks may not always relate directly to the preceding text. They do, however, provide a change of pace and an element of personal contact. Thus we present role models for the developing artist.

We were fortunate to be able to collaborate with New York stage manager and designer Joel Vig, who meticulously researched and co-authored Chapter 6 for us. The many photographs were acquired through a huge national and international search. They portray some of the most illustrative work of theatres for children around the world and of professional groups who produce presentational plays for family audiences. The wonderful whimsical drawings of artist John Traversa replace thousands of words, conveying the spirit necessary for working in young people's theatre.

Lastly, we have included quotations from famous names in the field of theatre, as well as amusing stories sent to us. These pertinent statements have been interspersed throughout the book to illuminate various points.

We wish to express our gratitude to the following people, who contributed to *Theatre for Young People:*

R. Michael Baker, who developed the initial report on the Repetition Exercise; Joanne Friel, who assisted with the index; Karen Head, who coordinated the mailings of our international search for photographs.

Thanks to Performing Arts Repertory Theatre—to its board, staff, creative teams, actors, and audiences, all of whom have provided so much useful experience and information about theatre for young people; thanks, too, for the permission to reproduce its photographs and forms; and special thanks to John Henry Davis for his tremendous help and advice on the manuscript.

Thanks to the professors and staff of Rutgers University Graduate School of Education for their colleagual support.

Very happy thanks to our editors at Holt, Rinehart and Winston, Anne Boynton-Trigg and Pamela Forcey.

Thanks to all our colleagues who gave generously of their time in the interviews and particular thanks to the members of the Producers and Presenters Committee for the National Showcase—Gayle Cornelison, Moses Goldberg, Carole Huggins, Carol Jeschke, Michael Miners, Bob Moyer, Jim Rye, and John Weil—for their support; also to Jinny Koste for her encouragement.

Many thanks to our typists: Nancy Allen, R. Michael Baker, Joy Blacksmith, Cheri Buie, Esther Glat, Sally Hopkinson, Dan Kirsch, Alvin Railey, Laura VanBuskirk, and Pam Walker, and to our proofreader, Constance Bahr.

And, finally, our personal thanks to our wonderful friends and family: Elva C. Shapiro, Alfred Hellreich, Jon Klimo, Pat Pinciotti, Geraldine Chrein, Rose

Castellano, David Frackman, Madelon Beyle, Suzanne Bixby, David Bixby, Lorraine Broderick, Glen Clancy, Stephen Coleman, Ron Delehanty, Karen De Mauro, Linda DiGabriele, Larry Engler, E. E. Griffith, Pamela and Jeffrey Hill, Ronee Holmes, Ellen Jacobson, Marcia Lane, Karen Lewis, Richard Lewis, Joe Melillo, Edward Moor, Anita Nager, Vivien Niwes, Carolee Pescatore, Marjorie and Stephen Prendergast, Mary and Larry Prendergast, Ellen Rodman, Norman Rosenhaus, Fred and Betsy Sokol, Nancy Stone, Fred Vogel, Karen C. Westman, Kate Evjen Whittaker, and Peter Falotico.

We are grateful also to the following people, who read the manuscript and made constructive suggestions: Patricia M. Harter, University of California, Los Angeles; Helen A. Manfull, Pennsylvania State University; Pauline E. Peotter, Portland State University; F. Scott Regan, Bowling Green State University; Julie Thompson, Adelphi University; Lin Wright, Arizona State University.

And, in conclusion, we dedicate this book to all children, present and future, whose lives can be enhanced through the vivid exercise of their imaginations.

H.S.R.
C.P.

CONTENTS

1·A PLACE TO BEGIN

At its purest, the impulse to create theatre for children is the impulse to give a gift, smiling, without strings.

Jonathan Levy, *playwright, "A Theatre of the Imagination"*

TO THE DIRECTOR: A SENSE OF OCCASION

Once upon a time in a small community there was a wonderful theatre production for children. All the townspeople were excited about this new event; they all eagerly bought tickets. Rehearsals progressed beautifully. The script was superb. The actors developed vibrant characters. The set was glorious, the costumes and props breathtaking. On the day of the performance everything went better than expected. The curtain rose. All the children and their parents were spellbound. The action on the stage was riveting. The audience laughed; they cried. The experience was sublime. The curtain fell. The audience, moved and enlightened, left the theatre. It was a true sense of occasion.

What we are describing is an extremely "once-upon-a-time" event. Unfortunately, a great theatre experience for young people is far from an everyday occurrence. In reality children rarely see the truly excellent theatre that should be made available to them.

Theatre for young people should offer this "once-upon-a-time" world to its rapt audience. The subject doesn't always have to be a fairy tale. Whatever the topic, however, the theatre must always capture this fantastical quality. Theatre of the 1980s must offer to its young

1

audiences something different from what movies, television, and life in general offer them. It must soar.

This book is dedicated to the unique nature of young people's theatre. Its primary objective is to give you a thorough grounding in all its aspects, so that you can make plays that have an excellence and a specialness that an audience of young people deserves.

HOW THIS BOOK IS ORGANIZED

In order to accomplish as eloquently and efficiently as possible our goal to cover young people's theatre thoroughly, we have organized the book in a very particular way.

> We should no longer speak and write about the necessity of the children's theatre, but also about such issues as how to stage good productions, how we can achieve steadily improving artistic performance.
> Ilse Rodenberg,
> President, ASSITEJ
> (International Association of Theatre for Children and Young People)

- **The book addresses you as a director** We aren't advocating that all of you become directors. We use this point of view, however, as an advantageous way to present the vast amount of material. The director is at the heart of the theatre. He or she is involved in all its aspects: from choosing the play, to casting, to acting, to designing, to managing, to preparing a total theatre package. Everyone must deal with the director, so it is important for you to understand exactly what the director's role is. In fact, with the generally limited budgets in theatre for young people, the director may have to take charge of most aspects of production.

- **The first part of each chapter is devoted to general theatre principles** One of the main causes of the poor quality of much theatre for young people is that many of its practitioners have not gone back to basics—to theatre itself. The artistic principles that make *all* theatre great certainly work equally for young people's theatre. Among the basics is a thorough understanding of acting, the script, stage space, stage mechanics, and principles of realism.

- **The second part of each chapter is devoted to the special nature of theatre for young people and the special characteristics of its audience** The key to theatre for children is that it must be *presentational* (non-realistic). In the latter part of the appropriate chapters we concentrate on the well-established principles of presentational style. This emphasis on presentational style may be the most vital aspect of this book, distinguishing it from previous texts on young people's theatre.

- **Also included in the second part of each chapter are *practical*, non-artistic considerations arising from the unique nature of the young audience** Children are not only short of stature; they are also often short of attention span and certainly of money. The procedures of running a theatre and choosing a script must be modified to suit their particular needs and situation in life. Financial considerations, school-time performances, and management decisions are among the issues discussed in the second part of each chapter.

Theatre has much in common with other arts. The impulse to create is the same in all artists. It is the particular ways in which the creative spark manifests itself that separate the art forms. As you begin your study of theatre for young people, it's vital that you understand the unique nature of *all* theatre.

THE NATURE OF THEATRE

- **Theatre is alive**   Like life, but unlike a movie or a taped television show, this particular event will never again occur in this particular way. Unlike film or television, the relationship between actor and theatre audience is a sharing, interacting one. On the surface, theatre seems to be much like live television. A closer look will reveal the crucial difference: though "live" television does take place at the moment it is watched, it does not take place in the actual physical presence of an audience; those who watch it are merely living-room spectators.

- **Theatre is a group experience**   Many of the other arts can be experienced alone. Reading a story or viewing a painting is usually a

This photograph conveys the excitement only live theatre can offer to an audience. Oregon Shakespearean Festival Association: *The Comedy of Errors* by William Shakespeare. *Photo by Hank Kranzler*

Nothing can compare with the magic of the real occasion. . . . the living actor appearing before the living audience; the silence, the tension, the entrances and exits, the laughter and applause.
Sir John Gielgud,
Stage Directions

We will always want that particular form of communication, which is the theatre, which we cannot get from those ''canned goods,'' television and films.
Helen Hayes

solitary activity. Even in a museum, where there are groups of people, the individual still responds separately. In theatre as in the other performing arts, such as ballet or a concert, the group is essential. In some ways theatre is like a sporting event or a religious service: each individual is separate but is also part of a collective, taking on a nature unique to that particular audience.

- **Theatre is transitory—another characteristic it shares with the other performing arts** A painting or a novel is finished when it leaves the hands of the artist. An observer can view these works separately from the creator, days or even centuries after the artistic products have been completed. Theatre, by its nature, is being simultaneously created and experienced. The event is ephemeral; it cannot be recaptured on instant replay. When it's over, what remains is a sensory image or a cognitive idea stored in the brain.

- **Theatre is a performing art: its scripts are written to be performed** Drama is of course a branch of literature available to be read and studied. But unlike a poem or a story plays are meant to be performed. Playwrights write a script not as an end product but as a stimulus for, and one element of, the theatrical production. So the reader of a play can study the script not only for its literary qualities, but also with an eye for how it will look when staged and with an ear for how it will sound.

- **Theatre is a merger of all of the other creative arts** It is a great collaboration of many forces and products. In fact some of the greatest poets have written for the theatre; some of the greatest visual artists have built sets; some of the greatest fashion designers have created costumes; some of the greatest composers have contributed their music to the theatre. Often the audience is unaware of the vast complexities of the production process. Children even think that the people they do see—the actors—bought these clothes and furniture and are making up their lines as they go along. It is only when children have more experience with the arts that they realize the magic of theatre is a planned effort.

THE ROOTS OF THEATRE

The origin of theatre is rooted in ritual and religion. Since earliest times people have developed rites and rituals to explain the natural functions of the world: the rising and setting of the sun, the waxing and waning of the moon, the changing of seasons, birth, death. By developing complex habitual activities primitive people (who by these actions seem less primitive) tried to understand, to record, and in a sense to control

their world so that it might seem less fearful. They accomplished this in part by acting out troublesome aspects of their existence.

Even today artists paint pictures, write poetry, compose music, and make films as a way of grasping the complexities of their world. By externalizing what is inside them, artists deal with their difficult or troubling situation. Oscar Brockett, well-respected theatre scholar, says that "Art is one way of ordering, clarifying, understanding, and enjoying our experiences."

These Bulgarian folk designs and the balalaika remind us of a time when theatre was more ritual and rite than rehearsal and performance. National Youth Theatre of Bulgaria, Sofia.

BASIC ELEMENTS OF THEATRE

Surprisingly, only four elements make up the complexity of theatre:

- actors
- space, usually a stage or auditorium, even a raised platform
- script, or idea if the play is not written down
- audience, regardless of age

Every form, every style, every production represents an investigation of the relationship among elements.

THEATRE AND ITS AUDIENCE

First and foremost, theatre can be entertaining—it can be fun. People usually go to the theatre primarily to have a good time. Secondly, theatre instructs its audience. Members of the audience often learn lessons about others and about themselves without realizing they are being taught. An adolescent girl probably has a much better chance of learning about herself by watching a play like Suzan Zeder's *Step on a Crack* than by reluctantly listening to her parents lecture her about the same issues.

People often attend the theatre as a means of escaping their current situation. Lavish, peppy Broadway musicals enable audiences to forget about the world for a while. Or people go to a sad tragedy and cry for the hero or heroine. In a sense they have identified with the awful plight and are crying for themselves. But, for whatever reason, this crying somehow purges them. Theatre transports the audience to other worlds; theatre focuses on the great panorama of human activity that everyone hopes to experience.

Theoreticians of the theatre have tried to explain the psychological nature of the theatre experience. Essentially two opposing forces are at work: empathy and aesthetic distance. **Empathy**—feeling close to and understanding the character, a feeling of kinship—and **aesthetic distance**—the ability to detach oneself from the drama with the realization that an artistic event is occurring—operate simultaneously and in various balances.

ANY AUDIENCE COULD CLEARLY SEE MY EFFUSIVE EMPATHY AND MY AESTHETIC DISTANCE IF THEY WERE WILLING TO SUSPEND THEIR DISBELIEF!

Sometimes empathy wins, particularly in audiences of children. These audiences often believe the action to be really happening and consequently call out warnings to the hero. Their inability to distinguish illusion from reality and their strong empathetic reaction to the hero prevent them from being able to distance themselves.

Sometimes aesthetic distance wins. No matter how wonderfully directed the production is, the audience should be aware, at least from time to time, that they are watching a play. They should be able to sit back and view the artistic elements and plot development in an objective manner. Too much objectivity, of course, is bad for the total effect. If an actor's mustache begins to come unglued (as happened in a recent New York production of *Hamlet*), the spell is broken. The seesaw of empathy/aesthetic distance is thus tilted too far to the side of what should almost be called unaesthetic distance. Even children can simultaneously wonder if Peter Pan (in the play by James M. Barrie) will conquer Captain Hook and how the technicians rigged the flying equipment. The key here is balance.

The poet Samuel Taylor Coleridge, who also wrote about the theatre, described the experience as a "willing suspension of disbelief." Notice that he did not call the phenomenon "willing belief"; this phrase would have implied ease of believing. He meant that the audi-

Perhaps the audience will wish to suspend their disbelief just as much as these young actors do as they begin their theatrical journey. Alliance Theatre Company, Atlanta Children's Theatre: *The Halloween Tree*. Directed by Wallace Chappell.

ence must want to deny their awareness that the action is not true. So, in a sense, the people in the audience *need* to immerse themselves in the magic of theatre.

HOW THEATRE ACHIEVES ITS AIMS

Because of their need to be immersed in the theatrical experience, audiences accept many conventions of the theatre. *Conventions* are devices by which the audience is induced to accept the play as reality. In the Western world some of the conventions that are particularly relevant to the child audience include:

Fourth wall removed In most productions, when the curtain rises, the world onstage seems to be facing one direction—the audience. Not only do the actors and set face one direction, but the fourth wall also seems to be missing. Children know that in real life furniture isn't arranged in this manner, nor do people always face one direction. Yet they accept the practice easily.

Compressed time   Stage time need not correspond to real time. Plays rarely portray just one or two hours of someone's life. In fact, an entire lifetime may be portrayed in this brief amount of time. Act and scene breaks may indicate the passing of many hours or many years.

Projected voice   Actors speak loudly enough even for those in the back row to hear. Before the development of the portable microphone, actors had to project their voices to the back row. Today, particularly in Broadway musicals, actors wear microphones to assist them. Even though an intimate scene may be happening onstage, the audience readily accepts the projected or amplified sound.

Plastic space   The stage space is transformed into one of many locales. Through the use of realistic and elaborate scenery or just a single small set piece, the audience accepts the fact that the stage represents a forest, or the inside of a palace, or even the surface of the moon.

This is an example of the use of the convention that a character is unaware of being observed by other characters who are "hidden" from him, yet in full view of the audience. Empire State Youth Theatre, Albany, New York: *Twelfth Night* by William Shakespeare. Directed by William Martin.

Photo by Joseph Schuyler

Acknowledged presence In many presentational plays the characters acknowledge the presence of the audience. Through single speeches—*monologues* or *soliloquies*—characters tell the audience how they feel and even what they are going to do next. During a scene a character may make one statement to the other characters and reveal to the audience, through an *aside,* what he or she really means.

PARTS OF A DRAMA

Plot: overall structure of the play; this structure should have a beginning, middle, end

Character: the people in the play; persons reveal themselves in several ways: what the character says, what he/she does, what others say about him/her

Thought: themes, morals, ideas, arguments; overall meaning of the action

Diction: language of the play; dialogue and stage directions

Music: not just instrument works or sound tapes, but all patterned sound; the actors' voices and their characteristics—stress, volume, tempo, duration, quality

Spectacle: all the visual elements of the production, such as costumes, scenery, props, lights, and, of course, physical movement

---

DRAMATIC FORMS

Tragedy: Presents serious action, maintains serious mood; attempts to ask basic questions about people's existence; the protagonist or hero should arouse sympathy and admiration

Comedy: Shows the humor and incongruity in events or in people; often based on some deviation from normal in action, character, thought, or speech; audience can remain more objective

Melodrama: Sometimes called *tragicomedy;* prevailing attitude is fusion of serious and comic; action usually contains a powerful threat to well-being of an innocent protagonist; also shows character's rescue from terrible ruin at ultimate last moment; good triumphs, bad is punished (most popular television form)

Farce: Comedy of situation, in which buffoonery, accident, and coincidence play important part

---

THE DIRECTOR: A RECENT PHENOMENON

Interestingly enough, the position of director did not exist until the 1870s. At that time the study of human behavior had begun to progress so rapidly that differences in opinion about character motivation began to surface during rehearsals. The variety of coaching methods and the differences in how actors wished to be treated began to sabotage the rehearsal process. Also, designers began to develop historically accurate sets and costumes instead of flat backdrops. The desire to develop these intricate sets, coupled with the technical discoveries of the time, made the design aspect grow in importance.

The rehearsal and construction period grew increasingly more complex as all elements—settings, lighting, costumes, and stage groups—needed to be harmonized. It became increasingly clear that someone must be in charge of integrating these elements. In other words, someone who could *direct* the production was needed.

In Germany in the 1870s the Duke of Saxe-Meiningen became the first individual to be totally in charge of a complex production. What the Duke did that was very different from those who had worked as actor/managers or stage managers before him was to merge both people and technical elements into a unified artistic creation. In the hundred odd years since that time famous and influential directors have explored all aspects of this interpretive and creative process, reflecting their own particular points of view.

The director's primary function is staggeringly enigmatic. The better the task is performed, the less the audience is aware of the director. He or she must take a strong stand throughout the entire process but not telegraph these decisions to the audience. In order to best accomplish this, directors must arm themselves with as much expertise as possible about every aspect of theatre. Finally, above all else, directors must understand that theatre is an event that celebrates life.

> *A good director is much harder to find than a good playwright.*
> Joseph Papp,
> *New York Magazine*

> *The ideal director is someone with a passionate interest in acting, plays, and the creative process that leads to performance, yet with no desire to take an active part in stage managing, acting, or design: a finger in every pie, overall responsibility for the artistic quality, yet bearing none of the burdens of the individual tasks; something of a dramatist, something of an actor, something of a technician.*
> Hugh Morrison,
> *Directing in the Theatre*

THEATRE FOR YOUNG PEOPLE: A SENSE OF A SLIGHTLY MODIFIED OCCASION

All the principles of good theatre in general apply as well to theatre for young people. Many talented practitioners in the field say that theatre for children is like theatre for adults, only better. However, they provide no guidelines to define what is better. Theatre practitioners in the 1980s must ask some penetrating questions about the organic nature of young people's theatre and provide some answers and procedures that can be put into practice *now*. To discover what exactly this nature is requires careful thought and clear logic.

DEFINING THE TERMS

The term *children's theatre* is often very confusing. It can refer to plays for audiences of children or productions performed by children for adults or those performed by children for children. Because of this confusion we will generally avoid this term.

The terms *theatre for young people* and *young people's theatre* will be used throughout this book to denote productions for audiences of young people aged five through fifteen, performed by adults.

The Children's Theatre Association of America (CTAA), the largest association of practitioners and scholars who work in university, community, and professional theatres for young people, has defined and elaborated on these terms. Theatre for young people "consists of the performance of largely predetermined theatrical art work by living actors in the presence of an audience of young people." It embraces the following characteristics:

- The performance may be based on written scripts of traditional form or may be adapted, devised, or developed improvisationally.
- The dramatic material of the performance may be a single story line or a series of sketches.
- The performers are highly skilled adult actors, with especially talented child actors in child roles.
- The full spectrum of theatrical arts and crafts is utilized to enhance the actors' performances: costumes, makeup, lighting, scenery, properties, sound, and special effects.
- The audience may be assembled in any configuration, utilizing a variety of spaces described by any number of theatrical forms.

*Theatre **by** children and youth* is a variant of theatre for young people in which the performers are children and/or teenagers rather than adults. Performers are usually no younger than ten; audiences are usually made up of children younger than the performers as well as interested adults.

The cutoff point between those who can attend theatre performances intended for a general audience and those who should attend theatre for young people is approximately age fifteen. At that age young people take a great developmental leap and are more equipped to view plays that have been directed for adult audiences.

In the practice of children performing plays for various audiences (the fifth-grade Christmas play) the emphasis is more on the developmental process for the actors. We have chosen to write about theatre for audiences of young people performed by adult actors. These actors may be professional, collegiate, or community. The primary focus here is on the development of a good final product.

A term that is often confused with children's theatre is *creative drama,* which describes the process of conducting drama activities with young people. According to the CTAA committee to redefine creative drama, "Creative drama is an improvisational, non-exhibitional, process-oriented form of drama in which participants are guided by a leader to imagine, enact, and reflect upon experiences, real or imagined." Creative drama rarely results in a formal production. How the participants grow, not how they perform, is the essence of creative drama. Often practitioners of theatre for young people are involved with creative drama. They feel that working on both the process of

The only factor that distinguishes youth theatre from the stage for grownups is the fact that the spectators are children.
Zenovi Korogodsky,
Director, Leningrad Theatre for Young Spectators

drama with children and the product of theatre for children helps give them a total picture of the field. Universities often award degrees in this joint specialization, called *child drama.*

THE ROOTS OF THEATRE FOR YOUNG PEOPLE

The current state of theatre for young people in America is the result of a number of factors. Its traditions, its relationship to education, its financial considerations, and the influence of American society have clearly affected what is currently being performed. Primarily a twentieth-century movement, theatre for young people has grown steadily, if fitfully, from a few isolated occurrences in major cities to a vast number of professional, university, and community-produced plays throughout the United States. Currently, on the positive side, the children's theatre movement can be credited with a large number of devoted practitioners, strong university programs, a recent upsurge in professionally produced plays, large-scale festivals and showcases, and bilingual companies.* But for the most part, as we stated earlier, what is being produced is often quite disappointing in contrast to its limitless potential.

Going back to the roots of young people's theatre in America is one way of understanding why the current situation exists. Many excellent

The Don Quijote Experimental Children's Theatre in New York presents bilingual productions (Spanish/English) with a strong emphasis on visual exposition that can be universally understood. *Peter and the Wolf.*

*A bilingual play appeals to audiences who speak one language (Spanish, for example) and are learning to speak another (English, for example). During each performance, both languages are spoken. One character, possibly an older adult, will speak in the foreign language. The younger character will answer partially in Spanish and then in English, as if to teach the Spanish-speaker the new language.

books and articles have been written that trace the development of the movement in America.* Instead of chronicling its history, we have isolated some specific factors that may help explain current conditions.

Children's theatre in America (1) has been strongly bound to the educational movement; (2) reflects the values of American society; (3) is often based on misinterpretations of children and theatre.

ROOTS IN EDUCATION AND SOCIAL WORK

Early practitioners of young people's theatre were social workers who had as one of their primary objectives the Americanization of immigrant children. Theatre was one way to teach these children in English about American social habits, through one of the "better things in life." Theatre was a great means to entice the children and their parents to come to settlement houses and arts centers in cities with large immigrant populations. Although these producers were well-intentioned and the movement owes them a great debt, some of the productions may have been less than good. These social workers and teachers were always enthusiastic, but they were untrained in theatre. An early book on children's theatre stated, "Children's theatre is distinct from adult theatre in motivation, writing, and interpretation." A statement like this expresses a real misunderstanding of the real nature of theatre for young people.

The close relationship among educators and people who desired social change continued to influence the growth of the movement. In the 1930s one of the largest influences was the Association of Junior Leagues of America, a service organization of women who, as one of their primary objectives, hoped to bring social and artistic reforms to the communities in which they lived. Again, these women were well-intentioned but often untrained in the theatre. Some of these clubs did eventually sponsor other companies instead of producing plays themselves. But until the late 1950s and 1960s these women's organizations continued to produce children's theatre, consequently taking it further from the mainstream of professional theatre.

One of the most significant influences on the children's theatre movement in America—still hotly debated today—is the relationship of theatre to schools. This relationship developed quite naturally: Children spend a large part of their days in schools. During the school day producers could take plays directly to the classrooms or auditoriums, or they could arrange for large groups of schoolchildren to come to the

*Two books are Nellie McCaslin's *Theatre for Children in the United States: A History* (Norman: University of Oklahoma Press, 1971) and Charlotte Chorpenning's *Twenty-one Years with Children's Theatre* (Anchorage, KY: The Anchorage Press, 1955).

Many productions, such as this participation piece, tour to schools, presenting their plays on portable stages in the school gymnasium or all-purpose room. Yellow Brick Road Shows, Newport Beach, California. At left is Rita Grossberg, who is interviewed in Chapter 3.

theatre. The logistics of selling became school-oriented, influencing not only the marketing of such productions but also the product.

Two school-related factors permanently changed the scope of children's theatre: the need to sell productions to schools, and the naiveté of school principals and teachers about the theatre. Companies often sold their plays in terms of their relationship to the curricula. Plays were often altered or completely rewritten to teach about American history or dental hygiene. Plays can teach. But when teaching objectives overwhelm entertainment objectives, the plays often diminish in artistic impact. What began to happen was that productions were strongly didactic and little else.

School officials often didn't know how to choose productions for their schools. Slick salespeople could easily convince a principal that a silly morality tale (or whatever else they were pushing) was the ultimate in theatre. The quality of the play was rarely discussed. Administrators, who were often uninformed and confused about what youngsters liked, booked plays sight unseen. Instead of trusting their own judgment about the artistic merits of a production, they somehow believed (because the producers told them so) that children loved anything as long as it was loud and fast and 45 minutes in duration.

In the late 1960s there emerged in England a movement called Theatre in Education (TIE), which tried to sort out educational and theatrical objectives. Several companies, most notably the Creative Arts Team in New York, were developed that utilize the British TIE model.

But not until the late 1970s in America did the majority of practitioners begin to separate and understand these two very different goals of theatre for young people: education and entertainment.

REFLECTION OF AMERICAN SOCIETY

As any theatre movement reflects the country and time of its growth, so American theatre for children cannot be insulated from the influences and objectives of our twentieth-century society. In general, three social factors strongly affect the movement. First, contrary to popular belief, America is not a child-oriented society. Second, America has a limited tradition of art-making. Third, America is a profit-oriented society.

America does not revere childhood. Of course, most parents love and care for their children, but America has been a society that has encouraged quick adulthood. In the early development of this nation many children were put to work; they were encouraged, by the puritanical society, to be moral and good or else face terrible punishments. For these economic and religious reasons children didn't remain children for long. Times have changed. Yet for different reasons today's children are encouraged to precociously embrace the sophistication of rock music, makeup, dating, and independence. Simply paging through contemporary magazines will show that America in the 1980s is a teenage-oriented society. (Even adults want to return to being teenagers.) Because childhood is seen as a dependent time, many American parents push their children to mature quickly. Consequently, theatre for young people is regarded as "baby stuff" for the very youngest children, who will soon grow out of it.

Also apparent is that the tradition of art-making in America has only recently come into its own and still remains on shaky ground. Theatre in particular, unlike some art and music, has not been valued. In contrast to a country like England, where a repertory theatre is the pride of many communities, Americans do not have theatres readily available to them. With the decline of vaudeville (variety shows) most theatres were converted to movie houses. The emergence of television further established the twentieth century as an unhappy period for theatre in America. The 1960s and 1970s saw a growth in number and quality of productions because of the money available through the National Endowment for the Arts, the federal agency that provided funding for arts activities. Cutbacks in the 1980s again threaten theatre's lifeblood. It is safe to say that the majority of Americans still choose to attend a sports event over a theatre event. Theatre often fights a losing battle.

Financially, America was founded on the principles of free enterprise and open competition. Moneymaking is one of America's biggest achievements. Children have few if any independent money sources. So, unless the parent can be enticed to buy what is being offered to children, the product of theatre will not be sold. The fact that the consumer of children's theatre is not the buyer continues to make the life of a producer very difficult. Good plays for young people cost as much to produce as high-quality adult plays. Yet adults will rarely pay the same price for their children's entertainment as they pay for their own. The result is that producers cut artistic corners to sell the play cheaply enough to be purchased by the family while also trying to appeal to the person with the money—the parent or school administrator.

MISINTERPRETATIONS OF CHILDREN AND THEIR THEATRE

Perhaps the biggest contributing factor to the current state of the art is what children's author Maurice Sendak has termed "adults' amnesia about childhood." Adults only remember selected incidents of their childhood, and these are colored by the passage of time, by subsequent experiences, and in general by adult sensibilities. Having been a child doesn't qualify an adult to be an expert on children. In fact, most

The Masque of Beauty and the Beast is an adaptation of the popular fairy tale. Because of their consistent popularity, fairy tales form a significant portion of the dramatic material for young people. Eastern Michigan University Theatre of the Young: *The Masque of Beauty and the Beast*. Written and directed by Virginia Koste.

adults have a very unrealistic view of what children like and appreciate in terms of art. They try to give children only what is sweet and delicate, based on how they recall their own childhoods.

The best authors of children's books and plays have a more realistic view of the inner torments of childhood. In *The Uses of Enchantment* noted child psychologist Bruno Bettelheim discusses the psychological value of violence and horror in fairy tales for young people.* James M. Barrie, the author of some of the most idealistic (yet conflict-ridden) stories for children, realized that children are often heartless, but he loved them, nevertheless.

Many in the field of young people's theatre try to please the members of the audience, whom they don't really understand, instead of trying to please themselves. What happens is that the production becomes increasingly more distanced from its creators. Not knowing exactly what to do or what principles to base their work on, these practitioners write scripts for, act in, and direct productions that are not based on any criteria of excellence and as a result are not exciting for any audience, children or adults.

Even critics don't know how to evaluate the work; few reviews appear in newspapers. It is conceivable that many people gravitate toward the field not for any real love of children, but because they know that there will be little censoring. George Thorn, theatre manager and consultant for the Foundation for the Extension and Development of the American Professional Theatre (FEDAPT), asks a very astute question, "Do people tend to go into children's theatre to a certain degree because there is that ability to be the one-person show and not to expose or test themselves?" Many self-designated "geniuses" have been drawn to young people's theatre as the last safe frontier of the 1980s.

Excellent practitioners who work in adult theatres often shy away because they don't realize that all theatre must be based on the same principles of excellence, whoever makes up its intended audience. Sadly, they miss the chance of experimenting with the vast possibilities of theatre for young people. They are frightened of, or disinterested in, having to please a young audience, instead of realizing that they need only please themselves. The ultimate result is that many less adventuresome artists enter the field, at least on the professional level.

This situation is not unalterable. As a new student of the field, you cannot expect to change the world—at least not tomorrow. In fact, many of these influences contributing to the state of the art are probably ingrained. America may gradually evolve into an art-loving, child-devoted society in your lifetime, but you can't control society and the

THE ESSENCE OF THEATRE FOR YOUNG PEOPLE

*Bruno Bettelheim, *The Uses of Enchantment: The Meaning and Importance of Fairy Tales* (New York: Alfred A. Knopf, 1976).

system. You can, however, completely control the artistic product. If you develop a solid artistic grounding in theatre for young people, you can make a great contribution. But, before you begin, you need to master two separate but interrelated sets of principles:

- **You need to understand the nature of the child audience** The special nature of the audience, however, need not become an obsession. The real key is the style.
- **More importantly, you need to master the principles of presentational style (non-realism)** These principles are chosen for their appropriateness and applicability to the child audience.

If you attend 100 plays for children—some good, some bad—you will notice that the common denominator of almost all the aspects that worked (for you and for the child audience) was the presentational style. The key to making theatre for young people is that it must be presentational. The principles of the presentational style, all time-tested, give you something very specific upon which to base your theatre practice for young audiences, instead of some of the current practices, which have grown up unaffected by the universal standards of good theatre. Then you can worry less about pleasing your audience, and worry more about pleasing yourself. Remember, all good theatre for young people is entertaining to adults as well as to children.

UNDERSTANDING THE AUDIENCE

Ideally, everyone involved with young people should have a firm grasp of child psychology and education as these fields relate to artistic principles. A strong knowledge of group dynamics, developmental levels, and other art forms for children can strongly affect the theatre production. We encourage you to read good books about children as well as for children. We also encourage you to watch television and movies for children, to attend theatre productions, and to talk with young people. What is absolutely essential for you to determine, before you can proceed, is how the audience of children differs from an audience of adults.

Some adults have an instinctive talent for dealing with children and keeping them mesmerized. Others, no matter how much they learn, don't relate well to children. Many practitioners in the field of young people's theatre have a special talent of knowing instinctively what children like. Even with this talent, you must understand these three basics concerning the child audience.

1. An audience of children is more homogeneous than an adult audience The producer of plays for children can know more about what to expect: a more uniform response. The child audience shares the common but limited experiences of being children. Knowing the age and experience level of the audience can be a helpful factor in choosing appropriate scripts. Many of the stories that seem old hat to adults are fresh and exciting to children. Classics and fairy tales continue to delight audiences of each succeeding generation.

2. Children have fewer personal, cultural, and social experiences to draw from

An audience of young people most likely has never been to college, never driven a car, never vacationed alone, and never held a full-time job. Children have not had the rich variety of life experiences that adults have had. Therefore, the subject matter of plays for children must take this into consideration. We're not suggesting that all plays for young people be about bunnies or princesses, but certainly a sophisticated satire in which the audience must first understand the reference point (for example, a satire about George Bernard Shaw) would be inappropriate. Also inappropriate would be a play about explicit sex or adult psychoses. However, there are topics children know very little about, such as political intrigue or societal problems, that can be the subject of plays, as long the issues are properly introduced.

Children are not as socially well-developed as adults. Consequently, they have not learned appropriate theatre behavior. They must be taught that they shouldn't run up and down the aisles or talk during the performance. They must learn to deal with ticket sellers, ushers, and programs. Practitioners in the theatre who do not understand this fact are often overwhelmed. After an excellent collegiate production in a large agricultural center in the Midwest, for example, the children did not applaud at the final curtain. They quickly filed out, laughing and talking. The actors were devastated. What they didn't realize was that the children didn't know they were supposed to applaud.

3. Children aged five through fifteen can be divided into three developmental levels

Some companies produce plays for general audiences of young people; some develop plays for a very small and specific age group. The decision to age-range is a very complex one that includes such factors as marketing, liaisons with schools, and audience numbers. Although all child audiences do have similarities, there are also specific differences in logic, language, behavior, and interests. Before you can make decisions about the possibilities of age-ranging, consider these stages of development, as outlined by Jean Piaget, noted theoretician in the field of child development:

Children under the age of seven are in the *preoperational stage* of development. Although they have language and are capable of symbolic thought, they have difficulty organizing these symbols into concepts and rules, and they really lack the ability to take the point of view of someone else. The choice of plays for the preoperational child should reflect these limitations. In the *concrete operational stage*, ages seven to

These are Nobel-Prize-winner Isaac Bashevis Singer's ten reasons why he writes for children:

1. Children read books, not reviews. They don't give a hoot about the critics.

2. Children don't read to find their identity.

3. They don't read to free themselves of guilt, to quench their thirst for rebellion, or to get rid of alienation.

4. They have no use for psychology.

5. They detest sociology.

6. They don't try to understand Kafka or Finnegan's Wake.

7. They still believe in God, the family, angels, devils, witches, goblins, logic, clarity, punctuation, and other such obsolete stuff.

8. They love interesting stories, not commentary, guides or footnotes.

9. When a book is boring, they yawn openly, without any shame or fear of authority.

10. They don't expect their beloved writer to redeem humanity. Young as they are, they know it is not in his power. Only adults have such childish illusions.

Nobel Prize Address

One group of elementary school children were so unused to live theatre that they kept touching the actors. They couldn't believe they were three-dimensional.
Patricia Snyder,
Director, Empire Youth Theatre, in The New York Times

twelve, the children are capable of logical thought about properties, facts, and relationships that involve real objects and events. Play material and staging can be more sophisticated for this level and reflect the increased development of the children. At the age of twelve and up, in the *stage of formal operations,* the children can transcend concrete reality and think about what might be. They can reason about hypothetical situations, detect inconsistency in propositions, and search for higher-order rules. Plays for this age can be detailed and complex and appeal to their growing development.

It is also important to remember that these stages describe the individual child, not the collective audience. The collective age of the audience is often brought down to the lowest common denominator. If many children in an audience of young people seven to ten are younger than eight, the older children (aged nine and ten) may be brought down to the level of the younger children. Conversely, if many teenagers are in the audience, the preteens wishing to emulate the older ones may try particularly hard to act more mature.

PRESENTATIONAL STYLE IS THE KEY

Although you must understand the child audience, in young people's theatre in America too much emphasis has been placed on audience and not enough on craft. Certainly, the children must be considered in such decisions as choosing the script or setting the ticket price. You must try not to be obsessed with the child during the creative process. (Of course the image of the rapt audience member will reappear in your mind's eye from time to time.) Your direct consideration of the child as audience member need not return until the final stages of production, when the play is refined and sold to the public.

In books on theatre for adults no such emphasis is placed on the audience. Likewise, theatre for young people must be put into the mainstream of theatre. It cannot be stressed enough that the essential issue is not how to construct a spinning wheel or how to stage a chase (although both of these aspects must be deftly handled). Dealing first with such details will set you off the track and leave you groping for a way to unify the production.

The key to theatre for young people, especially in today's world, is that it should be presentational in style. In order to direct, to act in, or to design for this theatre, you must study the principles of various presentational styles. This information will give you a basis for your major artistic decisions and will free you to consider craft instead of audience.

STYLE DESCRIBES THE WORLD OF THE PLAY

Style is one of the most misused words in the theatre vocabulary. To say an actor has "style" can mean that he or she is presenting a slick,

The innate exuberance of the presentational style works well for audiences of young people. Note the bold choices of gesture, stance, and facial expression which help to create a visually and vocally riveting performance. Indiana Repertory Theatre: *Scapin* by Molière. Directed by Sanford Robbins.

technically facile performance, or that the actor's personality or finesse is appealing to you. A description of a production as "stylized" can mean that it was not realistic and utilized much of the staging, characters, and costumes of a period different from today. Or "stylized" can refer to a production in which choices are made with no particular point of reference. Costumes and furniture from any period or staging chosen for its humorous aspects (not its appropriateness) characterize these productions—essentially assuming a "free license" to do anything.

When we talk about style, we mean the behavioral characteristics shared by the play's characters. Style is the precondition of the whole play; it colors every aspect of production—how the characters walk, what they say, what they value, what they wear, and how they move. At the core of the style may be a particular period, such as Restoration style. A playwright may also be so significant and prolific that his or her works establish a style that not only describes the period, but also embraces the characteristics of a body of work, such as in the style of Molière.

There are probably as many theatrical styles as there are periods in history and playwrights who view the world in a unique way. Style falls into two basic categories: *Realism* and *Non-Realism*. The division between realism and non-realism does not imply that one category of style is genuine (or real) and the other is not. The basic distinction between realism and non-realism is the manner in which the play portrays the world.

Realism in the theatre refers to what is recognizable from everyday life; events that follow an existing cause-and-effect sequence. Laws of gravity, for example, would hold true in plays of realism. Plays of realism could also be called **representational** in style because they try to *represent* the world to the audience: the actual place, the actual time, and real-life person. Performers in plays of realism are trying to convince the audience that they are not simply playing the character, but that they *are* the character (only during performance, of course).

One of the best examples of representational style is the television soap opera. Although some of the characters and situations are slightly exaggerated, and time is somewhat compressed to hold the interest of the television audience, most soap operas are realistic. Houses look like today's houses; characters wear clothes that might be purchased in department stores; lines that characters speak can be heard throughout the country. Soap operas are one art form that tries to *represent* a view of contemporary society.

Plays of non-realism do not always follow the logical principles of cause-and-effect. In plays of non-realism there are many conventions that do not mirror the world as it is. Laws of gravity may not hold true. Characters or props may fly through the air (James M. Barrie's *Peter Pan* and Mary Melwood's *Five Minutes to Morning*) or jump out of boxes (Suzan Zeder's *Step on a Crack*). Characters may speak directly to the audience in an aside (William Shakespeare's *As You Like It*). Characters may be animals who talk (Arthur Fauquez' *Reynard the Fox*). Costumes may be made of paper bags (The Paper Bag Players of New York). Actors may play many parts during the performance, showing the audience that they put on a simple costume piece to indicate their character change (Paul Sills' *Story Theatre*). Characters may sing and dance (Aurand Harris' *Rags to Riches*) or speak in poetry (Shakespeare's *Macbeth*).

The plays of non-realism are also called **presentational** in style because they try to *present* the world to the audience. No attempt is made to fool the audience into thinking that this place does exist; the idea is only that it could exist in the realm of the imagination. A presentaional play invites the audience to enter another world (adaptations of Lewis Carroll's *Alice in Wonderland*) which may be a suggestion or a symbol of life. The audience is often drawn in, even with actual physical participation.

Although there are many separate styles that fit into the categories of realism and non-realism, the chart may help you clarify the contrast. In the following chapters we will discuss specific styles in more detail.

Style is the way we make the world larger than our petty personal concerns and identity, waking us to a greater life both within and without.
Orlin Corey,
"Go Make Ready"

REALISM (REPRESENTATIONAL)	NON-REALISM (PRESENTATIONAL)
EXAMPLES	
Barefoot in the Park	*Macbeth*
Abe Lincoln of Pigeon Creek	*The Wiz*
STORY	
Events might happen in everyday life; logical cause and effect	Events occur that may never happen in real life; anything goes.
CHARACTERS	
People we could see every day	Characters who could exist, or even may have existed, but who have magical or larger-than-life properties, or who could never exist, like animals that talk or boys who fly
TIME AND PLACE	
Time as close to actual passing time as possible; place could really be visitied; locales are usually few in number because of logistics of set changes.	The action may take place over many years; the place may be imaginary or where we could never travel, like the sun; action may also take place in several different locales.
SCENERY/COSTUMES	
Scenery as close to existing rooms and houses as possible; clothes that might be worn on the street	Scenery just suggests places, (could even be boxes); clothes suggestive of other times; people may dress like animals or objects
DIALOGUE	
Ordinary conversation, although selected enough not to be boring	People may talk in verse, or sing, or use archaic language of another time, like "thee" and "methinks"
ACTING	
Actors portray people as they behave in real life—of course, with some selective artistic process; actors *represent* real people	Actors execute actions, such as singing and dancing, in ways not typically experienced; actors *present* their world to the audience
AUDIENCE	
Actors don't acknowledge the audience, except on isolated occasions	Often actors ask audience to respond or even participate; audience is almost always invited into the world of the play

AS YOU CAN SEE, I'M **PRESENTATIONAL** IN STYLE... WHEN YOU CAN SEE ME AT ALL!

The alteration of natural forms and phenomena is common to many of the scripts in the theatre for young people. This is the adaptation of Shakespeare's *Titus Andronicus* by the Actors' Theatre of Louisville: *Andronicus* by William Shakespeare, Jon Jory, and Jerry Blatt.
Photo by David S. Talbott

It is a hack's notion that a great work of art is something unbelievable every word of which is true; the artist knows the reverse to be art: something every word of which is invented but rings piercingly, sublimely true.
John Simon,
New York Magazine

PRESENTATIONAL STYLE WORKS WELL

Why style? Children get enough realism from television and movies as well as from life itself. To make theatre especially meaningful, as well as to ensure its place in a multimedia society, you must take full advantage of its unique potential. The presentational style helps young people focus because it often factors out complex motivation and transforms time and space. Theatre must help children make sense of the myriad of perceptions they are receiving every day. The practitioners of young people's theatre need to simplify the world, to eliminate the extraneous. Realism gives kids too much too soon.

It's not so unusual that many of Michel Saint-Denis' definitions in his book *Theatre: The Rediscovery of Style* have the word "secret" in them. He states, "Style does not lie. It is the expression of real understanding, of deep communication, of the world and its secrets." And he further explains that "there is something secret about style." There *is* something secret about style. It affords children a view of the world that can reach directly to their hearts. You can illuminate by paring away. By focusing and selecting for children, you present more, not less. Style can create a kind of "conspiracy" between the child audience and the performer.

This book is written from the particular point of view of the director, because the director is the artist who has the unique opportunity to become completely immersed in every aspect. We reemphasize that theatre for children cannot be as profitable as theatre for the general public. So it cannot afford a specialist to handle every aspect. This requires that the director assume a greater responsibility in the entire production. It would be easier, and certainly more passive, to learn the field from the critic's position. Instead, we offer you a point of view that places you in the thick of every decision, practical as well as artistic: acting, designing, sponsoring, managing, producing, educating, as well as directing. Thus this text is not only advantageous for students who want to direct, but is also particularly relevant for students who want to learn about each specialty in the field.

THE CHILD IN YOU

Director and publisher Orlin Corey terms theatre for young people "universal theatre." It is universal because all of you who attend theatre have a child within you. Some people have more of the soul of a child within them than do others. Getting in touch with that soul, yet retaining your adulthood, is the special talent required of the artists in theatre for young people. You must never cease to be taken in by the raw, touching drama of a girl's search for her dog or a boy's coming of age. The nature of these struggles must appeal to both the child and the adult in you. You must find interesting what children find interesting, or you will never be able to please yourself. Instead of looking for

TO THE DIRECTOR OF THEATRE FOR YOUNG PEOPLE

A real creation in the field of children's theatre can be done only by artists who have kept a child's soul, together with the intelligence, the formation, the experience, and the culture of an adult. Grigore Pognat, *actor, Director of Theatre for Young People in Romania*

In the presentational style, a characteristic is that the audience is "invited into" the world of the play. This actor, with props, costume, puppets, and media, is doing just that. Daniel Llords and Llords' "International": *Petrouchka* by Igor Stravinsky. Daniel Llords as the charlatan Puppet Master.

I think theatre for young people is a thrilling, thrilling field because the only boundaries are our own as artists. There are certain boundaries in adult theatre, bounds of text, bounds of place, that don't exist for young people's theatre, that you do not have to have anywhere at any time for any reason. So, it's very exciting and it's very challenging. And how do you meet up to that challenge? That is the question.
Zaro Weil,
former artistic director, Metro Theatre Circus

hidden adult meanings, if you direct to please that child within you, the kids will enjoy it too.

The process of directing for children is not static; it is not like going back again and being a child. It is taking that child forward with you into the new integration of things you've learned in college and in adulthood as well as of all the new modes of thinking that you've acquired along the way. As an artist in the field, you will realize that the artistic possibilities are boundless. The work is limited only by your own imagination. In no other field can you experiment with so much abandon, with so much acceptance by your audience. And finally, you can fulfill a dream of so many adults. You can relive your childhood, this time experiencing it with all the wisdom and sophistication you have acquired.

In this highly presentational piece, Alice grows with the help of the two men lifting her. Note how Alice is held by the two actors, with her six-foot legs dangling. Dallas Theatre Center: *Alice in Wonderland.* Designed by Irene Corey.

2·THE DIRECTOR AS INTERPRETIVE ARTIST

The directing of a play is a turn of the hand, a turn of the mind and of the heart, a function of such sensitiveness that everything human can enter into it.

Louis Jouvet, *"The Profession of the Director"*

Artists fall into two categories: creative and interpretive.* Creative artists include composers, sculptors, poets—those who conceive an idea and then through their respective media or instruments give form to their concepts. Interpretive artists are those who perform or interpret what has already been written, composed, or developed. Music, dance, and drama are art forms which are not complete until the interpretive artist interprets and/or performs what has already been created. Examples of interpretive artists include directors, conductors, musicians, dancers, and actors—all artists who do not produce a work out of the void, but who interpret what has already been created so that the work reaches complete fruition.†

The most traditional, and probably the most complex, function assumed by the director is the role of the interpretive artist. Reading a play script, developing an interpretation, communicating this interpretation to the actors and technicians, positioning the actors on stage,

And yet I think no artist worth his salt will feel he can rely on inspiration. Inspiration must be backed up by a very cast-iron technique.
Tyrone Guthrie,
"An Audience of One"

*Classifying an artist as interpretive does not signify that this artist is not creative, in the sense of original or clever.

†When directors or actors create their own scripts, they can be classified as creative artists.

27

and scores of other tasks must be accomplished by the interpretive artist, the director. At the core of the director's function as interpretive
artist are a knowledge and understanding of three separate but interrelated elements: (1) the stage space, (2) the actor, (3) the script.

MASTERING THE INTERPRETIVE ELEMENTS: SPACE, ACTOR, SCRIPT

The first step is to master the basic elements of your craft. These elements do not change when you interpret scripts for audiences of
young people. In fact, the best preparation is to develop an excellent
grasp of the basic elements and to investigate their possibilities. These
elements are at the core of the craft of directing, no matter who is in
the audience.

THE SPACE   Although each theatre space may seem very different from every other
theatre space because of locale, architecture, members of the audience,
lighting, and current production, there are only four basic types
of stage spaces and actor/audience configurations: (1) proscenium,
(2) arena, (3) thrust, (4) flexible.

Proscenium   A proscenium stage is the stage most typically found in
large theatres. In this type of stage the proscenium arch forms a picture
frame around the area of action. The audience sits in rows of seats
separated from the stage and looks directly ahead to a raised stage

area. The mood suggested by proscenium is often grand; audiences of young people often feel that proscenium staging is magical or larger than life.

Arena   Arena is also called *theatre-in-the-round* because the audience sits all around the outside of the round or rectangular stage where the action is taking place. The acting area is usually entered through the audience and may be higher, lower, or on the same level as the audience. Arena staging suggests a more intimate relationship between actor and audience. Young people say they feel more a part of the action. Because arena stages can be set up in any large hall, arena staging has become increasingly popular during the last decade. A director of theatre for young people must learn to exploit the arena, which has great potential especially because its pictures are so different from those of movies and television.

Thrust   Thrust is the stage that sticks out, or "thrusts into," the audience, who sit on three sides of the stage. The stage is usually higher than the audience. Actors enter from the exit to the wings on the one side where the members of the audience are not seated, or from one of two step units at the edge of the thrust, each called a *vomitorium*. Thrust is almost a combination of proscenium and arena.

Flexible staging   Flexible staging is a term used to describe any actor/audience configuration that does not fall into the above three categories. Stage spaces that include many platforms all around and through the audience, or a wheeled ministage that can be moved around during performance, or staging that involves the audience itself moving from place to place, all can be classified as flexible staging.

THE PROSCENIUM STAGE: AREAS

A standard orientation has been established to describe stage areas so as to avoid confusion when you communicate with actors and technicians or when the playwright or designer communicates with you. These stage areas are designated from the point of view of the actor on the stage, so you must learn to think as though you were standing on the stage (see the illustration).

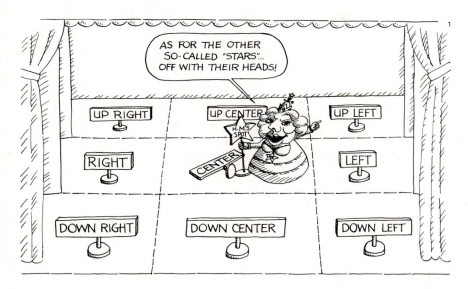

THE PROSCENIUM STAGE: PLANES

The proscenium stage is divided into series of imaginary lines parallel to the front edge of the stage, called *planes*. The closer the plane is to the audience, the stronger will be the effect of an actor positioned on it. Because of an optical illusion, a person or a chair placed closer to the audience will appear larger than that same person or chair placed further upstage. In plays for young people the director frequently positions more powerful characters downstage so that they appear "larger" to the audience.

THE PROSCENIUM STAGE: LEVELS

Levels mean height above the stage floor. Of course, no levels exist on stage if no pieces or units have been placed on the stage. Once such units have been placed, however, you will have various levels upon which to position actors. In general the higher the level, the stronger the position. If you wish a character, such as a conquering leader, to appear strong and important, place his throne on a level higher than

the stage floor. Perhaps one of the most commonly seen flaws in productions for children (particularly those that tour) is the failure of the director to exploit the potential of levels. Staging that doesn't utilize levels is not only spatially uninteresting because it is so vertically flat, but it also does not help visually reinforce the story.

right: An actor standing center stage commands the most attention. It is the strongest area. McCarter Theatre, Princeton, New Jersey: *The Taming of the Shrew* by William Shakespeare. Directed by Nagle Jackson.
Photo by Cliff Moore

far right: Note the variety of levels here. The focus, however, is obviously on the lowest figure, downstage center. Actors (top to bottom): Linda Kimbrough, Judith Ivey, Laura Esterman. The Goodman Theatre, Chicago: *Much Ado About Nothing* by William Shakespeare. Directed by William Woodman.

THE ARENA STAGE: AREAS

Another dimension is added to an arena stage: the audience may be seated all around the stage (up to 360 degrees). What is "upstage" for one viewer may be "downstage" for another. Orientation can be determined as for a map or a clock. Map or compass points can be described

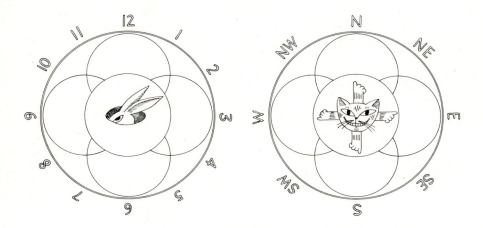

in terms of E, W, N, S. Circular staging is best described in terms of time—9 o'clock, 3 o'clock. In either case a fixed point (light booth or exit sign) must be designated as "north" or "12 o'clock." No longer do you think of downstage right or upstage center. Instead, think of placing actors at 9 o'clock or center or directing them to move northwest. Two charts that show both ways of classifying major acting areas are shown.

THE ARENA STAGE: PLANES AND LEVELS

Planes in the conventional sense do not apply to arena staging. Assigning concentric circles to the stage area does provide an orientation that is similar to planes. The weakest area is the center one; the strongest is the outside of the circle. If an actress is center stage in the arena, half of the audience sees her back. Placing an actor at the edge of the circle, preferably with his back to the aisle, opens him to face more of the audience.

The level above the stage floor obviously does not have much applicability to arena staging. Placing a large, thick cube in the center of the stage could block much of the action for the audience opposite the action. Occasionally, delicate trellis-like stairs help provide levels. Or actors stand on stools or on each other's shoulders to add levels to the picture.

THE THRUST STAGE: AREAS, PLANES, AND LEVELS

The thrust stage is a kind of combination. Often directors think of one half of the stage as a proscenium and the lower half (the part closest

to the audience) as arena. The diagram here illustrates this point. Thinking of the stage in this manner can result in some very lively blocking patterns.

THE FLEXIBLE STAGE: AREAS, PLANES, AND LEVELS

Because of the many variations in flexible staging—that's why the word *flexible* is so appropriate in describing this type of staging—generalizations are hard to make. Whenever traditional areas, planes, and levels do not exist, you must figure out a method of describing the space and then remain consistent. One director of plays for young people recently converted a long, narrow store in a local shopping mall into a circus-like performance area with three primary acting areas, which she termed quite simply: trapeze area, step unit area, and door frame area. When using a mobile unit, you obviously cannot refer to it by its position; you must name the unit. Flexible staging requires flexible terminology.

Before rehearsing his actors on the stage, our director must walk across it many times and conjure up all the action which is to take place on it.
André Antoine,
"Behind the Fourth Wall"

Actors work with three elements in the development of a role: body, voice, and mind/soul. This section focuses on the actor's body in stage space. Many inexperienced directors, in adult theatre as well as in theatre for young people, have not totally grasped the possibilities of stage pictures available with a single actor, pairs of actors, and groups of actors. An actor standing full-front, two actors always sharing scenes in the same one-quarter positions, and groups of actors clumped together are the choices over and over again. Actors speak as much with their bodies as they do with their voices. Audiences of young people read the pictures as well as hear the words. Before you can make talking pictures for your audiences, learn all you can about positions, areas, crosses, and turns available for your use.

THE ACTOR

BODY POSITION OF SINGLE ACTOR: PROSCENIUM STAGE

1. Full-front position: the actor's body and head directly face the audience.
2. One-quarter position (left or right): approximately 45 degrees away from the audience; the actor's head and body are halfway between front and profile.
3. Profile position (left or right): a 90-degree turn in which the actor's head and body face the side; the actor's side faces the audience.
4. Three-quarter position (left or right): approximately 135 degrees away from the audience; the actor's head and body are halfway between profile and full-back.
5. Full-back position: the actor faces the rear of the stage; the actor's back is directly facing the audience.

Actors move from one area to another by crossing ("Xing") in either a *straight* or a *curved* line. Actors move from one position to another by *turning*, which involves moving the feet as well as the body while facing the audience. When you assign actors their positions on, and their moves about, the stage, you are giving them *blocking*. Developing blocking as a way of visually interpreting the script is one of your basic tasks as director. (Principles of blocking are discussed in more detail in the latter part of this chapter.)

POSITIONS OF TWO ACTORS: PROSCENIUM STAGE

Although the possibilities for physical stage relationships are infinite, some basics about two actors in relationship to one another form the core of all that can prove helpful. If two actors are together:

- Actor A and Actor B may *share* the scene.
- Actor A may *give* the scene to Actor B.
- Actor A may *take* the scene from Actor B.

When a scene is shared, each actor is in a one-quarter position, facing the other. When Actor A gives the scene to Actor B, Actor A turns to a three-quarter body position to face Actor B, who is upstage of Actor A. When Actor A takes a scene from Actor B, Actor A moves upstage of Actor B and faces one-quarter front, thus forcing Actor B to face upstage.

BODY POSITION OF SINGLE ACTOR: ARENA STAGE

In arena staging there is no full-front, one-quarter, profile, three-quarters, or full-back because of the seating arrangement of the audience. What is full-front to one viewer may be full-back to another, so these terms no longer apply. Positions of one actor must be thought of in relation to the stage area. The actor should always try to face the greatest number of viewers.

BODY POSITIONS OF TWO ACTORS: ARENA STAGE

The factor to think about when positioning two actors is to try to give the entire audience as much face-to-face contact as possible with one of the actors. The shared position of proscenium will not work for arena because the actors will face away from a large portion of the audience. It is better for the actors almost to face each other without blocking one another. Not like this:

This is the way:

In arena staging actors approaching another actor or object almost always use the *curved cross,* not the *straight cross.* Actors sometimes even use the *S-cross* so that more of the audience can see more of the actor's face as he or she crosses the stage.

When actors turn from one position to another in arena, unlike in proscenium they turn so they will cover the greatest number of degrees to provide the majority of the audience with face-to-face contact with the actor. In addition actors can seem to face more of the audience by rotating the upper body in a different direction from the lower body.

THE SCRIPT

Play analysis is probably one of the most difficult tasks in your role of interpretive artist. Don't let the enormity of the responsibility prohibit you from attempting to do this job. Certain procedures and techniques for reading a play, as well as for analyzing its meaning, have been developed and tested by time. Remember, there is not just one way of interpreting the script. Children's theatre playwright Aurand Harris' scripts are good examples of plays that have had, and will continue to have, a great variety of interpretations. Probably the more complex the script, the more are the possible interpretations. What you must remember is that part of your role as interpretive artist is to find a unified, exciting interpretation of the script, one that challenges you and works well within your resources.

Many average scripts have been directed into exciting productions.

Through the use of space and actor and of insight the script begins to soar. Keep in mind that you are the audience's eyes and ears. As you begin to survey the literature of theatre for young people, note scripts that you favor and that you feel you can produce excitingly. Then, when an actual directing opportunity presents itself, you have a store of ideas ready to tap.

The specifics given to you by the playwright are the **given circumstances** of the play. You cannot change them; you must use them. They have to form the basis for any interpretation you develop. Ask yourself:

Who is in the play? What happens in the play? Where does the story take place? When does it take place? Why do the characters do what they do?

READING THE TEXT: FIRST STEP

The first step in directing a production of a particular script is to read the play all the way through without stopping. During this initial reading you will meet the characters for the first time; you will experience the story for the first time; you will identify with the characters' plight for the first time. The first impression you form will be similar to the only impression that the production makes on the audience. In your ultimate interpretation you can stress one set of scriptual circumstances more than others: you can interpret some characters more or less sympathetically.

SECOND READING . . . AND THIRD
. . . AND FOURTH

Now you get into the journalistic part: the investigation of the play. You must know much more about the play than an audience ever will. You must discover *everything*. You must penetrate everything so that you have all the information necessary to develop your own unique interpretation of the play. In these readings try to find out what the playwright has given you. Ask the questions a journalist covering an event asks: Who, What, Where, When, Why?

One particularly useful tool for script analysis is the development of an objective/subjective journal. Get a note pad and divide each page vertically in half. On the left half of each page write actual dialogue, actual stage directions, any actual textual reference that you feel will aid in your interpretation. Then on the right half of the page write how you feel about the line or direction. You may write, for example, during your first reading of *Reynard the Fox:*

<u>Ticelin:</u> You are interrupting my practice, Señor Brun. Caw!	Ticelin is very conceited; he probably is easily swayed by flattery—

The work of the production must include a written analysis of the play. The director must write it, and not despise the thankless job. The drafting of such an analysis compels the director to a clear and exhaustive knowledge of the play.
Jean Vilar,
"Murder of the Director"

As you continue to read the script, keep a running log of objective/ actual textual references and subjective ways that you feel or think.

During subsequent readings keep writing in your log. You may notice that your thoughts and feelings are beginning to change. How you feel about the character of Reynard or the set may be modified because you are acquiring more information and your subconscious is working on it. Thus, keeping the objective notes and the subjective thoughts separate will keep your interpretation from becoming hopelessly muddled. The actual script will be separated from your developing interpretation. At any time you can check back to see the germ of your ideas and the growth of your interpretation, as well as which exact textual reference helped you to come up with that particular interpretation.

PENETRATING THE GIVEN CIRCUMSTANCES

Your job is to interpret the play by investigating the characters, dialogue, conflicts, and actions. You must search the play deeply in order to form a well-conceived interpretation.

Character   As you read the play, you will begin to learn about the characters by:

- What the character says
- What the character does
- What others say about the character

Dialogue   The playwright has developed dialogue to show character. Note how the characters phrase sentences, what kinds of words they use, what they choose to talk about. People talk in specific ways because of education, experience, station in life, and personality. Notice everything you can about the dialogue.

Conflict   Plays are about conflict. The major conflicts in plays can be divided into categories:

- Person versus Person
- Person versus Self
- Person versus Nature
- Person versus Society

The hero or heroine, the person who is striving for something good, is called the *protagonist*. The person trying to thwart the protagonist is called the *antagonist*. Hero versus villain is a traditional person-versus-person conflict. ***Person-versus-person*** conflicts are the major conflicts of theatre for young people. Peter Pan versus Captain Hook in Barrie's *Peter Pan* is an example of a person-versus-person conflict.

Other plays are about personal inner struggle. This **person-versus-self** conflict is not often part of the literature of children's theatre because a conflict of this nature is usually deeply psychological as well as difficult to stage physically. An exception is Ellie in Zeder's *Step on a Crack,* who undergoes a great personal struggle. The "to be or not to be" monologue of Hamlet in Shakespeare's play is a perfect example of a person-versus-self conflict.

Person-versus-nature conflicts have become very popular in contemporary disaster movies, such as *Airport, Typhoon, Killer Bees,* and *Earthquake.* The major conflict of a play can be a person-versus-nature even if the natural disaster is not as vast as a hurricane or earthquake. People fighting the elements of nature can prove to be very satisfying for a young audience. In *Beauty and the Beast,* Beast has to struggle against the ugly appearance nature has given him. Hansel and Gretel in the play of the same name must struggle against the dangers of the woods.

The **person-versus-society** conflict, although sometimes political, can also form the basis for theatre for young people. Arthur Fauquez' script *The Man Who Killed Time* is about a man who battles with an entire town to live life more fully instead of watching the clock all the time.

Action As you continue to develop your interpretation of the play, you must begin to divide the play into workable pieces of action. Thinking of *Reynard the Fox* only as *one big chunk* will probably overwhelm you as well as your actors, your technicians, and the audience.

You needn't arbitrarily divide the play: The playwright has contributed some divisions to assist you. Plays are usually divided into acts, acts into scenes. Acts are usually divided into scenes because of a change in time or place or sometimes to provide a pause after a crisis. Many young people's theatre scripts, because they are shorter than adult plays (often approximately an hour in length) and not meant to have act breaks, are divided only by scenes.

Scenes can be further divided in two ways:

1. *French scenes.* French scenes are determined by the entrance and exit of a character. Since the arrivals and departures of characters are one of the playwright's major methods of developing action and character, dividing a play into these smaller units can be a valid method of dissecting the play.

2. *Beats.* Sometimes, however, characters remain onstage for a long time, through several idea or action changes; or the playwright may have divided a French scene even further through shifting the focus of conversation. One particularly useful way to think of the play's action is to divide the play into *beats,* or units of dramatic action. A transition from beat to beat is brought about by the entrance or exit of a character, a change in the subject or mood of the scene, or a change in time

or place. Each beat usually contains an underlying objective for the characters who appear in the beat. By dividing the scene into beats, you can begin to get an understanding of the subtleties of action and of character.*

MAKING USE OF BEATS

Assigning a title to each beat   Once you have divided the scene into beats, try describing the action of each scene in this form, for example:

Name of character	Action verb	Direct object
Reynard —	tricks —	Ticelin

Titling the beats in this manner can help you trace the dramatic action in a way that will facilitate an active interpretation and provide a good way to talk about the play with the actors.

After you have assigned a title to each beat, you can map out the action flow of each scene, then each act, then the whole play by listing the titles of the beats in order. This *play map* creates a total picture of your interpretation of the play that can be consulted by you throughout the development of the production process.

Assigning tempo to each beat   After you have titled each beat, designate the speed that you think describes how the scene moves. Is the scene slow, medium, or fast? Tempo describes how quickly the lines are spoken and how much time elapses between lines. Your first task is to assign a general tempo for each scene. You can become more specific after rehearsals have progressed. Many productions for children are fast, faster, fastest. Speed does not connote expert direction; even children need pauses for reflection.

Assigning mood to each beat   Next, assign to each beat a mood adjective that describes the general feeling of the beat. The mood may be scary, happy, delicate, or even depressed. Mood decisions color how the scene will affect the audience. Mood doesn't override the action: It simply adds shades or intensities to the already-existing thrust of the play. Mood decisions are important and can add subtlety when properly varied. Too many directors of plays for young people simply direct the scene to be ''happy'' instead of assigning titles to beats first. Harris' *The Arkansaw Bear* is a good example of a play that has a general mood of sadness but that contains many happy or bittersweet beats.

---

*A further discussion of beats, with appropriate examples, appears in the next chapter.

MAKING THE GROUNDPLAN

As you assign titles, tempos, and moods to the scene, a vague image begins to emerge in your mind's eye of how the play should appear. To sharpen this image, you must develop what is called a *groundplan*, a stage plan viewed from above, which helps illustrate the dramatic action of a play in terms of space. Although groundplans are often thought of as two-dimensional, they are actually three-dimensional: They add height to the width and length. Groundplans are also used to help actors visualize their actions before the set is built.

In conceiving the groundplan you have to determine how many acting areas are required to portray the action properly. The given circumstances will help you figure out what should appear on the stage; for example, a throne, a table and some chairs, a door, a tree, and a path. Try to have at least five separate areas, which can provide the focus of five different kinds of scenes. Experiment with different groundplans until you come up with a working plan to begin rehearsal.

FINDING THE SPINE OF THE PLAY

Finally, try to discover a unifying element—a superobjective—that ties the play together. The theme of a play may consist of a mood, an attitude, a sentiment, a visual image, a sound image, a line from a poem, or even a popular axiom. What is vital is that you isolate what you feel should bind the play together, make a verbal or visual statement about it, and then use this unified element to color all aspects of your interpretation.

The term often used to describe the unifying element is the *spine* of the play. Expanding the image of backbone may help you view what the spine actually does: It gives form and shape to the production, helping each scene add to the total theatrical statement. It unifies the production. And all characters have their own individual backbones, which should fit in with the larger spine of the play.

Harold Clurman, in his director's notes for Carson McCullers' *A Member of the Wedding*,* defines the spine of his production as "to get 'connected.'" This choice then affects all the characters. Clurman explains that Frankie, the tomboy character, seeks to connect but is not able to. So she tries "to get out of herself." The character Bernice tries "to do her deed (work) normally." For her just being alive is to be "connected." John Henry, the boy, tries "to learn to connect." The spine of Jarvis, Frankie's brother, is "to make the simplest connection with the first thing that's nice—a girl." Clurman discusses the implications of this choice of spine at length. It remains for him, of course, to "articulate" through *actor* and through *space*—through blocking,

On Directing (New York: Macmillan, 1972).

The visual articulation of the spine "to discover one's mirror image" is clearly shown. New Jersey Shakespeare Festival: *The Comedy of Errors* by William Shakespeare.

movement and gesture, set and costumes and lights—the *specifics* of the spine, so that the message is communicated to the audience.

Not only does each characterization fit into the main spine, but also the entire production—sets and costumes—comes together through the "articulation" of the spine. In a recent production of *Peter Pan* the director chose as the spine "to have an adventure." Various script references to adventure (for example, author Barrie's statement that Peter might say, "To live would be an awfully big adventure") helped the director make her choice. Each character, then, had as a spine (or superobjective) some aspect of adventure. Wendy's superobjective was "to grab an adventure." Captain Hook's and Mr. Darling's was "to prevent an adventure." Nana's was "to facilitate an adventure."

With the aid of the director the design staff also used "adventure" in their visual interpretation of the script. The set was particularly adventuresome for actors as well as for the audience. It was constructed of many levels and covered with soft foam; actors had to climb over the various bumps; frequent tumbling could take place because of the springy texture of the set. The costumes also were adventuresome— textures usually not combined (such as mylar and burlap) were juxtaposed, as were clashing colors. Nontraditional silhouettes were also used. For example, Wendy wore a very slinky dress in Neverland, signifying her "motherhood." The director made sure that all elements were consistent with the major theme—the spine of the play.

What to do to make direction become action is covered in the rest of this chapter. Choosing the spine is only the beginning of the interpretive process; transforming that spine into pictures on the stage requires great artistry from the director.

YOUR FUNCTION AS DECISION MAKER

Fortunately, theatre does not come in a kit. The director does not paint by number. Surely directing would be much easier if you could order Peter Pan No. 7. Then a truck would arrive with a prefabricated set, precut costumes, and pre-gelled instruments. Actors would be programmed like robots. All the fun would be taken out of the theatre; your primary duties as director would be as catalogue reader and computer programer. In the world of the 1980s technology has not yet superseded your job as director. You still serve a very real and a very needed function.

EQUIPPING YOURSELF TO DIRECT FOR YOUNG PEOPLE

Once you have a firm knowledge of the areas, planes, and levels of the stage, the potential body positions of the actor, and simple script analysis, you are ready to begin a more specialized direction—directing nonrealistic plays for young people. The principles and techniques presented in this part of the chapter are not replacements for those in the first section; they are additions to your craft as interpretive artist.

There are techniques and principles, *sometimes* appropriate for adult theatre, which *almost always* apply to theatre for children. It is these principles that we have factored out of general directing theory and emphasize here. In this section of the chapter we discuss the procedures for establishing the style of the production, and the development of a visual technique and picturization.

> ....
> *Children's theatre is theatre, just as children's food is food—served in smaller quantities, less spicy, simpler (perhaps), but basically the stuff that keeps grownups going.*
> Dan Sullivan,
> *critic, Los Angeles Times*
> ....

The one factor that makes young people's theatre extensively different from adult theatre is the manner in which the director chooses the script. When selecting a play for an adult audience, the director has a wide variety of plays from which to choose. Anything for which a budget can be secured and that will attract an audience is a possibility. When selecting a play for young audiences, budget and marketing are still factors, but now the director must also consider the appropriateness of a script for the developmental level of the audience.

Although choosing a script is not technically an interpretive art, you must be familiar with the types of scripts that are available to be interpreted.*

The most common error in choosing a script for young people is *under*estimating what the audience can appreciate. The following category system represents a sample of the types of scripts currently available and generally well-received by audiences of children. As in any category system, some scripts overlap classifications.†

CHOOSING A SCRIPT

*A discussion of how to judge quality in a script appears in Chapter 7.
†The design problems presented by these categories of scripts are discussed in Chapter 6.

Give the child something to discover. Often he is treated not as the quick, curious experience-hungry creature he is, but as a small moron. There is a vast difference between a young mind and a stupid mind.
Norman Nadel,
theatre critic

FAIRY TALES

Many of the scripts available for young people are based on fairy tales. Such stories as *Hansel and Gretel, Sleeping Beauty, Snow White, Jack and the Beanstalk*, and *Beauty and the Beast* have been adapted into theatrical scripts by countless playwrights. Although somewhat out of vogue in the 1970s because of the trend toward "relevance," fairy tales have continued to delight audiences of young people for generations. In fact, according to psychologist Bruno Bettelheim, "Nothing can be as enriching to child and adult alike as the folk fairy tale."* Although on an overt level these tales teach little about the specific conditions of life in the modern world, children can learn much from fairy tales about the problems of human beings and their possible solutions.

When selecting a fairy tale play for production, make sure the qualities necessary for deeper meaning—the good versus evil, the violence, the ugliness—have not been left out of the adaptation. Also important is that the playwright did not overexplain the story. As Bettelheim explains, "The fairy story is so captivating because the children do not know why they are so delighted." Overexplanations spoil this effect. In fairy tales internal processes are translated into visual theatrical images: The tales describe inner states of mind by means of images and action. Don't mitigate the excitement and violence of the action in your interpretation for fear the audience will be frightened.

Fairy tales can be appropriate for all ages, depending on the partic-

Sumptuous staging and careful period detail epitomize this production of *Beauty and the Beast.* PAF/Arts in Education, Huntington, New York.

Photo by Gerry Goodstein

*Bruno Bettelheim, *The Uses of Enchantment: The Meaning and Importance of Fairy Tales* (New York: Alfred A. Knopf, 1976); see this book for many excellent discussions of the psychological value of fairy tales.

ular treatment by the playwright. Moses Goldberg's *Hansel and Gretel* works well for children under seven because of its simplified plot and characters and the nature of audience participation in the script. Most fairy tale scripts are written for seven- to twelve-year-olds. A child of thirteen can still find deep meaning in a fairy tale, but peer pressure to act sophisticated may inhibit the young teenager from truly enjoying the play.

FANTASIES

Fantasies portray worlds that could exist only in the imagination. In these worlds animals talk, people fly, time moves backward—many of the laws of nature are totally disregarded. Unimaginative adults often have difficulty accepting a fantastical world; most children do not. Examples of fantasy plays include Melwood's *Tingalary Bird* and *Five Minutes to Morning*, Fauquez' *The Man Who Killed Time*, Cullen's *The Beeple*, and Mofid's *The Butterfly*.

Because of, not despite, the child's lack of abstract reasoning ability, fantasies work well for this audience. To the prepubescent child objects as well as animals and plants are often personified. The sun is alive because it gives light; animals understand children even though the dog or cat may not show it. Quite naturally, these personifications and

This has vindicated my belief that everyone loves a fairy story, particularly one told with action rather than chatter.
Yasha Frank,
director of Pinocchio *for children's unit of Federal Theatre project*

Two actors share focus in a fantasy. Asolo Touring Theatre, Sarasota, Florida: *The Tingalary Bird* by Mary Melwood.
Photo by Gary W. Sweetman

a world that has unusual laws of nature can become subjects for scripts.

Before age seven total fantasies may be quite overwhelming; children in the preoperational stage are just learning to distinguish between reality and illusion. A play that contains some limited fantastical elements (such as the talking animals in Nellie McCaslin's *The Rabbit Who Wanted Red Wings*) might be appropriate for the pre-seven-year-old. Many of the fantasy plays for the concrete-operational (seven to twelve) group begin somewhat realistically and then, through a dream, move to a fantastical world. After the age of twelve almost any fantastical play, perhaps even one based on science fiction, is appropriate.

Research shows that imagination in the developing child must be cultivated and is related to cognitive, behavioral, and social development. How appropriate, then, to choose fantasy plays for audiences of young people! Select those fantasy plays in which the playwright has developed a consistent world. Fantasy has its own requirements of consistency, perhaps more stringent than other types of plays. Develop your interpretation of these plays in an equally consistent manner.

CLASSICS

Fairy tales and classics are often grouped together, but for the purpose of this discussion a classic is a story, a novel, or a play that (like a fairy tale) has withstood the test of time and (unlike a fairy tale) was artistically conceived as a literary work receiving high acclaim. Examples of classics that have been turned into scripts are Alcott's *Little Women*, Baum's *The Wizard of Oz*, Carroll's *Alice in Wonderland*, Defoe's *Robinson Crusoe*, Dickens' *A Christmas Carol* and *Oliver Twist*, Stevenson's *Treasure Island*, and Twain's *Tom Sawyer* and *Huckleberry Finn*. Audiences, like readers, identify with the hero or heroine (well-drawn by the original author) who are leading exciting and dangerous lives. Usually the plots are complex and provide a positive view of the human potential.

When a playwright adapts a classic for the stage, the most commonly made errors are trying to cram as much action and as many characters into the play as possible, or paring away so much of the story and the characters that just a vestige of the original appears in the adaptation. Select scripts that keep the flavor of the original work and have action appropriate to budget and time limitations. Theatrical productions of classics appeal to the same audience who reads the works in literary form—children ten years old and above. In fact, teenagers also delight in theatrical productions of a classic, usually spending time comparing the theatrical adaptation to the original work.

Also included in this category are plays that have been established as classics, such as the works of Shakespeare or Molière. Many of these plays (and miniature versions of them) not originally intended for the

Children need and respond to truly universal theatre. . . . The finest audience for Hamlet, Macbeth, King Henry V *or any Molière play is the children from ages eight to twelve. . . . We must move toward the creation of a genuinely universal theatre, large enough to reach the young, deep and high enough to survey the human spirit.*
Orlin Corey,
Children's Theatre Assocaition banquet address, 1965

young audience work exceptionally well for children, perhaps even better than for adults. Unlike adults, children do not bring to the theatre the idea that this work is of major significance. They never follow along in the script during the performance as many adults do. The children simply respond to the excitement, the grandeur, the humor, and the images portrayed in such scripts. Children are used to not understanding all the words in adult conversations. They respond on a more perceptual level to the rhythm of the language and the sound of the words.

HISTORY PLAYS

Plays about people who actually existed and events that actually took place are very popular in the theatre literature for young people. The lives of such individuals as Daniel Boone, Benjamin Franklin, Thomas Edison, and Eleanor Roosevelt stand as positive models for children. A play like Kraus' *Mean to Be Free,* the dramatization of the Underground Railroad, helps young people personalize historical events.

Most historical or biographical plays are typically straightforward in their interpretive requirements. The only extensive problem is the manipulation of the often large casts in re-creating moments in history, such as the signing of treaties, or battle scenes. If the play is a musical, songs and dances must be staged. Producers of professional companies usually set the age range of plays of this type at seven through fifteen. Treatment of the material, as well as the nature of the historical figure,

above left: The classic *A Christmas Carol* is a family favorite, produced in many communities around the country each holiday season. Theatre Department, State University of New York, College at Brockport. Directed by Joanna H. Kraus.
Photo by Jim Gale

above right: A more recent children's literary classic is Madeleine L'Engle's *A Wrinkle in Time,* shown in an original adaptation by Gregory A. Falls. Actors (clockwise from left): Nina Wishengard, Richard Hawkins, Peter Kelly, David Colacci. A Contemporary Theatre, Seattle.
Photo by Chris Bennion

may narrow the age range. A play documenting the boyhood of Thomas Edison may not appeal to a teenager. Likewise, a play about Susan B. Anthony's campaigning for the vote would probably not appeal to children under ten.

ADVENTURE/JOURNEY

The quest and coming-of-age motifs are also popular in the literature of young people's theatre, particularly for children over seven. In plays of this category the hero or heroine must strive to reach a certain place, find a specific object, or master particular skills. The popularity of stories of this type can be traced back to primitive people, for whom the story had great symbolic significance as well as considerable teaching potential. Levy's *Marco Polo,* Falls and Beattie's *The Odyssey* (based on Homer), and Engar's *Merlin's Tale of King Arthur's Magic Sword* are examples of the adventure/journey.

Essential in the adventure/journey play are well-developed characters, action, and conflict. Stay away from "wishy-washy" adventure/journey plays: Scripts in which the significant deed happens offstage, or in which the climax occurs through a **deus ex machina** (a contrivance

The evil magician turns himself into a three-headed Hydra to fight the hero Aladdin. Asolo Touring Theatre, Sarasota, Florida: *Aladdin.*
Photo by Gary W. Sweetman

not integral to the action; literally, "god from the machine"), do not play well theatrically.

Many of today's playwrights write adventure/journey plays about a less physical, but no less powerful, quest. Based on internal searches, these plays provide the audience with models for coping with society and with their approaching adulthood. Aurand Harris writes of a young girl's quest to understand death in *The Arkansaw Bear*; Brian Kral's *Special Class* explores the handicapped individuals' acceptance of their limitations; Ellie in Susan Zeder's *Step on a Crack* must come to grips with a new stepmother; Frank Gagliano's *The Hide-and-Seek Odyssey of Madeline Gimple* traces a young girl's search to understand both the ugliness and beauty in contemporary society.

STYLE ANALYSIS: PENETRATING THE WORLD OF THE PLAY

What all these plays have in common is that, for the most part, they are scripts of presentational style. Before you can proceed to make strong visual statements—using the techniques in the first part of the chapter plus the more complex visual techniques yet to be presented—you must carefully analyze the script for its presentational elements. The first step in your script analysis is, of course, the traditional analysis already discussed. Now you must continue the penetrating interpretation of the script, with a careful consideration of the following elements, which form the basis for the stylistic world of the play.

This new world of the play may depict the past or the future. People may speak in verse, or sing, or dance. Characters may wear clothes of a different era. During the play much time may pass, and many places may be visited. All these considerations constitute the *style* of the play.

In dealing with a play that does not represent today's reality, you must make the world as specific as possible; **style must be a tangible component of your interpretation.** You should be able to describe the world of the play in concrete, operational action—that is, "viewable, do-able stage activity."

For a start consider these four factors in the development of a production style for all presentational plays: era in which the play was written, playwright, script, and (of course) you. You as director must blend these factors together to create the production style. You must consider each factor separately and order your preferences. You can then communicate these decisions to your actors and technicians. The beneficiaries of these decisions will be an audience of delighted young people, who won't comment on production style but will be entertained and instructed by viewing this enchanting world of the play.

ERA OF THE PLAY

Reading about the era that a play portrays can help you penetrate the given circumstances of the play as well as understand the behaviors of its characters. Examining other artists' work—paintings, music, and lit-

erature—can give you clues about the period. Also, actual documentation—histories, biographies, photographs, if they exist—can help you.
Find out as much as you can about the era in which the play takes
place. You won't transpose the specifics of period exactly as they existed onto the stage. You will make some selective decisions. But start
from what really existed.

If a play is written in a period different from the one it depicts, you
also should research the period during which the play was written.
Often this period influences the given circumstances more than the
time in which the play is set. For example, Shakespeare wrote *Macbeth*
in early-seventeenth-century England, but the action of the play takes
place in eleventh-century Scotland. More of Shakespeare's Elizabethan
British values than Macbeth's Scottish ones color the play.

Just view some 1930s films that portray great historical events to
understand how the artists' period often affects the work more than
the actual time the events took place. Observe Claudette Colbert as
Cleopatra in Cecil B. deMille's 1934 Paramount production of *Cleopatra*,
with her tweezed eyebrows and permanent-waved henna coiffure. In
her 1930s flounced gown she looks more like a stylish Depression-era
model than the Queen of the Nile.

Be aware that any historical era is evaluated by the current era. Keep
all periods separate: the period of the play, the period in which the
play was written, and, of course, the period of today.

Often plays for young people's theatre are not written about any
particular era. These fantasy and fairy tale plays take place in some
remote past. *Cinderella, Reynard the Fox, Sleeping Beauty, Jack and the
Beanstalk* provide a certain leeway as well as problems, since they can
exist in many periods of history. Consider first when the particular
script of the fairy tale or fantasy play was written. Then try to choose
an existing period in which the play might logically have occurred. The
decision to place *Reynard the Fox* in Revolutionary War America instead
of 1930s Germany will greatly affect the style of the production. You
may even have to create a world that is a combination of several times
or places. Always base your decisions on strong references in the text.
The style you choose should illuminate, not cloud, the world, whether
real or imagined.

THE PLAYWRIGHT

Find out as much as you can about the playwright. The truly great
playwrights—Shakespeare, Molière, Chekhov, Shaw—all have had
much written about their lives and their plays. Some of them have also
written their own extensive commentaries. For less-well-known playwrights, as those who write for young people's theatre often are, you
may find little, if any, information. Try writing letters to contemporary
playwrights, asking them about the scripts you may wish to direct.

Knowing what playwrights value can help you know their characters as well. George Bernard Shaw and Noel Coward valued verbal fluency and wit. Most of their characters speak quickly and facilely; a real clue about the world of the plays in which they appear. Playwright Jonathan Levy in a recent interview discussed how much the *commedia dell' arte* (a theatre form that developed in the sixteenth century) had intrigued him: "It's interesting because it's a combination of bright colors, very physical action and stock characters. That is, characters who are not stereotypes but archetypes: characters each of whom represent something deep in human characters."* Many of Levy's plays utilize commedia dell' arte either to a large extent, as in *The Marvelous Adventures of Tyl,* or in a less obvious way, with just a few of these conventions, as in *Marco Polo.* Knowing that Jonathan Levy is fascinated by commedia dell' arte can tell you much about the production style.

THE SCRIPT

Style is the collective characterization of the world. If one person sings all the time, then singing is a character trait. If everyone sings, then singing is a style factor. In fact, the better a character (not just the actor) is at singing, the more likely he or she will succeed in this world of the play.

When reading a play, list specific universal traits. For example:

How the characters talk Shakespeare's characters almost always speak in perfect iambic pentameter. Speaking iambic pentameter is a style trait. In Aurand Harris' *Rags to Riches* the characters speak in a comic-book-like, overly simplistic manner—a style trait of the script.

What the characters wear Most of the characters in Noel Coward's plays wear beautifully tailored clothes. Many references to this elegance appears in the text. Wearing beautiful clothes and moving elegantly is a style trait. Exaggerated costumes, both animal and human, exemplify the style trait of the Irene Corey design for Broadhurst's *The Great Cross Country Race.*

What the characters value Almost everyone in Chekhov's *The Three Sisters* wants to get to Moscow. They are all unhappy with country living. Longing for excitement is a stylistic value, then, which must be shown through action on the stage. In Barrie's script of *Peter Pan* all the characters, in one way or another, long for adventure. The director of the play should portray this value system through action on the stage.

Most of your clues about style are embedded in the text. You must

---

*The style of commedia dell' arte is discussed in detail in the next chapter.

distinguish the individual behavioral traits from the collective characterization traits that determine the style of the production. As you block the play, you will find ways to show how well or how poorly each of the characters executes the style of the world in which they live.

YOU, THE DIRECTOR

As objective as you may be, it is impossible, as director, to avoid becoming the fourth factor yourself. Your particular interests greatly influence the style of the production. What you see in the script and what you choose to emphasize affects the style concept for the production. As director, you must objectify your tastes: You must become aware of your likes, dislikes, and all your preferences, particularly in terms of periods and playwrights. A director who favors romance and sees the world as full of love may color any production by this preference. A director who favors daring and sees the world as full of adventure may also color any production in this manner. Each director will direct a very different production of *Peter Pan*. Remember, be aware that you may skew the world of the play by your own preferences.

A good example of a production that seemed too personally contrived is a recent summer theatre production of Shakespeare's *Midsummer Night's Dream.* Instead of setting the largely fantasy play in Elizabethan England, the director chose to change the period and set the play in the American South during the Civil War. When interviewed, the director elaborated her fascination with this time and location and explained that a single line from Act III, scene 2—Helena: "Lo, she is one of this confederacy"—had encouraged her to make this monumental period change. The audience, young people as well as adults, were

Many modern-dress productions, such as this one of *Twelfth Night,* work well in conveying Shakespeare's universal humor. Williamstown Theatre Festival. Directed by Marty Kapell.
Photo by Lawrence Sheinfeld

quite confused by the Southern accents, long hoopskirts, and Southern military uniforms. This choice clouded, not clarified, the world of the play.

DIRECTOR'S WORKSHEET

Here is a format that can help you in your interpretation of style. As you read the play, keep notes of the following categories:

DIRECTOR'S WORKSHEET

Choosing the Common Denominators of Style:
Play:
Playwright:
Relevant information about the playwright:
Era: Era in which the play was written
　　Period the play depicts
　　Period in which you will stage the play
Goals: What the characters want
Strategies: What the characters wear
　　How the characters move
　　How the characters talk (verse or dialogue, for example)
　　How the characters get what they want
Values: Why the characters want what they do
　　How far the characters are willing to go
You: How your particular preferences affect the style

A beginning worksheet for *Reynard the Fox* might look something like this:

Play:　Reynard the Fox

*Playwright:　* Arthur Fauquez

*Relevant Information:　* Belgian; interested in satire; interested in characters, not plot

*Era:　* Play was written in 1958, first presented in America in 1961. My initial feelings are that I will set the play in Pre-Renaissance France.

*Common Goals:　* To be King of the Forest; To eat well; To conquer Man; To unite against Man; To triumph over each other; To cope with change of seasons

*Common Strategies:　* Each character characterizes others as fools. All love trickery, cunning, daring. No one trusts anyone; One-upsmanship is supreme; "All for one and one for all, when convenient." Use of exaggeration and hyperbole; Each perceives Self as supreme

*Common Values:　* Love of sport; Need for pecking order; Use what's available; Always ready for a fight; Need to survive—will do anything to be King of the Forest and to eat well.

Me: I am particularly excited by the classic woodcuts of Reynard. These suggest to me something about the costumes—loose-fitting court costumes. The woodcuts also suggest the staging possibilities—postures, stances, and groupings. The style may be courtly formal, taking into consideration ritual and rites. Blocking will show each character's specific situation as it relates to the particular behavior of the period.

DEVELOPING VISUALIZATION SKILLS: COMPOSITION AND PICTURIZATION

An audience receives the message of the play through words (which the playwright provides) and pictures (implied by the playwright, but brought to fruition by the director). Despite a poorly staged production an audience of adults can grasp its meaning just from the dialogue. For audiences of children, however, words alone cannot suffice.

Research shows that visual imagery and nonverbal memory are separate from verbal memory and are retained longer and stronger in the mind. The memory capacity for pictures appears to be higher than for words. In order to make such strong, lasting impressions on the audience of young people, your production must be visually exciting. The symbolic meaning provided by artistically conceived groupings may even speak to a deeper part of the child's being. The abstract essence of the play often can only be expressed through pictures. Strong visual pictures may also compensate for the limited vocabulary of the child. The following principles of composition and picturization can help you develop your visual skills.

COMPOSITION: COMBINING ACTORS AND SPACE

When you look at a famous painting of a large group of people—for example, Leonardo's *The Last Supper*—notice how your eyes are drawn from one person to the other. Notice also how you focus on one group, then another, and then view the picture as a whole. How and where each character in the painting is positioned did not occur by accident, but is the result of the painter's well-developed sense of spatial relationship.

You must be able to manipulate the actors in space in a similar manner. Following are some of the principles of *composition*, the arrangement of people on a stage. We suggest that you think about this arrangement without any particular script in mind. Just as harmonious music creates an overall pleasing sound, so does a balanced spatial arrangement create a pleasing visual effect.

Emphasis Perhaps the most important element of composition is emphasis. Remember how many poorly directed productions you have attended in which you could not figure out what was happening on-stage, who was the most important character in the scene, or, even worse, which actor was speaking. All of these "disasters" could have been avoided by the director's understanding and proper use of em-

phasis. *Emphasis,* visibly reinforcing what is most important on the stage, is particularly vital in directing plays where the eyes can be distracted by large casts and elaborate sets so often encountered in plays for young people.

A television or movie director will use the camera to provide emphasis. By focusing on the action, zooming in to facial expressions, and panning strategically, the camera provides strength, variety, and contrast in emphasis. As you can see, the stage director has a much more difficult task. You must direct each member of the audience to "zoom in" to the appropriate spot on the stage.

The most obvious method of obtaining emphasis on the stage is by following an actor around with a spotlight. This method is not very subtle and highly impractical. The two most common, yet powerful, methods of obtaining emphasis are through strength and through contrast. Knowing and understanding these primary ways of obtaining emphasis can enhance your stage groupings. Some examples of emphasis through strength include:

- *body position:* position actor full-front
- *area:* position actor center

Theatrical staging often moves so fast that the camera cannot freeze the action, as in this battle scene. Oregon Shakespearean Festival Association: *Coriolanus* by William Shakespeare. Directed by Jerry Turner.

- *planes:* position actor downstage
- *level:* position actor on highest platform level
- *space:* position actor separate from others
- *repetition:* actor attended by three servants instead of one

- *focus:* other actors turn to, look at, or point toward actor

Emphasis through contrast is obtained by positioning an actor in sharp contradistinction to the other actors. A director can obtain emphasis through contrast in area, by placing an actor upstage center and all other actors downstage. Or an actor can gain emphasis through contrast in position—for instance, when all other actors are in the strongest body position—full-front—but the emphasized actor is full-back. Through contrast the actor in seemingly the weakest position obtains emphasis because he or she is different from all the other actors. An-

other way to obtain emphasis is through contrast in costume. Consider that seven actors are center stage in gray flannel suits, and one actor is up-left in a red and blue Superman costume.

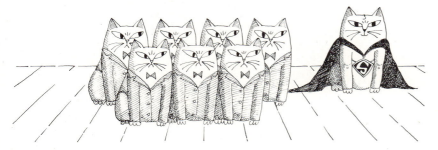

Balance Another important element of composition is balance. *Balance* is achieved when one part of the total stage seems to have equal weight in relation to the other part. A helpful visual image is the see-

Balance need not be symmetrical. Note here that the large group in the background balances the smaller group in the foreground. The Acting Company: *Il Campiello, a Venetian Comedy* by Carlo Goldoni. Directed by Liviu Ciulei.
Photo by Martha Swope

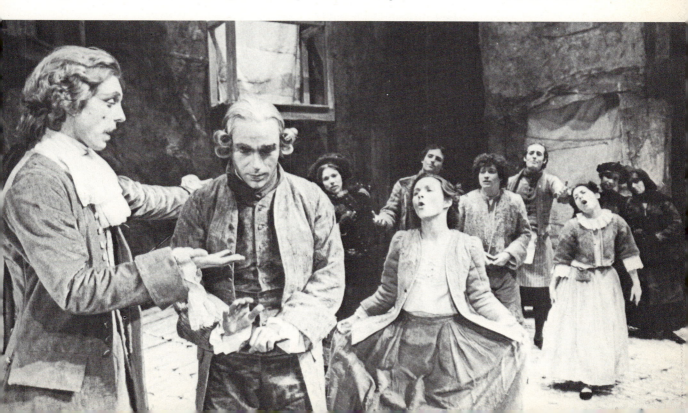

saw. The people on the right half of the stage, if placed on an imaginary visual seesaw, should seem to balance each other in a full-stage effect. As mentioned, because our eyes play tricks on us, a person standing downstage appears larger than a person standing upstage.

Therefore, in the balance of the stage composition one person downstage right may actually balance three people standing upstage left. Another example of optical stage illusion and balance deals with stage position. Because one-quarter is a stronger position than three-quarter, one person one-quarter right center of the stage can balance three characters three-quarter left.

Bodies are not the only element that contribute to balance. The set, furniture, costumes, lighting—and all their colors, shapes, and sizes—

must be considered. One actor suddenly appearing in a large yellow duck suit on stage left will disproportionately affect the balance of the composition.

Of course, stage composition is not static. Some scenes are balanced to the right, some to the left. What you strive for is overall "balance" in balance. Check to see whether the balance has been achieved by freezing the action. If not, you may be communicating something you don't wish to communicate. By constantly making unbalanced visual pictures, your composition may be stating that this world is misaligned, hectic, lopsided. Don't stage visually what you don't mean. Audiences of young people read much by what they see. Although they are certainly not conscious of balance, they are much affected by it.

Stability   The simplest way to define *stability* is as vertical balance. For example, if five actors all appear upstage center, you can stabilize the scene by placing one or two figures down left and down right. Otherwise the stage picture is displeasing; it seems to fly into the air.

TOO OVERDRAMATIC, BUT THEY DO ADD SOME **VERTICAL BALANCE!**

Sequence   Sequence is the most complicated principle of composition. It is the strategic placing of onstage groups in a rhythmic pattern. Even though the groups may be unrelated, the pattern can be linear, triangular, or semicircular. Proper sequencing creates a visual "beat" that provides a sense of order and connection to otherwise unconnected units.

PICTURIZATION: EVERY LITTLE
MOVEMENT HAS A MEANING . . .

After you master the techniques of composition, you are ready to consider picturization, or the storytelling aspect of the play. *Picturization* is the visual interpretation of each moment of the play. This involves placing characters on the stage so that the audience can understand the story and discern the character relationships without hearing any dialogue.

As director, you must learn to make pictures that not only interpret the action cleanly and clearly, but also add subtlety and bring out meaning hidden in the script. As director of plays for young people, you must make pictures that grab the attention of the audience, who often have short attention spans for dialogue. One of your biggest joys and hardest challenges in your role of interpretive artist is to use the elements of the stage and the actors to create action.

The function of director as picture maker begins logically. Surprisingly, many directors forget their common sense and obscure rather than clarify the story on the stage. People who like each other usually stand next to and touch each other. Murderers usually move toward, not away from, their victims. One hypothetical question to ask yourself as you create the stage pictures is this: If I could turn off the sound of this production, would I know the relationships of the characters and the nature of the action onstage?

If you have ever attended a production in a language you didn't understand, you probably experienced an excellent lesson in picturization. If you came away from the production wondering what on earth had happened onstage, the director failed as a storyteller. But if you came away knowing what had happened, even feeling you could almost understand the language, the director succeeded as a storyteller.

Remember, although the playwright is the author of the words, the director is author of the action.

Picturization begins with composition. Composition is the technique: picturization is the concept. In picturization you must use all the creative ingenuity at your disposal. Obviously, as many ways to depict a chase exist as there are imaginations. More than a simple matter of listing techniques is involved here. Therefore, here are some guidelines that you should consider as you picturize your scenes.

The play as a whole   Start by considering the intended impact of the play as a whole. Obviously, you don't want people dancing and strutting all over the stage in the middle of a death scene—unless you intend to present an absurd comedy. Know the type of play you're dealing with: comedy, tragedy, farce, or melodrama. Discern the general mood of the play. Feel the flow of the action. Align yourself with the main characters. Determine who has allegiance to whom. Consider ways to picturize the major conflicts without words. Refinement comes later. Remember, no absolutes exist. Comedy doesn't necessarily require rapid, staccato movements and larger-than-life characters. Love as a major theme needn't be pictured with hands over hearts.

Classify each scene according to type   Within the play each scene has its own life. Each type of scene requires a different sort of picture. In the play-analysis section of the chapter we detailed the breakdown of acts into scenes, scenes into beats, beats into moments. Now, for the purpose of picturization, we classify the scenes and describe them:

1. Scenes of main action   These scenes tell the big story and show the major changes in the cast of characters. The key objective is to focus the audience on these main characters and conflicts.

2. Scenes of background action   These scenes establish the place, time, and mood of the major action. They introduce the characters and situations and plant the seeds for the main action. The director must foreshadow the relationships of the characters and set up the story.

3. Scenes of secondary action   Scenes of secondary action give the audience a break from the intensity of the main action. A perfect example of scenes of this nature in *Peter Pan* are the scenes that take place in the home under the ground. In plays that have subplots the director must take care that the audience doesn't lose the thread of the story or the mood of the action.

4. Scenes of emotional relationships   These scenes are the most difficult to picturize because too much activity or movement can distract from the impact. For instance, often in musical plays for young people the action will come to a complete halt while the character sings about how he or she feels. These scenes unveil the mental and emotional state of the characters to the audience. The director must provide subtle gestures and movements to reveal the feelings of the characters.

Building scenes   Whatever the flow of the script suggests must appear in the picturization. Consider the variables—script, actor, and space—and work to build tempo and rhythm through the visual. Each scene must build to a climax pictorially; as director, you must orchestrate the dynamics of the picturization. Build each scene as well as scene upon scene. Static pictures do not suggest action or change. Think of yourself as an architect developing a blueprint for the action of the play. Speech, timing, and rhythm of action are all at your disposal.

Knowing and showing the nature of characters and their relationships   Part of picturization results from each actor's physical portrayal of the character. The gestures and movements of each actor

They cannot articulate it, but children do know when they are presented with inauthentic experiences, when the scary stuff is not really scary and the funny stuff is not really funny.
Richard Schickel,
theatre critic

tell the audience as much about the character's personality as do the words. You can't, of course, program your actors to move about the stage like robots. You can, however, give actors movement, business (activities with props), and gesture that show the audience their character traits and emotional states. As well as showing who each character is individually, the picturization must also demonstrate the changing relationships of characters toward each other.

We would be foolhardy to try to tell you *how* to picture the above types of scenes. Doing so would be like telling a poet how to write a poem on love or a painter how to paint a sunset. We've provided you with some specific information and a classification system. You must find the way.

PREPARING FOR THE IMPORTANT OCCASION

The way to prepare to direct for young people is to study the nature of directing for any audience and understand the presentational style. The principles in this chapter must become second nature. They form the core of all your directing for years to follow.

Is directing for children any different? It may be cleaner, clearer, more focused, more transparent. But certainly the basic principles of all good directing are the same. The main priority is that the directing must be fine. Ignorance of craft—not at all uncommon in the field of young people's theatre—is what we hope to reduce by providing you with a ''direction'' for the field of young people's theatre: the quest for excellence.

A professional is someone who gives his or her clients the best even though they may not appreciate the difference. Children will accept almost anything mockingly called *theatre*. To cheat them, however, is to deny the artistic spirit and the hope for the future that prompted you to direct for this audience in the first place.

In this production of the classic fairy tale *Snow White,* the ''mirror, mirror on the wall'' scene is staged in an unusual way. Honolulu Theatre for Youth. Directed by Kathleen Collins.

What steps do you take in interpreting a play?

In terms of interpreting a play, I look for three basic things. First of all I try to discover which character I am most empathetic toward. I try to see the play through his or her eyes: how do the other characters appear, how do the sets appear, how do they see the world, how do conflicts and obstacles impinge upon them? It's like *Alice in Wonderland* as seen through Alice's eyes; looking at the world through a character's eyes gives me a sense of style and also gives me a point of view. Secondly, I try to find out what the universe of the play is.

What do you mean by universe?

In one sense that's the society, the year, the kind of sociological behavior, the class of the characters, that sort of universe; but also I mean something more abstract. *Jim Thorpe, All American* is about Jim Thorpe and his growth as a human being and as an Indian. The universe of this play is not only the white society and the Indian society, but is more profoundly the dream world of Blackhawk. Blackhawk, an ancestor of Thorpe, was a great leader, teacher, warrior, and the play is his vision.

The third step is to discover what the play means: the theme. In PART's *Daniel Boone,* for example, written with playwright Tom Babe, the play showed very clearly the encroachment of civilization upon a wilderness, and about how civilization subverted and corrupted the people it came in contact with, especially Boone. After we understood that the theme is about the emotional tearing within Boone, we then got the idea for the set. It was to build the civilization scene by scene, so that at the end of the play we had a tacky, salesmanlike image "Welcome to Boonesborough." So I articulate the play's theme—in this case greed corrupts nature—and I interpret the theme by the use of the set.

What does a script have to have in order for you to direct it?

The people have to sound like human beings, even in a stylized play, and there is a certain unpredictability to human beings that I look for. The play must have conflict, real conflict that grabs me. And the dialogue has to show imagination.

How do you use space and actors to interpret the script in the rehearsal space?

INTERVIEW

with John Henry Davis, Director and Dramaturg for Performing Arts Repertory Theatre

First I have to get a central image. Let's look at *Teddy Roosevelt* for a moment. The central image of *Roosevelt* is of a man who is always seeking the arena, whether it be the boxing ring arena or the arena of politics. He always wants to get into the center. So, the important thing is to find an image that will translate the stage space into that image. I came upon the boxing ring, and I really stole it from Brecht. Brecht's notion was that theatre should be like a boxing match, with as much fun, as much spontaneity, as much reponse from the crowd as a real boxing match. Well, this is so right for *Roosevelt* because there just happens to be an *actual* boxing match in the middle of the play. So I created this set that looked like a boxing ring. It was also used as the arena of politics. In almost every scene Teddy is striving to get to the center, and he is constantly being pushed to the side by other people. Every scene is virtually blocked in that premise. Depending on the scene, I used the space differently. In the song "Stronger," when Teddy tries to build himself up, I deliberately put him in front of the platform. When he finally lifts the barbell, I put him upstage center, in the dead stage center of the platform, which is the *first* time he's ever been there in the play thus far. I didn't use the center before the end of the song. You see, part of directing is spareness, taking away. If you never use it before that moment and then you use it, it's powerful. But if you keep using everything in that scene, then you're dead.

Let's talk about style. Do you direct a presentational play differently from a representational play?

Oh, yes. A presentational play I visualize as a singer taught to sing so that the sound goes up through the head to the sky. I communicate the

65

play to the audience so it washes through them. So the presentational style is by very nature very forceful; it should have a lot of resounding waves, you know, like you throw a pebble in a lake, and all these shock waves go out from it. In a representational play you're trying to seduce the audience into believing in this world.

Why do you think Thorpe *works for children?*

Because it has powerful central images. And it taps something in a child that he or she can relate to. It has strong conflicts; the imagery is reinforced through the words, dialogue, and characters. Once you see something which has a kind of unification in its sets, costumes, acting words, intellectual concepts, and emotional feelings, I think the play has a certain power. And it's that power which translates itself to the child and leaves the child fascinated and fully involved.

In directing a play in presentational style, in what ways can you bring the audience and the play into one world?

I direct the actor to visualize who the audience is. Are they friends, are they enemies, are they merely watchers, are they partial participants? And I think in each play it's slightly different. In *Thorpe,* I think, we visualize the audience to be Indians.

Do you direct differently for an audience of children than for an audience of adults?

Yes and no. This is a difficult subject. No, in the sense that anything that is honest, that has power and conflict, will work in the theatre. If you don't have those things, you're not going to make it in either adult theatre or children's theatre. The child, especially the modern child who is exposed to so much more entertainment than we were, is very sophisticated and can take in a great deal— much more than a lot of people think. And if they don't get it consciously, they get it subconsciously. I think children are capable of very profound insights with profound and sensitive reactions to theatre. However, anytime you depend on the *words* to communicate your message to children, you are in deep trouble. The verbal, in and of itself, is too slight, too intellectual, and too unsatisfying to most children. Many playwrights get away with some things onstage because adults listen to those beautiful words, and they get fascinated by them. But a child will not. You can fool children less than you can fool adults. When

a deus ex machina occurs, I think the child is inwardly disappointed that the playwright hasn't found a more real and truthful way of solving the story problems. A child knows when you are being false and lying to him on the stage, and it is one thing you must never do. The play will lose its power, its mystery, and its excitement.

Why do you think so many plays for children are written without conflict and with simple solutions?

Because it is an adult's idea of what he thinks the child's world is like. It comes from the notion of childhood that children live in a kind of beautiful, fantasy world without real emotions and real feelings, and they love simplistic solutions to problems, and they love fantasy and imagination. Yes, they do love fantasy and imagination. But they also have complex emotional problems. And if we refuse to face these problems on the stage, why should they watch our plays? There's no reason to! But anytime you're running *toward* the problem, as a playwright, you're going to capture the children's imagination.

When do you consider the child in the directing process?

I try to forget about the child—I try to forget that the child is there, I really do. I do my plays for me, so that I am entertained, I am involved.

Has directing plays for young people affected the way you direct plays for adults?

Yes. I have learned to trust myself more. All directors need to really listen to the inner mind, listen to the inner self. If you train yourself to listen to that inner voice, you can often make tremendous steps forward in the direction of a play. I've learned this from directing plays for kids, because they have very spontaneous responses to things, and the structure of the play has to be so tight—it's an hour format—you can't let the audience's interest flag for a moment. And I'm not depending on lights, or sets, or costumes to give me focus. I'm only depending on my direction to give the audience focus.

Do you think that's a good rule to follow in children's theatre?

Definitely. You've got to be careful not to always make spectacles. If they want to see spectacles, they can go to the movies. There they have spectacle; what they often don't have is human stories with true conflicts that engage them. And I think that's what we have to work toward.

How do you respect the child audience in your interpretation of a play? If you're not thinking about the child audience, does this ever enter in?

Only in the sense that I'm always looking for a strong, fundamental image, which will guide them through the play, which they can hang on to. What I'm saying is that for a child audience the director has to distill a thing down to its essence. What is this play *really* about? What story am I trying to tell? Am I telling it *clearly*? And if you're telling the story clearly, the audience will be engaged. Something that a director should do, no matter what, whether it's an adult or child audience, is to watch the audience. Watch when they're bored, watch when they enjoy themselves, watch when they don't enjoy themselves. You'd be very surprised. You've got to watch them and pick up from them what is really happening on the stage. You've got to do that at least at one performance; you've got to really look at those children.

Last question: What is your advice to the new director working in young people's theatre? Where to begin?

Pick plays that you like. Pick plays that you relate to, that you will have fun with, that you can appreciate as an audience. Don't pick a play that you think other people will like. That's a big mistake. Secondly, try to find the truth of the human relationships, and try to find the truth of the essential conflict. Try to heighten the sense of opposite needs in the scenes. Thirdly, try to find a fundamental image which will carry through the play. Try to find several images that help that fundamental image, that are also physical and real. And, finally, don't strive for effects, strive for truth.

3·ACTING FOR YOUNG PEOPLE

*The actor is and must forever remain the frontier
guard on the border between dreams and reality.*
Max Reinhardt

WHAT THE DIRECTOR MUST KNOW ABOUT ACTING

To function competently as a director you do not have to be an actor,
but having worked as an actor at some point in your career helps. A
real ability to understand what the actor does and feels makes the bond
between the director and actor powerful. When a director outlines the
play to the actor and the actor brings to the work an excellent training,
each artist will spark the other and cause a creative spiral to begin,
moving them both toward the performance. When a director and actors are at cross-purposes and this bonding does not happen, the theatre experience is deadly for the artists and their audiences. The more
you as director know about your materials—your space, script, and
actors—the better equipped you are to create fresh and exciting theatre
for young people.

*I firmly believe that a director
should always be or have been
an actor.*
Eva Le Gallienne,
The New York Times

68

Four different acting techniques are discussed in this chapter: (1) The Stanislavski method of physical actions, (2) analysis of eight appropriate acting styles for young people's theatre, (3) The Super Six: Cybernetic Acting, (4) Outside/In Approach to character. They are different from each other in content and style but similar in purpose. Each technique provides the actor with a means to become specific, truthful, and interesting in the creation of characters for the stage.

The director's responsibility to a company of actors is to investigate thoroughly the actor's craft, which consists of three basic components: bodies, voices, and minds.

The basic physical movements required for any actor to execute are to walk, turn, kneel, crouch, lie down, rise, and run. Other more complicated movements in plays for young people are leaping, carrying another actor, and physical stunts such as cartwheels and handstands. Since scripts with words are made into productions with actions, the actor's body makes a very strong stage statement, even before the actor utters a sound.

The most obvious potential physical problem for actors who work in young people's theatre is the lack of disciplined training to the body. Actors spend hours on the lines, on the character, and on finding cute voices, but they rarely give thought to the physical image projected on stage. Costumes will not correct that image; often an elegant costume

THE ACTOR'S BODY

Actress Barbara Lockard in Oscar Wilde's *The Importance of Being Earnest* has learned to wear costumes and use props and furniture that are characteristic of a period vastly different from today. Theatre Arts of West Virginia. Directed by Ewel Cornett.

Of the basic elements necessary to acting, the most important are stamina and actual physical strength.
Sir Laurence Olivier

on an awkward body makes it appear even more awkward. Watching the early films of Katharine Hepburn and Laurence Olivier can provide a means for understanding the body's potential. Both Hepburn and Olivier move in a fluid, easy, articulated way. Young people's theatre actors need to acquire the same great control. A stage character will only be able to do what the actor as a person can physically do. The stronger and more disciplined the actor is, the greater potential the actor has for playing many different kinds of roles. With practice, actors will climb scenery with ease, perform choreographed fights safely and believably, as well as execute the smallest physical movement, such as the lifting of a teacup, with control and in character. A well-disciplined body is thus a prerequisite for the actor, just as a finely tuned concert grand is a prerequisite for the concert pianist. If actors are untrained, overweight, or physically awkward, you as director may suggest that dance, fencing, and acrobatic classes can help. These classes will tune the body as well as build skills and confidence.

THE ACTOR'S VOICE

The two basic components of the voice are the making of tone and the shaping of tone. The making of tone involves the addition of sound to the outbreath of air. Good tone should be rich and resonant without any hoarseness, stridency, nasality, or breathiness. Good speech is relaxed and rhythmic, without tensions or jerkiness. Breath inhalations are made silently and are well-timed. What is primary is that the voice should be easy to listen to and loud enough to hear.

The shaping of tone involves how the lips, tongue, and teeth work together with the rest of the vocal apparatus to make the tone into recognizable sounds. Sharp, brilliant consonants make an actor's speech precise and accurate.

COMPONENTS OF THE VOICE

There are nine separate elements that make up the voice. As director, you will be listening to your actors and asking them to produce the best possible voices they can. The following list may help you pinpoint vocal problems:

Component	Definition
1. Pitch	Level of the voice, low to high sound
2. Inflection	Rise and fall in pitch
3. Range	Distance between high and low pitch of comfortable speaking voice
4. Tone	Quality of sound of voice; includes resonance and timbre

Component	*Definition*
5. Diction	Word clarity, includes pronunciation (clear vowels and diphthongs) and enunciation (clear articulation of consonants)
6. Rhythm	Flow of speech; includes tempo, accent, emphasis, volume, pause, climax
7. Dialect/Accent	Manner of speech; the way words are pronounced, particular in a local culture
8. Intensity	Strength of inner feeling combined with manner of speech
9. Projection	Sending speech out a distance

MOST COMMON VOCAL PROBLEMS

As director, you want your actors' voices to be loud, clear, and interesting. The four most common vocal problems for actors in theatre for young people are (1) volume and projection, (2) diction, (3) range, and (4) accent.

1. Volume   Many inexperienced actors have not learned to speak on the breath; the only way they can produce a voice that will carry in a theatre is to shout. Shouting as a way of speaking is unpleasant and confusing to the audience and damaging to the actor's voice. An experienced voice teacher can train the actor to speak on the breath.

2. Diction   In pursuit of the clever character voice young actors will often neglect the clarity with which they speak. Poor diction is highly distancing for an audience of young people; if they cannot understand the words, they will "tune out" the play and the experience. Actors can learn to speak clearly through vocal exercises.

3. Range   Often young actors have not listened to their own voices or analyzed other voices; they may be producing a voice with very little color and depth. A flat voice is monotonous to an audience, particularly to an audience of young people, because children often listen to tone as well as to words. Suggest that your actors listen to their own voices, to one another, and to professional recordings.

4. Accent   Just as physical limitations restrict an actor from playing certain roles, regional accents will limit an actor, too. A Kentucky twang may be attractive and disarming, but Peter Pan in London in the early 1900s speaking like Daniel Boone will seem odd to the child audience. Encourage your actors to lose their regional limitations but to be able to summon them at will for certain character parts.

THE ACTOR'S MIND AND HEART: THE STANISLAVSKI METHOD OF PHYSICAL ACTIONS

Physical and vocal technique are important for actors to understand, explore, and practice. They are the first part in an actor's training. They are the outer aspect: the form of the actor. A method, a way of work to get to the inside—to the emotions and intellect of an actor—is also important to explore and practice. Regardless of how physically agile or vocally exciting an actor is, the actor will be empty and boring to the audience if the inner life—the emotional and intellectual reality—is not grounded in a full and specific method of working. Such a method of working was conceived by Constantin Stanislavski, a Russian director of the late nineteenth and early twentieth centuries.

UNDERSTANDING THE STANISLAVSKI SYSTEM

Until Stanislavski became a director in the 1880s, acting in the theatre was of the declamatory style. Broad, sweeping gestures, operatic voices, melodramatic poses, and "larger than life" behavior was at its core. This declamatory style had been in vogue for hundreds of years in many countries; it simply was what society understood acting to be.

Stanislavski changed that. He dreamed of a theatre in which real, recognizable human beings could be brought to life onstage through an actor's work. The remarkable element of the Stanislavski method is that it is not a random system; it is an orderly system based on the precepts of human nature. Stanislavski invented a way for an actor to re-create life under imaginary circumstances in an artificial situation, which is the theatre.

If you have ever had to speak or stand in front of a group of people, you know that you behave differently than you do in the privacy of your own home. Your head itches; you'd like to scratch it, but that isn't polite. People are watching. So you don't do it. You stop the impulse; you're watching yourself. Stanislavski knew that people behave in this way. He understood the actor's need to relearn how to live naturally in front of the audience.

Stanislavski also observed the phenomenon of an actor's inspiration: that actors onstage were able to cry, laugh, rejoice for no real reason. They are, after all, *acting*. Where do the tears come from? Stanislavski watched actors cry one night, because they were inspired, and be dry-eyed and empty the next night, unable to summon that "inspiration" again. Stanislavski knew that emotions cannot be summoned directly because they flee when scrutinized.

Stanislavski looked for a way into the actor's emotional and intellectual life. He looked for a means, a method, or a system that would allow the actor to deliberately and continually reach the emotional life and to touch it off, rehearsal after rehearsal, performance after performance. Stanislavski developed this method during his entire lifetime and named it his "method of physical actions."

The intensity of concentration of actor René Auberjonois and actress De Ann Mears in Molière's *Tartuffe* epitomizes the soul of acting. American Conservatory Theatre. Directed by William Ball.
Photo by Hank Kranzler

The link between the physical and the psychological behavior of every human being is the basis of Stanislavski's method of physical actions. People walk quickly to work for a reason: They are late. People listen for footsteps down a hall for a reason: They are alone and afraid. Children have temper tantrums for a reason: They are being ignored. Human beings do physical, "truthful" things for psychological reasons. Stanislavski knew that the only way for an actor to reveal those psychological reasons and to show real, not indicated, emotion on the stage was through doing actions in a truthful way.

Acting, then, is the reality of doing from moment to moment, living truthfully under imaginary circumstances.

AN ANALYSIS OF THE DEFINITION

Acting is the reality of doing   Plays are plays of physical actions, not merely of words. Playwrights craft plays about interesting characters caught in interesting circumstances. James M. Barrie wrote in *Peter Pan*, "Boy, why are you crying?" There are hundreds of ways to do that line. One actor may probe gently; another actor may attack and demand an immediate answer. Both probing and attacking are actions as Stanislavski defined them. However, doing does not mean gesturing. All actors use gestures, but the gestures must be organic and come from the reality of doing. For example, if Peter wants to impress Wendy, he may leap into the air with arms outstretched and begin to fly. The leaping and flying are the gestures; impressing Wendy is the reality of doing. Another actor may choose to impress Wendy by standing on his head rather than flying. An actor must know the given circumstances of the play before deciding on the appropriate, truthful actions for each line. The spoken lines come out of the physical actions, as though they are absolutely inevitable—the character could not possibly say anything else—and the physical actions come out of the given circumstances of the play. Making the right choice out of the hundreds of choices that exist for every line in a play often distinguishes the gifted actor from the average actor.

From moment to moment   A moment is a technical term that defines a do-able action within a time and place. Some directors prefer to call moments "intentions." One actor does something: She attacks her partner with "Boy, why are you crying?" This attack has a meaning to Peter, and the meaning is "defend." He does so with "What is your name?" His defense has a meaning for Wendy, which is "fight back." She does so, with "Wendy Moira Angela Darling," and a little snobby tilt of the head. This has a meaning for Peter . . . and so on, throughout the play.

Actors and directors discover moments or intentions in the rehearsal process, then set them; the actors can depend on each other to do the same actions each performance. However, since actors are human beings and the theatre is a live art, each performance will be ever so slightly different. Moment-to-moment work is especially exciting because of the tiny adjustments that actors make to each other to keep the performances fresh and alive. Note the phrase "tiny adjustment." If your actors are working moment to moment, this method does not give them license to change their blocking or actions during a performance. As British actor John Cleese of *Monty Python's Flying Circus* told talk show host Dick Cavett in a 1980 interview, "We do our improvisation during rehearsal. Why improvise in front of an audience? They've paid money!"

Living truthfully   If an audience is deeply affected by an actor's performance, it is because that actor has reached for the truth inside himself or herself and for the truth inside the audience. People respond because they recognize themselves in the actor's chosen behavior. Adult audiences are left cold by actors who do not reach for the truth; child audiences will get bored quickly and simply stop paying attention. Stanislavski realized that the way for actors to get to the inner truth is through an outer focus, the simple acts of doing.

Under imaginary circumstances   The imaginary circumstances are the given circumstances of the play. For example, child audiences (except for very young children) understand they are in a theatre in their hometown watching a play. But they also believe what they see—Lon-

"What does it mean to me?" are the most important words in the world to an actor. Act out what his slamming of the door means to you, and we'll believe you. The deftness with which you do this defines your art. No acting takes place in the head. It's all in the behavior.
Edward Moor,
master actor and teacher

don, around 1900, bedtime in a very cozy nursery, three children who have a *dog* for a nursemaid and a grump for a father. The director, the actors, the scenic, lighting, and costume designers all work together to create the imaginary circumstances.

THE CONNECTION BETWEEN STANISLAVSKI'S SYSTEM AND ACTING IN PLAYS FOR YOUNG PEOPLE

Acting needs to be specific to be interesting, and acting is doing, not just saying, the lines on stage. Because young people's theatre scripts are not usually as textually rich as plays written for adults, and the characters are not as full, the actors must be rich and specific in their actions to fill in the sense of the play. The Stanislavski system requires the actor to find specific actions to do. For example, Peter Pan cannot "act sad" when Wendy leaves—that is a general direction. But he can "say goodbye forever"—that direction is specific and actable. The way one actor may choose "to say goodbye forever" is by tossing the words over his shoulder in order to mask the sadness he feels. This walking away, the throwing away of the words, the "tough guy" voice all come out of his specific need to "say goodbye forever" and what that means to him.

In mastering the Stanislavski technique, actors will not have to depend on chance. For chance, as every artist knows, is the enemy of art.
Sonia Moore,
master actress and teacher

FOUR ELEMENTS OF THE METHOD OF THE REALITY OF DOING

The four elements of Stanislavski's method of physical actions that are the most applicable for actors to use in plays for young people are discussed below.

1. Given Circumstances   The Given Circumstances are the external environment of the play. It is the plot, the other characters, the super-objective (main thematic idea), the time and place, and the real space—the theatre or studio—in which the actors and director are working. The Given Circumstances dictate many of the available choices for an actor's physical actions.

2. The Magic If   "If I were King of the Forest! Not queen, not duke, not prince. My regal robes of the forest would be satin, not cotton, not chintz." E. Y. Harburg wrote the perfect Magic If song for the Lion in *The Wizard of Oz.* He is not the king of the forest—he's the Cowardly Lion. But what would he do *if*—how would he behave if he were? "I'd command each thing, be it fish or fowl, with a woof and a woof, and a royal growl."

No actor can truly believe he *is* the Cowardly Lion; if he did believe this, he would need a psychiatrist. But actors can make believe; they can put themselves into those imaginary circumstances and figure out what they would do *if.* "What would I do if I wanted Peter Pan to teach me to fly?" The Magic If helps to transform the characters' ideas and the playwrights' lines into the actor's do-able actions.

3. Imagination and subtext   As mentioned before, there are a hundred ways to do "Boy, why are you crying?" What this one line really means is in its subtext. The actor must make the subtext—in this case, "I want to know who you are!"—come alive by an interesting interpretation and do-able action.

4. Emotional memory/sensory recall   Actors bring *themselves* to the work in a play. They all have their heads filled with recollections of experiences, both wonderful and terrible. The Stanislavski system asks that actors use their memories, that actors match up something they know of themselves with something they know of their given circumstances, that they use their own memories to add to the imaginary circumstances of the play and to fill out the inner life. If you have ever spotted a mouse in your bedroom and bludgeoned it to death, you can understand American actress Geraldine Page in *Actors on Acting* when she says: "To play Lady Macbeth, you don't have to go out and find a king and kill him."

Every little moment has a meaning of its own.
Sanford Meisner,
master actor and teacher

FINDING THE SUPEROBJECTIVE

The superobjective is the main idea—the thread that ties the entire play together. To make the playwright's main point clear is the goal of the entire creative team. The job of each actor as character in the play is to find the actions that express the main idea. An actor expresses this superobjective in an active, expressive verb. As each actor works on a role, all actions can be logically checked against that main idea.

In working on a role, the actor's goal is to find out what the character does each moment onstage and why he or she does it. This process is shown in short, easy-to-work-with steps in Chapter 4.

I think it needs also actors who have in them a kind of wildness, an exuberance, a take-it-or-leave-it quality, a dangerous quality. . . . They cannot be casual for one instant. They must be aware. They must know how to do what they have to do. They must have style.
Robert Edmond Jones,
The Dramatic Imagination

WHAT THE DIRECTOR NEEDS TO KNOW ABOUT ACTING: A STYLIST FOR YOUNG AUDIENCES

In rehearsing a presentational, as opposed to a representational, play, actors must modify their rehearsal strategies. Still important, of course, is establishing a reality and believability of performance, talking and listening, learning lines, and blocking. Less important are emotional recalls, clarification of subtext, and all the other techniques that help actors with the development of three-dimensional characters. What becomes the focus of attention, for non-realistic roles, is the physical

manifestation of internal states. While never discarding the basics of representational acting, the actors must place more of an emphasis on outward shape than on inner focus.

No matter how much understanding an actor brings to the role, particularly in a presentational play, the actor needs a strong vocal tone, rapid and agile articulation, a good sense of rhythm and timing, an expressive, well-toned body, and a dynamic ability to focus. A sense of realism is not enough to convey the actions and needs possessed by larger-than-life characters. **Acting in *all* plays, but especially in plays of non-realism, has to be about *doing, not about being.***

A well-developed character, one that is as specific and interesting as Chris Kauffmann's portrayal of General Mitchener in George Bernard Shaw's *Press Cuttings*, is crucial to create and maintain the interest of an audience of young people. Asolo Touring Theatre, Sarasota, Florida.
Photo by Gary W. Sweetman

WHAT *NOT* TO DO

Failing to utilize a specifically conceived presentational approach for plays that are presentational results in two very different, but nevertheless disastrous, types of performances, which we have categorized as: (1) The slouch-and-mumble approach, (2) The perky, smiling approach. Spotting these two types of performances, analyzing the acting flaws as well as the audience response, and vowing never to establish these performances as role models can be the start for developing a positive, alternative approach to acting for young people.

SHOULD I UNABASHEDLY SCRATCH-MUMBLE-SLOUCH MY WAY IN, OR SUBTLY BIG-BRASH-LOUD IT ALL THROUGH THE SHOW?

Slouch-and-mumble approach   The performances in a recent New York production of *Alice in Wonderland* illustrate this lack of development of an approach to presentational style. Instead of a light, playful fantasy *Alice* became a ponderous, leaden piece. Most of the actors spoke slowly, moved carefully, and reflected intensely on every piece of business. The actress playing Alice, probably the worst offender in the production, mournfully stumbled from one episode to another, looking as if she were about to cry at any moment, constantly questioning the children about the whereabouts of the White Rabbit as if her very life depended on their answers. They were petrified. This lethargic and spooky Alice seemed more like Blanche in Tennessee Williams' realistic play *A Streetcar Named Desire*. The failure went beyond not meeting the children's expectations of a well-known literary character. Children in the audience kept asking their parents when Alice would enter, or they cried because this Alice seemed in such psychological pain. The effect was devastating; the children could not wait to leave the theatre.

Why this happened. This unfinished performance was probably more a result of ignorance than stubbornness on the part of the actors. Because the company was composed of student members of a resident theatre company, the actors probably did not know how to proceed to the next step. They just focused on their own reality, not on the presentational aspects of their script.

Ignorance is one reason that performances like the one described above may occur; *conceit* is another. Assuming that today's reality is the ultimate reality is the height of conceit. Actors who refuse to view the world of the play as different from the world as they know it are trying to make yesterday into today. They change lines to reflect current slang; they scratch, mumble, and slouch, when they should glide, sing, or soar.

The best remedy. Actors trained only in this misinterpretation of Stanislavski-based methods need to go the next step: to develop a technique for working in style. Actors must stop trying to contemporize yesterday by understanding the nature of *style* and viewing style as the vital core of the production. It is the job of actors to make themselves like the characters, not the reverse.

Perky, smiling approach   The other very common type of style problem results in a performance that is almost the exact opposite in nature. Superficially less boring to watch than the type of approach described above, but ultimately no less deadly to good artistry, is the "big/brash/loud" type of acting.

Every play is not a circus. The approach taken by bad actors in this category is to make movements bigger and faster, to project voices louder and stronger, and, of course, to smile through the entire performance. Famous, experienced actors as well as novice performers fall

But I cannot believe that intuitive imaginations in untutored bodies are somehow superior to disciplines and developed imaginations in skilled bodies, bodies with trained voices, accomplished speech, and brightly literate minds.
Orlin Corey,
"Go Make Ready"

into this trap. The audience seems to love all the pratfalls and funny faces. Critics often call this type of acting "overacting," but in fact such a performance is really *under*development of role.

Why this happens. The logic flaw in the development of a performance of this nature is believing that every period different from today (especially in plays for children) occurred long ago, took place far away, and is just lots and lots of fun. Plays that do not represent existing historical periods, like plays of fantasy or fairy tales, are often misinterpreted. Because there seems to be no grounding in actual reality, actors feel they can do anything as long as their behavior is amusing and slick.

The best remedy. In the perky, smiling approach actors realize they're in a larger-than-life world, but they must be directed to analyze the specific nature of this world. Being a young country, America does not provide a great sense of history. You as director can provide the actors with an image of the world they are portraying. They must be directed to analyze the unique style of each presentational play. They must study each particular period as it relates to performance.

You must provide actors with an understanding of the presentational style.

To work in presentational plays for young people, actors must first analyze the specific style of the play. Then they must adopt this style as their own, using one of the approaches, or a combination of approaches, presented in this chapter.

As we discussed in Chapter 1, the word *style* has many meanings. For the purpose of the following style analysis charts we have chosen to define style in this manner:

Style denotes the shared characteristics of a particular period in history.

In the following charts we have delineated eight major presentational styles. These eight styles have been chosen because:

- Mastering the skills delineated in these eight charts can prepare an actor for most of the requirements of theatre for young people, and
- Much of the current literature for young people's theatre is based totally or in part on these presentational styles.*

What these styles have in common is their intensely physicalized action, their non-realistic lines of dialogue, and their requirements of non-representational sets, costumes, and props. Presentational plays

> *The technique of acting can never be properly understood without practicing it.*
> Michael Chekhov,
> *To the Actor*

ANALYSIS OF STYLE: EIGHT CHARTS

*We recognize that some excellent scripts for theatre for young people are not entirely presentational in style, such as Suzan Zeder's *Step on a Crack*. Segments of this and other realistic scripts often contain material intended to be presentational, which can be analyzed with the aid of these charts.

The Beeple is derived in part from the comedies written in ancient Greece. Here actors portray bees in Alan Cullen's play. The Theatre for Young People, University of North Carolina at Greensboro. Directed by Linda Sirmon.

usually contain characters who are less psychologically complex. Mastering these styles will provide the actor with a storehouse of vocal and physical skills that can be called upon in any performance situation.

These styles currently exist, rarely in pure form, in the literature of plays for children. We have included at the bottom of each chart titles of plays for young people's theatre that are based on each style. Obviously, you and the actor must go to the original sources of style before you can analyze scripts that are derivations of these styles. (See sample plays included at the top of each chart.)

Remember that these charts give an overview of only eight presentational styles. For a more detailed discussion see the books listed in the bibliography at the end of the book.

OLD GREEK COMEDY
APPROXIMATELY FIFTH CENTURY B.C.

Representative playwright: Aristophanes; representative plays: *The Birds, The Frogs, The Clouds*

WHAT KIND OF CHARACTERS APPEAR IN PLAY
Probably caricatured, one-dimensional persons
Maybe a well-known figure who is being mocked
Possibly an animal or insect

WHAT CHARACTERS WANT OR VALUE
Usually a single obsession, like money or food and drink
Most characters value a sense of humor

WHAT CHARACTERS SAY
Mostly what they mean, even when a satiric idea is presented
Some may imitate insects or animals

HOW CHARACTERS SPEAK
In clean sentences filled with vocal variety, clear diction, and projection
Mixture of poetry and prose

HOW CHARACTERS MOVE
Highly exaggerated walks, gestures, and posturing
Athletic and disciplined
Extensive physical action and body involvement

PACE WITH THE WORLD
High energy level:
   On one end of the spectrum is a frenetic pace; opposite is frozen, caricatured posing, with underlying energy

EXTRA TECHNICAL REQUIREMENTS
Masks, half-masks
Complex makeup

SPECIAL PHYSICAL SKILLS ACTORS NEED
Singing, dancing, juggling
Pratfalls, somersaults, headstands, cartwheels

PLAYS FOR YOUNG PEOPLE'S THEATRE BASED ON THIS STYLE
Allen Cullen's *The Beeple* and *The Golden Fleece*

WHY ACTORS NEED TO MASTER THIS STYLE
Gives experience in playing animal characters that have human characteristics
Provides exercise in choral work
Provides opportunity to play obsessive/compulsive one-dimensional characters who say what they mean

right: Masks and stock characters, along with humor and sight gags, are characteristic of the commedia style. New York Baroque Dance Company: *Harlequins, Gods, and Dancers.*
Photo by Otto Berk

below: This is a modern adaptation of the commedia feeling, achieved without masks and period costumes. The Children's Theatre Place Company: *The Marvelous Adventures of Tyl* by Jonathan Levy. Directed by David Heveran.
Photo by Billy Cunningham

COMMEDIA DELL' ARTE
APPROXIMATELY 1550–1650

Actor-oriented theatre. Because performances were improvised, only scenarios exist.

WHAT KIND OF CHARACTERS APPEAR IN PLAY
One-dimensional stereotype; perhaps an archetype
Character types are inflexible, developed to a specific refinement, recognizable by audience
Characters include Capitano, Pantalone, Dottore, Arlecchino

WHAT CHARACTERS WANT OR VALUE
Each character wants one thing such as:
Old Miser wants money; Old Man wants Young Wife; Young Lovers want to marry

WHAT CHARACTERS SAY
Since characters make up lines, must be able to improvise verbally
Must have quick wit to improvise well

HOW CHARACTERS SPEAK
Vocal dexterity essential
Improvised prose, memorized poetry in songs

HOW CHARACTERS MOVE
Acrobatic
Forceful, but also with flexibility
With whole body, well-tuned

PACE WITH THE WORLD
Glib, quick
Fun-oriented

EXTRA TECHNICAL REQUIREMENTS
Homemade musical instruments
Masks and half-masks (except young lovers)

SPECIAL PHYSICAL SKILLS ACTORS NEED
Acrobatic techniques: juggling and tumbling
Singing and dancing

PLAYS FOR YOUNG PEOPLE'S THEATRE BASED ON THIS STYLE
Aurand Harris' *Androcles and the Lion*
Jonathan Levy's *Marco Polo*
Moses Goldberg's *Hansel and Gretel*

WHY ACTORS NEED TO MASTER THIS STYLE
Allows actors to develop finished pieces from scenario
Gives examples of *lazzi* (comic stage business) and *burla* (comic jokes) that still work today
Provides understanding of "stock" characters who still exist

ELIZABETHAN
APPROXIMATELY 1570–1620

Major playwright is Shakespeare; major plays include *Macbeth, Romeo and Juliet, Twelfth Night, As You Like It, Julius Caesar*

WHAT KIND OF CHARACTERS APPEAR IN PLAY
Characters vary from those who could exist, who actually did exist, to ones who could not exist, like witches
Most characters are truthful and believable, with complex personalities

WHAT CHARACTERS WANT OR VALUE
Often complex desires, rooted in Renaissance and Elizabethan social, philosophical, and theological thought
Often the necessity to fulfill their destiny

WHAT CHARACTERS SAY
Subjects are vast: Characters talk about love, death, jealousy, ambition, greed

HOW CHARACTERS SPEAK
How characters speak is as important as *what* they say
Tremendous range of tone and volume
Often in iambic pentameter
They may speak to audience through soliloquy or aside

HOW CHARACTERS MOVE
Use of full body; clear and fluid
Sometimes theatricalized for tragedy, more flexible for comedy
Action suited to emotion and language

PACE WITH THE WORLD
Varied: tragedies may require grand, noble, slower pacing; comedies more rhythmic, quick, light

EXTRA TECHNICAL REQUIREMENTS
Elaborate costumes
Foils, swords, weapons used for combat scenes
Intricate hand and costume props such as purses, hats, and candles

SPECIAL PHYSICAL SKILLS ACTORS NEED
Language requires vocal dexterity
Ability to work with iambic pentameter poetry
Singing, period court dancing

PLAYS FOR YOUNG PEOPLE'S THEATRE BASED ON THIS STYLE
Mostly adaptations of Shakespearean texts
Occasionally stories modified, but not purely in original style: for example, Graczyk's *To Be* and Harris' *Rude Mechanicals*

WHY ACTORS NEED TO MASTER THIS STYLE
Gives opportunity to work with complex thoughts refined through poetry
Affords practice in working with elaborate costumes and props
Provides a knowledge of the plots and characters upon which many subsequent plays and references are based
Enables actors to develop three-dimensional characters

FRENCH NEOCLASSIC COMEDY
APPROXIMATELY 1630–1670

Major playwright is Molière; representative plays include *Tartuffe, The Miser, The Imaginary Invalid, The Doctor in Spite of Himself*

WHAT KIND OF CHARACTERS APPEAR IN PLAY
From all levels of society
Vulnerable to human weaknesses, often to ludicrous extremes
Often based on the commedia dell' arte types; or magnified portrayal of person grounded in real life

WHAT CHARACTERS WANT OR VALUE
Abstract ideals are the concern, such as honor/dishonor, sin/innocence, loyalty/treachery, respect/contempt, authority/servility
Manners and customs of society

WHAT CHARACTERS SAY
Often satirize society
Often gossip about their smaller world
Speak about their needs, but with wit

HOW CHARACTERS SPEAK
Complex inflections, vocal variety because of Alexandrine couplets
With seriousness, even though what characters say is ludicrous

HOW CHARACTERS MOVE
Hands and heads dominant; gestures broad and punctuated by hand and wrist movement
At rest, character's weight on back foot with front foot forward
Characters move freely and elegantly; both sexes glide
Elaborate social movements: bowing, curtsying, greetings

PACE WITH THE WORLD
Characters interact rapidly
Characters deal with the world precisely

EXTRA TECHNICAL REQUIREMENTS
Long, full wigs
Elaborate costumes
Hand props such as fans, snuffboxes, canes, handkerchiefs

SPECIAL PHYSICAL SKILLS ACTORS NEED
Unusual vocal dexterity
Dancing and singing
Play such instruments as viol or lute

PLAYS FOR YOUNG PEOPLE'S THEATRE BASED ON THIS STYLE
Dale and Dunlop's *Scapino*
Harris' adaptation of *The Doctor in Spite of Himself*

WHY ACTORS NEED TO MASTER THIS STYLE
Many scripts for young people taken directly from Molière
Gives practice dealing with characters who appear to be serious to themselves but are funny to audience
Provides opportunity to work with lyrical, musical speech

TWENTIETH-CENTURY NON-REALISM
APPROXIMATELY 1890–1920s

Umbrella category for many specific styles, including expressionism and symbolism; representative playwrights include Maurice Maeterlinck, Elmer Rice, August Strindberg, Karel Čapek, and Alfred Jarry

WHAT KIND OF CHARACTERS APPEAR IN PLAY
Characters often representative of states of mind or all humankind
May symbolize abstract concepts such as "Love" or "Mother"
May symbolize place in society, like "Mr. Zero"

WHAT CHARACTERS WANT OR VALUE
Characters live in a world where reality and dreams mingle together
Motivated by ideas, themes, social and political functions
See selves as small representatives of a much greater function

WHAT CHARACTERS SAY
Talk about love or about society, particularly modernization of the world
Often characters speak from the playwright's point of view

HOW CHARACTERS SPEAK
Often staccato dialogue, machine-gun-like; or
Speech is ethereal and lyrical, with extensive pauses; or
Speech is filled with wild, piercing yells and/or loud chants and intonations

HOW CHARACTERS MOVE
Movements may be mechanical, staccato, robotlike;
Movements may be graceful, lyrical, as if in sleep, with a mystical quality;
Movements may be acrobatic and highly theatricalized in the manner of *biomechanics* of Meyerhold

PACE WITH THE WORLD
Varies greatly according to specific style
One end of spectrum is lyricism; other is wild, acrobatic freneticism

EXTRA TECHNICAL REQUIREMENTS
Masks
Constructivist sets such as ramps, trapezes, cylinders
Set pieces that merely indicate locale

SPECIAL PHYSICAL SKILLS ACTORS NEED
Acrobatics
Ability to chant and intone

PLAYS FOR YOUNG PEOPLE'S THEATRE BASED ON THIS STYLE
Maeterlinck's *The Blue Bird*
W. C. de Mille's *The Forest Ring*
Gagliano's *The Hide-and-Seek Odyssey of Madeline Gimple*

WHY ACTORS NEED TO MASTER THIS STYLE
Provides an understanding of basis for many avant-garde forms
Affords practice in playing nonhuman characters
Gives practice in dealing with plays with themes based on reality
Allows practice in moving on a constructivist set

left: *The Shape We're In,* an original script by Korty and Miller, owes a great debt to the twentieth-century non-realistic style. Theatre Department, State University of New York, College at Brockport. Directed by Carol Korty.

Photo by Susan Reger

below: Many of the conventions in Brechtian drama work well for audiences of young people. Masks and puppets help the director and designer make a strong visual statement. Hartford Stage Company, Hartford, Connecticut: *Galileo* by Bertolt Brecht. Directed by Paul Weidner. Designed by John Conklin.

BRECHT AND EPIC STYLE
APPROXIMATELY 1920s–1980s

Although Brecht died in 1956, he is the major playwright; major plays: *Caucasian Chalk Circle, Threepenny Opera, Mother Courage and Her Children*

WHAT KIND OF CHARACTERS APPEAR IN PLAY
May be a person who actually existed
May be a modern character reacting to the past, or a character of the past relating to the present
May be a character used as an example to teach something or as a symbol

WHAT CHARACTERS WANT OR VALUE
Must teach the audience a lesson
Must arouse and shock
Never allow the audience to become too emotionally involved

WHAT CHARACTERS SAY
Propose arguments; hope to effect change in audience
Must make audience think instead of feel
Must make audience know they are watching a play

HOW CHARACTERS SPEAK
Through long songs of dissonant tunes
Through "colloquial poetry"
Through combination of believable human speech and overtly theatricalized, humanized lines

HOW CHARACTERS MOVE
Both walking and gesturing, sometimes based on Oriental theatre
Use acrobatics, dance, mime, so body must be well-trained
Mix of many techniques including biomechanics, all intensely physical

PACE WITH THE WORLD
Extremely varied—from slow and ponderous to quick and agile

EXTRA TECHNICAL REQUIREMENTS
Screens with slides and films
Masks; music on stage
Visible theatre mechanics; set changes made in view of audience

SPECIAL PHYSICAL SKILLS ACTORS NEED
Ability to talk with and to audience
Use of alienation devices (placards and film clips, for example)
Need for physical and vocal flexibility

PLAYS FOR YOUNG PEOPLE'S THEATRE BASED ON THIS STYLE
Madge Miller's *Land of the Dragon*
Belgrade TIE's *Rare Earth*
Leeds TIE's *Sweetie Pie*

WHY ACTORS NEED TO MASTER THIS STYLE
Gives another approach to storytelling: utilizing a narrator whose primary function is to observe and report
Provides techniques that can stimulate an intellectual response
Affords familiarity with some Oriental approaches to theatre

TWENTIETH-CENTURY AMERICAN MUSICAL COMEDY
APPROXIMATELY 1940 TO TODAY

Representative composer/lyricists include Rodgers and Hart, Rodgers and Hammerstein, Lerner and Loewe, Sondheim; representative plays include *Oklahoma, My Fair Lady, Sweeney Todd, Annie*

WHAT KIND OF CHARACTERS APPEAR IN PLAY
All types: sometimes stereotypes, from all classes; common are young lovers, heroes and villains, both homespun and royal
Classifications include: ingenue, juvenile, leading man, leading woman, character man, character woman

WHAT CHARACTERS WANT AND VALUE
Gaining an ultimate goal, such as revenge or money
Changing social status
Winning, with a passion

WHAT CHARACTERS SAY
In songs, often speak beautiful rhymes or unrhymed poetry
In dialogue, make simple statements, usually to move the story along

HOW CHARACTERS SPEAK
In short dialogue sections interspersed with recitative and songs
Either in solo or with groups

HOW CHARACTERS MOVE
In and out of songs and dances believably, in character with agility
All types of movement required: tap, jazz, modern, ballet

PACE WITH THE WORLD
Two extremes: either very happy, quick, light movements, even the illusion of soaring, with resultant happy ending; very sad, heavy, aggressive, languid movements, with resultant tragic ending
Both with musical underscoring; extremes may be mixed together

EXTRA TECHNICAL REQUIREMENTS
Every possible type of property, from guns to parasols
Scenery that flies, turns, glides

SPECIAL PHYSICAL SKILLS ACTORS NEED
Strong singing voice; ability to read music; strong dance training
Gymnastic ability for tumbling, fighting

PLAYS FOR YOUNG PEOPLE'S THEATRE BASED ON THIS STYLE
Peter Pan (musical version)
Rodgers and Hammerstein's *Cinderella*
Aurand Harris' *Rags to Riches*

WHY ACTORS NEED TO MASTER THIS STYLE
Provides practice in singing and dancing in character, making these forms of expression inevitable, with orchestra/music
Gives opportunity both to stand out (solo or lead) and to blend in (chorus)

ABSURD

APPROXIMATELY 1950–1970, ALTHOUGH STILL SOMEWHAT CONTEMPORARY

Major playwrights include Beckett and Ionesco; representative plays include *Waiting for Godot, Rhinoceros*

WHAT KIND OF CHARACTERS APPEAR IN PLAY
A character faced with a moral dilemma
A character who feels that the world and human condition are senseless
Characters may be stereotypes or represent all humanity

WHAT CHARACTERS WANT OR VALUE
Ritualistic ceremonies of many sorts: eating, sleeping, most daily activities
Must find the meaning of life

WHAT CHARACTERS SAY
Reality often distorted: realistic, then situations or characters change
Words often used as sounds or noise, but must be spoken with energy, variety, clarity

HOW CHARACTERS SPEAK
Often berate or assault the audience
Often play the humor that arises from incongruity
May speak in excessively lyrical manner or shout overabbreviated sentences

HOW CHARACTERS MOVE
Movement may begin realistically, then evolve to robotlike, animal movements or into song and dance
Physical dexterity and timing stressed

PACE WITH THE WORLD
Important to search for humor in way characters deal with world
Although little time may pass, play does not move at slow pace

EXTRA TECHNICAL REQUIREMENTS
Costumes that dress actors like animals, machines, and other inanimate objects

SPECIAL PHYSICAL SKILLS ACTORS NEED
Vaudeville: dancing, tap dancing, soft-shoe
Magic and other circus skills
Slapstick and burlesque

PLAYS FOR YOUNG PEOPLE'S THEATRE BASED ON THIS STYLE
Mary Melwood's *Tingalary Bird* and *Five Minutes to Morning*
Joan Aiken's *Winterthing* and *Mooncusser's Daughter*

WHY ACTORS NEED TO MASTER THIS STYLE
Gives experience in transformations, not transitions
Promotes work in justifying non sequiturs
Provides experience in vaudeville/music hall interspersed with serious text

The Robber Bridegroom by Alfred Uhrey, based on the novella by Eudora Welty, brings exciting staging, energetic characters, and Appalachian melodies to a folk tale that children enjoy. Actors: Patti LuPone, Kevin Kline. The Acting Company. (See chart, page 89.)
Photo by Diane Gorodnitzki

Actors master these charts and develop their roles in one of two basic ways. They work either from: Inside/Out or Outside/In. These two alternative approaches are the result of two different philosophies and two different kinds of actor training. "Inside/Out" actors believe that they must first find the inner life of the character. These character justifications then set off in the actor appropriate and organic ways of manifesting the behavior. On the other hand, "Outside/In" actors first search for the shape of the character—the walk or the talk, for example. These physical responses set off appropriate inner feelings within the actor. Various techniques to master each approach have been developed by proponents of each philosophy.

An actor may be a dedicated follower of just one of the two approaches. Another actor may utilize the Inside/Out approach for the development of one type of role and embrace the Outside/In for another role. Or an actor may use a combination of these alternative approaches. The actor, for example, may start by developing a walk and a speech pattern (Outside/In), then work to justify character behavior (Inside/Out), and finally utilize specific props and costume pieces to give the final rhythm to the character (Outside/In).

In order for you to understand these two different philosophies of acting, we present these two approaches separately. Under each alternative approach we discuss some of the techniques that actors may utilize or that you can encourage your actors to embrace.

At the core of any Inside/Out approach must be an understanding of the principles of realistic acting developed by Stanislavski and his followers. Often, however, these principles do not seem to apply to the

ALTERNATIVE APPROACHES TO PRESENTATIONAL ACTING

INSIDE/OUT APPROACH

special demands of theatre for young people. Or actors may get bogged down in the transferring of the results of exercises to actual text. An Inside/Out approach can work with presentational plays and plays for young people. Good actors have always been able to solve the problem of using a reality-based method with presentational scripts. Instinctively they have realigned their thinking, reassessed their objectives, and refocused their attention. They have used the same Stanislavski-based information, but with a modified point of view. They have chosen to utilize a very internal but very *active* way to work on character.

Many Inside/Out techniques can work for presentational theatre. One particularly useful technique embraces the principles of *cybernetics* and offers the actor a clear viewpoint and practical perspective for character development. **Cybernetics** is a term coined by scientists to describe a system (or person) that reaches its goals by acquiring information from self as well as from environment.

Although cybernetics was developed in the 1940s to explain complex systems like computers, the principles upon which cybernetics is based have as much relevance to explain complex systems of human behavior. Cybernetic analysis is based on feedback from the *future* rather than cause from the *past*. For example, a rocket aimed for the moon is programmed to analyze in a cybernetic manner: It is not aimed directly, but analyzing new data as it moves on its course, altering its path as unexpected obstacles confront it, it ultimately reaches the desired goal. Human beings deal with life in a very similar manner. "Cybernetic" people have self-correcting systems that depend on feedback, sometimes expected and sometimes unexpected, gleaned by their sensing instruments (the five senses) to reach their target.

The cybernetic approach changes the focus from the more traditional "What has happened in the past?" to a more flexible "What will happen in the future?" This technique can assist the actor in dealing with the important actor/audience relationship so significant in presentational plays. It can help the actor to justify incredible actions, to flesh out incomplete characters, and to work with audience participation—often important factors in plays for young people.

THE SUPER SIX

Following are six principles based on cybernetic analysis* that actors can use in an Inside/Out approach:

1. Think ahead, not behind   Instead of trying to figure out what past events cause a character to do something today, think instead of what

---

*An excellent acting book based almost entirely on the cybernetic theory of acting is *Acting Power* by Robert Cohen (Palo Alto, CA: Mayfield Publishing Company, 1978). Many of the ideas and exercises in this section are derived in part from Cohen's lengthy discussions.

the character wants to have happen in the future as a stimulus for what the character does today.

With the core of the technique becoming the future, not the past, the main question for actors to ask becomes "What for?" not "Why?" The "why" and "what for" may seem initially to mean the same thing, but knowing and applying the difference can add subtlety to a performance. "Why" relates to the past and to prior motivation. "What for" asks questions in terms of the future and intended result. The following example from *Alice in Wonderland* (the many plays based on the book of the same title) may prove helpful. *Why* does Alice curtsy to the Red Queen? Because her mother taught her to curtsy to her elders. *For what reason* does Alice curtsy to the Red Queen? To stop the Red Queen from escaping before Alice can question her. "Whys" are given; "what fors" are what the actors figure out. Analyzing actions with "what for" as opposed to "why" will provide the actor with more *doing* as opposed to *thinking* actions.

Actors must imagine that their characters are pulled to the end of the play by the future, not by the past. Analyzing actions from a pulling perspective helps the actor make choices that are more focused. Another example from *Alice in Wonderland* may help explain the difference between being pulled by future and being pushed by past. Some actions, like searching for a familiar kind of food during the tea party scene or even comparing this world to the one above ground (both of which focus on the past), portray Alice as very neurotic. Actions like savoring the differences of this world or attempting to remember every detail to relate to friends back home make Alice more lively, more active, and more focused on the future. Actors in plays of non-realism must study the past only insofar as it guides and forecasts the future that lies ahead.

In theatre for young people, actors often must justify seemingly ridiculous physical behavior. Here actress Fredi Olster is about to hide in a large basket. American Conservatory Theatre: *The Merry Wives of Windsor* by William Shakespeare. Directed by Jon Jory.
Photo by William Ganslen

. . . .

Probably nothing so regularly typifies dull and deadly theatre as actors who insist, usually passionately, that characters wanted nothing but modest goals, pleasantly pursued.
Robert Cohen,
Acting Power

. . . .

2. Develop a positive and active world view Most characters do what they do because they expect that those choices will get them what they want. The actor playing the character must make choices that will likewise succeed. Remember, even though the actor knows that a character "loses" in the end, the character must conduct himself or herself with no prior knowledge of what will happen.

Actors also must figure out a "perfect ending" for their character. By doing this they set themselves up for a fall and open themselves up for feedback from others.

Finally, actors must like the character they are playing. Even bad guys don't think they are doing dastardly deeds. They (as characters) feel that they are doing what they need to do to survive, to be validated, to get what they need. Actors must never apologize to the audience for the deeds of their character.

Often characters in plays of presentational style and in plays for young people commit dreadful crimes or do illogical, silly things. The reluctance or, worse yet, the refusal to hold dear what a character holds dear (on the stage, of course) will result in a seriously debilitating performance. What the actor does on the stage is the director's, the other actors', and the audience's business. Actors who constantly comment to the adults in the back row of the house with winks and blinks and ho ho's to show that the character they are playing is silly should never have accepted the parts.

OH, MY INVISIBLE WITNESS IN THE AUDIENCE, I LOVE YOU!

3. Develop a private audience Another helpful rehearsal technique is for the actor to develop a person or group of people significant to the character who can then be invisible witnesses to the action by being stashed in the audience. In real life people often keep significant people with them in spirit at all times. When a person is in love, he or she may imagine that every deed is being watched by the lover. Pretending that the character's secret friend or greatest love is in the audience can enhance an actor's protrayal.

The person who might be essential for the character of Peter Pan in the play by James M. Barrie is his real mother. So the actor stashes this "imaginary ideal mother" in the audience and plays every action to her so that Mom will wish she had never deserted Peter. Another choice for Peter's imaginary private audience might be all cowardly boys and girls. Placing cowards in the audience will demand that Peter be especially brave so that these children will yearn to be as gutsy as Peter and never grow up. Planting and using these private audience members can create some very powerful characterizations.

4. Transform the seeing, not the being Transforming what the character *sees* rather than what the character *is* can equip the actor to deal with the problem of rounding out and playing two- or one-dimensional characters, who are often encountered in plays of presentational style.

For example, instead of an actor playing Reynard in *Reynard the Fox* by transforming himself into a bully, he can play Reynard by transforming the other characters in the play into stupid, naive animals, the way Reynard views them. Then the actor can use some of his own complex human reactions to stupid people to help fill in the performance of Reynard the Bully. The "Magic If" question for actors in plays of non-realism is not only "What if I were Reynard?" but also "What if *he* were *Brun* (another character in the play), what would I do?" In a similar manner the actress playing the character of Lendore doesn't play "humble" but characterizes others as powerful and knowing. The actor playing Epinard doesn't play hypocrite but characterizes the others as being too unworthy of receiving the words from God.

Instead of *becoming* another character, the actor sees others as the *character* sees them, and then plays his or her reaction to them, colored, of course, by what he or she knows about the character and script. Proceeding in this manner will help the actor to get outside self, so necessary in plays of presentational style, and to deal with the here and now, another necessity of working for unpredictable audiences.

5. Relish the style Actors must understand that the style of the play was not developed in a particular way just to give them trouble. Instead, actors should try to view the style of the play as a vehicle for getting the character what the character wants. Both the character and the actor may have trouble mastering the intricacies, for example, of iambic pentameter; neither the actor nor the character was born speaking blank verse. Elements of style are learned behavior for the character as well as the actor. Unfortunately, however, a character in a play by Shakespeare cannot exist without the verse. Take away the verse and only the remnants of the story remain. In plays where the world is so different from today's world it is urgent that actors master—and relish—the style. Romeo speaks beautiful verse to his love Juliet because he wants to woo her. Because everybody else speaks verse in this world, Romeo must do so, too, only much more wonderfully.

6. Bring the audience to the world of the play, not the play to the audience In plays of presentational style and plays that contain participation audiences are included in the world of the play. Actors, who have worked so carefully during rehearsal to develop this world, often make tragic mistakes during a performance. Instead of inviting the audience into their carefully conceived world, confused actors let the audience have the upper hand. Actors begin to work to make the audience laugh, instead of working to portray their wacky world, which should result in the audience laughing. Although these two statements seem similar, they are very different.

Under no circumstances are actors to relinquish control of their

> *We were on stage for the first time together, and I looked down into her eyes, and I saw that she was lost in total make-believe, which is the greatest gift an actor can have.*
> Helen Hayes, *speaking about working with her daughter*

In theatre for young people, actors often must play animals with human characteristics. Oklahoma City University Children's Theatre: *The Haunted Maples* by Eugene Schwarz.

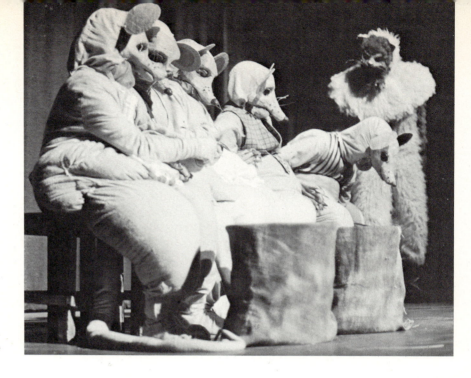

. . . .
You never get tired of playing for children.
Christopher Hewett,
describing his performance as Captain Hook on Broadway
. . . .

world. Actors do all they have planned during rehearsal and then let the audience into this wonderful world during performance. Laughter will be the natural response to this finely wrought performance.

OUTSIDE/IN APPROACH

Actors who utilize the Outside/In approach* believe that they must first explore the outward characteristics of their role before they work on inner feelings. Once the physical shape of a character has been established, the *in*ternalized feelings will be appropriately stimulated by this *out*ward shape and will flow naturally. Often actors who embrace the Ouside/In philosophy try on walks and costume pieces (discussed in the presentational charts) before they even know the specifics of their character. Outside/In actors use well-developed form to elicit feelings; they do not give form to feelings, which is the goal of the Inside/Out alternative approach. Well-trained Outside/In actors don't ignore the characters' thoughts and motivations, they simply believe that focusing first on the physical characteristics is a more efficient way to develop a character. Although this philosophy has physicalization at its core, vocal production and interaction with others are influenced by the Outside/In techniques.

Both of the following Outside/In techniques originated in the dance/movement field, but can work well with the development of two-dimensional or fantasy characters as well as with characters who are

*Many acting/movement approaches, such as Delsarte, Alexander, and Feldenkrais, are based in part on the Outside/In philosophy.

inanimate objects or animals—often found in plays for young people. Using techniques like these can also help actors master the physical and technical skills presented in the charts.

THE THREE-DIMENSIONAL BODY

Whenever a person moves, a *body* exhibits *force* in *time* through *space*. Actors must become aware of these four elements and develop character through a consideration of them. This specific knowledge can give focus and dynamics to a performance of a presentational nature.

Body   Body parts, body moves, and body steps are the three components of the body that actors must consider. Body parts include head, shoulder, rib cage, hips, back, arms, hands, legs, and feet. Actors must ask themselves how they can mold their body parts into the body parts that their characters might have; or in the case of an inanimate object— a machine, for example—how to make their body parts into the shape of the machine. Perhaps they need to stretch their necks or shorten their backs. The effect of changing their shape into the shape of the character may be infinitesimal to the casual observer, but the subconscious effect on the audience in the total portrayal of the character could be staggering. What parts of the body the character uses most reveals much about what kind of person that character is.

The next component is body moves: how the body moves while in place. What does the character do at rest? Stretch? Twist? Swing? Sway? Shake? In rehearsal, instead of just standing onstage fidgeting with their costumes, actors must choose movements that can characterize. They should experiment and try to summarize in two or three active, action verbs what the character typically does at rest.

Finally, actors decide how the body locomotes, or gets from one place to another. They figure out at what points in the script they change from one form of locomotion to another. Their choices are: walk, run, leap, jump, hop, skip, gallop, and slide. Although decisions of this sort seem very elementary, surprisingly few actors locomote very differently onstage than they do in real life.

Space   Even when the characters are not moving, they are making a *shape* in space at a certain level. When a character moves, that movement has *size, direction, focus,* and a *pathway.* Vital in the actor's portrayal is consideration of these factors. Questions actors might ask themselves are:

- *Shape:* Is the character round or angular?
- *Level:* Does the character move close to the ground or high in the air, like flying?
- *Size:* Does the character make large or small movements?

- *Direction:* Does the character move directly from point a to point b or make a zigzag move from point a to point b?
- *Focus:* Does the character look at something and move toward it, or focus behind, but move ahead?
- *Pathway:* If the audience were looking at the character from above, what sort of overall pathway might he or she be carving through space?

Actors who ask themselves questions like these help find specific character movements they might otherwise have missed with a less physically based approach.

Force All movements can be altered by changing *how* they are executed. Helpful factors for actors to consider are *contrasts:*

- If the character moves sharply, does he or she ever move smoothly?
- If the character moves loosely, what statement is made when the movements become tight?

How much, and what kind of, effort actors put into each movement adds subtlety to the performance.

Time Although time relates closely to force, isolating time as a separate factor may stimulate some exciting character movements. Actors may ask questions like:

- How does the character deal with time?
- What is the *speed* of the character's movements?
- What is the *duration* of the character's movements?

Allowing the character to complete tasks in a longer or shorter amount of time than other cast members makes a strong physical statement about the character's world view.

Once actors understand all these elements, making movement decisions becomes more finite because they have some concrete questions to ask. Each character movement becomes a question of which *body* parts move through *space,* making what shape with what kind of *force* utilizing what kind of *time.* This clear, practical method of movement analysis also offers actors a way to allocate and conserve energy—a very necessary factor in plays that are intensely physical, as are many plays for young people.

THE EFFORTFUL TECHNIQUE

Effort suggests a single action with a definite objective in mind. Rudolf Laban, who studied movement patterns of many varied cultures, concluded that in all the world there exist only eight sorts of physical ef-forts: actions with a specific objective in mind. He classified these ef-forts: *float, glide, slash, wring, dab, thrust, flick, press.*

In everyday life people utilize one form of effort after another. In making an "effort" to get out of bed a person may have to *press.* In preparing breakfast a person may execute three more efforts. Squeez-ing orange juice is *wring;* cutting bread is *slash;* buttering toast is *flick.* So goes the day.

After classifying these efforts Laban then separated the three vari-ables that go into each movement:

- *Tempo:* the timing of the movement, which could be smooth (called sustained) or quick (termed sudden)
- *Direction:* the aim, which could be toward a target (direct) or with no specific objective in mind (flexible)
- *Degree of weight:* the force used to execute a movement, which could be hard and strong (heavy) or delicate and easy (light)

An overview of effort and variables looks like this:

EFFORT	TEMPO	DIRECTION	DEGREE OF WEIGHT
FLOAT	sustained	flexible	light
GLIDE	sustained	direct	light
SLASH	sudden	flexible	heavy
WRING	sustained	flexible	heavy
DAB	sudden	direct	light
THRUST	sudden	direct	heavy
FLICK	sudden	flexible	light
PRESS	sustained	direct	heavy

One example of how this approach might work in a rehearsal im-provisation involves deciding which of the eight efforts best describes the character. One actor decides the character is Flick, for example. Then for the time being the actor sets aside the total characterization and concentrates only on personifying the essense of Flick. The actor explores ways of "flicking" with every part of the body. Once the actor finds some interesting ways to "flick," he or she goes through the script to find places where these movements can be utilized in con-junction with the dialogue.

Another example of a rehearsal improvisation utilizing the Effortful Technique might be the confrontation of two characters. Each actor chooses one of the classifications of effort to personify his or her char-acter. The actors then set up a conflict situation with each other; they each try physically and vocally to overpower each other. The conflict becomes, for example, Flick versus Press.

Actor 1 might ask: How can I as Press conquer Flick? The answers might be:

- through sustained, constant movement in contrast to Flick's sudden movements
- through direct, heavy movement, which overbears the flighty, unpredictable Flick

In essence Press can press Flick to death.

Actor 2 might ask: How can I as Flick conquer Press? The answers might be:

- through sudden movements that take Press by surprise
- through light, flexible movements that happen so quickly and from so many directions that stodgy Press is conquered

In essence Flick can flick Press to death. The actors then try to find places in the script to use these conflicts, in a modified way. As director, a provocative question to ask yourself is, which of these effort classifications best describes you as a person?

ASTONISH THE AUDIENCE

"You startled me and a good play has to startle people," wrote one ten-year-old critic of the Caravan Theatre of the Young's Medicine Show *last season.*
Virginia Koste,
director of drama for the young, Department of Speech and Dramatic Arts, Eastern Michigan University, Ypsilanti

Acting is a tough job. It is not simply a task that can be done competently. It is an art that must be executed brilliantly. Sergei Diaghilev, the famous ballet impresario, always said to his dancers: "Astonish me." That's what great acting must do: astonish the audience! Turn them on to the world! Make them see new connections and wild possibilities! Provide them with an alternate way of perceiving. Acting for anyone, but particularly for an audience of children, should never be ordinary. Acting is an affirmation of life, and who better than an audience of young people should witness such an affirmation?

I think you're a wonderful actress, and I want to talk to you about your acting. I want to know how you approach a role. What do you do?

I try to understand who the character is and why she does what she does. What is she feeling? What is this person doing that makes her behave this way? Just the way I try to understand anybody. I don't just accept a person's behavior on a superficial level. I really try to understand what's behind that person.

How do you transfer that thought onto the stage?

It's not just empathy; it's not just compassion. You can feel the feelings someone else feels; because as human beings we all share the same range of emotions, even though we are motivated by different circumstances in different ways.

How did you learn to act?

I studied with a coach. I had been told in undergraduate school that I was too bright, too big, too bold, too this and that, and I wasn't believable. Yet the same people who said my characters weren't believable described me later as a very honest actor. And that's because I also use my imagination. I try to be a very vivid and imaginative character who has an interesting personality with a lot of different facets.

Why do you like to perform for children?

The thing I like about performing in children's theatre is that your imagination can run wild. It's a very creative place because much of the material deals with fairy tales and fantasies and things that are magical. In anything that I do I try to achieve depth, to come from a place that's deep inside of me.

But once you have worked in a realistic style, does that work have any effect on the roles that are not realistic, like those for young people?

The coach showed me a way to be real in everything I do, even when I'm playing someone as crazy as a witch who lives in a tree. In one show I was a witch called Agatha. She lived in a tree. She was ugly, and therefore she couldn't stand to see anything that was not ugly. She had an evil potion and would put it on everything, so the plum trees in the forests turned to prunes. They shriveled and died, and a beautiful princess was turned into a gargoyle.

So you make that all real for you.

Well, it is real. Of course.

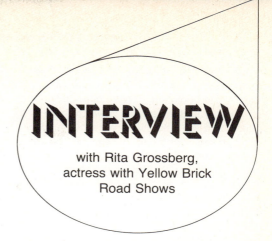

INTERVIEW

with Rita Grossberg,
actress with Yellow Brick
Road Shows

Is performing for children different from performing for adults?

You know, that's a funny question, because it is and it isn't. In a way it is, because an adult audience isn't going to respond the same way that kids are going to respond. The kids are spontaneous; they don't have a lot of the inhibitions of adults. So the rapport you develop with a child audience is more active and is a lot more alive because you are getting verbal, physical responses to what you're doing, whereas with the adult audience I have to sense the response.

How do you act for participation theatre?

The actor has to be aware. I do a thing with kids, an awareness thing, where I stand in the circle and I don't look at anyone in particular. I gaze at one spot and I know what everyone in that circle is doing. And I'm not looking at them. I can feel their energy working. I can feel the movement of their energy. And I can hear. And I can see peripherally. It's like heightened awareness. That's great fun for any human being, but it's really important for a performer, for an actor. What you need is that keen awareness to respond to their responses—how to act upon what the kids are giving you.

Did you ever lose control of an audience?

I think about times when I worked for the Asolo Theatre and I was touring in the Southeast. We did real heavy participation shows with lots of getting up and moving around, and some audiences would just get real crazy. I remember we were doing a story in which the prince was keeping a secret from the baker's daughter. He didn't want her to know he was the prince, and yet he was falling in love with her. Well, the kids decided that they were going to tell her that he was the prince. Right? One little boy, almost like a chant, started pointing, "That's him, that's him!" You know, you don't always have to respond to one kid, and the actors who were on stage—I wasn't on yet—chose not to respond. Before long there were ten kids going, "That's him, that's him!" Then the actors decided to respond, but it was too late. The whole side was yelling, "That's him, that's him!" The prince revealed himself to her, but nobody heard it and the whole audience was going, "That's him, that's him!" The baker came on stage and in a very large pantomime introduced his daughter to the prince. It didn't work. Everyone was pantomiming, but it didn't work. And my back happened to be to the little boy who started the whole thing. Well, the idea just came upon me during this mad chant, with the actors all frantic. I whirled around and directly said to that little boy, "We know it, and isn't it wonderful?" And he just went, "Ohhh," and the whole audience got quiet and we resumed the scene. Okay, so that's not a formula. It was do or die. It was direct confrontation with the instigator in a creative way. And that's the creative mind at work. It's the mind that doesn't get bogged down. It's the mind that moves, that keeps moving. Keep yourself positive. And keep your creative energy going. That's part of acting, but more than anything acting is being a hundred percent involved in the character. You are so totally committed and so totally concentrated as that character that people can't draw their eyes away from you, because the performer sets the level of concentration.

I don't care what kind of audience you have. You have the power to "suck 'em in." We did science fiction for a junior high school, down in L.A., and it was a rowdy, tough group. They looked like the type that would eat you alive, and the principal told us so. So before we even opened the door, the actors got together and said, "We know that they're going to love it. We know it. So go out there and act like it. And don't let them in that door until they know it, and they're going to know it by the way we act, by our attitude." You just embody that attitude when you first meet them at the door. And the space isn't their space; it's not their cafeteria. It's our space. It's magical, and we're in control. And the whole time you're there, you are totally one hundred percent there, totally concentrated, totally feeling everything you do. You're living it. How could anyone not watch what you're doing? You're so committed. They might not understand a word you say, but they'll be fascinated because you're so fascinated. This magical energy is happening because the people who are doing it are loving what they're doing.

What do you look for in an actor?

Honesty, warmth . . . and a sense of playfulness. You can be honest and warm, and you can be real dull, unless you have that spark of creativity. When you meet the person, you see it in their eyes. It's a creative spirit. There's a playfulness and there's sparkle. But they're talking to you and they're who they are. And when you are who you are, usually, if you're a certain kind of person, you're warm. But when you're trying so hard, nobody can see you. You have to relax. If you're not relaxed, people are seeing this fit of tension, this anxiety-ridden body and voice, and they can't see anything. When an actor comes to an audition really nervous, I say, "Please, I understand and I get really nervous, too, but I want you to relax because I want to see who you are, and I can't see if you're trying so hard."

Do you think your acting made you a better director?

Absolutely. Because I find a lot of directors can't communicate on a level that an actor is receptive to. You know, not to toot my own horn, but after every season people ask, "Where do you get those talented actors?" And I get them where everybody else gets their actors.

What do you do with them?

I find the places where they can do things and I start there. You know, talking about actors, there's so much potential there. My job as a director is to guide people to see the places where they can grow. It's opening doorways for them. "Here, look, you can do this."

How do you make the world real?

When you're performing, you have to believe that that fantasy is the way it is. You let yourself walk into it. You relax. You get yourself out of the way. Forget yourself. Be there in the environment. You know what my coach told me about auditioning? I used to get so nervous. I did things I never did on stage. He just said, "Be there, don't worry about the people much. Do what you know you have to do. If you understand the character and you know what the character has to do," he said, "do it. Don't think about yourself. Don't think about the people. Rather than losing your thoughts in those kinds of things, lose your thoughts in the situation that the character's in."

Do you want to be performing for children, as well as directing, in ten years?

I wouldn't mind. I don't want to be exclusive because I feel that when you have a gift, you should share it. I feel that it's a gift that I share, my talent, and I want other people to see how they can act. Another gift was to grow up in a family where I could experience the talent, where I could see my potential at an early age and begin

to realize it and express it. A whole lot of people weren't that fortunate. They haven't been guided by anyone else. So part of sharing my gift is to help other people with their gift. I am the kind of artist who feels I have a purpose: to communicate what I feel are important messages. And the messages that I feel are important have to do with morals and values and the human potential. And I don't just mean that everyone has the ability to create. Everyone also has the ability to be happy and to experience love in their lives and to live a life that's really full of positive energy. The world can be a really beautiful place if we realize as human beings that we have the power to make it and to show that on stage. Maybe that's the magic.

4
COACHING
THE
ACTOR

The director must never make the mistake of imposing his own ideas upon the actors. Acting is not an imitation of what a director thinks about a character.

Robert Edmond Jones, *The Dramatic Imagination*

YOU, YOUR ACTORS, AND DIFFERENT WAYS TO WORK WITH THEM

Chapter 4 explores the relationship between the director and the actors. One of the primary objects of the director is to elicit the best possible performance from the actors, individually and collectively. To accomplish this end, the director must develop a coaching approach that is based on a good understanding of the creative process, as well as on specific theatre skills. Working with actors is no easy task. Most actors would probably say that working with the director is often difficult!

The relationship between the director and the actors is more complex and less static than the usual relationship between boss and workers. Because the actors' personal lives must be delved into for material for character development, the director often knows all about traumatic events in the actors' past. Also, performers often put their egos on the line; directors must deal with the resulting nervous behavior. And finally, because the needs and desires of all must be merged into a collective, the relationship between director and actors grows increasingly more complex as the rehearsal process continues. Because each situation is unique, we've tried to provide a diversification of theories and approaches. If the director experiments with all of these ideas, something is bound to work.

The specific nature of the role of coach often eludes the director because what happens in the coaching process is based on such intangibles as excellence, ethics, values, and feelings.

EXPLORING THE ROLE OF COACH

WHAT IT'S NOT

Most directors view actors as nonpersons: They treat actors in the same way that a conductor treats his orchestra. The director fails to see each actor as having a specific way of working as well as a unique set of personal and theatrical experiences. Personality rarely surfaces in this rehearsal arena. If confrontations occur, the director tries to ignore the issue in the hope that the problem will disappear. Actors become tools in achieving a total effect.

Another way in which directors misunderstand the role of coach is to view the affiliation as a power struggle. The director devalues the actor by assuming a much more active position: that of dictator. The dictator-coach allows no discovery, no alternatives, and no opinions. As long as the actors do exactly what they are told, they remain in the production. One false move, however, and out they go; or life becomes miserable for them.

A third approach to the role of coach, equally disastrous, is to try to become guru/counselor. While more subtly manipulative than the dictator, the director who requires wholehearted devotion may also ultimately sabotage the production. The requirement of complete adoration from the actors will only increase the chances of developing a production that is self-serving.

What is faulty about all of these approaches is the way in which the director loses touch with self. The rehearsal arena should never be the place to find out who you are or to try on other personalities to see if they fit. Certainly, the rehearsal process is one of discovery, but first and foremost it is discovery in terms of performance. Many famous directors have been dictators or gurus or have shown total disdain for actors, yet they have been effective and even revered. As a beginning, you must try to promote a good actor/director relationship for the good of the production for young people. If you become a famous director someday, you can afford to be a prima donna. But you should know how to relate to your actors.

Many people outside the theatre world think all actors exhibit the same type of personality behaviors: extroverted, or extremely sensitive and childlike, or quiet and shy. People who have worked with actors real-

KNOWING WHO YOUR ACTORS ARE

Actor Jim Belushi leads a workshop session in techniques of improvisation for the Goodman Theatre, Chicago.

A good director has to be a psychologist. Some actors have to be told everything and others resent being told a single thing. Some you can yell at. Others you have to take to dinner and explain things.
Eva Le Gallienne

ize that this sort of generalization is unfair. Actors are of many different types and must be treated as individuals.

The scientific field of personality study has developed some categories that can prove helpful to the coach. These categories can help you develop the optimum method of stimulating a particular actor. Discerning what types of actors are in your production can assist you in knowing what kinds of approaches will work with them, individually and collectively. This doesn't mean that you should give a personality test to actors as soon as they are cast. But you can use this theoretical research in a practical manner to help the coaching process. Always remember, however, that you must use your judgment as well as some caution when adopting these techniques.

INDICATORS OF PERSONALITY

Katherine Briggs and Isabel Myers developed a test called the Myers-Briggs Type Indicator, which simplified Carl Jung's theory of human behavior and presented practical information about working with types. A coach can modify these four indicators into a checklist or category system for classifying actors into types.

First, the actor can be either **extrovert (E)** or **introvert (I)**. Extroverts usually relate more to people and things. Introverts relate more to the world of ideas and may be shy.

The actor can either be primarily a **thinker (T)** or a **feeler (F)**. Thinking actors usually consider their role and other actors impersonally, with logic and analysis. Feeling actors base their judgments on personal values and a more internalized system.

An actor can be a **judger (J)** or a **perceiver (P)**. Actors who are judgers usually make up their minds quickly; they also require more organization. Perceivers, because they reserve judgment, are more adaptable and make decisions about their role more slowly.

The final classification is the sensing/intuiting index. Actors who are **sensers (S)** depend on information they get through their five senses: They have to see it to believe it. **Intuitive** actors **(N),** on the other hand, emphasize ideas and associations made in the subconscious. Actors of this type often say they knew something without being able to point to a reason.

Which type of personality characteristics describes you?

WHAT TO LOOK FOR

Observe your actors in early work situations. Play detective. Set up a time reserved just to figure out what kinds of people they might be. Ask actors questions. Remember that everyone is a combination of the four variables. Sixteen distinct types exist in all. Early observation will be easier if you look at just one characteristic at a time.

During rehearsal break do your actors socialize with one another (E) or sit alone (I)?

When talking about their roles, do your actors analyze the script carefully (T) or explain how the script situation reminds them of their own life (F)?

Do your actors make choices quickly and refuse to modify decisions (J), or do they never seem to be able to make up their minds (P)?

Do your actors seem to be open to studying the costumes, props, and set designs (S), or do they seem to arrive at character decisions on some other level (N)?

Early in this observation process you may overgeneralize, but this search will at least lead you to focus on analyzing the traits of your actors and on finding the most appropriate techniques for working with them. Always remember that the ultimate goal of any director is to direct the best possible production; making everyone happy is secondary. But understanding how various people view the world does provide a handle on the working relationships that are responsible, to some degree, for the success or failure of the product. Even if you can't figure out which types the actors are, simply being aware of the many varied ways that actors deal with the world will make you more aware of the complexity of the group process.

Painstaking rehearsals are essential to produce ensemble performances of high quality like this one in Edmond Rostand's classic *Cyrano de Bergerac*. Center Stage, Baltimore. Directed by Stan Wojewodski, Jr.

Photo by Richard Anderson

EFFECTS OF EACH PREFERENCE IN WORK SITUATIONS

Type differences yield variations in interests, values, and problem-solving techniques that may facilitate or handicap the working relationship between the director and the actors. Understanding that sensers (S) like facts, intuitive types (N) like possibilities, thinkers (T) like logical principles, and feeling types (F) like a human angle may clue the director into an approach. A good idea can be presented in many different forms. It's up to you to communicate your ideas so that the production concept will be easily understood.

HELPFUL REHEARSAL HINTS BASED ON PERSONALITY TYPES OF ACTORS

INTROVERTS (I)
- Like quiet for concentration
- Tend to be careful with detail
- Dislike sweeping statements

FEELING TYPES (F)
- Enjoy pleasing people
- Relate well to people of all types
- Need praise

EXTROVERTS (E)
- Like variety and action
- Make decisions quickly
- Dislike complicated process

THINKING TYPES (T)
- Tend to hurt people's feelings without realizing it
- Relate best to other thinking types
- Need to be treated fairly

INTUITIVE TYPES (N)
Like solving new problems
Dislike doing the same thing over
    and over

PERCEPTIVE TYPES (P)
Don't mind keeping things open
    for alternatives
May postpone unpleasant jobs

SENSING TYPES (S)
Dislike new problems
Like established routines

JUDGING TYPES (J)
Like to have distinct plans
May make decisions too early in
    creative process

MERGING THE GROUP

Two distinct theories exist about whether or not to reveal type during
the group creative process. Some theoreticians believe that group leaders should not even reveal to the group that they have typed the actors, no less into what category they have placed each actor. The other
theory is that the director can be frank with most group members in
revealing each member's type. Most people's favorite subject is themselves. Finding out more about self, particularly when the information
may prove valuable, is interesting and fun. In conflicts during rehearsals, pointing out the types of each actor and the mutual usefulness of
opposites may assist the development of group cohesiveness.

To turn a script like Judith
Martin's *Dandelion* into a stage
presentation, the director must
focus on developing an
ensemble. The Theatre for
Young People, University of
North Carolina at Greensboro.
Directed by Tom Behm.
Photo by W. C. Burton

For example, during a particularly heated controversy about character relationship, explaining that intuiting types need sensing types to bring up facts, and that sensing types need intuiting types to see possibilities, may calm the actors. In a similar manner, pointing out that thinkers need feelers to arouse enthusiasm or to persuade, and that feelers need thinkers to analyze and organize, may help put out the fire of a particularly heated argument. Contrary to the opinion that opposites not only attract but get along better (in a group creative problem-solving situation, at least), research shows that opposites fight and may even destroy. The coach has to work hard to meld the different types with their differing world views into a working ensemble.

One final point about type: The last variable to consider in this process is how your type affects the dynamic of the group. Although you must balance all the givens concerning the actors, you must also consider what will work best for you. Your personality, your training, and your experience also are a part of this synergistic process. Giving up too much of yourself can be as deadly as remaining stubbornly dogmatic.

AN IDEAL ACTOR/ DIRECTOR RELATIONSHIP

Once you begin to know about yourself and to draw conclusions about your actors, and once the rehearsals commence, some type of relationship between you and your actors begins to emerge. During these rehearsals what will happen will be that you, keeping in mind your prerehearsal decisions, will figure out how and in what way each actor will add to your original concept. The actors will figure out how they will contribute to the total concept of the play. They will begin to evaluate you. Before the honeymoon period is over, begin to develop a clear mental picture of how this relationship should continue. A particularly useful image, which takes into consideration both the necessary positive and realistic negative factors as well as the mutual benefits, might be a strong tree full of branches and foliage. Picture the director's contribution to the final product as the trunk. With the director's help the actors provide branches first and add foliage next. Neither part of the tree can exist in a fully realized state without the other part.

THE LAST PEP TALK

According to Anselm Strauss, an expert on role training, "A coaching relationship exists if someone seeks to move someone along a series of steps, when those steps are not entirely institutionalized and invariant and when the learner is not entirely clear about the sequence." Interestingly enough, this statement can be made about all coaching relationships, from vocal coach to athletic coach. What the director must try to do in the coaching of a theatrical production is to:

Remember (particularly during the irritable stage) that you must not tell an actor too much at once.
George Bernard Shaw,
The Art of Rehearsal

- Throw the actors into situations to elicit certain responses, thus giving the coach the opportunity to interpret, predict, and challenge actors' desires and skills
- Not only base the work on the current ideas and skills of the actor, but seek to create new skills and desires
- Strike a balance between two poles; not pressuring the actor with impatience, yet pushing the actor when the actor appears ready but is reluctant to move
- When necessary, resort to such tactics as accusations, challenges, and dares
- Undergo a change as well, which is described by psychologist Nelson Foote as "a winning pattern for each," when both people in the coaching relationship have something to gain, and they make those gains.

So, you may have to be a little like Mom, a little like Svengali, a little like a good buddy, a little like a groupie head, a little like a super guru. You become a product of what you are already—a healthy, stable, talented director—and what your actors are already—a group of artists with various personalities.

The actors in your productions may have difficulty in physicalizing their part, in vocalizing their part, or with the rudiments of developing a role.

PRACTICAL ASPECTS OF COACHING THE BASICS: SOLVING BASIC ACTING PROBLEMS

COACHING THE BODY

You may encounter different types of physical problems with your actors. We have provided some simple exercises to help eliminate three basic difficulties.

Problem 1 You yell "cross down right," and your actors stare at you. If they cannot execute your directions, review the stage chart in Chapter 2 with them. An exercise you can do is to line your actors up onstage and give them different directions, moving them around very quickly. If you keep up this practice, they will be able to find their way around the stage easily.

Problem 2 You look at your actors and see how awkward they are. They don't know how to walk gracefully. They lope; they round their shoulders; they move only from the waist up. What to do: Review the principles of body mechanics with them; do some basic relaxation exercises with them; suggest they take a dance class. Impress upon them again the need for a strong, graceful body.

Problem 3   They don't know what to do with their hands, and they handle props clumsily and incorrectly. The clumsiness can be alleviated by a dance class; the correctness will come out of character work. The way they handle the teacup, the steering wheel, the cake, depends on their character. Leave this "hands" problem alone, and work on the exercises in the next sections on improvisation and character development. The handling of props and what to do with awkward hands will come out of the work and become quite natural.

COACHING THE VOICE

The voice is a critical tool for an actor. In the best of all possible worlds your actors have full, open, round, trained voices. They can do any dialect easily. They can be heard in any size theatre; they can go from a whisper to a scream in a long or short amount of time, with tremendously interesting and startling intonation.

Not so? The accompanying chart may help.*

THE ACTOR'S WARMUP EXERCISES

The following is a series of simple exercises you may use as a 5-minute warmup for your speech, so that you may rehearse or perform without strain. Repeat each exercise five to ten times.

1. *Preparation.* Feet apart, stretch up tall. Bend from the waist, loosely but vigorously. Try to sag the fingers to the floor. Raise the trunk, stand erect, and swing arms in large circles, one at a time.

2. *Relaxation.* Yawn, inhaling deeply and stretching the jaw as wide open as possible. Vocalize as you exhale—aaaaah!

3. *Breath control.* Breathe in deeply and fully. Exhale as slowly as possible through rounded lips.

4. *Humming.* Starting at a low pitch easy for you, hum one octave up the scale slowly, four prolonged mm's to each breath.

5. *Singing.* Sing with wide-open mouth, on a do–me–sol–do–sol–mi–do tune (C–E–G–C–G–E–C),

```
                        mah
                mah           mah
            mah                   mah
        mah                           mah
```

Repeat, starting one tone higher each time. Vary the exercise by using *moh*, *maw*, or *mee* instead of *mah*.

6. *Intoning.* Repeat the above exercise, intoning the syllables and keeping the speech pitch at or near the sung tone.

7. *Resonating.*
   a. Say the phrases below loudly, one to a breath, lengthening the underlined vowels.

D<u>ow</u>n and <u>Ou</u>t   H<u>e</u>re tod<u>a</u>y
N<u>ow</u> and Then   G<u>o</u>ne tom<u>o</u>rrow

*The chart was developed by Evangeline Machlin for her book, *Speech for the Stage* (New York: Theatre Arts Books, 1966).

Who are you   A loud sound
Me and mine   A round tone
Far away   Hold your vowels

b. Repeat the following, lengthening the underlined words.

The moon on the one hand, the sun on the other.
The moon is my sister, the sun is my brother.
The moon on the left hand, the sun on the right.
My brother, good morning; my sister, good night.

8. *Articulating.* Say the following limerick, or any that you know by heart, in less than 10 seconds. Keep the consonants sharp.

A tutor who tooted the flute
Tried to tutor two tutors to toot.
  Said the two to the tutor
  Is it harder to toot, or
To tutor two tooters to toot?

9. *Projecting.* Say the following or any similar group of lines in full voice, with lengthened vowels, lengthened m's, n's, and ng's, and with well-opened mouth.
  Now entertain conjecture of a time
  When creeping murmur and the pouring dark
  Fills the wide vessel of the universe!

10. *Interpreting.* Use the following, or any speech from a current role of yours, to complete the warmup. Say it in full voice and with clear emphasis where needed.

SONNET XXIII

As an unperfect actor on the stage,
Who with his fear is put beside his part
Or some fierce thing replete with too much rage,
Whose strength's abundance weakens his own heart,
So I, for fear of trust, forget to say
The perfect ceremony of love's rite,
And in mine own love's strength seem to decay,
O'ercharged with burden of mine own love's might.
O let my books be then the eloquence
And dumb presagers of my speaking breast,
Who plead for love, and look for recompense
More than that tongue that more hath more expressed.
  O learn to read what silent love hath writ;
  To hear with eyes belongs to love's fine wit.

Shakespeare

Often you find that your actors have little experience in developing their roles. They have difficulty in simple acting skills: talking, listening, and responding truthfully to the other actors on stage. Young actors who have not been trained in an acting technique often will indicate emotion rather than let themselves respond naturally in the rehearsal process. The following exercise forces actors to leave themselves alone, to focus all their attention on their partners, and to stop

COACHING BASIC ACTING TECHNIQUES: LOOKING, LISTENING, RESPONDING

acting cleverly in their heads. The Repetition Exercise is based upon Stanislavski's system of physical actions and is taught by Sanford Meisner of the Neighborhood Playhouse and Edward Moor of the Edward Moor Acting Studio in New York City.

The Repetition Exercise is sequential. Your actors practice each step until they are responding with their basic impulses, and then they add one step at a time, until they are doing all seven steps. Your actors can practice this exercise on their own; you can also begin a rehearsal with one pair doing the exercise for a few minutes, as a warm-up.

THE REPETITION EXERCISE

Step 1: Simple repetition   Each actor concentrates all attention on the other actor; this frees each from thinking about himself or herself. The basic rule is that the actors can only do what their partners make them do.

Example of the Simple Repetition: Two actors sit comfortably in chairs facing each other in the front of the rehearsal room. Actor A begins the exercise by making a statement about Actor B. This is a true statement that A is "getting" from B, but it has no point of view attached. Upon hearing the statement, Actor B repeats it word for word, and this line gets batted back and forth between the two actors.

(Actor B is really bald in this example. Actor A is not.)

Actor A: You have a bald head.

Actor B: You have a bald head.

Actor A: You have a bald head.

Actor B: You have a bald head.

After a few minutes stop the improv (short for improvisation) and have the actors start over, reversing the starting order.

As coach, you should let the improv go on for as long as both actors are repeating and exploring each other's behavior. In Simple Repetition the improv generally lasts a few minutes. Once the actors have put together all seven steps, an improv may last as long as 30 minutes.

The reason for the repetition: By repeating the words the actors get away from improvising intellectual verbal responses. The repetition forces them to explore behavior. Acting is doing, not talking. The playwright always provides the words; what actors and directors must find is interesting behavior, a way to do the words. Actor A works from what he or she is getting from the partner and states it simply; that statement has a meaning for Actor B. Actor B must then repeat the words, but in a different way that reflects what those words mean to him or her.

Step 2: Truthful repetition   This step adds the actor's personal point of view.

> *Actor A:*   *I like* your bald head.
>
> *Actor B:*   *You like* my bald head?
>
> (*several repetitions*)

At this point in the exercise something very interesting happens, which is the Change. The Change is an induced transition that comes from within because of what one actor is doing to the partner at that moment. The improv continues:

> *Actor A:*   That's right, I like your bald head!!!
>
> **The Change:**
>
> *Actor B:*   I *hate* my bald head!
>
> *Actor A:*   You hate your bald head?

It is the insistence of Actor A that provokes Actor B into the Change of words.

The questions "Why?" and "What are you doing?" are never allowed in this exercise, as they evoke new answers and get the actors off the repetition.

Step 3: Adding behavior with the three-moment game   Step 3 introduces behavior; there are only three moments in this step.

> *Moment 1:*   Actor A makes a comment to Actor B, based on what he or she is getting: "You have beautiful eyes."
>
> *Moment 2:*   Actor B responds behaviorally *only*, no words: for instance, by laughing.
>
> *Moment 3:*   Actor A responds verbally to the nonverbal response: "Oh, that amuses you."

The game is over, and the actors begin again, this time with Actor B starting off with a verbal comment.

Step 4: Adding the independent activity   This step involves the addition of a difficult task that one actor must accomplish within the improvisation. The task must involve a real object; for example, a model airplane. The actor must find a difficult task to do with the object; say, glue the plane together. Using imagination, the actor must invent a reason for performing the task immediately, such as "entering the plane in a contest worth $500, and the deadline is in one hour." Actor A begins gluing the plane, and Actor B begins the repetition, based on what he or she is getting from Actor A. For example, "You're involved." From this step on encourage your actors to leave their chairs and make use of their physical environment. (Important: In the heat of an improv an actor never knows what he or she will have to do to achieve the Objective. Therefore, sharp objects used as part of an Independent Activity can be dangerous and should be avoided.)

Step 5: Adding the knock and entering   Actor A begins the Independent Activity in the rehearsal room; Actor B knocks on a door to try to get into the room. Actor B should have a simple reason for entering, such as "dropping in for a cup of coffee." The improv could go like this: Actor A ignores the knock, causing Actor B to pound on the door. This pounding in turn annoys Actor A. Remember, Actor A's desire is to complete the Independent Activity; Actor B's desire is to enter the room.

Step 6: Adding the objective   Actor A has the Independent Activity. Actor B tries to get into the room with a new aspect, the Objective. The Objective is what Actor B wants to make Actor A do, such as "Give me back my ten dollars." The Objective gives Actor B the same sense of urgency that the Independent Activity gives to Actor A. Actor B should not tell Actor A what the Objective is before the exercise, and Actor B can never say the words, "Give me my money," since by following one of the repetition rules, he or she can only follow the partner's lead.

Step 7: Adding the relationship   This last step involves the addition of an imaginary personal relationship. For example, Actor A and Actor B may have continually fallen in love with the same girl. Those are the given circumstances. The improv begins as before: Actor A has the independent activity; Actor B enters with a strong objective. Caution your actors that they must not play an "attitude" such as, "I am angry with you because you love Heather." They must continue to work moment to moment, but having the relationship inside both actors should color the work. This cumulative final step in the Repetition Exercise begins to prepare actors for working on roles, since all characters in plays have relationships.

SCORING A ROLE

Often inexperienced actors need your assistance in breaking down large chunks of a script into workable segments. You can provide them with another Stanislavski-based method that simplifies the action of the play.

Plays are divided into acts; acts into scenes; scenes into beats; beats into moments, or intentions. Just as the director carefully scores a script, so must an actor analyze and divide the script into moments. The first choice each actor must make, in conjunction with the director, is to figure out the character's ultimate goal. Called the *superobjective,* this goal may or may not be met by the end of the script, but it colors everything the actor does as the character by providing a clear, specific focus. For example, the actress playing Wendy in *Peter Pan* may choose "I want to control all males" as a *superobjective.* Notice that the sentence reads "I want/infinitive/noun." Stating the superobjective in this way is fairly standard; however, the choice of superobjective for each production is not absolute, but depends on the specifics of each production.

Next the actor must decide what the objective is for each act, for each scene, and for each beat. A beat is a section of a scene that has an overriding objective and several actions that the actor utilizes to pursue this objective. In the first act of *Peter Pan* the actress playing Wendy, for example, may choose "I want to mother Peter Pan" as an objective for the whole act. Then, breaking down into the first beat, she may choose "to open the conversation" as her objective for that beat. Within that beat there are moments, or units, which indicate the smallest action unit of character development. For each moment she chooses an action to get her objective. She may try to charm Peter into choosing her to mother him; she may wheedle; she may force. All these choices are options the actress might consider in working out her role.

When an actor develops the role of a Spider in Mofid's *The Butterfly*, he must begin long before he gets into the costume. Actions and objectives, as well as the use of body and voice, must be discussed and refined by actor and coach. The Everyman Players, Dallas. Directed by Orlin Corey. Designed by Irene Corey.

Photo by Beth Odle

20   PETER PAN   ACT I

fairy language. PETER *can speak it, but it bores him.*)
Which big box? This one? But which drawer? Yes, do
show me. (TINK *pops into the drawer where the shadow
is, but before* PETER *can reach it,* WENDY *moves in her
sleep. He flies onto the mantelshelf as a hiding-place.
Then, as she has not waked, he flutters over the beds as
an easy way to observe the occupants, closes the window
softly, wafts himself to the drawer and scatters its contents to the floor, as kings on their wedding day toss ha'-
pence to the crowd. In his joy at finding his shadow he
forgets that he has shut up* TINK *in the drawer. He sits
on the floor with the shadow, confident that he and it
will join like drops of water. Then he tries to stick it on
with soap from the bathroom, and this failing also, he
subsides dejectedly on the floor. This wakens* WENDY, *who
sits up, and is pleasantly interested to see a stranger.*)
WENDY. (*Courteously.*) Boy, why are you crying?

Beat # 1

(*He jumps up, and crossing to the foot of the bed bows to
her in the fairy way.* WENDY, *impressed, bows to
him from the bed.*)

PETER. What is your name?
WENDY. (*Well satisfied.*) Wendy Moira Angela Dar-
ling. What is yours?
PETER. (*Finding it lamentably brief.*) Peter Pan.
WENDY. Is that all?
PETER. (*Biting his lip.*) Yes.
WENDY. (*Politely.*) I am so sorry.
PETER. It doesn't matter.

Beat # 2

from

Wendy's

point of

view

a   WENDY. Where do you live?
      PETER. Second to the right and then straight on till
morning.
b   WENDY. What a funny address!
      PETER. No, it isn't.
c   WENDY. I mean, is that what they put on the letters?
      PETER. Don't get any letters.
d   WENDY. But your mother gets letters?
      PETER. Don't have a mother.
e   WENDY. Peter!

The actress playing Wendy must search the script for indications of when one beat ends and the next one begins. We have marked the first two beat units in the Peter Pan/Wendy meeting scene. In Beat 1 Wendy *opens the conversation,* so that she can become Peter Pan's mother so that she can control all males. In Beat 2 Wendy *investigates* Peter, so that she can become Peter's mother so that she can control all males.

Each beat is further divided into moments; implicit in each moment are:

- Actions: transitive verbs that indicate what one character does to get the objective
- Activities: physical means to carry out actions
- Personalization of moments: the use of an actor's own memories of a similar nature to the character's, to stimulate both actions and activities—a way to *find* what to do.

We have divided Wendy's Beat 2 into moments. Each moment is indicated by a letter and is from Wendy's point of view. Remind your actors that the principle of the Repetition Exercise still applies in this work. The actress playing Wendy cannot choose actions to do on stage if they are not motivated by her partner. For example, she cannot embrace Peter if he does nothing to make her want to do that. The definition of acting as described in Chapter 3, "the reality of doing from moment to moment" is critical in this stage of the work, and these choices are worked out between actors.

Actions: *What I do*	**Activities:** *How I do it*
a. To win Peter	With a big smile
b. To reconsider Peter's possibilities	With a cock of the head and a puzzled look
c. To impress Peter with my knowledge of the world	With shoulders squared and head up proudly and formally
d. To investigate him further	With a press forward on the bed
e. To comfort with my love	With a leap forward and a warm hug

As coach, you must help your actors score their roles from their own point of view. Remember, score the role only into subdivisions that are able to be internalized by the actor. If your actors are novices, simply clarifying major objectives may suffice. More experienced actors may be able to score the role into precise moments. However, since the more specific performance is always the more successful performance, encourage your actors to work in these terms. Your job as coach is to help them define their moments clearly and execute them deftly on the stage.

LEADING THE WAY INTO STYLE

Coaching actors to work in a presentational style requires that the director develop some techniques and approaches to help actors *focus both internally and externally*. Although coaching plays of presentational style would appear to involve mainly cues and group run-throughs, ignoring the reality-base will result in a technically facile, but hollow and dead production. Actors most certainly need to master all the appropriate external behaviors presented in the charts in Chapter 3, but they must also learn to utilize all that is inside them in order to give life to the charts.

Actors must relate to the play's issues, values, and language, which may seem at first glance to be very different from the today world. As coach, you will have to help actors to see the relationship between the distant world and the more familiar reality inside their heads. They must see how what is inside the character may also be within them. What is so important for actors to grasp is that, once the *internal* search has begun, the *external* portrayal becomes much easier.

Another difficulty that actors voice in portraying two-dimensional characters is that they feel unchallenged by such roles. They do not see how these characters can be made believable. In fact, many actors turn down parts in young people's theatre because they cannot bear the thought of playing another two-dimensional prince or princess. Certainly, one of the current weaknesses of the field of young people's theatre is that there is no large body of excellent scripts.

It is very difficult for adult actors to portray children for audiences of young people. Successful portrayals like these begin with a careful internal search for the unique nature of each character. Metro Theatre Circus, St. Louis: *Mud Weavings.* Written and directed by Zaro Weil.

One of the best tactics to keep really good actors interested is to stress what Polish director Jerzy Grotowski calls the "grappling with self" nature of acting. Grotowski believes that actors do not need to identify with the character, or live the part they portray, or portray the part from the outside. Instead, an actor "houses the character as a means to grapple with his self." This exploration of self has a twofold purpose: to improve the specific performance and to improve the actor's craft in general.

You must point out to actors that they view this portrayal not merely as acting a fox or a king, but as an active means to self-discovery. In this case actors are permitted freedom not found in more clearly developed scripts, and so they can utilize more extensive possibilities in their character development. Actors must supply part of themselves to help characters become specific. The coach must be very definite about how to work with weak or nonrealistic scripts. Coaches must never apologize to actors because of script limitations; they must establish procedures that clarify how their craft can be developed through intensive internalized search and externalized behavior.

Although the cybernetics-based system described in the acting chapter offers actors a way to work from self, many actors have difficulty applying this approach to presentational-style scripts or scripts with poorly developed characters or conflict. Actors must make a connection between their inner selves and the outward behavior of the character. Your job is to help actors connect. Without personalization of the role, actors might as well be machines. Every actor portraying Hamlet or Reynard will play the role differently, in part because of the vast differences in their personal experiences. Actors must never feel that there is some absolute definitive Hamlet or Reynard. The following *image-based procedures* offer a way to zero in on the use of an actor's personal storehouse of experiences.

MENTAL IMAGERY FOR THE INTERNAL SEARCH

THE IMAGE AS THE CORE

This coaching approach* is based on the theory that an image is at the core of all learning, behaving, and communicating. These images—mostly visual (sight), possibly also kinesthetic (touch), auditory (hearing), gustatory (taste), or even olfactory (smell)—form the basis for everything we do. They are transmitted to the brain and stored there for a lifetime. We have a conscious or subconscious memory of everything we have experienced through our five senses. As coach, you must:

- help the actor retrieve his or her images
- help the actor utilize memory images

*The research that provided the theory for this approach was funded in part by a Rutgers University Junior Faculty Fellowship.

- increase the actor's storehouse of images
- merge the actor's singular images into a group collective image
- work with actors to get the images out of their heads and onto the stage

Using the image as the base of the coaching process provides a focus for both actors and director. Rather than engaging in some generalized rehearsal process, the actors can work to find specific images within themselves that can be enacted. Instead of evaluating some intensely personalized portrayal, the director can objectify the critique to some extent by discussing the success or failure of the portrayal of an image.

RELAXING AT THE BEGINNING

Psychologists in the field of mental imagery (the study of the image-related processes) agree that relaxation and concentration are necessary for the retrieval of memory images. Once actors are in a receptive state, they can push aside the freneticism of daily life and turn their focus inward. During the early stages of the rehearsal process, especially at the beginning of each day's rehearsal, help your actors reach a receptive state. It is during this state that you may also help increase the actors' storehouse of images by showing them specific objects, pictures, photos, costumes, or props.

(One interesting sidenote: If you are having difficulty in solving a directorial problem, you may try to relax yourself, so that you can reach inwardly for answers from your own personal image storehouse.)

You can use one or both of the following types of relaxation training. One is primarily physical, involving alternate tension/relaxation. The other is more internal, involving a series of open-ended questions. The following two charts are models for these two approaches.

Many actors, through negligence or especially because of shyness, use every possible excuse to try to get out of working, as a thorough-bred sometimes refuses to jump over a hurdle. It is quite an art and also a pleasure to persuade them—for they are almost always the most gifted and most interesting actors.
André Antoine,
"Causerie sur la mise en scène"

ALTERNATE TENSION/RELAXATION EXERCISE

Most imagery procedures are more effective if the actors achieve a state of general muscle relaxation. Here is the basic flow of an alternate tension/relaxation exercise. Try saying this text or modifications of it to relax your actors before rehearsal. Encourage your actors to relax at home before working on their roles. You might even have them tape-record one of your relaxation sessions so that they can replay it at home.

Lie down in a comfortable position. Begin to get in touch with your breathing. Breathe in. Breathe out. Breathe in. Breathe out. I'm going to ask you to tense and relax various parts of your body. When I say tense, I'd like you to tense that body part. When I say relax, I'd like you to let go of all tension. Try to focus on the one body part at a time.

Get in touch with your breathing. Breathe in. Breathe out. Imagine that as each body part is relaxed, all tension is gone. Tense your toes.

Relax. Tense your knees. Relax. Remember your breathing. Tense your right leg. Relax. You should feel your whole leg relaxing and settling into the floor. Tense your left leg. Relax. Now tense your buttocks. Relax. Tense your lower back against the floor. Relax. Tense your stomach. Relax. Tense your rib cage. Relax. Feel the tension gone in your lower body. We're working up. Push your shoulders back. Relax. Pull your shoulders forward. Relax. Now work on your arms. Make a fist. Relax. Tense your upper arm. Relax. Tense your whole arm. Relax. Now let's work on your face and head. Clench your jaw. Relax. Open your mouth wide. Relax. Grimace. Relax. Scrunch up your whole face. Relax. Eyes closed. Relax. Eyes wide. Relax. Now feel all the tension gone from everywhere in your whole body. Keep breathing. Breathe in. Breathe out. Now slowly begin to rise. Use just enough tension to allow yourself to stand.

Familiarity with the relaxation technique has distinctly positive effects on most people.

OPEN-ENDED QUESTIONING EXERCISE

Another approach for helping actors relax is to ask them a series of questions that they answer silently. The questions deal with possibilities, and they are to be considered internally. Ask the actors to lie down. Again, use a pleasant, soothing voice. Between questions allow from 5 to 10 seconds for the actors to answer.

Is it possible for you to feel yourself lying on the floor?
Is it possible for you to feel the floor with your whole body?
Is it possible for you to feel the floor supporting you?
Is it possible for you to feel your lower body only?
Is it possible for you to be aware only of your head?
Is it possible for you to close your eyes and still be aware of yourself?
Is it possible for you to become totally relaxed?
Is it possible for you to imagine that you are outside yourself watching yourself?
Is it possible for you to picture a beautiful outdoor scene?
Is it possible for you to feel good about yourself as an actor?
Is it possible for you to feel that your performance will be successful?
Is it possible to feel warm and secure in the rehearsal environment?
Is it possible for you to allow your eyes to open?

You can do this exercise daily at the beginning of rehearsal. In fact, the relaxation results are cumulative. Don't vary these questions. Don't change the order of questions.

FINDING AN IMAGE

Once actors are relaxed, they can more easily retrieve previously perceived images. For example, an actress playing Wendy in *Peter Pan* may suddenly remember during relaxation an incident where she met an intriguing stranger she hoped to know better, in a manner similar

No play should move in an
efficient straight line between
first rehearsal and
performance. This time of
survey and discovery is the
time, too, when the first
tendons are being formed
which will come to unite the
actor's personality with the
crescent figure of the character
itself.
Harley Granville-Barker,
"The Exemplary Theatre"

to the way she feels intrigued by Peter in their first scene together. A remembered look on the stranger's face, or the way light and shadow moved about the room during the incident, may trigger a whole series of useful, valuable emotions. This kind of memory image could be called an *emotional memory image*. It is particularly useful because the actress can retrieve this image whenever she wishes to feel that way again.

Images used in role development may be simple or complex. Early in the rehearsal process the coach must assist in the search for these images. Through creative questioning the coach can help actors retrieve these memory images. Using questions like

Did you ever feel like . . .
Have you ever seen . . .
Have you ever experienced . . .

can be the spark that stimulates the actors' initial finding of exciting images.

Once the actors have found the image, encourage them to stay with that image. Coach with encouragements like:

Stay with the image.
Really see the image.
Look for detail.

The more detailed the reexperiencing of the image, the more specific will be its usefulness in developing the role.

ADDING NEW IMAGES

Sometimes actors have difficulty finding images within themselves. For whatever reason they are not able to come up with images that they feel are important. What you then must do is use an object to stimulate an image. For example, you may show the cast of *Canterbury Tales* a thirteenth-century knight's shield. Also, share with the cast costume sketches, set colors and textures that may evoke exactly the image needed. These concrete objects may help the entire cast retrieve images of a similar tone, color, or type. Therefore, you can provide the basis for the development of the cast's collective imagery storehouse. You want all the actors in the play to develop characters who live in the same world.

Once your cast is well into rehearsal, you may wish to share other artistic works of the period with them. You want the actors to get a visual and kinesthetic sense of the world they will be portraying for the audience.

Play music from the period   Playing music is an ideal way to stimulate images. Music often reaches deep into the unconscious to assist actors in finding a knowledge of the period.

Show paintings to the cast   Share paintings of the period with the cast, particularly those that are stylistically similar to the production style. The way the painting depicts a particular stance or a gesture of the hand may be all that is needed to unlock a whole series of memory images.

Gather photographs   Another possibility, if the period of the play takes place in the last hundred years or so, is to show photographs of the times to the actors. Candid shots of people and buildings or streets may help, but even more stimulating are portraits, which represent how the individual wanted to be viewed by the world. In a sense, then, as the actors view the portrait, they see the "ideal man or woman" of the time.

Attend to pre- and post-sleep images   Often just before people drift off to sleep or just as they awaken, images that have been stored in the subconscious reveal themselves. Encourage actors to keep a pad and pencil beside their beds so they may detail any images that appear in this manner.

ADDING SELF TO THE IMAGE

What is happening now in the early stages of image-related processes is that the actors are acquiring as many images as possible that will form the basis of their enactment during performance. Finally, just be-

A director must have very clear images in mind in order to stage a battle scene as intricate as this one. The Goodman Theatre, Chicago: *Richard III* by William Shakespeare. Directed by William Woodman.

fore the actors begin to experiment physically with the character (which may occur almost immediately in the rehearsal process, or not for several days or even a week), ask them to begin to form an *imagination image* of self being character. Essentially what they will do is overlay their image of self with the image of character. They will imagine themselves doing what the character does and saying what the character says. Now that the actors have imagined the character portrayal, they are ready, poised at the brink when thought becomes action.

COAXING THE OUTWARD FOCUS

Once this initial internal search has begun, the actors are ready to begin the leap to the actual doing. Making this leap seems to be the hardest part of acting. Many potential actors have detailed images in their heads but are unable to get them out of their minds and into their bodies. They can tell you what they want to do, but they cannot do what they intend. As coach, it's your job to do all in your power to assist these actors in making this giant creative leap. In a sense, the actors really make two leaps: (1) from imagining to enacting, and (2) from an image of character to an image of them being character. Therefore, you must structure the actors' performances into a fully blown, totally realized theatrical experience through the use of image as the focus. Reviewing some of the Outward/In techniques presented in Chapter 3 may help.

The rehearsal process should never be a battle between internalized process and externalized product. Your coaching should be a merger, a balance between what is happening inside the actor and what behavior is revealing itself outside. Although the external may seem to take precedence, the actors should never turn off their image-making process.

DIRECTORS NEED A KNOWLEDGE OF THE CREATIVE PROCESS

Fluency is the ability to generate many similar ideas. Researchers in the field of creativity say that any group leader working creatively will stress *numbers* of *ideas* early in the problem-solving process. Telling actors to make original behavioral choices is like screaming "Relax!" at tense actors. Early in the rehearsal process, when actors are experimenting with character, encourage them to try out many possibilities for behavior based on the images they have been finding.

At this point don't inhibit the actors in their problem solving; don't judge; encourage them not to judge. Push them to come up with lots of possibilities. Remove the brakes; provide the individual with complete freedom for emotional and physical exploration. Ask the actor playing Reynard, for example, to come up with one way, then another way, then a third way to move like Reynard. Psychologist Carl Rogers

Don't criticize. If a thing is wrong and you don't know exactly how to set it right, say nothing. Wait until you find out the right thing to do, or until the actor does. It discourages and maddens an actor to be told merely that you are dissatisfied. If you cannot help him, let him alone.
George Bernard Shaw,
The Art of Rehearsal

believes in providing a climate in which external evaluation is absent (at least early in the creativity process).

The next stage in the creative process is **flexibility,** which is the ability to generate ideas in many categories outside of the usual one. Flexibility is internal but is manifested externally. Internally, the actor is using the *imagery process,* which describes the rotating, shifting, and transmuting of the perceived picture in the mind's eye. Externally, the actor may be trying one approach, and then a similar one, and finally throwing out both approaches while experimenting with an entirely different idea. Once the actors have reached the stage of flexibility, they are more receptive to comments and evaluations from the coach. It is during this stage that you can steer the actors away from clichés or stereotypic behavior.

If an actor playing Brun in *Reynard the Fox,* for example, shows hunger by licking his lips or patting his stomach, have him try to find, in his storehouse of personal memories, a picture of the actions of someone who was experiencing hunger. Have the actor play with that image, modifying it to include the givens in the script and his own givens as an actor (such as how tall he is or the pitch and power of his voice), and finally to portray hunger in a way that avoids the cliché.

Finally, the actors must be able to develop **elaboration,** the ability to implement or spell out ideas. Once the actors experiment with varieties of choices, they must be able to detail and refine the performance. Particularly in scripts that are not themselves well elaborated, the actors must find ways to develop full-blown characters by adding three-dimensionality from their own storehouse of experience. If the actors are having difficulty with elaboration, encourage them to return to their original (internal-search) image for detail.*

> *You must ask questions of these images, as you would ask questions of a friend. Sometimes you must give them strict orders. Changing and completing themselves under the influence of your questions and orders, they give you answers visible to your inner sight.*
> Michael Chekhov,
> *To the Actor*

EVALUATE THE PERFORMANCE, NOT THE PERSON

The most important aspect a director must remember in coaching through imagery is to evaluate the enactment of the image, not the personality of the actor. Notes given to actors should not describe abstract goodness or badness; rather, they should delineate what needs to be done to improve the performance of the image. Being as specific as possible about what you see and hear is always valued by actors who wish to improve. As you evaluate, show the actors what they did and how they can improve what you find unsatisfactory. Some directors talk too much and never provide alternatives for what they did

---

*Another category of creative behavior is *originality,* the ability to generate statistically uncommon responses. Often novelty is confused with originality. Actors choose actions simply because they are uncommon, idiosyncratic, and therefore possibly unjustified in the script. As coach, you do encourage your actors to be original, but you also must ask them to justify their choices.

Both these actors in *Moby Dick* have such strong, clear images of what they are seeing that every member of the young audience sees the same fearful images. PAF Playhouse Youth Theatre, Huntington, New York. Directed by Richard Harden.

Directing can be thought of in two ways—"direct," as a dictator directs you to do something, or "direction," as in pointing out the general idea of where you want to go. Wilfred Leach, director, Broadway production, *The Pirates of Penzance*

not like about the performances; others just smile during rehearsal. It's better to be upfront and specific. Try to focus the evaluation on the image, not the person.

Tell the actors who play the Lost Boys in *Peter Pan* that during the Wendy Bird scene, for example, you were unable to tell how each one felt about the death of Wendy. Explain that the theatrical image was unspecific. Ask them how they might show what they feel through externalized actions. Encourage them to return to their original images to look for more details and "how's." Focus on the external enactment of the internal image.

IMAGERY TECHNIQUES FOR LATER IN THE REHEARSAL PROCESS: BALANCING INTERNAL AND EXTERNAL

The internal search continues even after the actors have begun to externalize their choices. Many valuable imagery-based techniques, which were developed for use in therapy, can also be utilized during the later phases of the rehearsal process. The following other imagery-based approaches can help actors work through their difficulties, utilize their time more efficiently, and prepare them for the varied audience responses.

Compressed Rehearsal This technique suggests that the actor can benefit by going through the entire rehearsal in his or her mind's eye. Each movement, each sentence is initiated only in a compressed manner. Gestures are made, but only the kernel of the gesture can be observed by the outsider. For example, instead of a sweeping gesture of the arm, a simple twitch of the shoulder may appear to indicate internally the appropriate somatic response. Research has shown that musicians and dancers who utilize this technique have essentially experienced the benefits of an additional rehearsal. Also, actors may "run through" their specific performance in their minds by utilizing the compressed-rehearsal technique about 30 minutes prior to performance.

Self-Desensitization This technique, modified from Arnold Lazarus' book on Imagery Therapy, *In the Mind's Eye,** can prove very helpful to actors who are inexperienced at performing for young people. If the actors feel frightened that during performance the child audience will do something dreadful, have your actors picture the worst possible imagined occurrence. For example, the actor may picture what to do if the children screamed during the entire performance, or ran up to the stage, or didn't respond at all. Usually the fears are more terrible than the real thing. Actors, then, have prepared a repertoire of behaviors in response to those imagined fears and can cope with the actual dreadful circumstance, should it arise.

POTPOURRI OF IMPROVISATIONS

The Repetition Exercise in the first part of this chapter was presented so that the director could help actors develop a grounding for good acting in general. The more gamelike improvisations in this section are more prescriptive in nature: They are script-related and performance-related and offer the director some specific exercises for specific actor difficulties.

Removing the performance context frees the actors from the ruts in which they are stuck. Interest in improvisation resurged in America in the 1960s, when many companies, most notably the Second City, The Compass Players, The Premise, and The Committee, began to develop entire pieces improvisationally. Improvisations have been utilized as far back as commedia dell'arte and more recently by such directors as Copeau in the Vieux Columbia of the early 1900s.†

Games are often easier for blocked actors to cope with than scripted roles because the players' ignorance of the future is genuine. Improvisations can be used by the director to draw the actors into deep situational and character involvement better than can a scripted scene, particularly one with which the actor is experiencing difficulty. This

*(New York: Rawson Associates Publishers, 1977.)

†A more detailed presentation of improvisations used specifically for the development of original theatre pieces appears in Chapter 5, "Creating a Play for Young People."

approach can have an eye-opening effect on the actor. The director, however, must realize that often the effect of the improvisation is so intense because the *theatrical* moment of the first time is the *actual* moment of the first time. Experiencing the same feelings or getting the same effect again and again is the trick. In the evaluation of the improvisation the director must focus on the transfer of the result of the improvisation to the performance context. Sometimes what is being transferred is an *attitude*—feelings of group solidarity, for example. Other times what is being transferred is *behavior*—a specific movement or a line reading, for example. But if no focus is placed on this attitude or behavior, improvisations are simply fun and games—a great therapeutic aid in making rehearsals pleasant and exciting, but of no specific value to the performance.

THE EXERCISES

Here are some improvisational exercises for use in the coaching process. Remember, these exercises are prescriptive aids for the actor. Actors who are wonderful at improvisation may still not be able to act, and excellent actors may have difficulty mastering the exercise. Being good at the exercise is not the goal. These exercises should be viewed as tools in the rehearsal process.

Concentration techniques

In all plays, but especially in plays intended for audiences of young people, actors must develop intense powers of concentration. Child audiences can be unpredictable; actors must develop an ability to listen and talk at the same time. The statement, "He's so dull he can't walk and chew gum at the same time," had better not describe your lead actor, or your production is in for big trouble.

EXERCISE: WINTER IS MY FAVORITE SEASON

Justification: This exercise stresses talking and listening at the same time and requires actors to think about what they are doing, to be aware of what is happening at the same moment, and to play for the next moment.

Description: Choose two actors. Assign to Actor A a topic such as "Winter is my favorite season," "Green is my favorite color." Assign to Actor B a topic with an opposing point of view: "Summer is my favorite season," "Yellow is my favorite color." When the start is called, each actor must talk simultaneously on the assigned topic, at the same time listening to what the other actor is saying. If, for example, Actor A, speaking about winter, mentions cold, Actor B, speaking about summer, must respond by mentioning the warmth of summer. The first actor to pause for 5 seconds or the first who gets confused and begins to speak on his or her partner's topic is declared the loser.

Selectivity techniques

Part of being a good artist is developing the ability to make selections. *What* is selected to be portrayed is as important as *how* that selection is performed. Actors often have difficulty in choosing appropriate behaviors from the charts in Chapter 3, or they try to do *everything*. Less is often more, so help your actors learn to compress, to pare down, to eliminate for the purpose of developing a finely chiseled performance.

EXERCISE: REDUCING THE SCENE

Justification: In plays of presentational style playwrights often use words and lines for expository reasons, for character development, or just simply to amuse the characters and, ultimately, the audience. Actors must be able to get at the core of each scene.

Description: Time the regular rehearsal. Set a timer for that amount of time minus one minute. Explain to the actors playing the scene that they must play that same scene again, at the same speed, with the same rhythm, but with less dialogue or less movement. Set the timer and proceed. Tell them that they will have to cut lines and improvise dialogue somewhere. Actors must pay rapt attention so they know when to respond to each other. When the actors have finished, ask them why they left out what they did. Continue giving the actors less and less time until they pare the scene to its barest bones.

Characterization techniques

Actors playing one- or two-dimensional characters often stress the obvious in their portrayal. Consequently, character motivation becomes predictable and boring. Actors do not need to "hit us over the head." Finding ways to add contours and depth to characters should be part of an actor's repertoire. You may need to help.

EXERCISE: PLAYING THE OPPOSITE

Justification: In real life people often refuse to acknowledge their vulnerabilities; they won't be seen crying or angry. They force an opposite reaction—a false smile. On the stage actors often need to portray more of this resistance. If they don't cap the emotion, they telegraph their feelings or give an overindulgent performance. If you encourage the actor to fight the emotion, the audience will have a stronger empathetic response to the performance through viewing a compelling internal confrontation: between actual grief and the internal decision not to show the emotion.

Description: If an actor seems to be playing the character in too obvious a way, encourage him or her to play the opposite action. Use the example of a drunk. If the character is playing a drunk, encourage the actor to be as undrunk as possible: to walk and talk with precision. A real drunk tries hard to suppress drunkenness. Assist the actor in feeling the difference between acting drunk and fighting being drunk. If an actor is playing a very happy character, have him or her search for sad moments in the text.

Text-expansion techniques

Sometimes actors become locked into vocal and inflectional patterns early in the rehearsal process. They say their lines in exactly the same way each time without ever considering other possibilities. As observer, you get the impression that even if the person to whom they are speaking fell through the floor, they would remain unaffected. Also, actors sometimes seem to wait patiently to speak until the character who speaks before them has finished. They don't respond in any way before their cue; they don't seem to be *compelled* to communicate. Many of the patterns and habits that actors impose on the text can be broken with the aid of some simple exercises. Here is one example:

EXERCISE: SEIZING PERMISSION TO TALK

Justification: Often actors speak only because the playwright wrote something for them to say. But, in fact, the character seizes the opportunity to speak and, when finished, must give up the floor. Actors cannot assume that it is their right to speak just because their lines are next. As in life, characters must seize the opportunity to say what they need to say.

Description: Set up a rehearsal process based on an actual scene in the play. A large group scene is most appropriate for this exercise. During this improvisation actors must try to keep the stage. An actor who wishes to speak must wrest the stage from the speaker. Encourage actors to get attention by physical means—changing positions, touching other actors, using props, or by vocal means, such as speaking loudly or deliberately. They must use whatever will grab the attention of others onstage. When they have finished speaking their mind, they should give up the floor in a similar manner. This is an exercise that embellishes the text to an extreme degree. What is discovered will not be transferred directly to the actual performance, but the feelings of seizing the stage can be the focus of future rehearsals.

What kind of actors do you like to work with?

The main thing that I look for in actors is that they have something to teach me, some area of skill or expertise, something that I don't know about that they can really teach me. That's the reason I hire people, not only because of the usual skills and abilities and spontaneity, but I really hire them because I want to learn from them.

How do you blend different kinds of people in achieving an ensemble?

In a way I do want them to blend in, and in a way I want them to be somewhat autonomous. We have a group point of view and a group approach based on certain concepts of aesthetic education. I want people to be on the same crusade bandwagon that I am. That feeling has to be very strong in each one of the actors, that kind of dedication, because the job is so hard. The hours are long, and the work is arduous.

Do you relate to the actors in the same way during rehearsals and offstage?

We always have a personal trust. I think it's really important that they like me, that they respect me, that I respect them. Because of that trust, they're able to divorce themselves from me as a friend and see me as a director. It's a tightrope walk, really, because they do have to listen to what I say and at the same time feel the freedom to contribute and also have the grace not to sulk when their ideas are not accepted. In the total concept of the show we really do work together.

In teaching, if you want to create a response from the class, you have to ask a creative question. You as teacher have to take that risk. That philosophy of teaching carries over into the way we work together. We're continually asking each other the question, "What could we do here?" We may ask, "What are we going to do with this tablecloth that's on the floor from the last scene? How could it be used as an introduction to the next scene? Maybe it could have a piece of reverse material on it . . . "

How do you conduct rehearsals later in the rehearsal period?

I have very specific plans that I come to rehearsal with based on overall goals, on what happened yesterday, and on what we have to do. I keep a journal.

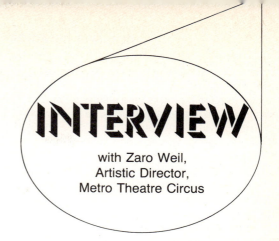

INTERVIEW

with Zaro Weil,
Artistic Director,
Metro Theatre Circus

As you coach your actors, when does the idea of the child audience come in?

Oh, I don't think about it, you see, because the child is in me. I pay close attention to my own "kidness," my own ability to synthesize and create; what's the child in me is the child in the audience.

What about the child in the actor? Do you try to find that?

Good point. Absolutely, I try to nurture and find that child and create that safe environment so that the child can come out, but I also temper that child with a strong adult. I hope the actor can assume the responsibility for his own adult in the rehearsal process. I help by setting up a model as adult and child.

Do you ever talk about the child's response?

Yes. But the child response would be like mine—would be turned off if something is boring, or the rhythms are dull, or there's no increase in tension. What's boring to me is going to be boring to a child. I honestly don't talk with my actors about doing a show for children except in the beginning, when we first decide what kind of content is going to be in our show, and then finally at the end, when we rearrange it and recontour it.

The reason we choose the kind of theatre we do is because of what we feel personally committed to explore. And that's probably how I keep my actors. Many actors don't want to work for the child audience because they consider it so boring. The form that we take is children's theatre, but the content is for the children in ourselves. I want people who really do continually question and who find children's theatre a way to find meaning in their own lives.

133

How do you cultivate a working relationship with your actors?

I try to have a private time with each one of the actors. Actors, especially in the kind of work we do, find the work tenuous at times. They don't know if the whole thing's going to topple over, and they'll be left flat after two weeks with no decent idea. Actors become insecure and concerned. So I find it important to continually reassure the actors. One thing I've learned not to do is to ever talk about one actor with another member of the company. That's one thing that frightens actors. If they think the director is really buddy-buddy with someone else, they think their work is going to be disparaged in some way. So I think it is really important for a coach to make sure the actor knows the work is valued.

Is the way you work with actors different in each situation?

The process, the questioning, is always the same, no matter who is in the company. In fact, that grows stronger and stronger with each show. My actors always have the permission to continually question. That's what our actors learn after a period of time in our company: not to be satisfied with the given. They're just right along with me, and ahead of me sometimes.

You're not scared to have them ahead of you?

Well, sometimes I am, but it doesn't matter. Creating theatre is not blind inspiration. It's a series of decisions. All of the group works in the artistic process. If you make decisions that don't go along with your original intent, you must have sense enough to modify your intent or the decision.

How do you do that?

You select. You have to be very focused in what you present. And it's the audience that interprets that experience according to their stored memories and their stored experiences. We all have experiences that we bring to the theatre. We shouldn't do plays that are realistic for kids. I think you should make a decision to do non-realism, something that is very selected and very focused. Therefore, what I try to do in the coaching process is to make sure the actor's every muscle and every sense is totally aware and responsible.

How do you facilitate that?

They have to bring to me a certain amount of training and understanding or I won't hire them. Certain things can be taught, but it takes a long time to really develop that understanding of the physical and vocal self. Every single moment is accountable on stage. That's what art is about. The actor should be like a one-celled amoeba; the whole amoeba just shoots over and creates a new form. I want actors to be that responsive. If the actor is kinesthetically aware and captures the essence of what he's doing, then the audience perceives him that way. And the audience doesn't just hear the music or see the action, but becomes sensorially involved with the whole experience. The stronger the sensory experience is, the stronger the tracing on the central nervous system, and the more input goes into the stored memory. The stronger the stored memory is, the more fertility there is for creativity. So creating theatre for young people is the planting of seeds. If the kids see us leaping into the air, they don't just watch us, but their whole upper torsos leap and move. So I work with my actors to always capture that joyful quality.

What we try to do in Metro's shows is broaden children's movement experiences by offering different kinds of movement textures and qualities. Some are lyrical and slow; some movement is fast and hard, like *Sesame Street.* We try to reassert that multitude of words physically through sounds and visualization. We try to create new levels of experience for children. Our actors must be equal to that challenge.

5·CREATING A PLAY FOR YOUNG PEOPLE

There must always be room to adopt an
unforeseen stroke of inventiveness, some
spontaneous effect which may occur at a good
rehearsal and bring a scene suddenly and
unexpectedly to life.

Sir John Gielgud, *Stage Direction*

Working without a script can be your greatest challenge as director. The decision to develop a piece of theatre through the group process occurs for a number of very specific and often interrelated reasons. Often no current scripts exist that speak to the needs and talents of the director or group of actors; a particular adaptation of a famous fairy tale or classic may not represent the way in which the company has pictured the stage version; perhaps the group feels the desire to make a strong personal, political, or social statement; maybe even the royalties payable to the publisher are more than a new group can afford to pay, particularly if a long run is intended. Whatever the reasons—philosphical, personnel-oriented, script-related, budgetary, or educational—a decision of this magnitude will result in great changes in your role as director. Suddenly, no script is available to which you can refer; no plot or story exists with which you can lull yourself to sleep; no lines are written with which you can drill actors. You are now faced with developing a whole production: from idea to opening night.

135

UNDERSTANDING THE BASICS OF YOUR DECISION TO CREATE A NEW PIECE

Looking at other companies throughout history, evaluating your rehearsal process, and analyzing the craft of playwrighting may help you in making up your mind before you decide to develop an original piece.

HISTORY REPEATS ITSELF

Throughout theatre history groups have developed pieces of theatre, sometimes with the help and skill of playwrights, sometimes without. The actor-oriented companies in sixteenth-century Italy, for example, developed a form called *commedia dell'arte* in which much of the business, called *lazzi*, and most of the jokes, called *burla*,* were improvised. Although most of the characters had been established by tradition and the audience usually knew the outcome of the play, there was no formal script, merely a scenario. Probably much company infighting occurred right in front of an audience, as each actor tried to take center stage.

*The term *burlesque* derives from this word.

A Broadway production of *Strider*, an adaptation of Russian folk tales, was developed by a group of actors who played many parts with only minimal costumes. Playing horses here are (stage right to left): Gerald Hiken, Skip Lawing, Pamela Burrell. Directed by Bob Kalfin and Lynne Gannaway.

More recently, as part of the radical theatre movement in America and Europe, groups of artists have developed pieces of theatre that expressed a strong point of view. In the 1930s in the United States a New Deal program created the marvelous Federal Theatre Project. This spawned such companies as the Workers' Laboratory Theatre, the Group Theatre (probably the most distinguished), and the Theatre of Action, all devoted to their artists' needs to make strong sociopolitical statements. Most of these companies had the services of playwrights who translated their ideas into produceable scripts. Such plays as Clifford Odets' *Waiting for Lefty* and Maxwell Anderson's *Both Your Houses* are excellent examples of two companies' search for truth. The children's unit of the Federal Theatre Project pioneered in using adults, rather than children, to act in plays for young audiences.

Even more recently, the 20-year period between the late 1950s and late 1970s saw tremendous growth in companies that chose to develop their pieces of theatre improvisationally. Companies like the Second City of Chicago improvised right in front of an audience. Company members were more interested in experimenting with the theatre media than with the ideology of social revolt, although many of their pieces were full of social commentary.

Other groups chose to make a strong statement about society, using the theatre and their interpretation of it to express their anger. Jerzy Grotowski, a famous director of the Polish Laboratory Theatre, chose to strip away the trappings of theatre in the same manner that he wished society to become simpler. Peter Schumann of the Bread and Puppet Theatre wished to make theatre a more communal experience. He broke bread with the company before (and with the audience after) the play, which utilized larger-than-life puppets—hence the term "bread and puppet." Julian Beck and Judith Malina, directors of the Living Theatre, shocked American theatregoers in the late 1960s with pieces developed by the actors, in which with much angry language and total nudity they tried to get at the core of what was wrong with society.

Because many of these companies did not have a playwright, and because each piece was developed for a particular actor in a particular time in history, most of these scripts are not produceable today either by the originating company or by any other company. Creative theatre pieces are even more ephemeral than scripted theatre pieces. These performances can be viewed as a moment in time, never to be reproduced with different actors in a different period for a different audience. Very few great pieces of theatre literature came out of these radical companies. The power lies in the passion of the group, the specificity of the roles developed for each person, and the current needs of the audience.

Our first objective is to entertain children. We thought at first this would be difficult because they have been conditioned by movies and the radio to quite different things. Much to our surprise, our productions were greeted with enthusiasm by both adults and children.
Yasha Frank,
director of Pinocchio for Children's Unit of Federal Theatre Project

A SHOULD-I-CREATE-A-PIECE-OF-THEATRE QUESTIONNAIRE

You must consider six basic elements before you decide to develop an original piece of theatre: Personnel, time, space, audience, money, as well as your own capabilities.

PERSONNEL (already assembled)
- Who is the group? • What are the skills of each? • How were they trained? • Do they balance each other like idea people and performance people? • Do they work well together? • Do their ideas spark each other?

PERSONNEL (to be cast)
- What sort of performer should I cast? • What skills should I look for? • Do I want similar or dissimilar sorts of experience in cast members? • Can I tell if they will work well together?

TIME
- How much time do I have? • Do I have long daily rehearsal periods? • Do I have four weeks or four months? • Can the company begin germinating ideas a few weeks prior to the beginning of actual rehearsal?

SPACE
- Do I have a rehearsal space with various physical areas for discussion, improvisation, rehearsing, set and costume construction, all of which may be occurring simultaneously? • Do I know where I will be performing? Permanent house? Touring? In schools: theatres or gyms? In libraries, arts centers, churches?

AUDIENCE
- Do I know for whom I will be performing? • Can I meet the needs of my audience by developing a piece, or are more traditional scripts more satisfying to this audience? • Can I predetermine the age range of my audience? • Do I want to produce a play for general audiences or for specific age ranges?

MONEY
- Will the money I save on royalties pay for salaries and technical requirements? • Can I develop the desired effects within the existing budget? • How can I best utilize my budget—interpreting a play or creating a play?

MY OWN CAPABILITIES
- Do I feel secure without a formal script? • Do I understand the difficulty of the improvisational process? • Am I confident as the leader of a group creative endeavor? • Does my talent lie in creating a script?

These questions needn't have any specific answers, but they should force you to think about your decision in a clear, logical manner. If you feel you can artistically and practically utilize your personnel, your money, your time, and your space to develop a script for your audience, and if you feel particularly adventuresome, proceed!

You may decide to develop your play improvisationally with the aid of a playwright. Or you may choose to become the director/playwright yourself. Or you may assign this position to a member of your company.* No matter who develops the script, the characteristics of a good play include, at the very least:

- a major conflict
- characters who want something and try to get it
- dialogue that sets characters apart from each other
- scenes that build one upon the other
- play length appropriate to its theme
- ultimate resolution of major conflict

The steps in the playwrighting process don't change even though the play is being developed to some extent by a group of artists. In the following discussion we have highlighted thirteen steps (of the many that may actually occur) that can serve as guidelines for the development of your piece of theatre.

THE PLAYWRIGHTING PROCESS

THE THIRTEEN-STEP PROCESS

1. The need to create Many needs and desires exist that compel the artist to create a piece. Philosophers and psychologists have tried to analyze the creative process, yet the need to create often defies such probing. You and your company must have a burning desire to say something in a way that has never quite been said and done before.

Too many plays, particularly in the history of theatre for young people, have been written not because of a need to say something, but because of an opportunity to speak. It's possible that you have a deep-seated need to speak out about highway safety or dental hygiene, but before you begin to develop a creative piece, make sure that what you create might not be better stated in an essay or through a lecture.

What comes out in our programs does not come out of thin air. It can only come from confirmed belief and deeply held opinions about life and of kids, who are the receivers of what we're talking about.
David Pammenter,
team leader, Belgrade TIE, Coventry, England

2. An idea Idea and need are related; often having a clear idea makes the need stronger. Many kinds of ideas can form the core of a piece of theatre. The following ideas have clear applicability to theatre for young people. We have also provided examples from the current literature of plays that can be produced for young audiences. Some of

*Sam Smiley's *Playwrighting: The Structure of Action* (Englewood Cliffs, NJ: Prentice-Hall, 1971) is an excellent book on playwrighting that details the making of a good play.

these plays were developed improvisationally, but many of them were written singly by a playwright. Remember the idea for your play should develop into a piece of about 45 minutes to 2 hours running time.

- A Person. A particular person or category of person, such as a king or a thief, can be the core of the play. Examples: Brian Way's *The Toymaker* or Ed Graczyk's *The Amazing Mr. Pennypacker*.
- A Place. A particular place, like an airport or a hotel, where unrelated people come together is a good stimulus for an exciting drama. Examples from the literature of theatre pieces that can be produced for children are Agatha Christie's *The Mousetrap* and Kaufman and Hart's *You Can't Take It with You.*
- A Catastrophe or Natural Disaster. A volcano or flood can stir the creative juices, because much action is compressed in events of this nature. Examples: Belgrade TIE's *Rare Earth** and Bix L. Doughty's *Noah and the Great Auk.*
- A Conceptual Thought. Beauty, love, truth, or even the vote for women can also form the basis of a piece of theatre, but converting such abstractions into specific theatrical action becomes difficult. Metro Theatre Circus' *Commedia Cartoon*, Grey's *Beauty and The Beast*, and Performing Arts Repertory Theatre's *Susan B.!,* are scripts dealing with conceptual thought.
- A Situation. A wedding, funeral, or holiday can form the basis for a play. The thrust of the play might be on how the incident irrevocably affects people's lives. Examples: Eugene O'Neill's *Ah, Wilderness!* (about the Fourth of July) and adaptations of Dickens' *A Christmas Carol.*
- A Historical Event or Person. Remember that you can't cover the person's entire life in the amount of time of one play. Part of a someone's life or a single event can be at the core of the play. Apply artistic selectivity to the choice of what you show and don't show. Don't show *everything*. Examples: Saul Levitt's *Jim Thorpe, All-American* and Jonathan Levy's *Marco Polo.*
- A Fairy Tale or Children's Classic. Fairy tales and adaptations of classics form a large part of the current literature of theatre for young people. One of the main reasons why many of these scripts are so dreadful is that the narrative of stories doesn't translate well into the medium of theatre. Make sure you don't just lift whole chunks of the story, but select judiciously with an eye and ear for what will work on stage. Examples: Moses Goldberg's *Hansel and Gretel* and Sara Spenser's *Little Women.*

*Rare Earth was developed improvisationally by the Belgrade Theatre In-Education Team in 1973–74, and is available from Methuen Press.

This unusual adaptation of *Alice in Wonderland* is set in the American West and re-titled *Alice in the American Wonderland.* Looking Glass Theatre, Providence, Rhode Island. Directed by Bernice Bronson.

Photo by Johanne Killeen

Often companies will narrow down their choices to two or three ideas and then make the final decision after they have researched the alternatives.

3. Research Doing research is not cheating. No person or group of people has all the pieces of necessary information inside their heads. Consulting original or secondary sources, interviewing people who have specific knowledge about an issue, researching the period, reading various versions of a fairy tale, reading an entire classic, and studying already scripted plays on similar topics will only make your piece better. Many so-called artists say they like to remain "pure" and simply create out of the air. Learn from the scholar: Add some authenticity to your work.

An interesting facet of the group creative process is what each member chooses to investigate. One way to proceed is to narrow down the topic, then send each company member away to bring back various materials, books, interviews, photos, paintings, and records that they feel could be relevant. This potpourri of information can then be pooled and explored during brainstorming sessions. Ultimately, however, some decision about content must be made. Probably you will be the person to make choices; however, feel free to rely on the good judgment of other members of your company.

4. Establishing the initial improvisation   Once the material is stacked on the desk, initial decisions take place about making thought into action, ideas into theatrical conflict, and abstract themes into walking, talking characters. The best way to begin is to list ideas that need to be expressed, scenes that need to be staged, characters that need to be presented. If your actors have lots of experience with improvisation, they can assist you in making this creative leap. If not, you may have to set up improvisations by assigning characteristics and objectives to actors and then placing these actors in specific situations based on the materials you've gathered. Many fine exercises exist for this purpose as well as for the development of group cohesiveness.*

5. First set of improvisations   An important rule of thumb is to let each improvisation go on about 45 seconds longer then you comfortably feel you should. Often the subconscious takes over during verbalization, and actors then come up with perfect lines and well-developed characters. Always tape-record the daily improvisations. Try to let go of some of the control during this phase. During improvisations the director does not direct in a specific sense, but plays a significant role in bringing the work to its best group expression.

6. Group evaluation of improvisation   During these evaluation sessions the company must trace where the piece is going, deciding which scenes, which characters, and which directions will be eliminated and which will be elaborated. You must help arouse a strong, clear point of view by what you say during this evaluation session. Limits of time and of technical and performance staff all are considerations that must be taken into account. Unfortunately, only a few companies have unlimited time, and so decisions have to be made that simply cut out part of what the group had hoped to develop. You will be the "bad guy," the one who cuts favorite characters, favorite scenes, wonderful turns of phrase for the ultimate good of the final product. Time is often the biggest limitation in the creative process.

7. Preparation of final scenario   In this scenario scenes are ordered, characters are delineated, and conflicts are clarified. The choices made

You are so complete as an improvisationist. You understand the working of an action. You understand the beats which make up the action. You understand the entire structure of an entertaining or communicative action. You know it from every possible viewpoint. You know it as a playwright would know it, you know it as an actor knows it, and since you are self-directed, you know that, too.
Comedian Shelley Berman

*Perhaps the most utilized book on improvisation is Viola Spolin's *Improvisation for the Theatre* (Evanston, IL: Northwestern University Press, 1963). This may provide you with a good method for developing improvisations. Other improvisations were presented in Chapter 4.

in this phase will completely color the final result. Imbedded in this theatrical syntax is the essence of the final production. The decisions to be made are not offhand and can't be left to the group. You must act as the writer of the final scenario, or you must assign one of your trusted company members to do so.

8. Final improvisations   At this point the only directing you may be doing is to side-coach during improvisation, helping the actors focus while they are working. Again, record improvisations and evaluate each improvisation after it is completed. You may also have time for the group to evaluate the improvisation.

9. Draft of script   Keep in mind the resources of your group and the reasons why you chose to develop a play in this way in the first place—because no existing script seemed appropriate for the needs and skills of your group. Now you must finalize "a script" that represents these desires and skills. The script must now begin to look like a traditional one—with dialogue and essential blocking and technical requirements. During this phase your playwright in residence, your leader of improvisation, or probably you, must sit at the typewriter, command inspiration, as well as your many pages of notes, and *write*.

It's not just a question of listening and taking in. I must formulate a way in which rehearsals go, so questions will be answered.
David Holman,
writer/researcher, Belgrade TIE, Coventry, England

The Alliance Theatre in Atlanta has developed many of its plays through improvisation. This is a production of *The Gadget*. Directed by Charles Abbott.
Photo by Charles M. Rafshoon

10. Rehearsal   Now you conduct a traditional rehearsal* period, although much of the blocking and characterization work has been done during the stages of improvisation. Many companies feel they have completed the work when the script is finished. Good companies continue to work, refining the theatrical effect so that the production is brilliant. One process you do continuously during rehearsal is evaluation. A quick way to evaluate how the production is shaping up is to look at the rehearsal in four ways:

1. What the actors say (Is the dialogue interesting? Have you selected the right word for the right moment?)
2. What the actors do (Are they working moment to moment in a specific way? Are they making sense?)
3. How the actors move (Are their physical movements carefully choreographed and structured? For example, if they need to move quickly in one scene, are they moving quickly enough?)
4. How the actors and the technical effects sound (Do the voices fit the characters? Are the sound effects—slide whistle, drums, etc.—timely? Is the music appropriate?)

11. The practice audience   This is the stage where you perform your almost-ready production for a trusted class or invited audience to see what needs work and what works well. This is the "out-of-town tryout," when the director and actors can gauge the audience reactions in order to make the final adjustments.

12. Final cleanup rewrite and rehearsal   Here you put the final touches on the script and production during your last rehearsal. Modify a few lines; clarify some blocking; tighten the pacing; adjust the costumes.

13. First performance   At this point you should be ready to present your original piece to your audience.

THE THIRTY-DAY GAME PLAN

A thirteen-step timeline for the play development process is shown on the next page. The steps also are listed there, with times. This timeline is only a framework. You may discover in a particular step that you need more time to complete the task than illustrated. Or you may find you have completed the task in less time. A timeline may be the antith-

*The rehearsal process is discussed in more detail in Chapter 7.

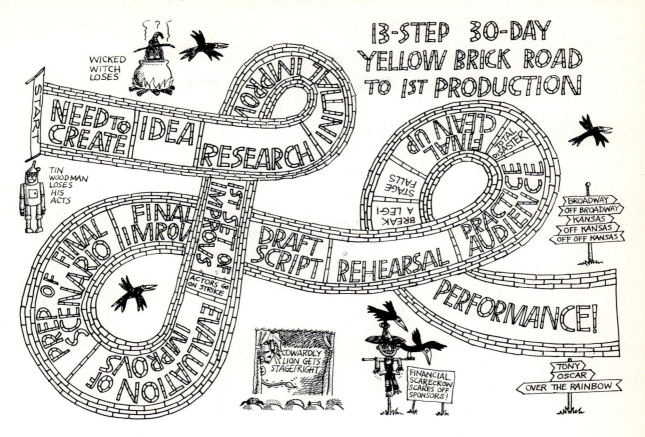

esis of the creative process, but you should be aware of the existence of such an external structure. Tailor the timeline to your creative impulses and particular situation.

1. The need to create .... Day 1
2. An idea .... Days 2, 3
3. Research .... Days 4, 5, 6
4. Establishing initial improvisation .... Day 7
5. First set of improvisations .... Days 8, 9, 10
6. Group evaluation of improvisations .... Days 11, 12
7. Preparation of final scenario .... Days 13, 14, 15
8. Final improvisations .... Days 16, 17, 18
9. Draft of script .... Days 19, 20, 21
10. Rehearsal .... Days 22, 23, 24, 25
11. The practice audience .... Days 26, 27
12. Final cleanup .... Days 28, 29
13. Performance .... Day 30

INVESTIGATING FORMS AND RELATIONSHIPS

Once you know the pros and cons concerning the group creative process and understand the basics of developing a piece, you can begin a more thorough investigation of what is expected of the director, what to look for in casting actors, what forms of scripts lend themselves to the development of original pieces, and how to utilize improvisation in the creative process. The following sections of this part of the chapter cover: (1) the director, (2) the actors, (3) the forms, (4) music, (5) the improvisational process.

THE DIRECTOR

Mike Nichols came once and directed us a little. He didn't do that much, but what he did was just so brilliant. Don't ask me what he did or how he did it, but he made you think that you were the best and the funniest and the most brilliant, and so you gave a little more. He made you think you were better than the best. He had this way of drawing it out of you, which is what a good director does.
Comedian Joan Rivers

The decision to develop a play from scratch will affect the director first. No longer will you have total control of the rehearsal process. Although you probably have some ideas about what the final script might be, much of what occurs will be a combination of the creative spirits of the artists with whom you have chosen to collaborate. No longer will you be able to rule with an iron hand. If you feel you cannot relinquish some of your control or are unable to trust your actors and technicians to share the responsibility, you should probably scrap this project before you begin.

You will have to acquire rehearsal skills and coping behaviors that you may not have needed in your role of interpretive artist. The important thing to remember is that you must balance freedom with control, encouragement with evaluation, your artistic vision with their artistic visions. As Paul Sills, perhaps one of the most respected directors of improvisational theatre, has said, "Somebody has to help the group become a group. There is a need for a teacher or leader when you are dealing with these forms." You cannot just sit back and watch your talented group improvise. Although many groups may be run democratically, a committee cannot produce an excellent artistic piece without a leader.

HOW TO PREPARE YOURSELF

• **Read as many plays as possible, young people's theatre scripts as well as scripts for adults**   Note as you read these plays how characters are delineated, how dialogue is developed, how conflicts are set up and resolved, how scenes are ordered. Scripted plays serve as models for your play.

• **Attend every play you can**   Although a good director of traditional theatre scripts should also attend the theatre often, viewing as many plays as possible is essential for you. Each time you attend the theatre, focus on a specific element: plot, character, climax, blocking. You are in a sense going to become a playwright, a facilitator, and a psychologist in the creative process. You must arm yourself with as much theatre knowledge and experience as possible. Then, as you begin to work in each new situation, you will be able to pull out surprising pieces of business, apt ideas, and interesting combinations of characters from the recesses of your brain.

• **Practice improvisation yourself**   Later in this chapter we discuss improvisation in more detail. Try to take a course or participate in theatre games so that you will have as many points of view and experiences as possible. Once you have experienced improvisation, you will be able more easily to understand its nature and potentials. And you will feel more comfortable.

• **Become a scholar**   You should have the ability to trace trends in research and focus on the most effective way to tell a story. During the early research time you must make quick decisions about the direction the script will take. Read philosophic essays, look at history texts, study articles in psychology journals. Notice how scholars develop a hypothesis and then try to prove or disprove the theory. We're not advocating that your plays be deadly dull, just that they be clearly defined, logically developed, and dramatically interesting.

• **Learn to be assertive**   *Assertive* became a popular word in America in the late 1970s. Remember, being assertive doesn't mean being aggressive, nasty, or obnoxious. An assertive person is able to take charge when taking charge seems necessary. Being assertive means saying what you mean, even though you may hurt some feelings. You are in charge. You are the director because you have a clearly developed point of view and an ability to communicate what is necessary in order to achieve the final production. Don't forget that you are the leader of this creative process.

I find that the best directors are the ones who know what you're thinking when you go through the scene. They know what went wrong, they know what you were going through, they know whether you forgot a line or were taking a wrong choice or whatever. An improviser reads people so well that he can read the actors and know what is wrong and what to go for to improve things.
Actor and director Alan Alda

The decision to develop a play may arise because of the needs of a company that has already been assembled. Or the decision may have arisen because of your own strong feelings. No matter what the reason, actors who find themselves part of this process must exhibit particular skills not always found in actors who are cast in more traditional productions. Before you make the final decision to proceed, take a hard look at your company, or make sure you have realistically evaluated the casting process.

THE ACTORS

EACH COMPANY MEMBER
No matter how similar or dissimilar the company, certain individual ways of working are important in developing plays improvisationally. These skills are not exclusive to any sort of training; they depend on

the personality types of the actors and on what kind of working conditions they each favor. Among many other characteristics, to be successful in the creative process, the following are essential for an actor:

● **Each actor must have a strong sense of space**   The best improvisatory actors can make what Viola Spolin calls "a where." They are so clear about establishing the space that the audience can immediately tell what is being shown, even in the absence of a set. Mime skills have a lot to do with sense of "where," as does an ability to remember exactly where objects have been established. Many plays developed improvisationally, such as *Story Theatre,* are composed of several short pieces. It is vital for the actors to establish, as well as to distinguish, each new place quickly.

● **In comedies actors concentrate on tasks rather than "being funny"** Moment-to-moment work is essential. The sense of doing needs to be very strong in actors whom you must trust to work from scenarios. Particularly in script segments that are not fully written out, or in moments of audience participation, the actor must never strive to *be funny* but must continue to stay in role and work moment to moment. The humor will come from the doing something in a funny way, not in "acting" funny.

A related requirement is that the actor not feel a need to speak at length onstage: not to do playwrighting but rather to *do*. What is important is not exposition, but a real ability to establish a quick conflict with each other. As actor/director Alan Arkin explains: "The only way a scene can work is if the first person comes up with a very strong objective and the second person comes on with a very strong objective and they hang onto very strong ideas of what they want to accomplish in this scene."* Actors must co- and self-edit simultaneously.

● **Each actor must exhibit a strong ability for characterization**   When a playwright creates a script, the heart of the play is dialogue. The actor must find actions and behaviors to show what the character is doing. When a company develops a play, the actors create the behavior that is at the core of the play. The dialogue is an extension of the behavior. Actors most often develop believable people in a very short amount of rehearsal time and play these characters in an even shorter amount of time onstage. Mike Nichols, Broadway and movie director, in describing an actor who is good at developing characters that work well, writes: ". . . He has what few actors have—a sense of character observed from without. The ability to comment on a character with some humor and a little bit of distance and . . . to be able simultaneously to comment from without and fill it from within."†

*Jeffrey Sweet, ed., *Something Wonderful Right Away* (New York: Avon Books, 1978), p. 22.
†Sweet, *Something Wonderful Right Away*, p. 87.

● **Each actor must provide a sense of here-and-now reality** Actors must also accept reality moment to moment from each other. If Actor A says, miming an ice cream cone, "This is a terrific ice cream cone," Actor B must not reply, "You ninny, I don't see an ice cream cone." Actor B must say something like, "Yummy, give me a taste." If Actor B mocks Actor A, the play and indeed the company are finished.

● **Each actor must develop a personality that works well under stress** Although many traits make up a personality, two basic types of dealing with stress exist: There are those who rise to the occasion and become more than they are, or at least are able to dig more deeply into the subconscious, and there are those who cringe from stress and block the creative flow. When casting, try to find out through improvisation which type of personality each actor exhibits.

● **Each actor must show an understanding of the child audience** The actors need not necessarily have acted for children, but some kind of experience with children certainly helps. Also, look for actors with a real childlike sense—a sense of fun and a sense of humor. Actors should have respect for children. If participation will be included in your production, make sure your actors have some creative drama experience, or provide them with creative drama training.

The theatre which scorns its audience is doomed, is, in fact, no theatre at all.
Harold Clurman,
"The Audience"

THE COMPANY AS A WHOLE

Many opinions exist about the similarity/dissimilarity quotient of the company as a whole. On the one hand, groups who have worked together for a long period of time share vocabulary, sets of experience, point of view, maybe even political or social convictions about issues. They also know whom they can count on for certain kinds of characters, certain kinds of decisions onstage and, sometimes, even offstage. Often, however, groups of people who have been together too long, who have similar training and similar experiences, continue to develop similar pieces, which are static and boring. Despite their acquired facility in improvisation their familiarity and similarity may ultimately kill future productions.

On the other hand, one can have actors with varied backgrounds. Meshing a Stanislavski-trained actress with a theatre games person, or a psychologically oriented person with one who is intensely interested in politics, can provide striking and exciting results. Sharing skills can be the focus of early group development. Probably in this case more time will be required to develop a piece because the early rehearsals must be used to develop group cohesiveness. Also, the finished piece will probably turn out more unpredictable—perhaps, excitingly, falling right into place, perhaps full of chaos and discord. The decision about similarity/dissimilarity of company experience is one you must carefully consider.

When a company works as closely together as this team in Ireland, its members develop a strong ensemble quality necessary for success in improvisational methods. Team Educational Theatre Company, Dublin: *The Wind of the Word* by Mary-Elizabeth Burke-Kennedy.
Photo by Beth Ridgell

THE FORMS

Any form of play can be developed improvisationally. At one end of the spectrum you can develop the well-made play, with complex characters who have complicated wants and needs. The play is carefully constructed in its plots and themes and is completely put in writing. At the other end of the spectrum you can develop a play totally improvisationally: The actor may go onstage and pick the elements of a scenario out of a hat—person (king), place (fair), adjective (angry), verb (attack), conflict (nobody pays attention to him). Then the actors improvise on the spot in front of the audience.

In the middle of the spectrum of types of plays that can be improvised are story theatre and participation. The play *Story Theatre* itself is not a traditional well-made play, even though it is scripted. It has simple, short plots and uncomplicated themes. The characters are one-dimensional: the king is always the essence of royalty, not a King Lear. In participation plays a lot of the script is established before performance, but segments of the script are developed with the audience.

THE TRADITIONAL SCRIPT

Companies that choose to develop a traditional theatre script through improvisation usually have the services of a playwright and a director of improvisation, both of whom are skilled and experienced, as well as actors who have great facility in improvisation. Developing a traditional three-act play will take more time than most companies have.

ON-THE-SPOT IMPROVISATION PIECES

The 1960s saw a resurgence for adults of nightclub-style skits that the performers seemed to make up as they went along. Audience suggestions, social/political themes, verbal wit, and split-second timing characterized the performance. Behind all the spontaneity, however, were intensive rehearsal periods—working on cataloguing audience suggestions as well as setting many specific pieces that could be modified on the spot to fit various situations.

The concept of total improvisation pieces was embraced in the 1970s and continues to be used in the 1980s by theatre companies producing plays for young people. Companies usually intersperse improvisational pieces with scripted pieces to balance the production. As in performing for adult audiences, a company member would ask for suggestions from the audience, and the group would enact the piece. Unknown to the young audience, the improvised animal or scene had actually been partially rehearsed and staged. Companies like the acclaimed Magic Carpet of San Francisco mime audience suggestions of animals, toys, famous people, and other such categories.* Usually pieces that are based totally on audience suggestions are fillers, inserted between longer, more rehearsed stories.

STORY THEATRE

Story theatre is another form that was developed in the 1960s. *Story Theatre* is the title of a production developed by Paul Sills at Second City Company in Chicago.† The original production was a collection of Grimm's fairy tales and Aesop's fables, in which the company of seven actors played various roles in each story. In the original production actors narrated the stories and then assumed the roles of the characters about whom they were speaking. Costume pieces indicated character, music played by an onstage band helped establish the mood, sound effects made by actors onstage punctuated movement, and locales were established through mime.

The script of *Story Theatre*, published by Samuel French, can be directed by you or utilized as a model for your own story theatre production, a term that has evolved to mean any production that takes the form and structure of the original. Because the original production uti-

> *There was a narrative technique that was developed by Robert Breen at Northwestern University called chamber theatre, and that was a technique very similar to story theatre where the actor could speak about his character in the third person. Except they used a narrator. So I just cut out the narrator twenty years later and that was story theatre.*
> Director Paul Sills

*Other categories that can be rehearsed are current events, the seven deadly sins, variations of good versus evil, television shows and characters, nursery rhymes, the ten commandments, and fairy tale characters.

†Original company members include Valerie Harper, Richard Schaal, and Paul Sands, all now well-known television actors.

What you have to understand when you do story theatre is that, though these words come out of the mouths of different people, the story is one voice. So when you do a story, you don't tell it to an audience, you don't play a character. And the story doesn't just take place on the stage. The feeling is that the story is all the space you can fill, and therefore you share the story among the players on the stage, among the audience, among the musicians, among the lighting man and the lights—among everything.
Richard Schaal,
actor in original production of
Story Theatre

lized music of the period in which it was produced and was developed to reflect the talents of that specific company, many directors have found that they would rather use their own material to create an original story theatre production.

Because of the young audience's theatrical needs for strong visual statements and the often-experimental nature of actors who choose to perform for children, story theatre is an excellent choice for young people's theatre. Often inexpensive, easily tourable, this actor's theatre continues to grow in popularity in the 1980s. By adding their own ingredients—rock or electronic music, live sound effects, elaborate costume pieces or simple leotards, stories from other countries or local legends—many companies experiment with story theatre form.

Drawings sent to companies reveal that the audience readily accepts the conventions of story theatre. Although one actor may play several roles, children depict the many roles of the same actor as played by actors with varying physical characteristics. The drawings also add detail to locale and props that had been merely mimed during performance. The only limits of story theatre seem to be in the ingenuity of the performing company.

The following characteristics distinguish story theatre form:

1. Many short incidents or stories, rather than one long story, are presented.
2. Material is based on existing fairy tales, folk tales, fables, myths, legends, or nursery rhymes. Occasionally letters from young people are used as material.
3. Actors play many roles, and characterizations are often one-dimensional; particular walks or voices are the distinguishing character elements.
4. Actors begin narration in third person and then become the character in the first person. For example, an actor might begin by speaking, "Once upon a time there lived a king. He spoke to his kingdom, saying . . . " At this point the actor would become the king and speak, "People, we are in grave danger. . . ." Actors switch between narrating the character and portraying the character.
5. The production is performed on one set, which may be the arena stage floor with small pieces to indicate place. Or the set may occasionally be an elaborate constructivist set. What is primary, however, is that the actors use the set in specific ways to establish place. Variety in areas, planes, and levels of each story is vital.
6. Actors wear a basic costume, such as leotards, tights, or jeans. Costume pieces such as hats, capes, and accessories are used in various ways to differentiate the characters.
7. Props are usually mimed.

8. Sound effects and/or music punctuates the action and sets the mood.
9. Stories are varied in terms of length, mood, and pacing for the sake of variety.

AUDIENCE PARTICIPATION

Participation* is a general term that in itself does not constitute a form, but encompasses a number of types of scripts in which the audience is asked to contribute to the action in various ways. These contributions can be as simple as being asked by an actor to applaud to awaken a sleeping hero or as complex as the audience's assembling an intricate prop during the performance (a performance for which they have been previously prepared). The potential is unique—the direct involvement of the young people creates an intense actor/audience relationship. The children become part of the action; when this is done well, a powerful empathy results.

Directors often embrace participation because of its positive selling points. Sponsors are attracted to participation because they think they are getting double for their money: a theatre piece and a drama lesson. Drama lessons are not intrinsically bad, but participation stuck onto an inappropriate play or involving actors who know woefully little about responses of children can only continue to give theatre for young people a bad name.

Participation requires a cast that will not break its trust with the audience nor pander to it. Some misguided actors actually tease the children by not responding consistently to a prearranged signal. If you establish that three claps by the audience will awaken the hero, then three claps should expediently accomplish that result, or you have cheated them.

Another common pitfall to avoid is whipping up the audience to a state of hysterical excitement and then leaving them with no theatrical outlet for their emotions. One particular company developed a piece of theatre about water pollution in which they pointed out that all the streams in the children's playground had been polluted. The children participated in a political rally in which revolutionary action was encouraged. On this frenzied note the actors departed, leaving the teacher to deal with the hysteria. Again, the company did a terrible disservice in the name of participation.

The following discussion of types of appropriate scripts should help you make decisions about what participation can be. The loss/gain chart can also help you decide if you want to use participation at all.

*Even if you decide not to develop your own participation piece, this section will help you in preparing an already scripted participation play.

....

After we perform a show for a school group, we frequently answer questions from the audience to add to the educational value of the experience. The questions frequently asked involve the props and costumes, or acting in general, and as children can be especially demanding in their questioning, one should be well prepared before embarking on this activity. Following one performance, we requested questions from the overflowing audience. One young man's hand shot up and he was acknowledged. The question rang out, "How do you get down from a forklift?"
After years of pondering that question, I finally did some research about industrial machinery, and now feel completely prepared for anything an audience member might ask. Almost.
Director,
Happy Times Children's Theater
....

above left: Direct actor/ audience contact can stimulate audience participation. Volunteers from the audience help actor James Donlon look through his telescope.
Photo by William Patterson

above right: The excitement of participation can be seen on the faces of these children who are helping actor Michael Locklair. Looking Glass Theatre, Providence, Rhode Island: *Metricks!* by Peter Miller and Rebecca Linn. Directed by Peter Miller.

PARTICIPATION

GAINS
For the audience
- added physical dimension
- experience in learning by doing

For you and the actors
- exploration of script/audience relationship
- altered perception of actor/ audience relationship

LOSSES
For the audience
- the aesthetic distance component of empathy/aesthetic distance balance
- one kind of formal sense of occasion

For you and the actors
- a bit of your sense of power
- control of the total theatre product

The following seven categories of participation* represent most of the currently existing major types:

1. Do you believe in fairies? (DYBIF) Deriving its title from Peter Pan's plea to the audience requesting their applause in order to save Tinker Bell's life, the DYBIF type of participation is the most superficial type. In this type of participation:

- Actors in character request unison vocal or unison seated physical participation from the audience (for instance, "All bend forward").
- Production is staged in a proscenium arch stage.

*John O'Toole has also developed a classification system for types of participation. In *Theatre in Education* (London: Hodder & Stoughton, 1976) he divides participation into three genres: *extrinsic*, *peripheral*, and *integral*. Extrinsic participation indicates that the element of participation is separated from the theatricality. In peripheral participation the audience is invited to contribute in order to add to the theatricality without affecting the structure. Integral participation is where the audience perspective also becomes the perspective of the characters.

Certainly the moment when Peter requests the audience's applause is magical, but probably no audience in the history of *Peter Pan* ever failed to applaud. In less well-conceived participation segments, failing to receive an answer to "Which way did he go?" or a response to "Everybody, whistle when you see the villain," happens often and rarely affects the rest of the play. The actors still muddle through, continuing their actions, mumbling under their breath, "Funny kids." Participation of this type takes very little time to prepare and rarely jeopardizes the theatrical experience. Choosing DYBIF is safe but rarely innovative.

2. Berry bushes　　In the berry-bush type of participation plays:

- Actors, sometimes in character role and sometimes in a role of creative drama-like leader, move into the audience area.
- Play is usually presented on arena stage.
- Audience is divided into sections for various kinds of participation activities.

An example of this type of participation is Moses Goldberg's *Hansel and Gretel,* in which the audience during one segment is asked by the actors playing Hansel and Gretel to grow into berry bushes. The children are encouraged to stand up in their seats, make their arms grow into twigs, and then grow berries on their hands.

　After the berries are picked, the audience members are asked to sit down. Actors, moving into the audience, use creative drama tech-

In this production of *Raduz and the Three Clouds*, audience members are encouraged to take a group role. Note that most of the children have raised their arms in this "berry bush" type of participation. Asolo Touring Theatre, Sarasota, Florida.
Photo by Gary W. Sweetman

niques like side-coaching, modeling behavior, and positive reinforcement.*

3. Fly or die   Another type of participation play may or may not involve some berry-bush type of participation, dealing primarily with the audience's chosing between various alternative endings. In this type of participation:

- The action takes place on either arena or proscenium stage.
- Actors make requests of the children while in role, but again oscillate between actor role and creative drama leader role.
- Audience choses between two or three alternative endings, all of which have been rehearsed by actors.

Our plays encourage appropriate audience participation. During a performance of Kaspar at the Crossroads, *a little girl stood up to deliver an impromptu lecture to two of our adult actors (who happened to be arguing at the time) on how we should be friends and live together in harmony. The little girl (age seven or eight) was so forceful and well-spoken that she captured the total attention of the whole audience (300 or so in a school gym). Then she sat down and after a moment the play went on as if the interpolation had been scripted.*
KIDS Theatre,
Madison, Wisconsin

In one production of a play about space travel the pilot of the ship asked the audience, who had traveled with the cast to the moon during the play, if they would like to (1) remain on the moon and try to colonize the area, although facing possible death, (2) return to a safer earth and lose the colony, (3) travel to another less hostile planet to try to make a colony there. This particular audience voted to remain on the moon, and this ending was then enacted.

Occasionally, this type of participation play is taken a step further. The audience is sent back to a classroom to work out and script an alternative ending. The actors are given a few minutes to study the script. The audience reenters the auditorium to watch the ending they have just written.

The next four types of participation plays have been derived from the landmark work of the Belgrade Theatre in Education team in Coventry, England. In that company, team members, called actor/teachers because they have been trained both in theatre and in education, worked together to develop these script types. The scripts discussed represent the interests of the actor/teachers and the needs of the young people of Coventry.† They have served as models for similar scripts developed in America.

4. Kenilworth   The name of this type of participation derives from a program that Stuart Bennett, a leader in the field of Theatre in Education in England, has termed "the first TIE program." The Kenilworth type of participation method is more complex than the previously discussed types because two separate periods of time, as well as two sep-

---

*We encourage berry-bush participation primarily for groups, not for individuals. Some companies, however, have found single participation successful.

†Belgrade TIE scripts that have been published are mentioned with reference to the particular publishing company. Unpublished scripts may be available from the Belgrade Theatre, Theatre in Education, Coventry, England.

arate spaces, are needed. In this type of program, during the first section:

- The action and training take place in the classroom.
- Actors as themselves prepare young people to participate in the second half of the program, somewhat in the manner of a creative drama leader.
- Actors usually present a brief overview of the historical event that will be enacted in the second half of the program, somewhat in the manner of a classroom teacher.
- Participants usually number thirty to sixty young people.
- The group is divided into smaller groups, with each group prepared to do a specific task in role, such as working on auto bodies or constructing an engine.

During the second section:

- The drama usually takes place in the school hall or gymnasium, where an arena stage has been set up.
- Actors assume roles of actual or composite historical characters.
- Young people in group roles physically participate—doing actual tasks in the production.
- Young people are asked to share an "emotional stake" in the drama, having been assigned roles as weavers, car-makers, etc.
- The climax of the drama is a group decision to effect a change of some kind.

An example of the Kenilworth type of participation is a production developed at the Belgrade called *Car-Makers.* In that program the actors, as themselves, present a history lesson on the car-making industry, a major industry in Coventry. Then, still in the classroom, the class is divided into several sections and trained to work on various assembly-line tasks. They work with prop pieces to put together cars. They are told that these parts are just props, but that the work is to be treated as representative of reality.

After a break the class assembles in the school hall. A play begins in which the actors assume roles of actual composite characters in the history of the Coventry car-making industry. The young people are asked to participate in the making of the cars. The situation becomes difficult as the lights in the school hall are turned off, as noises on tape recorders are turned on louder and louder, and jeers from the actor playing the boss constantly criticize the workers' ability. The intent is to simulate actual conditions in the automobile industry. Finally, one of the actors sets up a strike, during which time the young people figure out how they will form labor unions to represent their needs. The play ends with the presentations of the young people's demands for more unions.

5. Adventure/journey   The major premise of this type of participation program is the quest for something good or the search for someone evil. Participation of all thirty to sixty children, ages six through eight, takes place almost throughout the entire program. In a typical adventure/journey program an actor enters the classroom, introduces him- or herself as an actor, and then explains that a play is about to take place.* The actor exits briefly to put on a costume piece, then returns in role and explains that a villain has stolen an important secret code book. The actor asks the class to help him find the villain. Meanwhile a note, written by the villain to his accomplice, somehow appears in the classroom. The note mentions that important information is hidden in the gymnasium. The members of the class, now deputized as detectives, accompany the actor to the gymnasium.

In the gym an arena stage has been set up. After a series of clues—all unraveled by the actors and the young people—and a major chase, the villain is caught. In fact, often one of the young people telephones the success to a "police station" (the theatre office), where a waiting actor receives the call. Characteristics common to all adventure/journey programs are:

- Actors establish that a play will take place.
- Actors assume roles of characters in the drama.
- Class participates in a group role (for example, that of themselves as detectives).
- The optimum age of participants is six through eight.
- Action takes place in many areas throughout the school.
- Clues are set prior to the start of the program.

6. Simulation gaming   Similar in nature to adventure/journey, but involving older children (nine through fourteen), simulation gaming usually constitutes a segment of a longer two- or three-part program. In this type of program:

- The major premise is the playing of a game, which simulates a large sociopolitical issue such as disarmament or global food distribution.
- Action takes place in a school hall.
- Intricate game rules that have been established prior to the program are explained to the young people.
- Action takes place on a game board or similar surface that is set up in the school hall.

*Initially, the actor/teachers did not utilize this introduction. Many young people thought that they were participating in an actual event. They were unable to distinguish reality from illusion, and they felt betrayed when told at the end of the activity that they had just been in a play. Therefore, the team added this introduction to clarify the dramatic premise.

- Actors take peripheral roles, such as game-show host or roulette-wheel spinner.
- The resolution of the game is illustrative of a world situation; for example, preventing the world's oil supply from running out.
- After the play the participants are encouraged to discuss the results of the program.

7. Proscenium participation Perhaps the most technically intricate type of participation play, the proscenium type, was developed by Belgrade TIE because of the opportunity to utilize a large proscenium stage and the desire to involve an entire audience of 400 to 500 young people. The best way to explain proscenium participation is to describe *Ice Station Zero One,* a fine example of this type of participation.

Several weeks before the production the classes whose teacher chose to book the performance receive a team-developed letter from a character named Eddie, which tells the children that they will be traveling to the North Pole on a hovercraft. The Belgrade Theatre auditorium will become the hovercraft. Included in the letter is information on hovercrafts and other materials to be distributed by classroom teachers. This preparation aids in the development of the theatrical illusion that is necessary for proscenium participation to be effective.

When the children arrive at the theatre on the day of the performance, they are met by actors dressed as hovercraft attendants who collect tickets, hand out emergency drill cards, and direct the young people to their seats. The theatre has been designed to give the illusion of a hovercraft—theatricalized, of course. As the children enter the au-

This is the stage portion of the production of *Ice Station Zero One* developed by the Belgrade Theatre in Education team in Coventry, England. The control panel of the hovercraft, shown here, is the focal point from which the story is created by both actors and audience members. Directed by David Pammenter.

ditorium, they see windows on each side of the auditorium, through which films are shown of the sights on the journey to the North Pole. Also, a large lighted control panel is set up on the stage, above which are large screens displaying various slides illustrating the trip. At each seat is a seat belt.

During the performance the actual participation experiences include passing various crates from the back of the house to the stage, leaning in seats from side to side to help loosen the hovercraft from an iceberg (accompanied by slides rotating from 45 degrees left to 45 degrees right, to simulate a view from the hovercraft), and enacting a seated emergency drill. The core of the effect is the simulation of being transported on a hovercraft to the North Pole; however, there is no actual physical participation in that the children never leave their seats.

Generally, a proscenium-participation type includes these elements:

- The production is staged on proscenium stage with traditional actor/audience seating arrangements.
- Audience of young people participate while seated.
- As many young people as can be seated in theatre are able to participate, either as one unit or divided into smaller groups.
- Some of the actual participation is physical, such as passing objects, marking ballots.
- Much of the effect is achieved by preproduction materials and theatrical staging of a central premise, usually based on transporting the audience from one locale to another to aid in a disaster of some sort. (Premises have included turning the theatre into a submarine to go underwater to stop radiation poisoning, or turning the theatre into an airplane.)
- Much of the effect is achieved by slides, films, sound effects.
- Actors participate in character role, with some degree of creative drama-like side coaching built into the dialogue.

"SOMEDAY MY PRINCE WILL COME": CREATING OR CHOOSING MUSIC FOR THE THEATRE

One of the most important considerations in creating your own play is whether or not to include music. Theatre for young people without music is a recent phenomenon and has so evolved that current catalogues of scripted plays list almost three straight plays for each musical, probably because of the practical considerations of budgets and cast requirements. However, most straight plays also include incidental music and dance.

By its very nature, musical theatre is presentational, constantly proclaiming the total theatricality of the play to the audience and the performers. Music and dance can express the feelings of a scene better than a thousand words, especially for children. Musical numbers can add sparkle and quicken the tempo, but if they are not well done, they just interrupt the flow of the story. One of the joys of theatre can be the infectious quality of good music. However, it is much harder to define what is "good" music than to define what is good theatre. Nor can this book teach you the elements of music—namely melody, rhythm, harmony, form, dynamics, tempo, and tone color. Even if we did, it is doubtful whether this knowledge can be of any significant value to you in creating or choosing appropriate music for children's productions.

MUSIC FOR THEATRE FOR YOUNG PEOPLE

When we discuss music for theatre for young people, we do not refer to "musical comedy," the extravaganzas staged on Broadway. These may be excellent family (or universal) plays—*Sound of Music* or *Annie*, for example—but they are clearly out of the scope of young people's theatre. These types of musical performances focus on song and dance scenes and huge "production numbers" that require singing and dancing choruses and a professional choreographer, music director, and chorus director, in addition to a large orchestra and conductor, a sound engineer, and elaborate stage and rehearsal areas.

Music is the universal language of mankind.
Henry Wadsworth Longfellow

What is appropriate for you to consider in your creative process is what is referred to as "incidental music." This usually requires just a piano, or portable rhythm instruments with kazoos, or even a nicely balanced four-piece ensemble of piano, string, wind, and percussion. "Incidental" should not mean merely *sticking in* a song; music should never *interrupt* the flow of the story. A "show-stopper" number is distracting to young people and usually results in confusion and restlessness. Music should beautifully express the deeply felt emotions and conflicts of the characters and should enhance the plot. For example, if you cannot appropriately include music within the story and you wish live music, you can utilize such devices as a singing troubadour, bridging the scenes with timely ballads accompanied by a guitar.

Young people today are much more sophisticated in music than in theatre, so there is little need to restrict the type of music to simple, romantic, or bouncy tunes. Any numbers, jazz to rock to classical to pop, may be appropriate, as long as the song is not too long or elaborate for the story and does not stop the show. In fact, a song can better express deep or complex feelings to children than words.

For the youngest audiences only (ages five to seven) short numbers and simple, sweet tunes are usually well-received, but you or the songwriter have more leeway in your rhythmic composition than you may realize. The well-known research of composer Carl Orff has demonstrated that preschool children respond not only to simple melodies and words but also to a wide range of rhythms.

Taking "adult" music and jazzing it up or watering it down for young audiences does not work. Even the youngest theatregoers rec-

This company based on improvisation develops pieces of theatre with strong music and dance components. Metro Theatre Circus, St. Louis: *Mud Weavings.* Written and directed by Zaro Weil.

ognize when they are being pandered to. Today's teenagers seem to respond almost primitively to loud, dissonant music, but this does not preclude the universal appeal of pure, harmonic melodies. For example, what could more perfectly capture the glowing simplicity of a fable, appeal to the inherent idealism of children, and enhance the romance and mystery of another world than a song like "Someday My Prince Will Come" from the movie *Snow White and the Seven Dwarfs?*

The music must always be consistent with the *spine* and *style* of the play. In *Do You Love Me Still?* by Metro Theatre Circus, the music (and dance) is the prime accomplishment; whatever diminishes the music lessens the performance. In *Reynard the Fox* incidental jazz music inappropriately inserted only distracts from the story. You, your company, and your playwright must make certain that the numbers are not only apt, but *extend* the theme of the performance. Good music takes the audience into the world of the play and enhances that world.

ONE LAST NOTE

Additional considerations enter into creating musical plays beyond the demands of making straight plays:

1. As director, you must determine the musicality of the play and the musicianship of your company. If either the play or the company doesn't measure up, avoid the pitfalls of music altogether (except perhaps during scene changes). If you're insecure about your own musicianship, appoint someone else to be music director.
2. Each and every performer must be *musical*. Forced singing or danc-

ing is easily perceived even by young children. The talent of a fine singer or dancer transcends words: It creates the magic that charms the audience.

3. When creating a piece of theatre, you may use original melodies or well-known tunes. But they must be properly placed. As a rule, it is much better to complete the book first, even with lyrics, and then have the composer create the appropriate music. If you start with the songs, you encounter the problem of finding a place to *insert* them or of writing the script *for* a number. This often results in distracting from, rather than enhancing, the story.

4. As director, you must assume the responsibility for the unity of the production. Make sure the music is consistent with the spine of the play. Make use of the dance rhythm and melodies of the period and locale.

5. You must also consider such aspects as staging areas (especially for dance), availability of piano (or side area for combo), and acoustics. Strict limitations of budget and stage may even necessitate the use of background music tapes.

As director, you need not be a songwriter, choreographer, or performer of music or dance, but you must understand how, where, and whether to include musical numbers in your artistic product. You must ensure that the numbers are subservient to the total effect of the work. If so, your production will be energized by the life-affirming qualities of music and movement, song and dance.

Perhaps the most difficult stages in the creative process are those where your company must improvise to make the ideas come alive theatrically. To assist you, we will present specific improvisation techniques, some axioms for good improvisation, and some play-development hints.

THE IMPROVISATIONAL PROCESS

PRIVATE AND PUBLIC IMPROVISATION

At the core of the group creative process is the improvisation. Two basic categories of improvisation exist: private and public. Private improvisations are used by actors to "tune their instruments" and to develop their roles. They are usually conducted by an acting coach during the rehearsal of a scripted play. The objectives of private improvisations are to help the actor develop a character for an already-scripted role and to get in touch with a personal storehouse of images to be used in role development.*

Public improvisations may or may not be performed in front of an

*The Repetition Exercise in Chapter 4 is an example of a private improvisation.

audience. Their main objective is to work out the plot or the conflict. Here, actors must create the behavior that will form the core of the piece. Actors should not simply talk, they should also do, in the theatrical sense. Public improvisations have as their ultimate goal "the instruction and entertainment" of an audience. Thus, product as well as process is important.

Three examples of public improvisations are demonstrated that we have found to be successful in the development of our original pieces. Improvisation 1 is for a single actor, Improvisation 2 for two actors, Improvisation 3 for a group of actors.

EXAMPLE 1: EMPTY CHAIR*

Justification: If an individual actor is having difficulty with character justification, this exercise can help justify complex character or situational motivations.

Description: Place two chairs facing each other. Actress A sits in Chair 1 and asks a question based on script ideas of the imaginary "alter ego" in Chair 2. The question might be: "How did you become interested in nuclear power?" She then moves from Chair 1 to Chair 2 and answers the question. Actress A moves back to Chair 1 and continues to probe. Then she returns to Chair 2 and answers the question. Essentially, the actress plays two parts of the same person, asking questions to which she subconsciously knows the answer. The actress is probing into other levels of consciousness.

EXAMPLE 2: JUMP

Justification: When Actress A is not developing different actions to win her objective from Actor B, Actress A must be trained to "jump" Actor B.

Description: Assign Actress A the task of getting a specific objective from Actor B. What Actress A might wish to get is a book of magic spells that is in the possession of Actor B. (Actual physical props should be used.) Actress A tries to get the book first by demanding it. If Actor B will not give up the book, then Actress A may try to plead for it. If Actor B is still not about to give up the book, Actress A may try to wrestle the book out of Actor B's hands. Actor B must understand that if he is convinced during any one of the three actions, he should give the book to Actress A.

EXAMPLE 3: ADVERTISEMENT PHOTO

Justification: If the group is having difficulty finding appropriate group enactments.

Description: Show the group an appropriate photo of a group scene. (Begin a collection now of interesting group photo advertisements in magazines. Advertisements that look like candid photos of weddings, funerals, waiting

---

*This exercise is based on J. L. Moreno's psychodrama exercise of the same name, which has therapeutic, nontheatrical objectives.

rooms, parties, graduations, etc. are good stimuli for group improvisations.) Discuss the photo. Figure out who each character is, what the relationships among characters are, and what has just happened. Then position actors in the exact positions in the photo. Have the group improvise what they think will happen next. Discuss and improvise again. Then, ask the same group to improvise what happened just before the photo was taken. Have the group finish the scene in the exact positions of the photograph. Discuss the reenactment.

WHAT TO TELL YOUR ACTORS

Just as we can't tell you everything, neither can you prepare your actors for every eventuality. They must develop a general sense of improvisational craft from which they can cope with each individual situation.

Actors should refer to the following Ten Helpful Hints as they begin the improvisation process. These hints apply to improvising in any of the previously discussed forms.

For instance, if we're improvising a scene and you choose a position, if I want to make it a scene, I've got to take the opposite position. If I agree with you, we don't have a scene.
Director Mike Nichols

ACTOR'S HINTS FOR THE IMPROVISATIONAL PROCESS

1. You must always have something to say. Don't just take the stage for the purpose of taking the stage.
2. You must always be able to answer the question: Why are you telling the other actor this?
3. You must take a strong position. In two-character scenes that position must be in opposition to the other character.
4. You must always be doing something. If no situation exists, you are just mouthing dialogue.
5. You must always be aware that you know. At no time in the play is it more interesting not to know what will happen than to know.
6. Don't poke fun at something or somebody at the height of the dramatic conflict. Satire is too sophisticated a concept for an audience of young people.
7. Remember, if it's spoken, it's real. If Actor A establishes something, Actor B must not deny the verbal reality.
8. Make the active, as opposed to the passive, choice.
9. No matter how difficult it may seem to do so, the actor's business is to justify whatever he or she is doing.
10. Go with your impulses. Even if eventually the choice may seem wrong, go with the current flow. You can change your choice next time around in rehearsal.

IMPROVISATIONAL SCRIPT DEVELOPMENT PITFALLS: THE CRAFT OF CREATING A PLAY

Sometimes in your haste to zip through improvisations and get the show finished, simple playwrighting skills are forgotten. It may be helpful to refer to a list of some of the important playwrighting principles. Unfortunately, we have viewed plays in which these principles are totally ignored. Remember, even though your play is improvised, make your finished product as well-crafted as possible.

- **Scenes must be about conflict, not about exposition** At the opening of a melodrama a maid and butler spoke at length about the master's and mistress's past life. Try not to replicate boring scenes of this nature. Have necessary plot information revealed indirectly through action.

- **Plays are about people, not about issues** Try to illustrate the issue through person. For example, Belgrade TIE made their point about housing projects by developing an excellent play on one particular old woman's plight of losing her house. Called *Home Sweet Home*, the piece grabbed the attention of the audience and made its point because of the audience's identification with a particularly well-developed and well-acted characterization. If the piece had been a didactic treatise about the housing needs of the old, the point would not have been made. Good theatre first; good moral second.

- **Keep plot and character separate** Characters should not merely be functions of the drama, they should be people with needs and objectives. Another example from Belgrade TIE illustrates how to differentiate between characters who are simply functions and characters who have clear needs. In *Ice Station Zero One*, the proscenium participation play discussed earlier in the chapter, the team originally developed a character named Atuk, who was to represent primitive man's use of resources. The first drafts of the scenes with Atuk never seemed to work. After much contemplation the team realized that the character of Atuk was just a generalized primitive man who spoke out in a general way about all of the world's abuse of nature. The character merely served the drama by contrasting technological scientists with simple people. Later drafts made Atuk more believable as the company developed scenes for him in which he tried to stop technological advances in a very specific and compelling manner.

- **Important scenes must occur onstage** In ancient Greek and Roman plays messengers would arrive onstage to describe the complex battle that had won or lost the war. This practice was employed mainly because the battle was impossible to stage. Leaving out significant scenes for this reason today is inexcusable. Since you are developing your own play, don't make the resolution scene unstageable. If you can't afford to stage the scene of the witch dissolving in a puff of smoke, think of another way for the witch to die. Don't use the device, which

Children don't want to feel you're trying to push something down their throats, so when I have a moral, I try to tell it sideways.
Author Theodore Geisel
(Dr. Seuss)

we have seen too many times, of having an actor point offstage, saying, "Oh, look, the witch is dissolving."

• **Don't use deus ex machina**   In ancient plays, when the end of the play seemed unresolvable, out of the sky (but really on a stage-pulley system) would appear a god in a basket who would save the day. Unfortunately, many playwrights and companies end plays in a similar manner. No gods come from the sky, of course, but often unexpected, undeveloped characters suddenly appear to announce a lost legacy or to concoct a magic spell. Make sure your endings have been set up logically during the drama.

• **Dialogue can come from interviews, but make selections carefully**   If interviews are one of your primary forms of research, you can use actual words from interviews. Occasionally these words can be lifted directly from the tape recorder and made into dialogues or monologues. Usually, however, the hand of an artist must trim down the statements and make composites of the sentences of many people. Don't overlook interviews as sources, just be selective.

In a play about the elderly developed at the Belgrade, the eighty-four-year-old doorman who had spent a lifetime at the theatre was interviewed. Maybe because he had been near the theatre, or maybe because he was a particularly literate man, his taped interview was played in its entirety during one segment of the show, as a voiceover. Examples like this are rare, but when they do happen, don't be afraid to use them.

The child-like quality achieved by Judith Martin (second from stage left) has made The Paper Bag Players in New York one of the foremost original groups in theatre today. Directed by Judith Martin.

I miss Second City so much. Throwing a hat on and being a whole character, or sitting on a chair and pretending it's a car, or bringing on a stick and pretending it's a gun. I miss when you could just pretend anything in the world.
Actress Gilda Radner

LAST WORDS OF ADVICE

"Go to it!" Seriously, we close this chapter with a quote from A. J. Antoon, who worked with story theatre form at Yale University. These words are our final words of advice to a director who hopes to create new pieces for young people's theatre:

"A storyteller who doesn't believe his own story soon starts talking to himself; nobody wants to listen."

So, director, the last step as well as the first step is: Believe.

Why do you direct?

You mean in the theatre at all? There are two ways I would answer that, or divide directing into two things. One is interpretive, and the other is more all-encompassing and in which I'm more interested. This is to make plays, of which directing is just a part. I'm sometimes also involved in the designing and writing and composing and the choreography. I like to make theatre pieces. I suppose I'm most fond of that, more than interpreting. When I was involved in the arts, I was going to be a painter and a print-maker. I realized that theatre allowed these things, these images that I brought together and organized in my prints and paintings, to live, to have time. I think that's what leads me to the theatre. I bring other things with me to the theatre, but primarily I like the idea of bringing images to life. So that's why I'm here. And in this field I love the fact that over the years I have been able to do things for and with an audience who didn't care ahead, who could come with a marvelous openness.

And that's why you do plays for children?

I think so. I realize, among other things, that a great deal of my childhood lies with me.

I think that's so common with people interested in children's theatre.

I suppose. It's not simple to talk about it, is it? It's all wrapped up in my associations with my childhood, the fantastic illustrations in books and the rush of sensations I somehow recall encountering. I remember what it smelled like in the first painting studio I went into when I was eight, which thrilled me.

When you do your plays, do you try to please yourself?

Oh, yes, I have to be true to myself as an artist and hope that what I make will be enjoyed by, and have meaning to, others. Of course, in dealing with children, I don't deal with the same subject matter I would with adults. At least, there are certain things that children are not so interested in and aren't appropriate for them. And generally speaking, I just try to make the work that is there.

In creating your plays, when if ever do you consider your audience? For example, you don't assign age range. What are your feelings?

I guess I feel that what I need to do is make

INTERVIEW

with John Clark Donahue, Artistic Director, The Children's Theatre Company of Minneapolis

something that is something. This is a shell [holds up a seashell], with its myriad of mysteries and complexities. It's undeniable. So, who is it for? It's for all of us to come to many times until we die, and it'll never be within our grasp. I like to think that what I'm supposed to do is make a piece which is truly something and which can then be come to by anybody. They take away what they take away. I don't worry about whether or not it's right for here, or here or here—except, as I said, I wouldn't discuss things in the same way for younger people between five and fifteen, perhaps, as I would for older. Some people will come and say, "I don't think my child understood it. I don't know whether my child got anything out of it." Of course it's nonsense, because that isn't how children come to things. Unless they're taught to think that way, they will let a thing roll and rush over them. Or if they could become tiny, they would crawl around this shell and get to know it and not wonder what it was for or even why they were doing it. So, I would make it shorter, perhaps about an hour and fifteen minutes.

You do a lot of classics. Do you like that?

Part of our philosophy here is to do the classics and to do them pretty true. So that, in juxtaposition to the new work, you have the classics and vice versa. I think they should be kept alive and revered.

Do you find new things every time you do something like Hansel and Gretel?

I think so. We did it the last time in German with an English storyteller, which was very nice. This is a totally different mounting. We've done it three times now. Of course, *Legend of Sleepy Hollow* is the same mounting we did in 1969. This

169

is the fourth time we've done it. Certain productions which we think are good approaches, we honor and keep alive, hopefully, over decades. Others we will do differently. So it depends. We have people in this production of *Sleepy Hollow* who were in the original one and they are ten years older, including the leads, but we also have children who were twelve and are now twenty-two. I'm trying to make a theatre that has a depth of patina to it. Somebody that you can see at the age of sixty who was performing here at twenty.

What do you look for in the people that you choose to make part of this family?

We've grown our own, mostly. The ones who came early on liked my work and wanted to work with me; the younger ones . . . I guess we look for the illusive quality that we all can recognize . . . people that are saying behind their eyes, "I must be there. I must work, I must do." I'm trying to build a certain aesthetic here—people being able to do many things: move, dance, sing, play instruments, be humble, work toward an ensemble, have humility and vulnerability, be very demanding and highly trained.

Tell me what happens when you do improvisations?

Oh, my! I think the point of improv, the reason for working improvisationally, is to discover how to work and how to discover, so that the work is totally discovered by the participants, all the way along the line. That's when the work has true life. You build a climate, an understanding, a sense among the participants that discovery is possible. And once you learn that, it becomes glorious because true work is going on. The whole company works together every Tuesday for three hours in the morning. And then, I'm working improvisationally with students twice a week for six hours.

Do you work on a theme or on a picture?

Many, many ways—phrases, poetry, music, masks—a single prop, a haiku.

You also seem to know the people very well. You seem to know their possibilities. That takes a long time.

Yes, now that we've been together—the people who are between twenty and thirty—I've known them for ten to fifteen years, since they were wee ones or since they were teenagers. I don't even have to speak English sometimes, or just do this [gesture] or just make sounds, and the people respond. We've learned to communicate on many levels.

It's interesting, when asked about your success, you talked about the people who come to your theatre. You don't feel that it's your vision or your genius?

Well, I have to do what I do, and if they respond to it, that's great. I have the wisdom now as I enter my middle age to know that we must always be free. By that, I mean we must be able to give it up. Of course I sensed that. I wrote about that in my play *Old King Amalfi,* when I felt the country needs to know that it could give it up, give up that direction.

But now the times are very different, and you still exist. And you're so unconventional. That's what's incredible. Hasn't anyone ever made you accountable?

Well, I've tried to balance things. We sometimes do things that are quite conventional. But now you realize it's $1,300,000. I have a board of fifty people. I'm going to have a seminar later this year on risk-taking and the right to fail as being at the very center of the nature of the art process. People can't always feel that they're constantly in danger. They have to be able to feel free.

Your success with Hansel and Gretel must make you feel safe.

Oh, yes. That production will allow other things to go into dangerous territory, to take tumbles.

Your use of blood packets in Treasure Island— did you consider that "dangerous territory"?

The healthy thing about theatre is that theatre is medicine. It's meant to be done: It's healing to see that. It's different than television and motion picture. The theatre is ancient in its ritual. It has to do with medicine and healing by acting out. We are more cleansed by theatre. Theatre is the gathering. Both forces are live. So I think it's good, and it should be dangerous. It should be theatrical. It should be high or heavy. It needs to be.

Of course you have the blood packets, and you have the Japanese theatre where the slit throat is just a red ribbon. Now the latter is even more powerful and more awful: the red ribbon. Once you get out of the phase of the blood packet and into the more awful reality of the ribbon, you're really learning to celebrate the theatre. I hope over the years, too, that seeing these plays told in various ways will somehow clarify the journey we can make to seeing and hearing and being. I'm hoping that I'm beginning to get toward the threshold of people realizing that theatre also is important as healer, so that people will begin to realize that the arts are vital, central to healing. And we are taken seriously.

I am sure a lot of people take you seriously.

I'm working on *The Little Mermaid* now. That's why I have all these fish. I'm studying fish; and more will arrive: sea horses, angel fish. We have a twenty-piece orchestra, beautiful strings, an original score being developed. I'm setting it in an ancient land, a combination of Ethiopia and Egypt, but it's mystic, too. It's very exciting to work on. The physical setting is evolving now. It is a true tragedy. I've been listening to it over and over. Really deeply moving. And if we can put it on well enough so that the whole community attends it, just as they go to see *Hamlet* because of the terrible dilemma of Ophelia's love for something she can't have, then it is children's theatre in the best sense of the word *children*. Right? What Pablo Picasso and Cocteau knew, and Fellini celebrates in *8½*.

6·SETTING THE STAGE: DESIGN FOR YOUNG PEOPLE'S THEATRE

One of the most striking similarities between directors of theatre for young people and directors of adult theatre is the embarrassing lack of understanding of technical theatre and the design process. Directors quite openly admit to having no knowledge of lighting boards, scene shops, or costuming and makeup methods and materials. The problem is, if anything, compounded by the fact that in the field of young people's theatre shoestring budgets and lack of trained personnel are more the rule than the exception. The director of theatre for young audiences must all too often assume a combined position—director/designer/technician—responsible, by default, for all these diverse tasks.

A good indicator of a director's ability to relate to the technical elements of production is to watch the director backstage. Here many a director picks nervously through the maze of escape stairs, scenery braces, and prop tables. The technical end of production is like a jungle: overhead, like vines, lighting cables loop back and forth; chains, ropes, and cable hold curtains, lighting pipes, and scenery aloft. Unaware of the terminology, not wanting to deal with the technology, this director is constantly afraid of touching the wrong thing or stepping in the wrong spot. And of course, as in every jungle, the last great fear is the unfriendly natives.

When faced with what seems to be an overwhelming workload involving all the elements of production, a not-uncommon reaction is to reason, "We'll just do without," or, "I'll see what they come up with." When broken down into logical areas, the technical process—from sketch through execution—becomes comprehensible, approachable, and much less frightening. A thorough understanding of this process is important for any director and critical for the director who, by necessity, is responsible for the practical end of one or more of the technical areas.

Both in the preparation stage and in the running stage of a theatrical project you must be the final artistic voice. Your realistic goal is to arm yourself with the most basic understanding of technical terms and processes. But the greatest skill a director needs does not involve the actual doing but rather the supervision and guidance of those on hand. Your job is knowing what can reasonably be expected from the production team.

WHAT EVERY DIRECTOR NEEDS TO KNOW ABOUT THE DESIGN PROCESS

This chapter will provide a framework for understanding the creative and technical processes in the major specialized areas of scenery, lighting, costumes, and makeup in order to equip you, the director, with a working vocabulary of equipment and procedures.

The creative projects of John Clark Donahue have made The Children's Theatre Company widely known for both original scripts and non-representational scenic designs. Note the scope this design gives for unusual entrance and exit points, stage picturization, and spectacle. The Children's Theatre Company, Minneapolis: *A Circle Is the Sun* by Frederick Gaines and John Clark Donahue. Directed by John Clark Donahue. Scenic design by Donald Pohlman. Costume design by Gene Davis Buck.

ORGANIZATION OF THE PRODUCTION STAFF

The successsful production of a play is not the achievement of a single individual but the composite result of a number of artists and craftspeople, each of whom contributes to the total effect. These areas of activity provide the basic breakdown of job responsibilities within a theatrical production staff.

Obviously there are many variations of this basic breakdown. However, the more important positions, their work duties, and their responsibilities remain fairly constant. These are the people who immediately surround the director. Let's take a closer look at who they are and what they do.

....

The director without a sound knowledge of backstage organization or a clear picture of the duties and responsibilities of various members of his or her production staff is poorly equipped to assume the authoritative leadership required of the individual who must synchronize all phases of production.
A. S. Gillette,
Stage Scenery
....

Director   You, the director, assume your role as technical supervisor. Through your analysis and interpretation of the play you establish the style of the production. The same style that determines the actors' choices of vocal and movement techniques carries through and determines settings, costumes, makeup, and lights. Everything should work together to express your idea of the play.

Put out of your mind the idea that theatre is a democracy. It is not. Decisions cannot be made through voting or through committee or parliamentary procedure. You, the director, must supervise and synchronize the talents of the artists and craftspeople working on the project.

Stage manager   The stage manager acts as the director's virtual right hand. Because the relationship between the two is one of mutual dependence and trust, many directors on the professional level will demand a particular stage manager with whom they have established a working relationship. The stage manager acts as the liaison between the director and the acting company, the director and the scenic designers, the director and the technical department heads and their crews. The stage manager must keep accurate records of all these various areas and constantly keep the director informed as problems arise. For elaborate productions the stage manager usually must have one or more assistants.

Designers   Like any visual artist such as a painter or a sculptor, the theatre designer deals with the variables that constitute the component parts of an art piece, such as color, balance, and perspective. On the practical side, the designer is little more than a problem solver. On the artistic side, the designer is creating a unique and personal statement: the visual expression of the play, as focused through the particular perception of the director.

The scene designer provides the sketches for all the settings required for the production. These drawings include ground plan, sightline drawings, front elevations, and detail drawings. The scene designer also provides general information for shifting the settings and super-

Shown are the design sketch (left) and the actual costume and mask for the character of the Fly in Mofid's *The Butterfly*. The Everyman Players, Dallas. Directed by Orlin Corey. Designed by Irene Corey.
Photo by Beth Odle

vises the set construction and painting as well as the purchase and building of props.

The lighting designer collaborates deftly with all the other designers, for in many ways the lighting is the unifying force in the overall design. Duties include planning the lighting plot, determining the number and types of instruments to be used, seeing to the placing and mounting of these instruments, setting up the control board, and developing a control board cue sheet.

The costume designer submits sketches to the director for all costumes to be used in the play. After the director approves the designs, the costume designer reviews stock inventory to determine what may be altered for use in the current production. The costumer then buys remaining fabrics and accessories and supervises the actual making of the costumes. When the costumes are rented or shopped, the designer has the responsibility for placing orders, viewing samples, and overseeing final fittings, adjustments, and alterations.

The makeup designer must work closely with the director, the lighting designer, and the costume designer. The makeup designer must provide sketches that delineate makeup colors. Hairstyles, whether using the actors' own hair or a wig, are also the responsibility of the makeup designer.

STAGE SCENERY

Of all of the areas of technical theatre, stage scenery has perhaps the longest history. When the first hammish caveman pushed a stump, some branches, and some rocks together to form a crude representation of place for his story, he set the stage. In the 2,500-year history of the theatre stage settings have been doing much the same. Certainly things have changed, especially in the last hundred years in terms of new materials and high technology, but a great deal has also remained the same. Perhaps upwards of 75 percent of all stage scenery used today is a variation of the flat—a movable stage wall used since the Greeks.

The history of scenery is fascinating but not vital to your task. As the director, you must understand what sets can and cannot provide, and you must know some basic facts about their function.

WHAT SETS MUST BE

All sets must be: (1) portable, (2) reusable, (3) durable, (4) affordable.

1. Portable   Scenery is most often built in a shop, rather than on the stage for which it is intended, and moved into position only when the crew completes it. Both directors and designers must always keep in mind the weight and awkwardness of the scenic units, not only in terms of mounting the production initially, but also for eventual strike and storage. A common mistake is building units that don't fit in to and out of access doors.

2. Reusable   Scenic units should be designed in such a way as to be readily available for future shows. Flats and platforms should be built in standard sizes well-suited to the theatre stage where they will be used.

3. Durable   Scenery, especially weight-bearing scenery, must be built to last through the rigors of rehearsal and performance.

4. Affordable   Scenery should be constructed out of materials readily available and inexpensive, yet still fulfilling the other criteria. Inferior and shoddy building and painting materials may be cheap, but they will prove to be more expensive in the long run.

WHAT SETS MUST PROVIDE

The most common misconception about scenery is that it is a decorative picture in front of which a play takes place. While decoration does play a part, a set has to do a lot more than look pretty. A well-designed set provides a visual springboard from which the play may take off. Actors work on, around, within, and through a set.

To be successful, a set must provide: (1) visual exposition, (2) machine for action, (3) mood, (4) aesthetic picture.

1. Visual exposition   Visually, sets must tell who, where, and when in a single eyeful. This enumeration of details, the given circumstances of the play, is of primary importance in the conveyance of the play's information. Whether the hall of the troll king, a pirate ship afloat in a midnight storm, or a secluded glade in a dark and spooky forest, the basic questions an audience wants to know will be the same.

Who? Of course, the actors tell the audience this, but not until later on and with words, which are much weaker communicative tools than images. You must therefore make sure that what they see is telling the story you want told. A place—whether a palace or a cottage—can tell a great deal about the people who live there. Is it someone I would like? Would they like me? Are they like me? What does a living room filled with chrome and glass suggest that is different from one filled with heavy Victorian furniture? How would the palace of the Evil Queen in *Snow White* differ from the palace of King Arthur in *Camelot?* Is the forest of Neverland different from the forest of *Alice in Wonderland?* In each of these cases an audience looking at the scenery will be asking, "Who lives here? How has this place left a mark on this person? How has this person left a mark on this place?"

When? There are several whens that a set should answer—or at least provide clues to. The period of the play is perhaps the first and one of the most important. Other whens that must be answered are time of day and time of year. Each time carries with it a whole storehouse of denotations and connotations, both subjective and objective. Why is it that 11:59 P.M. isn't spooky, but one minute later, at midnight, is? What is it that makes Mary Melwood's *Five Minutes to Morning* such a magic time—just as night draws to a close and the reasonable, rational light of day restores the predictable order of things?

The importance of the seasons has certainly diminished in our modern day, but they should not be underplayed. No less than two generations ago, and for the centuries before, the seasons and their changes had great significance and application to people's lives. Spring, summer, winter, and fall have personalities and character traits that have become less apparent in our day, but the seasons have been used by playwrights for centuries.

Where? There is a specificity about location that must exist. Years ago, stock scenery was the mainstay of a theatre. The wooded glen drop, the grand ballroom drop, the humble cottage kitchen drop, were all standard. Such stock scenery is no longer the case. Every show has its own particular atmosphere, which should be reflected in its settings.

2. Machine for action   A machine for action should be exactly what the name implies: a set that does what it's supposed to do efficiently and smoothly. Where actors enter and exit, the number of actors entering and exiting at the same time, the speed and manner in which they come on or go off, are all factors that determine the specifics of the stage machine. A common problem is to design the stage machine around one or two of the major "grabby" scenes in a show, ignoring its impracticality for the rest of the action.

Certain types of plays have almost been locked into certain scenic styles. Story theatre is almost synonymous with the staging convention of the plastic stage, making use of the ramps and stairs, the platforms and levels to create the various stories. Musical comedy also has its more-or-less stock approach to stage scenery, making use of both wing and drop scenery, of wagons and revolves that can quickly shift from scene to scene. Before abandoning these choices, make sure the sets you have chosen work as well as, or even better than, these more commonly used sets.

3. Mood   Mood is the visual music that underscores the action in a theatrical piece. Capturing the mood of a play in visual terms is a difficult and highly subjective job. The theme of the play, the treatment of the characters by the playwright, the handling of the dialogue, and the tone of the scenes each contribute to the overall impression of mood. How is this quality captured in visual terms when it is so difficult to pin down and verbalize? The use of color, line, textures, scale, symmetry, or asymmetry can create a visual interpretation of the emotional feelings within a play. Because of the ephemeral quality of mood, everyone concerned should have the clearest possible picture of what is being sought after in order to maintain a similar mood focus. When handled correctly, mood is perhaps the most powerful, evocative tool.

4. Aesthetic picture   The final criterion for stage scenery is that it should exhibit qualities that please the eye. This is not to say that sets should be "pretty" to look at; in fact, that is too often a problem with stage sets. Rather, stage scenery, like any other visual art creation, should exhibit principles of good design and execution.

HOW SETS MOVE

The shifting of scenery is one aspect with which every director must have a working familiarity. The smooth running of a show, the effortless move from scene to scene, the expeditious movement of actors, scenery, and props will ultimately be a director's responsibility. Many a promising production has fallen apart because of scene changes of interminable length, full of loud noises and frenetic activity. Efficient technicians will help a director by making suggestions concerning timing and traffic patterns. To be most efficient, actors should be worked into the shift, if only to help in removing hand props and readily movable pieces of stage furniture.

Scenery is shifted in one of three ways: (1) running, (2) rolling, (3) flying.

1. Running   Running scenery is carrying or sliding sets on and off manually. In cases where wing space is at a minimum and flying capability does not exist, running is the most efficient, if not the only method to shift from scene to scene.

2. Rolling   Rolling scenery is exactly what the name implies. Scenic units are built as platforms with fixed or swivel casters. These platforms on casters are called wagons and may be rolled on and off stage manually or mechanically. Some theatres are built with full *slip stages*, full stage platforms that are rolled on permanent tracks into playing position.

Rolling scenery requires adequate wing space to be shifted out and be clear of sight lines. The *revolve*, a round platform that can be divided into segments for different scenes and pivoted to new playing positions to accomplish shifts, is one solution to quick set changing.

3. Flying   Flying scenery is the quickest and quietest method of scene shifting. Scenery is raised and lowered vertically by means of ropes and counterweighted lines. A fly loft is an obvious requirement for this form of shifting. Flown scenery is almost always two-dimensional; drops and flats are the most common flown units. Flying scenery requires the greatest care in order to prevent serious accidents. Actors must be constantly aware of where scenery is coming in or going out; scenic units must be counterweighted accurately so as to be easily managed; technicians must be well rehearsed so as not to bring in the wrong line, say, lowering a third act drop at the end of the first act finale.

LIGHTING

Lighting helps the audience to focus. As we have said before, one of your responsibilities as director is to assist audiences in knowing where to look. Lighting can be a primary tool in making visual pictures that tell the story.

The use of light in dramatic production is a relatively new phenomenon. Only in the last 500 years has a production been moved into formal indoor spaces and become dependent on light sources other than the sun. The use of oil burners and candles had obvious disadvantages. Gas burners were a step in the right direction, but only the development of electric light made for a radical change. Early electrical lighting had many of the same limitations and was used in much the

....

There is something to be said in the theatre in terms of form and color and light that can be said in no other way.
Robert Edmond Jones,
The Dramatic Imagination
....

same way as previous light sources. Burning lime was used in the nineteenth century to create an intense, though hard to control, light; this is the origin of the phrase still used today: "play the limelight." Rows of lights, hung overhead and/or placed at the foot of the stage, were roughly controlled for dimness or brightness. Carbon arcs were crude but revolutionary in that brilliant light could be projected from a distance. Soon after World War I, however, the use of spotlights, coupled with the development of dimmer boards to control them, created a capability for specific illumination: controlled, focused light thrown over a distance. The use of light in this way is the single most important factor in the development of our modern theatre.

Lighting is not only the newest element of technical theatre, it is also the most technically sophisticated. As if *ohms* and *watts, amps* and *lumens,* were not enough, the introduction of computer technology has thrown a whole new wave of chips, bits, and integrated digital circuits into the vocabulary. To most people whose familiarity with light is limited to the flipping of a switch and the changing of a bulb, anything more complicated than this seems intimidating. If you are to harness and control the incredible power of light, you must begin by gaining a modest understanding of what lights do and how they are rigged and controlled. If you can drive a car without being a mechanic, you can deal with the lighting board without being an electrician.

PROPERTIES OF LIGHT

Light is electromagnetic radiation visible to the human eye. In regulating light, you must deal with four separate and controllable properties: (1) brightness, (2) color, (3) distribution, (4) movement.

1. Brightness   Brightness refers to the intensity of light, which can cover a wide variance from a faint glimmer to a blinding flash. Brightness is the result of many factors, including types and sizes of instruments used, bulb (or, technically, lamp) wattage, dimmer levels, color mediums, filters or other special-effect devices, focus, and masking devices. Brightness is a highly subjective quality and is influenced by several factors. The brightness of a previous scene, the speed of changes in lighting, which may or may not allow the audience time to adjust their eyes, the distance of the audience from the stage, the reflective qualities of the colors and textures of the costumes and set (and even the actors' faces), all are factors to consider. In general, bright light makes an audience more attentive and alert—an important factor to consider when the success of a scene depends on attention to verbal and visual detail.

2. Color   Virtually every color of the spectrum is available through the use of various readily available color mediums. Sheets of colored gelatin or colored plastic material may be used singly or layered to provide any shade. Special attention must be paid to the way in which colors complement each other; a careless choice may completely destroy the subtle palette that a costume or set designer has used. Often designers use warm colors (oranges and reds) for comedies and cool colors (blues and greens) for tragedies. The human eye is most sensitive to color in the yellow/green (middle) portion of the spectrum. Scenes using light predominantly from either the red end or the blue/violet end provide visibility problems.

3. Distribution   Distribution is the directionality and form of light. The form of the light can vary from a full flood to a full spot; the former is a general haze or wash light, the latter a specific sharp shaft of light. Moving the lamp closer or farther from the lens regulates the form of the light.

The direction of the light is of great importance. The designer may chose to light from any angle in the 360-degree range. Light from directly below or directly above causes strange shadows but can be highly effective for dramatic purposes. Light from sharp angles above, or directly to the side of, the actor tend to reveal the almost sculptural qualities of the human figure in motion. (This explains why much of ballet and modern dance relies so heavily on side light.) Even backlight has its uses for silhouette special effects; the actor stands out from the background by being surrounded with a halo of light.

4. Movement   Movement is the change or variation of any of the other properties: brightness, color, or distribution. These variations may happen at any speed, singly or simultaneously. Over the course of several minutes the brightness in a sunrise, for example, will increase from a faint glow to a bright, full stage wash. The light colors, meanwhile, will shift from a violet or steel blue to the reds and oranges of the first rays of the sunrise to the lemon yellows and amber tones of early morning. These changes may be coupled with a distribution shift from a general flood to a specific spot or sun special.

WHAT LIGHTS DO

Lights have four main functions: (1) visibility, (2) revelation of form, (3) composition, (4) establishment of mood.

1. Visibility   Light must help the audience see the action on the stage; this visibility is essential. Audiences straining to see often become restless and feel that they cannot hear the dialogue. An audience will instinctively focus on the brightest spot on the stage. For this reason the light of greatest intensity should be on the actors' faces.

2. Revelation of form   Light also gives three-dimensional form to the actors and sets on the stage. In the theatre, unlike in films or on television, actors really are three-dimensional, living beings in front of the audience. Lighting should assist this revelation of form by heightening the three-dimensional nature of actors apart from the backgrounds.

3. Composition   Light also acts as a factor of composition. The same scene, for example, can look radically different with differing degrees of intensity, color, and distribution. Make sure you and your designer are working for the same stage picture.

4. Establishment of mood   Light should establish mood. Not as simple as turning up the lights or dimming them, mood is really the result of combining the previous three factors. Audiences who cannot even verbalize the mood are greatly affected by the visual effects of light.

LIGHTING EQUIPMENT

A great deal of equipment exists for stage lighting, known both by technical and brand or company names. Rather than getting bogged down in the technicalities of supertroupers or lekolites, we will discuss only the simplest necessities for understanding the process of lighting a stage.

Lights are classified into three basic types:

1. **Spots** or **spotlights** throw a well-defined, concentrated shaft of light. Instruments may be mounted in a fixed position or may be mobile to move with the actor. In this case the term *follow spot* is used.
2. **Area lights** or **floods** provide general illumination in the form of pools of light to specific small areas.
3. **Border lights**, also known as strip lighting, are rows of lights, either hung above or placed below, that give general illumination to acting areas or scenic pieces.

These three kinds of lights are controlled by a dimmer board, which, by means of separate controls, allows for increasing and decreasing the illumination of individual lights, selected groups of lights, or all the lights as a unit. Through the dimmer controls we are able to achieve all variations, from all lights at full intensity to a full stage blackout. Lights can fade up (increase in brightness), fade down (decrease in brightness), or cross fade (the intensity of one group of lights is raised as the intensity of another group is lowered).

COSTUMES

The clothes that actors wear seem very similar to everyday clothes. In many ways the costumes seem even better: more beautiful, more ornate, more spectacular than any "real" clothes could be. Many girls in the audience covet the princess' robe; many boys long for the prince's armor. Offstage and in natural light, these costumes appear somehow strange: oddly colored, full of spray-painted folds, cardboard clumps glued onto the material, with huge snaps and zippers instead of dainty hooks. Theatre clothes are not everyday clothes.

Theatre, by its very nature, deals with heightened action and moments. Costumes must often be put on and removed quickly and in unconventional ways. Because of this increased activity, they must withstand tremendous wear. In one limited run a costume can go through more traumas than any street garment does in its lifetime. Yet, onstage, costumes must simply appear like clothes.

A stage costume is a creation of the theatre. Its quality is purely theatrical and taken outside the theatre, it loses its magic at once.
Robert Edmond Jones,
The Dramatic Imagination

WHAT COSTUMES MUST HAVE

Costume design takes into account three variables, treating each with equal concern: (1) durability, (2) practicality, (3) the visual aesthetic.

1. Durability Durability refers to the inherent strength of the garment. Even in a normal realistic show costumes must have stronger seams, fasteners, and fabrics in general than clothes worn by the person on the street. Actors work in a state of heightened energy, and as a result they have the unfortunate habit of literally "bursting their britches." In plays for young people the need for durability is even more crucial.

2. Practicality Practicality involves the commonsense approach to choosing fabrics and construction methods that best meet the staging requirements of a show. Shop for fabric with a critical eye. Look beyond the surface colors, textures, and patterns. Consider colorfastness, wrinkle qualities, shrinkage potential, and methods of cleaning and pressing. Although antique garments and accessories are lovely to look at, they generally fail to be practical for stage use.

Also, practicality takes into consideration the inherent limitations of the individual actors. If you think an actor will not be able to walk around the stage with the weight of a particularly heavy costume, for example, don't buy the fabric, no matter how cheap or beautiful it may seem.

3. The visual aesthetic The visual aesthetic comprises the combination of lines, colors, and textures that captures the style of the production. The principles of good design should be the basis of the visual aesthetic. This aesthetic is most obvious in a flashy, "glitzy," elegant show with lovely ladies in satins and chiffons, men in well-tailored suits and evening wear. Often an audience will oooh and aaah, even burst into applause for costumes of this kind. For example, in one mu-

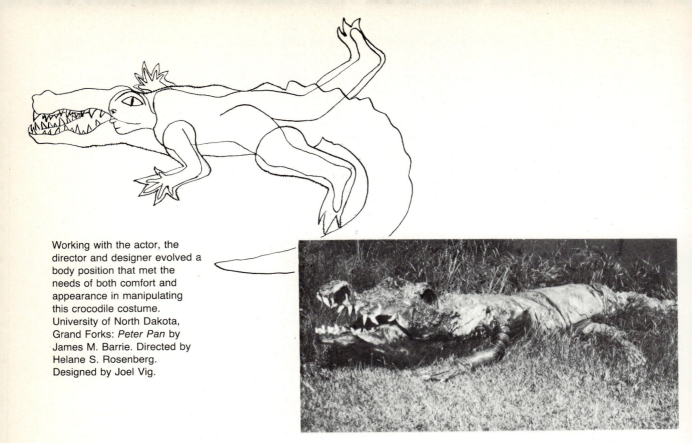

Working with the actor, the director and designer evolved a body position that met the needs of both comfort and appearance in manipulating this crocodile costume. University of North Dakota, Grand Forks: *Peter Pan* by James M. Barrie. Directed by Helane S. Rosenberg. Designed by Joel Vig.

sical number in the Broadway musical *42nd Street*, designer Theoni Aldredge actually stopped the show with her dazzling costumes, which spanned the stage with the colors of the rainbow. But even in shows where rags and tatters take the place of velvets and sequins, the sense of a strong visual aesthetic must be present. All costumes for any show—whether the ragtag garb of peasants, soiled and torn garments of prisoners and slaves, even the seeming "noncostume street clothes" in a modern dress play—must measure up with the same aesthetic yardstick.

TYPES OF COSTUMES

There are three basic types of costumes, any of which may be called for in any given script: (1) historical, (2) modern dress, (3) fantasy.

1. Historical Historical or period costumes must honestly reflect the fabrics, lines, decorations, and ornamentation of the specific fashion from any given time. Many directors think of any clothes before 1920 as fairly similar in a "long ago and far away" manner. All women wear

184

long full skirts, and the men carry canes and wear top hats. In point of fact, each period has its own unique silhouette and accessory requirements. A period show must be dressed from the shoes to the hats, from undergarments to overcoats. A pair of saddle shoes peeking out from a medieval peasant skirt, while barely visible, can shatter the fragile reality that you have worked so hard to establish. A well-costumed period show is a virtual feast for the eyes. Whether the mystical simplicity of ancient Egyptian robes and headdresses, the wild and whimsical extremes of Restoration court costumes, or the sleek, modern lines of the hats, coats, dresses, and shoes of the 1930s, a period show is a piece of fascinating living history.

2. Modern dress Modern dress implies clothes that make no period statement; they are the here-and-now fashions of the times. A common mistake is to assume that shows calling for modern dress really need no designers. The director can simply let the actors wear whatever they might choose. But a costume is not a random garment pulled from a character's closet; it is, rather, the statement made by all of the garments collectively in the closet! Modern-dress costumes should provide the same sorts of visual clues to characters as period or fantasy clothes. The designer is still concerned with the interplay of colors, shades, and hues for each character and for the play as a whole, as well as with the lines and silhouettes and the various textures.

above left: Production design for this Gertrude Stein piece for children was based largely on inspiration from the Bauhaus school. Note how the visual aesthetic incorporates geometric forms—circles, tubes, cones, spheres. University of North Dakota, Grand Forks: *Oh Where Oh Where Is There?* Directed by Sue Pratschner. Production designed by Joel Vig. Costumes designed by Karen Thornburgh.

above right: Animal costumes vary greatly. Contrast this realistic Nana with Irene Corey's Lion and Fox on page 194. University of North Dakota, Grand Forks: *Peter Pan* by James M. Barrie. Directed by Helane S. Rosenberg. Designed by Joel Vig.

185

3. Fantasy Fantasy covers a wide range, from almost realistic, futuristic science fiction characters to fantastic creatures of myths and legends: witches, demons, trolls, and fairies. Designers have a fairly free hand in creatively outfitting these imaginary beings. For fantasy characters to achieve a total effect, cooperation between the lighting, set, makeup, and costume people is vital. You, the director, of course, must oversee this process.

COSTUMES CONVEY IMPORTANT INFORMATION

The costumes for a show must do more than merely dress the actors. A costume designer must dress the whole play in order to convey all sorts of important visual information. Costumes should address six specific areas: (1) establish the society, (2) delineate individual place in society, (3) create focus, (4) denote relationships/interrelationships, (5) illustrate progressions, (6) provide beauty and aesthetic interest.

1. Establish the society Every society throughout each period in history has created its own fashion statement, based on all of the sociocultural values of that particular time and locale. The surface effects are easily noted. Choices of colors and materials, types of decorative motifs, and the degree of decoration are only the reflections of a deeper and somewhat more obscure truth: how this society felt toward itself and toward the world. Fashion in Victorian England, for example, reflected a self-assured conservatism. Victorians felt that theirs was the ultimate achievement in evolution and civilization. This was a time for optimism, with no room for self-doubt. All sorts of elements were drawn together from Egyptian to classical Greek to French rococo, all freely adapted to suit the Victorian frame of mind. While today this look may appear to be dowdy, stuffy, and old-fashioned, to the Victorian it was a new and uniquely modern style that incorporated and reflected all of known history, even improving and surpassing it.

Each society somehow displays its social, religious, and cultural values. To visually capture these qualities is to capture the spirit and soul of a period, and this should be a major priority for the director of a period piece.

2. Delineate individuals' place in society Costumers strive to make every character an individual. Who a character is, the character's gender, occupation, position, and relative status, should all be reflected in the choice of garments. Society's view of various occupations has changed throughout history; no area reflects this more than fashion. For this reason careful consideration must be given if a play is to be moved from one period to another. The way in which any given society has viewed such professions as soldiers, doctors, or moneylenders has gone through radical shifts. A costume should reflect both how the society perceives a character and how the characters perceive themselves.

3. Create focus   Costumes are potentially one of the strongest eye-grabbers, and they should be utilized to their fullest potential. Imagine a stage set in muted beige and grey, restaurant tables covered in white cloths, waiters in black and white, patrons in muted greys and pastel tones. Suddenly, at the top of a center-stage staircase, a curtain opens, and there stands a woman in a bright-red sequined dress. Virtually every eye in the audience will move to this focus point—and "Hello Dolly!" Focus can be achieved by a variation not only in color but also in silhouette or texture. A leading lady may seem to be wearing the same costume as the chorus she performs with, but careful observation will often point up subtle variations that help make the costume, and thereby the performer, stand out from the ensemble.

4. Denote relationships/interrelationships   Members of a group, whether ideological or family, should dress alike in some way; similar colors, textures, or lines help an audience to identify and delineate characters and relationships. This may be extremely subtle or blatantly obvious: for example, with one family, the Montagues, in blue and the other family, the Capulets, in brown. While this costuming technique works well, especially in shows with large numbers of characters, it is also important to distinguish each character. For example, in *Peter Pan* all of the lost boys should look alike, yet be different from each other. This feature is known as individualizing the ensemble.

5. Illustrate progressions   As a character develops, changes in costumes can point out and reinforce this development. In *Dracula*, for example, as the character Lucy gradually falls more and more under the power of Count Dracula, her clothes reflect these changes. As she is transformed from an innocent heroine to "an unclean thing," a depraved creature of the night, her costumes may shift from starched white cotton and linen to slinky, sexy black silk and satin. Costumes are helpful in illustrating physical and emotional changes and changes in age and health.

6. Provide beauty and aesthetic interest   Costuming is a kinetic art form. The costume, when joined with the actor, moves through space in time. The costume really exists only in motion, only for the brief moments of the performance, and even then only in the minds of the audience. The garment on the hanger is merely the empty shell of this memory.

MAKEUP

No aspect of the theatre is more amazing, fascinating, and downright magical than stage makeup. The makeup artist, using materials that for the most part go back hundreds of years, makes both subtle and bold use of color, highlight, and shadow to create the most startling and astonishing effects. The creation of witches, trolls, and fairies is but one area of a makeup artist's art. With makeup, the aging process is speeded up or reversed, the beautiful can become ugly and the ugly beautiful. One face can actually be transformed into another, even in cases where no similarity existed.

WHAT MAKEUP MUST ACCOMPLISH

Makeup in the theatre is used to accomplish three primary goals: (1) projection, (2) correction, (3) characterization.

1. Projection An essential function of makeup is to transmit facial characteristics by means of highlight, shade, and shadow to compensate for both the distance of the performer from the audience and the flattening, "washout" qualities of bright stage lighting. Almost all of the expression in the face occurs within a triangle from the eyebrows down to the mouth, at the apex of the triangle. In general, the makeup artist attempts to accentuate these features and deemphasize the areas around them.

White is used to highlight the area under the eyes; a dark line is drawn beside each lash line (upper and lower) to accentuate the eye. Shadow is used for the eyelids, with a lighter color above to delineate the eye sockets. The eyebrows are darkened, with highlights above and below. The bridge of the nose is highlighted, the sides shadowed. The lip line is defined both by darkening and coloring. A highlight is placed above the top lip, a shadow below the bottom lip. In this way the various planes of the face are broken up to add depth and dimensionality. Although the effect from the distance of the makeup stool to the makeup mirror may seem rather startling and severe, the distance of stage to audience compensates for this. In general, actors have a tendency to apply makeup too subtly rather than too broadly.

2. Correction Makeup involves the altering of less-than-perfect features, changing the real to the ideal. In the musical *The Apple Tree* little Ella, the chimney sweep, is transformed by her fairy godmother into Passionella, the ravishing movie star. The real fairy godmother was not a magician but a makeup artist named Joseph Cranzano. There is a little Ella and Passionella in everyone; makeup tricks allow everybody to exploit their ideal selves. No one has a perfect face. One eye may be lower than the other; one side of the mouth may droop and the other turn up. Correction is the skill of using both painting and sculpting techniques to create the ideal.

The makeup base itself is a primary correction device, evening out the skin tone (with its irregularities, freckles, and blemishes) to an overall standard color, whether it be cream-rose or light Egyptian. A little extra highlight between the eyebrows can widen the space between eyes too closely set. A slightly crooked highlight down the bridge of the nose compensates for a less-than-perfect nasal bridge. Even though Hamlet chastised Ophelia, exclaiming, "God gave you one face and you make yourself another," one of the major objectives for makeup design is to make one face into another.

3. Characterization If actors were only to play themselves, correction and projection techniques would be wholly sufficient. Because they portray other characters, actors must be skilled in transforming their own faces into the faces of these characters. The wide range of makeup materials now available offers even the amateur a vast range of possibilities for radical makeup changes. False noses, chins, forehead pieces, even eye bags and lids are made commercially, or they can be made easily and with a minimum investment of time and money with readily accessible materials. Richard Corson's *Stage Makeup**[*] text, especially in its revised format, provides easy and specific step-by-step instructions for creating not only foam or latex rubber prosthetic pieces, but virtually all two- and three-dimensional special effects.

In creating characterization makeup, it is important to create a statement of a character in the simplest way possible. Often characterization such as this can be achieved with a single well-executed effect rather than a combination, or more often a conglomeration, of effects. Think of a character in terms of a caricature. Ask yourself what single feature of the character captures the visual essence. Cyrano has his nose, Queen Elizabeth I her forehead and curly red hair, Benjamin Franklin his bald pate and bifocal glasses. Often this one effect can make more of a statement than two arduous hours in front of the makeup mirror.

MASKS

Masks are makeup carried to the ultimate extreme. Here again our three makeup principles can apply:

1. Projection The use of masks allows the designer to create extremely large features. The primary purpose of masks, in the huge amphitheatres where they were originated, was to project the form of the actor. Building a modified megaphone into the mask accomplished vocal, as well as visual, projection.

2. Correction With the face of the performer totally hidden, the mask makes a total character statement uninfluenced by the similarities or

> *This brave theatre of ours will accept limitations—be it budget, corset, or mask—as a challenge. Working within the confines set up by these restrictions, we shall find new solutions, create new departures. What is wrong with a theatre of poverty, if it is rich in imagination?*
> Irene Corey,
> *The Mask of Reality*

*[*]Richard Corson, *Stage Makeup* (Englewood Cliffs, NJ: Prentice-Hall, 1981).

Masks and costumes need not have human inspiration. Here Irene Corey interprets plant life to form these fantastical characters. The Everyman Players, Dallas: *Wiley and the Hairy Man* by Suzan Zeder. Designed by Irene Corey.

Photo by Karl Stone

disparities of the performer to the role. Masks allow the design element full freedom to determine the correct features and their placement for any given role. Features can be exploited or distorted for symbolic significance.

3. Characterization   The use of masks allows for the portrayal of all forms of natural and supernatural creatures such as gods and goddesses, devils and demons. Masks have virtually no artistic bounds. They need not even be figural, but may instead be an abstraction of a face, facial feature, body part, or even an inanimate object totally unrelated to the human form.

PRACTICING THE DESIGN PROCESS: YOUNG PEOPLE'S THEATRE

The practical problems that arise in theatre for young people and, in fact, in all theatre often cannot be solved as simply as they seem to be in textbooks. Also, we cannot prepare you for all eventualities or arm you with every fact. You must evaluate any situation in which you find yourself. We do, however, have a handy triangle that can help you develop a realistic attitude about your limitations. It's a general rule of thumb passed down from an old Broadway designer. Keep it in mind at all times.

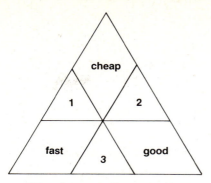

1 If it's done cheap and fast, it's no good
2 If it's done cheap and good, it's not fast
3 If it's done fast and good, it's not cheap

The remainder of this section deals with specific examples. First, we will present a case study of designing a presentational piece for young people. We will show you how the director can shape and mold the design process from idea to completion. We have chosen *Reynard the Fox* for our example because of the universal nature of its problems: how to costume people as animals, how to picture change of seasons, how to design a flexible playing space. You will face specifics like this constantly if you continue to direct plays that are presentational in style or are for the young audience. Second, we will analyze some of the other categories of scripts currently in the literature of young people's theatre, detailing specific design ideas for each type.

The design process involves: (1) analysis, (2) deduction, (3) imagination, (4) creation, (5) adaptation. These processes occur separately or simultaneously, depending on the design team's method of working.

You've decided to direct *Reynard the Fox*. What will happen in terms of design?

REYNARD THE FOX: A CASE STUDY IN DESIGN

1. Analysis   Analysis lays the foundation for the whole process that is to follow. Shortcuts here lead to disastrous results later on. The first reading tells the story and the plot; in this early stage a designer makes every effort to keep a completely open mind and not lock into premature design choices. The first reading has given the designers a gut feeling—an intuitive reaction to the spirit of the play.

After the first few readings, with time between each for reflection, your designers will have made their observations and preliminary notes and will be ready to sit down and chat. Be forewarned: Good designers will put you on the spot with to-the-point questions and will want specific answers. Nothing turns a designer off more than a director who has failed to do the necessary homework and background research. A director who can't give straight answers to production questions isn't helping anyone.

Here's one possible way to present your interpretation of *Reynard the Fox* to your design staff: The play takes place in the very heart of the forest. Four scenes corresponding to the four seasons take place. There are seven speaking characters: Ticelin, the crow; Rev. Epinard, the hedgehog; Brun, the bear; Ysengrin, the wolf; Noble, the lion; Reynard, the fox; and Lendore, the marmot. No era is given. This will be a point to discuss. The script has a fairly light and lyrical quality to it, without seeming whimsical. Each of your designers may have different reactions to the literary form and will look to you to redirect or reinforce their initial reactions.

At the first production meeting there will be a discussion. You may wonder why the set designer can't just build a forest set, why the costume designer can't just sew seven standard animal costumes. You know, of course, that the set can't be just any forest. The action outlines particular and specific requirements that a designer must incorporate:

- where characters enter and exit
- physical requirements, such as a tree that must support a person
- picturization potential for groups of from one to seven actors

The costume designer uses all of the same information to answer questions:

- requirements of costume to perform special effects
- quick changes
- number of characters in each scene

Some of the initial questions are answered in this production meeting; others are not.

There's more to design than just these practical considerations. Designers will want to know the spirit, the aura, the atmosphere that you are looking for. Don't be afraid to make any kind of statement that might illuminate your point of view. Designers are used to dealing with abstract concepts and translating them into concrete patterns. Telling your designers that you see *Reynard the Fox* having the qualities of a Monet painting, a Rachmaninoff concerto, or a Victorian valentine may seem silly to you but will give your designers food for thought. Whatever you can see or feel, try to express—the palette of colors, the sounds, the smells, the sights, the lights, shadings, and shadows. By talking through your ideas, you help to clarify your thoughts for your design staff and also for yourself.

Be specific. Delineate what you consider to be important moments. Discuss special effects: how the beehive incident is to be handled, ideas

AM I CREATING BELIEVABLE FANTASY OR JUST CANNED SOUP?

for the thunderstorm effects, the changes in seasons from every stand-point. Do the trees lose their leaves? Do the animals change in appearance from season to season? How do you want the quality of the light to change from fall to winter, from spring to summer?

Any technical information you can give is needed now. Blocking choices and patterns, use of specific character walks, ideas on the combat scene between Reynard and Ysengrin, Reynard's desperate run for his life at the finale—all of these moments require specialized scenic, costume, lighting, and makeup tailoring. As the first production meeting draws to a close, try to encourage and maintain an open area for artistic expression.

2. Deduction   The designers are now armed with the information needed to go back to their respective drawing boards. They build on your analysis; they deduce specifics from your concept of the production. You may have them researching medieval court costumes and manners—the general feeling closely connected to the quality of the early woodcuts of the classic characters. You may have them thinking along the lines of a very presentational style—hand-held masks, non-realistic scenery, an almost Oriental flavor to the controlled movement patterns and stances. You may have them searching for the ultimate archetypal trappings of the character types that they represent; bits and pieces of symbolic meaning, not attached to any historical time but evoking a more or less "floating period." Your designers may begin to draw from both historical and contemporary sources. Could not Reverend Epinard be a Billy Graham-style evangelist? Noble, the lion, a Richard Nixon-style monarch? Ticelin, the crow, an Al Capone-type scribe? At this stage designers may bring multiple suggestions to you. Together you will create a vision.

3. Imagination   Now is the time for imagination. The designers assimilate all the information and distill it into visual form. Generally the set designer takes the lead, creating the basic ground plan—the playground for the play. The costume designer takes the preliminary plunge concerning the colors, textures, and lines of the show, then making thumbnail sketches of the animals and their costume accessories. The makeup designer in a situation such as *Reynard* works closely with the costume designer to achieve a unity. The lighting designer follows the steps of the other designers in order to create a lighting plot to consolidate and enhance all of the elements of their various designs.

Once these preliminary "exalted images" have been captured, it is time for a second production meeting. Now the discussion becomes livelier. You and your designers are all talking; everyone's wheels are in motion. Your designers have come back, having translated your verbal ideas into visual realities. Don't be surprised if they are not right

Invite your imagination to conjure the most exalted image and, once it has been captured in paint on paper, accept the challenge that it can be realized on the stage.
Irene Corey,
The Mask of Reality

the first time. This is the time to change things. If you're unhappy, don't be afraid to ask for changes. No fabric has been bought, no lumber cut; so now is the time to send the technical staff back to the drawing board, if need be. By the next time you see your designers, they will have final sketches and models awaiting your approval. Let them know exactly what you want. Maybe the set doesn't have the flexibility in the play areas that you had hoped for; perhaps the costumes are right in color and texture but have a somewhat cartoon quality that must be changed; you want additional lighting specials for the echo scene; you hope for a sense of contemporary political satire but don't see anything as literal as a spoof on the Nixon presidency. Don't be afraid to make legitimate requests: Your designers will be happy to accommodate you. Be specific. Designers can have short tempers when, later in the production process, you request major changes that require long hours of reconstruction. Remember, imagination is the creative end of the design area and certainly the reason why any designer sticks with this crazy business.

4. Creation   Creation is the transforming of the ideas and two-dimensional drawings into what is real and three-dimensional. Here is where the end products, conceived by analysis, deduction, and imagination, are constructed: the sets, costumes, masks and wigs, lighting arrange-

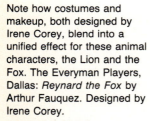

Note how costumes and makeup, both designed by Irene Corey, blend into a unified effect for these animal characters, the Lion and the Fox. The Everyman Players, Dallas: *Reynard the Fox* by Arthur Fauquez. Designed by Irene Corey.

Photo by Jerry Mitchell

ments, and props. Creation involves careful consideration of detail, collaboration with others, and knowledge of machinery and materials. The goal of each designer in the creation process is to create something tangible that contributes to a total effect and has that magical quality.

5. Adaptation   Directors make discoveries. Actors make discoveries. Designers observe these discoveries and maintain a degree of flexibility to accommodate changes. For example, a lighting designer will watch rehearsals with an eye to reinforce the director's blocking by punching points with corresponding light cues. Set designers have a responsibility for getting actual set pieces, or reasonable facsimiles, for rehearsal. They will adapt set pieces if the need arises. Costumers notice when an actor has difficulty with a costume or rehearsal piece and make the necessary alterations.

Because the **Adaptation** and **Creation** steps are closely linked, in our discussion of *Reynard* we have chosen to speak of them simultaneously. For example, the huge cape designed for Noble works well for all scenes but the turkey chase. Here it tends to inhibit quick movement and even tangle and trip the actor. The designer discovers that when the lining fabric is removed, the cape flutters harmlessly. Ticelin, meanwhile, has trouble getting up and down the tree. Additional hand and footholds are scabbed into the trunk, solving the problem in a practical way without making changes in the design aesthetic. In this way the creating and the adapting are combined to form a continual process—the adaptation of two-dimensional ideal designs into three-dimensional kinetic images.

The show is now in its final technical rehearsals. All of the elements are here; the paper plots and thumbnail sketches are as large as life or bigger up on the stage. Last-minute alterations occur, but that is why you hold rehearsals. All of the elements are blended harmoniously; you've worked out problems. Your designers will be on hand to adjust and adapt the minor incongruities in order to achieve production unity. The show opens; the design process is complete.

You now have a basic understanding of how *Reynard the Fox* is designed and put on its feet. The endless problems somehow find solutions. All areas of design can work together to develop a total, unified visual effect.

But what if your show is not *Reynard the Fox?* You are doing *Abe Lincoln of Pigeon Creek* or *The Wizard of Oz* or an original piece that you yourself have scripted about a pioneer family moving across the country. All the problems seem to be different; all of the focus points have shifted; you feel lost.

The design process still holds true, but areas of concentration and

SPECIAL SCRIPTS: SPECIAL NEEDS

A wire form mask (similar to those used in Peter Shaffer's *Equus* on Broadway) allows the actor's face to remain totally visible while still creating an animal character statement. The Nebraska Theatre Caravan: *A Midsummer Night's Dream* by William Shakespeare. Directed by Bill Kirk. Designed by Stephen Wheeldon.

particular problems change. Each specific type of script has its own set of trouble points and calls for a specific technical approach, a different bag of tricks. Design is, of course, still design, but design with differing emphasis and objectives.

We will present some basic script types you are likely to encounter and the technical requirements common to them. Once you become aware of the differences, you will see that the design ingredients change, but the design recipe remains the same.

Far more in theatre for young people than in theatre for any other audience, available scripts fall into types, in regard to both form and content. Although we can lay down no universal rules to handle all design choices, we can give you a way to classify scripts that may help you begin the design process.

We will discuss five types of scripts: (1) classics, (2) historical plays, (3) adventure/journey, (4) fantasy, (5) story theatre.

CLASSICS

Children recognize the names of classics; parents buy tickets to classics. In fact, you may even have fond memories of your childhood viewing of *Cinderella*. But your picture of the production is through a memory made hazy by time. You probably don't remember how the designers created the visual design. From a pleasant memory like this you may even choose to direct a classic before reading the script. Then, when you read the script, you realize that the production will be scenically impossible.

Most fairy tales and classics are stories passed down through generations. When they are told, the storyteller or author relates visual requirements and describes the various locations, splendid attire, and pageantry. Neither plots nor effects were ever meant to be staged—except in the mind's eye, where all magic is possible.

As you read the existing scripts, you will find that the adaptors have made one of the two choices. The magic effects may be left out entirely. Many of the scripts of *Alice in Wonderland*, for example, leave out the shrinking and growing scene. Or the author may describe the effects, "the dwarf explodes," but give you no clues for staging.

Knowing that many of these script adaptations have problems shouldn't dissuade you from producing these classics. Just be both ruthless and realistic in your initial reading of these scripts before you make your choice. Many of the early adaptations are less technically feasible than the more recent ones. When you choose to stage a fairy tale or classic, decide what it is about the story that delights you, then shop around for a script. You may have as many as ten versions of *Alice* or five of *Beauty and the Beast* from which to chose.

To do justice to these plays, you and your design staff must address two main areas: (1) script requirements, (2) audience expectations.

Script requirements   As you read these scripts, you will notice that many of them have similar requirements. In terms of scenery you and your design staff can pare down busy scenery choices to the bare essentials; a throne room to represent a kingdom, a leafy bough to indicate a forest. To counteract the often-wordy scripts, you can keep scene-shifting time to a minimum. You and your costume designer can simplify period silhouettes, maintaining the color and line but with less bulk and cheaper fabrics. You may chose one costume piece to act as a symbol for each character; you may dress the company in neutral garments, with one differing costume piece used as a symbol. The king may wear his crown, the jester his belled cap, the queen her cape. Although these choices are possible, they may not be desirable. It is, however, better to execute these costume designs well than to do a poor job on a more elaborate scale.

Makeup is generally straightforward. Just be sure that your actors follow guidelines for character makeup and that each cast member is part of the general makeup scheme. Lighting is straightforward as well. Concentration is mainly on visibility, creating the slightly surreal, almost iridescent quality of the metaworld. You and your lighting designer must also accommodate the practicalities of quick scene shifts, split focus, and magic and illusion. In this regard it makes sense for both you and your designer to familiarize yourselves with the methods of stage magicians and illusionists in terms of levitations, disappearances, reappearances, or transformations. Such classic effects as the disembodied head, the sword basket or cabinet, the woman sawed in half, or even the levitating lady are all dependent on apparatus that may be rented, bought, or built. It pays, in this regard, to make the acquaintance of local magicians and magic suppliers. Impressive magic effects must be incorporated early, since each effect has very special requirements that must be included in the set and lighting designs.

Audience expectations   As Dickens might say, "Children come to the theatre with great expectations," especially if they are about to see *A Christmas Carol*. You must consider these expectations in your design choices. Because of their familiarity with the stories and characters from sources such as picture books, movies, and television, children come into the theatre with a whole preconceived notion of how the play will look. If you choose to create a design different from Tenniel's *Alice in Wonderland* or Disney's *Cinderella*, you must make a strong initial design statement. This design supersedes the preconceived notions and creates its own reality. Novelty for novelty's sake makes no sense; you should make choices that best portray the characters and the story. By breaking new ground and making nontraditional design choices, directors and designers work together to help the audience see old material in a new way.

HISTORICAL PLAYS

Biographical plays of heroes and heroines throughout history have always been favorites in the repertory of plays for young people. Plays such as *Abe Lincoln of Pigeon Creek, Daniel Boone,* and *Jim Thorpe, All American* are not only exciting and entertaining, they are also educational and can be utilized within the curriculum. The primary consideration from a design standpoint in this kind of play is establishing the time frame within which the action takes place. What people wore, how they talked and walked, the manners and mores of the day are all important factors that should be apparent in the visual elements of the design. You and your design staff must read about the period in which the person lived as well as about the person.

Because the time frame holds such importance, you and your set designer probably won't choose a plastic stage. Portraitive settings for each locale, complete down to the period furniture, are expensive and impractical choices. A setting that captures the spirit of the period through suggestion is the best choice. Materials and methods of construction and use of colors, line, and form create visual echoes of the symbols and motifs that epitomize any given period. If the set can capture the flavor of the period, then each specific scene need not establish that period. Freed from this task, the designer can then establish different locales with small pieces: a podium for a political rally or a captain's wheel for a riverboat. Lights require little if any special consideration except for follow-spots and special mood lighting. Use period light fixtures whenever possible.

Costumes, too, should strive to be more evocative than portraitive. Certainly period silhouettes, hairstyles, hats, and shoes are important, but you must sacrifice a degree of realism for practicality. You and your designers must identify the fashion trademarks of the period and incorporate them into the design: for example, the bustle of the 1890s, the hoopskirt of the antebellum South, and the men's high-heeled pumps of the Restoration. Research will tell you that most period costumes were not constructed for ease of dressing and undressing. You must create an illusion of hooks and laces and stays, in a costume that is practical for quick changes.

Color can help your audience know who's who: to distinguish and identify a single character from the ensemble as well as to know something about his or her personality. Because many actors are double cast, costumes must also make a quick, strong, symbolic statement. If accessories alone are to indicate the character change, make sure the changes are drastic. The subtlety of a bow tie, handkerchief, or apron isn't enough.

The makeup designer works to achieve a balance between period realism and production practicality. One specific problem encountered is achieving a likeness of a famous and recognizable person. Facial hair, nose, chin, and lip lines are the points to alter in making one person's face into another's.

Authenticity invariably lacks artistry, yet there are still people who confuse art and archaeology, and allow their admiration for scientific research to interfere with their intuitive reactions to an artistic experience.
Douglas A. Russell,
Theatrical Style

ADVENTURE/JOURNEY

The adventure/journey format is as old as theatre itself. *The Iliad* and *The Odyssey* have much in common with Maeterlinck's *Blue Bird* or Ibsen's *Peer Gynt*. Each involves the quest, the search, be it for golden fleece or the bluebird of happiness. Running parallel to this quest is the progression of character self-discovery, the growth of child to adult, the raising of consciousness. The design challenge here is more than just in portraying a large number of locales, as is the case in historical plays and in many children's classics. Each design area should have a sense of fluidity, of constant movement and transformation.

Movable sets and set pieces are a strong and obvious choice. Audiences in general love to watch scenery move; audiences of kids are mesmerized. Revolves, slip stages, wagons, and treadmills are all applicable. As the director, you should explore the use of movement and mime tricks. Actors swaying precisely from side to side look for all the world like they are aboard a moving ship. Add to this scenery moving past them slowly and the illusion of movement in static space is complete. On land, this same illusion may be created by having the actors mime walking in place while the scenery moves on or off.

Costumes must reflect changes in seasons and climates encountered on the journey. On a more subliminal level they also reflect the character's internal changes. Color progressions and symbols incorporated into the designs help to illuminate the character's subtext. Because adventure/journeys are progressive in nature, costume pieces are often added or subtracted in layers.

Lighting is a very effective tool in portraying the rites of passage as well as the gradual passing of time. Spots and specials work well for the adventure/journey. They can be used to enhance the natural and supernatural trials of snow, sleet, or dark of night. Special lighting effects can also point up the internal struggles with which a character is coping and that he or she finally resolves. Have your lighting flow from cue to cue like visual music, underscoring and punctuating the changes and progressions in set, costume, and character.

Makeup designers can literally pull out the stops. On the practical side the design has to show the effects of struggle and turmoil, as faces age because of the harsh treatment of the elements, illness, disappointment, and despair. The makeup should also echo the internal changes: The audience should be able to see a character gradually coming to peace with him- or herself. Masks may be used instead of makeup, with a progression of masks to illustrate character aging, growth, and development.

FANTASY

Fantasy plays are not rooted in our factual world, either in the "here and now" or the "there and then." You are dealing instead with a whole new metaworld—a world of make-believe, mystery, and magic. Here anything is possible and not only can, but most likely will, happen. *The Hide-and-Seek Odyssey of Madeline Gimple*, *The Tingalary Bird*, and *A Midsummer's Night Dream* all portray fantastical places and events, yet seem almost as though they could happen.

The greatest problem in creating believable fantasy (and what fun is it if we can't believe in it?) is arbitrary and inconsistent design choices. Designers should use the same criteria for creating fantastic designs as for realistic designs. You may want to steer your designers to think of fantasy as nothing less than extraordinary reality. Since the worlds of these plays are places that don't exist, the designers have great freedom of expression but must always keep an eye for consistency. Depending on the material, development of design choices for fantasies may be the result of one of three separate processes: (1) evolution, (2) transformation, (3) creation.

Evolution is merely a process of extrapolation. You are projecting into the future or into one of the possible futures. The design of science fiction fantasies is perhaps the most common use of evolution. You are creating a period that does not exist but is based on a direct evolutionary line from a period that does exist. Very successful design concepts using this process are the television program *Star Trek* and the motion picture *Star Wars*.

Transformation is not nearly such a linear projection of given circumstances. The transformation process is used in scripts that begin in a recognizable time frame and step off into the area of the fantastic; for example, *Alice in Wonderland* or *The Wizard of Oz*. In both cases the successful design of the fantasy land should have some stylistic tie to the real world, be it Victorian England or dust-bowl Kansas.

Creation is the process with the least bounds, allowing the designer ultimate freedom but also maximum responsibility. There is no anchor to any specific time or place. Therefore, it is up to the designer, consulting with the director, to establish all of the stylistic determinates based solely on the metaworld created within the script. Designing a production of this nature involves a great deal to think about, rationalize, and justify.

The sets for a fantasy play must establish places unfamiliar to the audience. Because the audience has never been to this fantastical

It does no good to say Shakespeare's Sicilia and Bohemia are fantasticated, nowhere places; fantasy has its own requirements, in some ways more stringent than those of other genres.
John Simon,
New York Magazine

The use of nontraditional materials in creating costumes and masks characterizes the Mummenschanz productions.

world, your set designer's obligation is to portray this world with originality and, most of all, with consistency. You may wish to work with strange sculptural forms or with reinterpretations of existing materials. You may exploit color, line, and texture to their radical extremes. The sky's the limit for the fantastical world.

The primary task of the costume designer is to alter the human silhouette. One possible approach is to think how you want the final costume to look and then fit the human into it. One actor may make a terrific rock; two actors may portray an octopus. You may utilize seven actors to make a dragon. Also, the costume designer may work with nontraditional materials—metals and mylar, foam and fur. Encourage your designers to break down stereotypes: All witches don't have to wear black. Many insects, plant forms, and inanimate objects appear in these plays. Remember, all dogs in fantastical plays are not alike, but all animals in the same production must look like they live in the same world. Look upon the costume design as a challenge, not one big problem.

Related to the costume-design process, makeup design involves the altering of the human face. The face should flow into the silhouette of the costume. An excellent example is the design of *Reynard the Fox.* Irene Corey designed both makeup and costume. Notice how both blend together to create a unified visual effect. Encourage the makeup designer to use not just traditional materials, but also spangles, feathers, and fabrics. Think of the face as a blank canvas and proceed. The makeup design, like the costume design, should be consistent for the production.

Lighting for fantasy plays is highly theatrical. Scripts call for intense colors, many specific lighting cues, and special effects. Because colors of costumes and sets are often intense, the lighting designer must coordinate all designs. To pull off the unusual effects, you may need special equipment like black lights, strobes, or projection machines.

STORY THEATRE

Unifying the production is the most important design task for story theatre productions. Too often scenes seem unrelated; actors appear to be in different productions; the overall effect is like a night of one-act plays. Designers can aid you in creating a strong, unified visual effect.

Settings must have a great deal of built-in versatility. Elaborate constructivist sets with ramps, stairs, levels, and movable parts make for an exciting and workable playing space. Because of its potential for varied stage pictures, simultaneous staging, and interesting movement transitions from story to story, a constructivist set is one of the best choices. Whatever the set design, it should be a clean, clear space with simultaneous staging potential. Achitectural elements that suggest spe-

The human silhouette was successfully altered by using a leather harness to hold the actor's legs comfortably in the position in the diagram. The result was a dog, Nana, that many children believed to be a real dog with human intelligence. University of North Dakota, Grand Forks: *Peter Pan* by James M. Barrie. Directed by Helane S. Rosenberg. Designed by Joel Vig.

cific playing pieces must be included. For example, a pole can be a tree or a ship's mast; a hinged ramp can be a drawbridge or a gangplank.

Lights call for specific visibility. Highly theatrical use of specials works well in story theatre. Take care that individual areas are tightly focused. In this way you can shift from story to story with the speed of a cross fade. Lights should fulfill two functions. They provide the basic framework and focus for each individual story, and they provide the transitions and bridges from story to story.

Costumes can be a major factor in holding the stories together. First, they must create a visual ensemble. Encourage your designer to break some new ground in making a visual statement. To costume yet another company in dyed tank tops and bib overalls without searching for other options lacks imagination. Once your costume designer has arrived at the ensemble statement, the next task is to individualize the ensemble. The audience must be able to identify each actor. The ensemble is held together by a similarity in one area: line, color, or texture. Individuals are made different by variations in one or both of the other areas. If everyone wears leotards, thereby having the same line, they are individualized by changing the color. If the costumes are all in one color family, you will differentiate by strong variations in texture and silhouettes.

Costumes must also be durable because they are whipped on and off, pulled out of trunks, and tossed offstage. Costume pieces should exploit symbolic and archetypal images; the pieces should be big and broad. Instant identification is your goal. Makeup is generally corrective. Sometimes makeup pieces such as beards, noses, and wigs denote character change. These makeup pieces should be as broad as the costume pieces.

THE END OF THE LINE . . . AND COLOR . . . AND TEXTURE

The design and technical areas for young people's theatre differ very little in their execution from those of any other theatre project. The differences that do exist are primarily due to the given circumstances within the plays in the repertoire for children and the varying levels of verbal sophistication and understanding of dramatic convention that exist in different age groups.

To an audience whose major limitation is this lack of sophistication with language skills, what better way to transmit information than through visual means? Theatre is a temporal art form. It exists only for the moment, and in that moment it must not only convey but be received. For communication in any form works only when the signal transmitted is the signal received. By presenting a unified, selected, and focused set of visual images, you steer your designers to complement your use of actors and space. Together you give the playwright's vision a life. You now have a fundamental framework of skills, terms, and principles of technical theatre and design to serve you in this capacity.

We wanted to talk with you about design because of the impact you've made on the field of young people's theatre, particularly with your non-realistic designs. Where do you start?

I always start with the script itself. I start with reading the script to see what's happening that wants to happen. The second step is to talk with the director to see what concept he or she has, what he wants to stress, what direction she wants the play to take. And those things also are tempered by the staging: Is it to be a touring show, is it to be stable, where is it happening? The next step is to deal with the limitations of budget or spaces. And then after that is research. I visit any place that is necessary to research a given play. In the animal plays, *Reynard the Fox* and *The Great Cross Country Race,* it's a matter of going to the zoo, of really watching the animals, seeing how they move, and capturing them with pen and pencil. It's easier to be immersed in them than to just look at photographs, although I can just look at photographs and work from there if I have to. In that case I would gather materials and read about the quirks and characteristics of that animal, so that I would know what their basic rhythms are: Seeing the animals affects the basic choices in the costume itself. It affects my choice of fabric. To give you examples from a past production of *Reynard:* There's the porcupine, Epinard, who is a very prickly character. That costume was done with sharp folded spears of organdy, which is a very crisp fabric. But the marmot, Lendore, is a very warm, cuddly kind of character, so she was placed in a cocoon of fur, only it wasn't fur cloth. Fur cloth wouldn't work; it would be too heavy. What I chose was a sheer, bubble kind of material. So once I have all of this together and obtain a character analysis from the director that augments my own, I'm ready to start designing. It's really like putting all the factors into the pot and letting them stir around and coming up with the ideas from there.

Interestingly, you haven't said the word "child" yet in terms of your designing. Why?

I never think of terms of, will this please or displease the child. I don't think any of the great literature for children is written from that viewpoint. Lewis Carroll's work or any of the lasting great classics of children's literature do not talk down to the children. This is why Maurice Sendak is so incredible; he is not talking down to children, he is talking from a place children understand. I think there's the difference. I approach things in a similar way. If you're fresh and if there's honesty in what you're doing, children recognize it. If it's sham, they recognize it as sham and turn off from it almost immediately. It's a strange thing, but I think it's true; I think they recognize this honesty. And campy, cute things for children are not received well, and not long-lasting. They're like froth; they go away, and we don't know about them tomorrow.

What do you think children want scenically?

They don't really demand detail. And that perhaps is why in their drawing they get right to the heart of things. They don't have to have all the feathers, for example. So what I always try to do is get to the essence of the animal, and what visually represents the animal. I'm doing essences, I'm going to be giving animal characters strong, distinctive shapes which are stripped of the exterior fur. And children accept that, and adults look at that and say, "Oh, that's highly stylized." I've always made a special effort to approach each play to try to see its distinctive quality. Design is giving visual form to what are basically abstract ideas. And to do that you have to be pure in line and color, for communication.

Designing animal costumes must be particularly difficult, because we see so many dog costumes with the zip up the front in fluffy shag.

They don't think, you know, some designers don't think! If you're going to do a squirrel, it's going to be a six-foot human squirrel. You can't use the same size of hair on a six-foot squirrel that you use on a one-foot squirrel. You have to enlarge all of it: you have to rethink. Does his body look slick? Then you must make a slick body. Does his tail look fluffy? You don't generally use hair in the tail. I guess you could go out and get a horse's tail. You have to enlarge it to scale.

I don't know why designers don't think about that concept.

I think it's partly Walt Disney's fault that they use those bag suits. It's part of a stereotype of those characters . . . Mickey Mouse and so forth . . . that if you've got a sloppy suit and tail and two ears, you're a dog. But you're not a *specific* dog; if you can get the "Benjiness" into Benji, you succeed in your design. I would rather see less than too much. Just put on tights, strap on a tail, and give them two ears. You see, I go to the stylization; that's what I always do. You could take a clown nose, you know those little round balls, paint them black, stick on two ears and a tail, and you have more dog than with an actor stuck in a bag.

You work outside children's theatre and then you come back to it. How do you feel about that?

I don't find there's much difference in the way I'm working. I don't approach it in any different sense. I'm designing *Christmas Carol* for the Dallas Theatre Centre, and I think of it the same as *Reynard*. It's a family piece, one that anyone can come to and enjoy. And it's traditional to take children to *A Christmas Carol*. I was surprised; I had never really read the subtitle, which is *A Ghost Story.* You look at those early illustrations, and you read the original story. You've got this little Scrooge, and you have these spirits that loom up all over him. They're taller and bigger than he is. I mean, this is *"I am going to tell you a ghost story."*

How were you trained?

At Baylor University with Paul Baker. I give him great credit for his creative approach to teaching. He has been phenomenal for students who come through his courses. They don't just become copies of him; he opens them up, and they do their own thing. I think it was crucial that I had an art major before I became interested in theatre. And then I did my master's work in theatre. But I've gone back and forth . . . taken a year of art and then taught art. Both are important. Right now I'm taking a life drawing class. It's a matter of keeping your seeing sharp; it's so easy for it to get dull.

When you see things, do you keep a journal or do you sort of file them in your brain?

A lot of things I see I should write down and I don't. You never know where an idea will come from. If it's not back there [points to head], you can't use it. It's the way things come together. That's the real creativity. It's the surprise combination of things that makes a new answer, or what seems to be a new answer.

Do you ever have trouble with directors because you have such a strong image? There seems to be that division between actors and technicians on a university campus, and it always makes me sad. There seem to be two different camps.

Unfortunately, it ends up that way a lot of times. My theory is everyone should understand all aspects of theatre, so that you don't have such a narrow view. Not to be a specialist who can only see his own problems, but one who is able to interrelate, is ideal. Of course, Orlin Corey and I worked together for so many years; there were never any problems. I have since worked with other directors—for example, Keith Trinity at Memphis State—with whom I also had a perfect working relationship. There was give and take— even my adding directorial input or his adding design input—so that it went back and forth that way. I think that's ideal. If you don't have an open line of communication, the relationship is not going to work.

How do you begin communicating with a director?

I think my first question to any director is, "What is the overall mood or atmosphere that you want this play to have?" Is it bright and light? Or is it dark? What are its values? Is it oppressive? Is it pageantry? I want to know the overall feel, because it's the overall feel that's going to govern all selection of fabric, texture, color value, and so forth.

If you were to give advice to people who were interested in designing, what would you tell them?

I think they need all the art training they can get. That's really basic. That's a continuing process. I'm talking about life drawing, sketching, landscaping, painting, anything that you can do in those areas. Then I would say, learn to sew, learn to use wood, learn to weld, do anything that teaches you about materials. Learn to love factories. Go to places where they make things; just have the world's resources at your fingertips. I love to visit factories. I love to go where things are being done. I am always picking up new ideas, "Oh, that cable does *that.*" There are so many possibilities. Unfortunately, some designers get carried away.

I know. I had a designer once who foamed everything.

Yes, I've seen that, but still maybe you have to do that to get it under control, then you can ease out of it. Know your materials, know your medium, keep experimenting. I don't think it's enough just to know how to draw.

7
PRODUCING PLAYS FOR YOUNG PEOPLE

*The mechanics of play production are most
effective when they are least apparent.*

Elmer Rice, *The Living Theatre*

THE OVERALL PRODUCTION PROCESS

Chapter 7 deals with a vital creative leap in the theatre-making process: bringing the dramatic script to life on the stage. You can read thousands of plays, write thousands of diaries, recognize the spine of these plays in a flash, but unless you transform all that intellectual-emotional work into the practical production of theatre for the sake of an audience, you are performing only one part of your job as director.

When asked "What does a producer do?" most people don't know, or they suggest something to do with raising the money. In the commercial Broadway theatre this is absolutely true; plays are produced by producers, directed by directors, designed by designers, and acted by actors. The producer's job is clear-cut: find a property to produce, raise the money (often in the millions) to begin the project, lend financial-management expertise, hire the best artists, directors, designers, and managers available to help ensure the project's success, and oversee the entire operation.

208

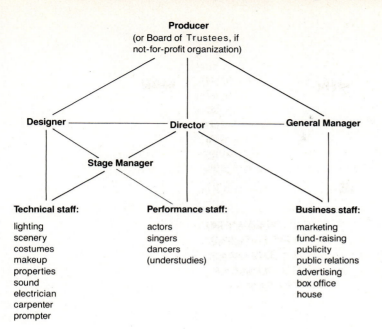

Producer
(or Board of Trustees, if
not-for-profit organization)

Designer ——————— Director ——————— General Manager

Stage Manager

Technical staff:

lighting
scenery
costumes
makeup
properties
sound
electrician
carpenter
prompter

Performance staff:

actors
singers
dancers
(understudies)

Business staff:

marketing
fund-raising
publicity
public relations
advertising
box office
house

Production diagram: flow chart of production personnel.

However, in theatre for young audiences the producer may also be the director. Raising the money is important, but budgets are smaller than in the commercial theatre and may be handled easily enough by the theatre manager or a producing organization. So, in this chapter we are not defining producing as wheeling and dealing at the Broadway level; we are defining producing as what the director must do to get the young people's script produced in a theatre for an audience. We have organized this chapter in a sequential way—starting with "initial considerations" and moving toward "closing the play."

PRODUCING THEATRE FOR YOUNG AUDIENCES: MAKING A CREATIVE LEAP

Up to this point in the theatre process the director has either worked alone, as in interpreting a script, or worked with actors while preparing them to work on roles. When you reach the production stage of the work, you have reached the truly collaborative stage. Theatre is a collaborative art form; we have discussed how all its aspects, from the pitch of an actor's voice to the color of shoelaces, can affect the final product and the sense of occasion. This stage of the work can really test a producer's mettle, as the producer is ultimately responsible for the whole production, yet without control when the curtain goes up. The play is in the hands of the actors, the technicians, and the audi-

The actor, the playwright, or the director, when he turns producer, becomes a deputy of dramatic art. And it is according to the power conferred on him and the manner in which he exercises it that we are going to judge him as a producer.
Louis Jouvet, *director*

above left: Budget and facility limitations on theatre companies performing for young audiences often make sparse scenery a necessity, but this need not limit the success of a production as theatre. Actress: Deborah Mayo. PAF/Arts in Education, Huntington, New York: *Wise and Wonderful.*
Photo by Joan James

above right: In deciding on a play, consider not only the classics but also new scripts. Consider commissioning a script from a known playwright. The commissioned play shown here, *La Morena* ("the dark one"), poignantly explores a Puerto Rican family's adjustment to their move to New York City. Actors (clockwise from lower left): Miluca Rivera, Lucy Vega, Carlos Carrasco, Antonieta Maximo. Commissioned and produced by Steve Tennen and the Henry Street Settlement, Family Matinee Theatre, New York. Written by Beth Turner. Directed by Raul Davila.
Photo by Bert Andrews

ence. However, there are ways that the producer can attempt to ensure what happens when the curtain goes up, and this process is presented here.

Before you read on about the process, look at the differences between producing theatre for adults and theatre for young audiences:

- The age and experience level of the audience affect your choice of script; for example, *Hamlet* will not work for five-year-olds.
- The repertory of scripts available for production for young audiences is limited, since "children's theatre" is a relatively recent phenomenon. Also, the field does not attract "star" playwrights, since there is little money or glamour attached to it.
- The economics of producing plays for young audiences are vastly different from producing plays for adults: Adults may choose to pay $50–$100 to see a Broadway show, but they are unlikely to spend that amount for a child to see *Cinderella* at a local university. Thus, production budgets are generally small.
- The acting talent available for theatre for young audiences is often not the best; the adult legitimate theatre in the United States offers more prestige and more money than most children's theatres. Therefore, the talented and ambitious will take the Broadway job, or national tour job, over a job performing for young audiences. Of course, there are exceptions to this; some actors make a commitment to performing for young audiences and choose this field for their life work.

The producer of theatre for young audiences needs to be aware of these limitations in order to overcome them. The first step in the production process is the choosing of a play to do, and with that choice, the hiring of a director. This chapter assumes that the producer *is* the director, in essence hires him or herself, as this is the way it often happens in young people's theatre.

AUDIENCE

A producer of adult plays rarely considers the audience in the selection of the play. However, the producer of theatre for young audiences must initially be concerned with the audience, particularly with its age and collective experiences, because these factors will help determine the choice of dramatic material presented.

If you are producing a play for young people to which you are selling tickets, it helps to choose a play with a familiar title which will appeal to your young audience and its chaperons. If you are producing a play to tour to schools, the popular title is less important, as you are not appealing to the single ticket buyer as much as you are selling the play as a commodity to one sponsor, such as the PTA or school board. Two aspects of your audience—their age and their commitment and access to you—affect your choice of what plays to produce for them.

PLACE OF PERFORMANCE

The producer must look realistically at the space available, since it will dictate to some extent the type of production mountable. If there is no fly space, or rigging, and you believe the only proper way to produce *Peter Pan* is with "flying by Foy,"* you cannot choose this play. If the

*Peter Foy is a well-known specialist in the mechanics of rigging actors to fly.

INITIAL CONSIDERATIONS IN CHOOSING A PLAY

All plays for young audiences have subtext that actors can act, regardless of the nature of the play. Plays for young people do not have to be trite, simple, or simplistic. In fact, some deal with complex, serious topics. An example is Franklin D. Roosevelt's battle against the polio that crippled him and threatened to end his political career, as portrayed in Performing Arts Repertory Theatre's *First Lady.* Actors (stage right to left): Marcia Savella, Richard Kind, Christina Denzinger, Lee Welch, Bijou Clinger. Directed by John Henry Davis. Written by Jonathan Bolt. Music by Tom Tierney. Lyrics by John Forster. *Photo by Gerry Goodstein*

In a vital, living theatre, the role of the audience is functional and creative.
Elmer Rice, *The Living Theatre*

theatre seats 3,000 and the stage is enormous, an intimate four-character play may get lost in the space. Chapter 8, "Managing Theatre for Young People," covers all the management considerations of space, such as gross receipts from the number of seats sold. But the director as producer must also view the space for its artistic merits when choosing a play to produce.

BUDGET

The budget determines many things, including the choice of script and final look of the production. If the budget is very small, paying high royalties and attempting a lavish production of a play such as Rodgers and Hammerstein's *Cinderella* are foolish. You would not have the budget required in order to make stage magic. A better choice might be *Reynard the Fox*, as discussed in Chapter 6, which has a smaller cast than *Cinderella* and which can be designed simply but effectively with leotards, tights, and wire masks.

POTENTIAL CAST AVAILABLE

The director must evaluate who is on hand to cast and what their collective abilities and talents are, as this may affect the choice of play. If singers are available, a musical might be a good choice, for it is best to capitalize on actors' strong points. If only young or student actors are available, it makes sense to avoid those plays with severe casting demands in age or character. The commercial theatre almost always casts by type, because personality closely matched with character gives the actors an edge toward success.

ANALYZING AND SELECTING THE PLAY

By now the producer has collected all of the information needed to select the play to be produced. Below is a script analysis chart. This checklist provides a means of actively thinking about a play and therefore covers the criteria for evaluating a script. This checklist can be used to evaluate any play.

A producer really puts the whole package together; the creativity is in trying to make sure the pieces fit. Your job is to trust your own judgment, make a decision, and go with it.
Carole C. Huggins,
producer, Kennedy Center for the Performing Arts

SCRIPT ANALYSIS CHECKLIST

1. Story (the whole idea): Is it interesting? _____
2. Plot (the actual events that occur in a particular order on the stage): Is there clear, interesting plot development? _____
3. Any subplots? _____
4. Action (what the characters do and why they do it): Is there interesting action? _____
5. Theme: Is there a clear, well-developed, easily recognizable theme? What is the theme? _____
6. Characters: Are they specific, well delineated, well drawn? _____

7. Type of drama: Tragedy _____ Farce _____
   Comedy _____ Melodrama _____
8. Styles of theatre: Old Greek Comedy _____
   Commedia dell'Arte _____
   Elizabethan _____
   Absurd _____
   French Neo-Classic _____
   20th-Century Non-Realism _____
   20th-Century Musical Comedy _____
   Brecht and Epic _____
9. Dialogue: Is the dialogue appropriate to the characters? _____
   Does every word *count?* _____
   How skillfully does the playwright handle exposition, giving
   us the facts we must have? _____
10. Structure: Does the play have many characters, two or three plots,
    many years covered? _____
    Does the play have few characters, one plot in a short
    amount of time? _____
11. The Central Image: Does the play have a central image? _____
    How could it be manifested on stage? _____
12. Conflict, or Dramatic Tension: Person vs. Person _____
    Person vs. Self _____
    Person vs. Society _____
    Person vs. Nature _____
13. Does this script have integrity to a total idea? _____
14. Does this script have a climax? If so, where is it? Is it active enough? __
15. Does this script require music or choreography? _____

(continued on next page)

The Sheffield Ensemble Theatre capitalizes on the known talents of its actors in creating a certain type of story-theatre/revue. This is *Beans*, directed by Rita and Buddy Sheffield. Their other productions—*Bananas* and *Feats* and *Videosyncrasies*—have different content but similar formats.

. . . .

The Director remains as good as his play—no better. He should remember that unless he has a good play he is predestined to failure.
John Gassner,
Producing the Play

. . . .

16. Does this script stimulate thought? _____
17. Does this script stimulate emotions? _____
18. Does this script have a sense of humor? _____
19. Is this script written in good taste? _____
20. Is this script suitable to the age and general experience level of the audience for which it is intended? _____
21. Can the potential cast execute this script reasonably well? _____
22. Is the potential cast musical? _____
23. If not, will omitting the music and dance hurt the script? _____
24. Summary: Does this script have:
    • dramatic worth, with good plot, characters, theme? _____
    • educational worth to lead young audiences to their emotions, to challenge, enlighten, and entertain? _____

Analyzing the components of a script is one task; evaluating the talents of the playwright is another. We have included two scenes from Performing Arts Repertory Theatre's *Susan B.!*, the story of Susan B. Anthony, with the permission of the producer, the playwright Jules Tasca, and director John Henry Davis. The first scene doesn't work well; the second scene replaced it. These two scenes illustrate the difference between dramatic writing that fails and dramatic writing that succeeds. The first scene fails because it introduces a new but dull character, the minister, and it is a relatively friendly discussion. There is no dramatic conflict; the scene never rises above a discussion. The

In writing lyrics for young people's theatre the lyricist needs a certain spareness in the work, and needs to say in one or two lines of a song what previously had taken the playwright two pages of dialogue.
Ted Drachman,
lyricist, Performing Arts Repertory Theatre's Susan B.!

This is a scene from Performing Arts Repertory Theatre's original production of *Susan B.!*, the story of Susan B. Anthony and women's struggle for equality under the law. The scenic metaphor selected by the director was doors and doorways, through which women could not "go." Actors: Kay Wallbye as Susan and John Canary as her suitor, Parker Pillsbury. Directed by John Henry Davis. Written by Jules Tasca. Music by Tom Tierney. Lyrics by Ted Drachman. Choreography by Haila Strauss.
Photo by Gerry Goodstein

reason the second scene succeeds is its economy: the playwright uses characters the audience has already met. The scene also contains a challenge of wills, which is suspenseful and actable. Susan talks in the first scene about the issue; she *acts* on it in the second scene.

FIRST SCENE: SUSAN B.!

SUSAN *(Exiting)* And it can take you, Aaron McLean, straight down to ——

MARGARET Susan! *(MARGARET stops GUELMA, who wants to go after her)* Let her go.

GUELMA I've never seen her with such an edge. What's the matter with her, Margaret? Did she lose one of her gentlemen friends?

MARGARET You know she doesn't talk much about that sort of thing, but I suspect that might be a little part of her mood.

AARON Well, it's too bad, because she needs a good husband. Someone to keep her in tow. When she gets one you won't see so much of this high-handed behavior.

GUELMA I think Aaron's right. Has she ever mentioned the name of this gentleman she favored?

MARGARET Never, Guelma. Never even a hint, Cousin.

AARON Well, with the attitude she's developed, maybe the fellow's lucky he got away.

(GUELMA sits on the riser and begins sewing in pantomime. AARON is lighting a pipe. A clergyman, REVEREND BARRET, enters and sits on the riser between AARON and GUELMA.)

REVEREND Married life certainly has agreed with you, Aaron. You're putting on weight.

AARON It's her fault, Reverend. Guelma makes all my clothes so big, and then I kind of have to gorge myself to look nice. *(He laughs)*

GUELMA You'll find I do all the work around here and get blamed for all the mistakes. The successes are Aaron's, Reverend.

REVEREND There's a lot to do now that God's blessed you with children.

GUELMA I'm spoiled this month with Susan here to help out. I'll dread it when she goes back to teach in September.

AARON It is nice seeing her again as long as you don't bring up women's property rights.

REVEREND She can't have much of an argument because . . .

(SUSAN enters, drying her hands)

SUSAN Well, it was a stack tonight, but finally the dishes are done.

GUELMA Thank you, Susan. You just indirectly helped make a christening outfit here.

SUSAN I'm sorry I interrupted the Reverend when I came in. Who can't have much of an argument about what?

AARON Nothing, Susan.

REVEREND Oh, let's not tell fibs to a house guest now.

AARON Wasn't a fib. More of a self-defense.

REVEREND I spoke, Susan, of women's property rights.

AARON Close the shutters! Get the hens out of earshot!

SUSAN So that's what I can't have much of an argument over, is it? And, Reverend, why?

GUELMA   Why. It should be spelled W-H-Y-E, so you could add it to the other four-letter words she's not allowed to say.

SUSAN   It's an honest question.

REVEREND   So it is. The Bible tells us everything has its place. That is why there is so much harmony in nature.

SUSAN   That's what the slave owners say, Reverend Barret: Negroes were made by God to be slaves.

REVEREND   Now I agree with you, *they're* wrong. God never said *that*. But he did make woman from the rib of Adam as a helpmate.

AARON   Helpmate, Susan. Rib. Adam. Helpmate. Don't look at me. The Reverend just gave you God's word.

SUSAN   And that's the reason why a married woman can't own a home in her own name? Where in Genesis does it say "and God said let married helpmates be forbidden to have a home in their own names"?

GUELMA   You shouldn't joke about the Bible.

AARON   That's right. If lightning strikes you, my mortgaged house'll go right up with you, woman.

SUSAN   I'm not trying to make light of any religious thing. I'm trying to say that just as the idea of slavery is bothering most men's consciences, well, so is the idea of women being less than human before or after marriage. God loves us all, or he loves none of us.

REVEREND   The Bible shows us that women have well-defined duties of housekeeping and child rearing. Saint Matthew tells us that the wife is subject of the husband. Why, a husband could even sell his wife to satisfy his debts.

SUSAN   Let's bring that back then too.

REVEREND   These are modern times.

SUSAN   Bad luck. If you could get a hundred dollars for Guelma, Aaron, you could clear your mortgage. I'll make up the price tag, you dust her off.

REVEREND   You're starting to sound like that Elizabeth Cady Stanton woman.

GUELMA   That's because she reads everything that crazy woman writes, Reverend.

SUSAN   Guelma, please. You know Mrs. Stanton is not one bit crazy.

GUELMA   As Aaron says, "crazy as a cat in a sack."

SUSAN   Women's property rights are a crazy cause? God, even our own mother couldn't inherit land left to her.

AARON   Your uncle held it in trust. It all worked out, Susan. Forget this Stanton woman's ideas about equality. Just look at the way she dresses.

GUELMA   I blush to say it: in bloomers.

REVEREND   Godless, that's what bloomers are, Godless. Breeches on women.

SUSAN   God doesn't see bloomers. He only sees a person's heart.

REVEREND   He certainly does see bloomers, and He must cringe.

SUSAN   Why?

REVEREND   Because . . . because . . . because *I* cringe when I see bloomers.

SUSAN   Then you might cringe when you see me because I've had . . .

GUELMA   *(Rising)* Had what?

SUSAN   Had . . . had a bloomer outfit made for me.

REVEREND What?

AARON I told you, didn't I? Let women start fighting over property rights in public, I said, and the next thing you know they'll be wearing pants. Lock my cedar closet.

GUELMA Susan, I insist for the honor of the family name that you stay sane.

REVEREND Why would you dress up in an outfit like that?

SUSAN Well, I . . . I . . . I've . . . I've been invited through the women's organization that I joined to meet Mrs. Stanton and . . . and I want to meet her dressed as a modern woman.

GUELMA If pants mean modern, I forbid you to be modern! As your older sister, *I forbid* you to associate with the Stanton woman! *I forbid* you to hobnob with a woman who is crazier than yourself! That's the final word on it!

(As the others exit, SUSAN removes part of her costume, and she is, presto, dressed in a 19th-century bloomer outfit; she puts on a matching hat to complete the suit. ELIZABETH CADY STANTON, also dressed in a bloomer outfit, enters. She and SUSAN simulate taking a stroll.)

MRS. STANTON I've enjoyed this walk. It's been so pleasant.

SUSAN The pleasure was all mine, Mrs. Stanton. All you've done at the antislavery conventions—you'll go down in history.

MRS. STANTON I do what I think is right.

SUSAN It's a gold mine to find someone like you who thinks the same way I do on women's rights; it's such a relief not to have to shout and argue.

SECOND SCENE: *SUSAN B.!*

SCENE 4

(GREELEY steps forward and speaks during scene change. GUELMA Xes up on wagon steps, freezes. SUSAN moves R., freezes. ELIZABETH and PARKER exit L., return with table, angling L. of C. ELIZABETH exits R. PARKER exits L. AARON exits L., changes and returns to L. of table. Newspaper on table.)

GREELEY *(Brushing off pants)* Pants! Pants to men were something sacred. For most men the sight of a woman in bloomers was a slap in the face. Aaron almost wept when he found his wife in . . .

(GREELEY Xes to AARON, taps his shoulder, action begins. GREELEY exits L.)

AARON Pants! My Guelma in pants! *(He is mopping his brow with handkerchief.)*

SUSAN Aaron, don't yell. It's the fashion.

GUELMA Aaron, don't yell. It's the fashion.

SUSAN This is the look of a modern woman.

AARON This is the look of a modern man, and I can hardly bring myself to look at you two.

SUSAN *(Xes C.)* Aaron, I don't mean this disrespectfully, but you're going to have to get used to the changes in . . .

AARON *(Xes to R. of table)* I will get used to nothing! You will both go upstairs and change out of those devil's clothes and we'll burn them.

GUELMA *(Xes to AARON)* Now, Aaron . . .

SUSAN Guelma, you're free to dress as you please.

GUELMA (*Xes to L. side of table*) I know. That's right, Aaron. The modern woman is free.

SUSAN And we have work to do.

AARON (*Looking at both*) Work? What work?

SUSAN Aaron, Guelma has agreed to help the women's organization. We're going to see Horace Greeley right now.

AARON (*Xing around table, backing* GUELMA *up to* SUSAN) Oh, no, she's not!!

SUSAN Oh, Aaron, Guelma and I always used to do things together. What harm is there in that?

AARON (*Has reached U.C.*) 'Cause she's married now, and I will not have it. You . . . you took marriage vows, *Mrs.* McLean! And you, Miss Anthony, while you are on vacation from teaching, are living in my house! (*He steps up on wagon;* SUSAN *Xes to table.*) Now I repeat, both of you go upstairs and change those Godless getups!

GUELMA Aaron, please. I promised Susan and Mrs. Stanton that I would go and . . .

SUSAN Guelma, he's angry over nothing. Let's go, it's getting late. (*They start out, Xing to D.R.*)

AARON I will not be a man disgraced! You go out that door, Guelma, don't bother coming back!
(*Pause.* GUELMA *becomes uncertain.* AARON *Xes to table, his back to them.*) I mean it! The door will be bolted forever! I swear it!

SUSAN Guelma? (*Pause*) Guelma?

GUELMA (*Looks at* SUSAN, *then* AARON) I . . . I . . .

SUSAN This is your chance to start thinking for yourself!

GUELMA I . . . I'm sorry, Susan, I can't. I just can't. (*She runs up wagon stairs, exits L.*)

AARON You better follow her if you know what's good for you, Susan. I can lock you out just as well. (*Pause*) I mean it! Go ahead, woman! (*SUSAN looks at him and slowly walks up the stairs.*) Thank God, now you're showing some sense for a change. I knew you'd see reason.

SUSAN (*Yelling to* GUELMA) Guelma, pack my clothes and send them to Elizabeth's. (*Xes back to C.*) Aaron, you can't lock the door on someone who's never coming back.
(*SUSAN exits R.* AARON *slams newspaper on table.*) (*End Scene 4.*)

One last point about selecting a play: choose a play that you find interesting and that sparks your imagination. If you think a script is poorly written and the plot is dull, you will probably produce a dull play. Maintain a healthy self-interest as you select the play on which you will spend hours and hours of work.

The appendixes include a list of the major publishers of plays for young people as well as a selected list of playscripts.

I produce plays because I think they're going to be successful. When you're producing plays, you have to be emotionally involved with them or you shouldn't produce them.
James Nederlander,
Broadway producer

EARLY PRODUCTION DECISIONS

Many novice directors assume the production process moves from play selection to audition. Actually, there are several essential steps between these two important stages.

An American carnival in the 1920s is an unusual but interesting period choice for Shakespeare's *The Comedy of Errors.* Such an extreme design decision must be made early in a production by the producer, director, and designer in collaboration. Actors: Barry and Brian Mulholland as Antipholus and Dronio. Oregon Shakespearean Festival, Ashland. Directed by Will Huddleston. Designed by Richard L. Hay. Costumes by Jeannie Davidson. Lighting by Thomas White.
Photo by Hank Kranzler

. . . .

Once in 1967 our theatre group Los Grillos (The Crickets) went to Iquitos, a city in the east part of our country, in the jungle of Peru. We went with our children's theatre plays; one of them was The Toy Symphony, *with two characters in the play who play opposite ways of being, the Viola and the Flute. We did our presentation and the children seemed to follow it perfectly well. But the most glorious moment I ever had was when I was walking up an Iquitos street and I heard: "Señorita Viola, Señorita Viola." It was a thin girl in a window who was calling me by my name in the play. This call in the street was for me the real compensation for the work that I did from my heart.*
Sara Joffré de Ramon,
artistic director, Los Grillos, Peru

. . . .

INTERPRETING THE PLAY AND CHOOSING ITS STYLE

Refer back to earlier chapters for initial references to style. A director must choose one style for the play and stay with it; a hodgepodge of styles can be very confusing to any audience. Remember, one of our premises is that almost all plays for young audiences are presentational in style.

ACQUIRING THE DESIGN TEAMS

After the producer acquires the theatre, the play, and the playwright, but before the play is cast, the producer hires the designers. Brilliant designers can rarely bail out a rotten script or a poorly directed production, but brilliant designs can do much to enhance the production's artistic statement and sense of occasion. Designing for the theatre is as much an art as acting or directing; the producer needs to have trained designers working on the production in order to give it the best possible look. The previous chapter detailed this design process.

The producer chooses one designer over another by looking at the designers' portfolios of representative work and by interviewing the designers. Once the designers are hired, they will need a copy of the play to read immediately so that they can begin work on their designs; they must have several options available to discuss with the producer as the play approaches the rehearsal process.

HIRING THE STAGE MANAGER

A good stage manager has to be very well organized. If you're not organized, how can you organize everyone else's time and keep the production on schedule?
John Galo,
professional stage manager

The stage manager assists the director in running the auditions; during rehearsals the stage manager takes notes in the prompt book on every movement and bit of stage business; during the run of the show the stage manager runs the show from backstage, calling the light, sound, and scenery cues, and coordinates the timing of curtains and intermissions with the house manager. An efficient and competent stage manager is indispensable to the success and sanity of the production.

PLANNING THE COUNTDOWN
PRODUCTION CALENDAR

One of the most important jobs for the producer to accomplish thoroughly and clearly is the writing and scheduling of the production calendar. The calendar is a useful organizational tool that helps the flow of work. Everyone connected with the production sees the deadline dates and can work toward them. (See the sample calendar on pages 242–243.)

THE AUDITION PROCESS

The director has two objectives to realize during the audition process: (1) to assess actors' abilities in voice, body, and character work; (2) to get to know and feel as much about the actors as possible, in order to determine their suitability for particular roles and for working with the rest of the cast.

Following are some useful methods for auditions.

PRIVATE INTERVIEW

The private interview gives the director a chance to investigate actors as people. You do not have to discuss the actor's background or experience: presumably that is on the résumé, or if there is no résumé, on a form that the actor fills in. Discuss instead the subject nearest to the actor's heart—him- or herself. Michael Shurtleff in his book *Audition* writes, "Garson Kanin is the best interviewer I've ever watched. He gets people to open up and reveal themselves because he's really curious about every human being that crosses his door, so he really talks to them: about cooking, baseball, do they sew? . . . anything that comes into his head that interests him and them . . . the résumé he can always read later."*

However, one thing the producer of theatre for young audiences will want to explore is the actor's previous experience in performing for such audiences and how the actor feels about that experience. At an audition in New York City one young actress, when told in the private interview that the job was touring for young people, said, "Oh, you mean *children's* theatre? Can I get out of rehearsals to audition for commercials?" She was not hired. The private interview may be used as an "ice-breaker" before the general audition, or it can be used as a final, in-depth wrapup after the general audition.

GENERAL AUDITION: COLD READINGS, PREPARED MONOLOGUES, OR BOTH

Publicize your audition dates a week or two in advance. You can run admittance to a general audition in two ways. At an *open call* actors arrive and sign up with the stage manager; then you see a different actor every 10 to 15 minutes on a first-come, first-served basis. For *appointments* you can post a sign-up sheet with times listed at 10-minute intervals.

Within the audition itself you can have a cold reading, in which you ask the actors to read, unprepared, scenes from the play with the stage manager, or you can require the actors to bring prepared monologues. There are pros and cons to each, and you might want to do both. The advantage of a cold reading is that you can begin to see, or not see, the actor in the role; the disadvantage is that if the actor is simply a poor reader, the audition may go badly, and the cold reading is deceptive. A prepared monologue will show you an actor at his or her very best, but there is little spontaneity.

If you do use the cold-reading approach, allow the actor to look over the script while waiting to audition; this may help a reading problem. Once an actor reads for you, ask for a second reading, but with another objective such as, "This time ridicule your partner to make him give in to you." By assigning objectives, you'll see if the actor can take direction.

If an actor reads with any affectations, remove them. For example, actors auditioning as Boone for Performing Arts Repertory Theatre's

*Michael Shurtleff, *Audition* (New York: Bantam Books, 1979), p. 29.

Actors performing for young people must know their craft very well because children quickly perceive what is real and what is false. The actor's attitude toward the child audience is immediately seen for what it is, whether respectful or condescending. Jack Tale Players, Ferrum College, Ferrum, Virginia. Directed by R. Rex Stephenson.
Photo by Don Scott

Daniel Boone often latched onto a Kentucky accent. One particular actor was tall, strong, very good looking, with a nifty Kentucky twang. The producers loved him immediately, but the director gently asked the actor to drop the accent. The actor did, and it was clear he couldn't act the role; without the accent "crutch" he couldn't make sense of the character.

You can dismiss actors once you've seen them, or you can ask them to wait outside in order to be seen again. (Try not to keep actors waiting for hours.) You can have actors read again, as you begin to match actors up with roles and with each other. This process will begin to give you an idea of how the members of the cast might balance each other.

At this point run an improvisation session, as shown in Chapter 4. This exercise will tell you a lot about the actors' imaginations and how well they translate creativity into stage action.

MOVEMENT AUDITION

Since most good plays for young audiences are somewhat physical in nature, a movement audition will show how the actors stand and move, and if they are coordinated. If you have a choreographer working with you on this production, let the choreographer run this part of the audition by giving a group a series of simple steps that form a routine. If you do not have a choreographer, any of Viola Spolin's physical warmups or improvisations will work.

SINGING AUDITION

If you need to cast singers, you need an accompanist and a tuned piano. Each actor must bring a prepared song with the sheet music in the proper key.

CALLBACKS

Once you have auditioned everybody, you will need to decide whom you want to see, hear, and talk to again. The stage manager will then schedule callbacks. During callbacks take your time to really evaluate the potential of each actor. The following checklist will help you to evaluate each actor's audition. As you evaluate the *total* person and performer, you can use these categories to pinpoint specific weaknesses or strengths. All directors look for different qualities in the audition; director Jay Harnick describes what he looks for as "a certain radiating energy." You will need to define for yourself those qualities that actors must have in order for you to cast them in your productions.

Of Mice and Men is a play written for the adult audience. However, this photograph shows the recognizable artistic intensity that can be generated by a fine professional actor. Such truthful intensity is just as necessary in productions for young audiences; it is therefore a quality that a director must look for during auditions. Actor: the late John Norwalk as Lennie. Oregon Shakespearean Festival Association: *Of Mice and Men* by John Steinbeck. Directed by Pat Patton. Sets by Jesse Hollis. Lighting by Robert Peterson.

Photo by Hank Kranzler

ACTOR AUDITION CHECKLIST

Voices: Evaluate:
1. Diction _____
2. Volume _____
3. Voice development and variety _____
4. Rhythm _____
5. Dialect/accent _____
6. Projection _____
7. Breath control _____
8. Suitable voice to character _____
9. Singing voice: Soprano ____ Contralto ____ Tenor ____ Baritone ____
10. Musicality _____

Bodies: Evaluate:
1. Movement: disciplined, controlled, graceful, or awkward? _____
2. Physical relaxation _____
3. Acknowledgment of other actors on stage? _____
4. Use of body in improvisation _____

Character Work: Evaluate:
1. Moment-to-moment work: justified, truthful, interesting choices? _____
2. Character investigation: believable? _____
3. Inner life: alive or empty? _____
4. Concentration _____
5. Any stage fright? (lack of concentration) _____
6. Any indication? (nontruthful work) _____
7. Personal discipline (no ad libs) _____
8. a. Attitude toward audience _____
   b. Attitude toward scene partner _____
9. Good taste in personal choices _____
10. Energy _____
11. Ensemble work _____
12. Takes direction? _____
13. Creates empathy in the audience? _____
14. Personality complements or contradicts the character? _____
15. Imaginative, active choices? _____
16. What is stage personality like? Warm? Cool? Compelling? Dull? _____

CASTING THE PLAY

Casting is matching what you see inside the actor with what you see inside the character, including the relation of the character to the other characters in your play. Remember that you are trying to create a sense of family, a sense of unity. The ensemble has to work as a whole.

FIRST STAFF MEETINGS

The director must also work with the various staffs, meeting with them to discuss the development of the production.

PRODUCTION DESIGN TEAM MEETINGS

The first meetings between the director and the designers have a specific focus and purpose: the director and designers must forge a mutual vision of the play. They then coordinate their focus to achieve that vision. A director may have a very specific look or approach in mind, but the director/designer relationship works best when it is a partnership with mutual respect, rather than a directorial dictatorship. The following issues should be covered in the first meeting:

- Director's interpretation and vision of the play, and discussion of the spine.
- Style of the play.
- Mood of the play: What senses are the playwright, director, and designer attempting to share with the young audience?
- Budgets: Producer/director must be able to tell the designers what their budgets are, particularly if the budgets are limited. The amount of money not only will determine the materials used to execute the designs, it will influence the designs themselves.
- Restrictions: For example, Performing Arts Repertory Theatre tours the United States in maxi vans; therefore, the scenery for any PART show must fit into a maxi van and be of sturdy material to withstand difficult touring conditions (for example, ten performances a week in ten *different* locations).
- Problem-solving: The best time to anticipate and solve problems is in this initial meeting. Equipment shortages, staff problems, or any out-of-the-ordinary requirements can lead to a crisis if not dealt with in the beginning of the production period.
- Ground plan: Where and how actors will enter and exit; what furniture or set piece will appear on the set.
- Schedule: The director and designer fix the production dates when work is due.

Also, all designers should come to the first reading of the play to show the cast sketches, swatches, and a scale model of the set. This will give the cast a feeling for the style and ambience of the world of the play.

ORGANIZING THE TECHNICAL STAFF

This is a job that most designers in the professional theatre take care of themselves, but often in educational theatre the producer-director recruits the crews. The most important aspect is to expect nothing less than excellence in their work. The staff members need to realize that their contribution is just as powerful and important as the actor-in-the-limelight's contribution. The production of any play cannot work as an art form without a crew's hard work and cooperation.

MANAGEMENT STAFF MEETINGS

The producer-director meets for the first time with the management staff in order to discuss the strategy for selling the play. Planning the

A good producer can be the person who knows how to select all of the important people who will do their jobs in a remarkable fashion, and in selecting the people, to select those whose chemistry works together, who vibrate on the same wave length, and who together make magic.
Donald C. Farber,
From Option to Opening

When you do a play something always goes wrong that you didn't think was going to go wrong. So if you spend time up front correcting what's correctable, you have time to take care of the last-minute emergencies.
Liz McCann,
Broadway producer, The New York Times,

steps of the promotional campaign is the objective of this first meeting. Chapter 8, ''Managing Theatre for Young People,'' covers a complete management plan. Also, the management jobs which must be accomplished before opening the play are detailed in the countdown production calendar on pages 242–243.

FIRST READING OF THE PLAY

The entire cast and crew should attend the first reading. The stage manager should have prepared the room by taping the stage area on the floor, marking the stage exits and entrances. Make sure that everyone is seated comfortably, then have the stage manager begin by reading stage directions. Ask the participants to concentrate on these things:

- Actors should focus on their own characters: what others say about them, and what they say about themselves.
- Small-part actors also focus on themselves and begin thinking of specific ways that they can make a statement in the play.
- Designers and technicians focus on the play, evaluate the dramatic metaphor, and consider how they might realize it in their work.
- Management staff focuses on the play, looking for any thematic material or catchy lines they can use as the basis for the marketing campaign.

After the reading have a discussion, and let everyone contribute. Rehearsals should run about three to four hours. If time allows, read the play again, this time with another focus, such as looking at the spine of the play and how it influences each character.

Reading the play can take as much or as little rehearsal time as you like. Some theatre companies will sit and read for several days, exploring character, values, relationships, and subtext. The advantage to reading for so long is that the actors get a real grasp on their characters *before* they have to articulate the character physically. They may even be thinking of blocking and movements as they sit, and this time can prepare them for blocking rehearsals. All the actors, even ''walk-ons,'' need to feel valued during this process, to be convinced that their contribution doesn't depend on the number of lines spoken, but on the quality of stage work created for the audience.

REHEARSING THE PLAY

All rehearsals should begin promptly, so that no one's time is wasted. Comic Woody Allen says that 90 percent of life is just showing up. In this case it's showing up *on time*.

The purpose of rehearsing the play is to achieve the interpretation of the play through dramatic action. In the analysis of the play the director has divided the script into acts, acts into French scenes, French scenes into units, units into actor's beats. Then the director must de-

Careful planning of all details contributes to the "feel" of a play, as in The Acting Company's production of Bertolt Brecht's *Mother Courage and Her Children*. The tattered clothes, Katrin's obvious exhaustion, the dirt on Mother Courage's hands—*everything* furthers the truthful impact of the playwright's words. Actresses: Frances Conroy and Mary Lou Rosato. Directed by Alan Schneider. Sets by Ming Cho Lee. Costumes by Jeanne Button. Lighting by David F. Segal.

cide what he or she wants to accomplish each day of the rehearsal period, then create a comprehensive rehearsal schedule. This schedule should be posted and given to the cast at the first rehearsal of the play.

According to director Milton Smith there are four discernible stages in the rehearsal process:

1. Preliminary study, during which the actors become familiar with the play
2. Blocking out the movements, or deciding and learning the entrances, exits, and changes of position
3. Working out the details of characterization, or learning the roles and how to act them most effectively
4. Working for finish, or pulling the whole play together to give unity and effectiveness of performance*

*Milton Smith, *Play Production for Little Theatres, Schools, and Colleges*, 1948.

WHAT KIND OF ACTOR DO YOU HAVE: INSIDE/OUT OR OUTSIDE/IN?

Listening to your actors read, you'll be able to tell whether an actor starts with the externals—tries an accent, say—and will work in to the character or if an actor starts inside—appears to be passive and quiet in the readings, and once the character is inside, the external characterizations of speech, walk, posture, and gestures will come. Inexperienced actors with little training will often leap for externals as a quick and painless solution—a funny voice, a silly walk—and then force their character to fit these externals. If you see this happening, ask the actor to try ten other ways to walk and talk and to create character, to see if the actor can let the organic process happen.

IMPROVISATION

Improvising around material in the play is an excellent way to begin rehearsals the first week. In a relaxed way the actors will begin to make interesting discoveries about their characters. This is a good time to use the Repetition Exercise from Chapter 4.

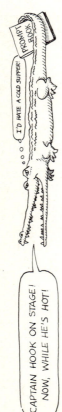

BLOCKING: PRE-BLOCK, OR THINK ON YOUR FEET?

The director can pre-block at home and come to the first rehearsal with the script detailed with exits, entrances, crosses, etc. Or you can let the actors improvise blocking, then look at it, see what you like, throw out what you don't like, and create new blocking with the actors. Director John Henry Davis says, "It is highly crazy to pre-block. Pre-blocking doesn't work because it is prepared and therefore does not respond to the needs of the actors at the given moment. You can pre-block if you feel insecure—then you always have something to fall back on. But blocking becomes most alive when you let the actors stimulate you, and you stimulate them."

Also, when you do specify blocking, ask your actors to write it in their scripts; they are responsible for their movements. Also, ask them to cross out all printed stage directions from previous productions. Leaving these directions there on how to say particular lines will interfere with their inventing original and truthful behavior for each moment.

HOW TO GET YOUR ACTORS OFF BOOK

"All actors off book by X Date!" should appear somewhere in your production calendar. Insist that this rule be followed, and on that day do not allow anyone on stage with a script. No actor, no matter how talented, can begin to explore the character fully while still reading a script, as the script interferes with the reality of doing from moment to moment.

The best way to ask actors to memorize their lines is by *rote,* in a complete monotone, with no meanings. Otherwise, if they imbue the lines with meanings that they haven't really thought through, then learn the lines with an inflection, these lines will be locked into a vocal pattern, and these patterns are hard to break.

Also, if you have actors whose characters must speak with an accent, advise them to learn the accent away from the part. Have them practice reading magazines in the accent until the accent is perfect. Then they can bring the accent to the part. This way they will not be predetermining any moments by an accent; the moments will come out of rehearsal, and they can add the accent to the moment.

REHEARSING THE SCENES

This is one way to rehearse: Say the play has two acts, with seven scenes in Act I, five scenes in Act II.

- Run the first three scenes hard; block them; run them again.
- Run the next logical group hard; block them; run them again.
- Run this entire grouping hard.
- Run the remaining scenes in Act I; block them; run them again.
- Run the entire act.
- Start with Act II the same way.

Important point: Never give a line reading to an actor, even if the actor asks for it. Once you do, the actor will never be able to create that moment any other way. Instead of a line reading, suggest the actor try different behavior—such as "cajole her," "threaten her"—to find the right action for the line.

WORKING WITH SUBTEXT AND CHARACTERIZATION

Subtext is the meaning under the lines; it is *not* paraphrasing. For example, if the line is, "If you believe, clap your hands!" paraphrasing is, "If you want Tink to live, clap your hands." Subtext is, "I was careless. I can't let Tink die. Help me out, please!" Helping your actors to find interesting and honest subtexts will imbue the play with life. People mistakenly assume that since many young people's theatre scripts are simple, they have no subtext. In fact, since the language is not as rich as Shakespeare's and the plots may not be as well developed, the actor and director must work harder to find interesting choices.

MAKING CHOICES AND NAILING THEM DOWN

Rehearsing is a creative process, and since you are creating a production of a play, you and your cast will be making many decisions. As

The purpose of producing theatre for young people is to provide them with a first-class live theatre experience. I am a puppeteer, and a master puppeteer taught me this many years ago—if a live actor can accomplish the moment on stage better than a puppet, there is no reason for that puppet to exist. Think about that! The only reason to use puppets is to add a different dimension to the theatrical experience. Puppets must project the abstract, or project a cartoon; puppets must leap beyond real life. This is what I try to do in my work, this is what gives my work meaning. Picasso said it took him a lifetime to be able to paint like a child again. I become a child when I create for them.
Marshall Izen,
master puppeteer

Scenery and properties alter an actor's performance. The director introduced the door and the pole early in the rehearsal process. Actors: Harriet Bass (center), Scott Depoy (stage left, above), Skip Foster (below). Alliance Theatre Company, Atlanta Children's Theatre: *The Halloween Tree.* Directed by Wallace Chappell.

decisions are made that you are happy with, nail them down. The stage manager records the move, the cross, the action in the prompt book. With inexperienced actors you must set choices so that they do not feel they must improvise when they perform; they are secure in the dramatic choices that have been set in rehearsal.

WORKING WITH SCENERY AND PROPERTIES

The usual practice in play production is to rehearse in one room and perform in another. But start working with some scenery that approximates the set, and start working with real properties as soon as the company is off book. Scenery and props will feed the inner life of the actor in that they are specific objects to which to relate. An actor might "find" the beginnings of a character through the methodical mending of a sock or through saying good night to a Teddy bear. Anything that supports the creative process is valuable at this stage of the rehearsals.

THE RUN-THROUGH

The run-through is important because it is the first time that the actors will get a feel for the entire show; it also gives the director a chance to see the entire show and to decide what needs fixing. However, running through just for the sake of running is not particularly useful. Instead, have everyone focus on one problem per run-through so that each time there is a separate purpose. For example, each character focuses on his or her dramatic through line—"Reynard wants power" or "Wendy wants to control all men"—and checks to see if all choices take him or her in that direction.

The cardinal rule during a run-through is not to stop, unless it is impossible to proceed. Then you stop, fix it, and go on.

MAKING CHANGES, AND THE DIRECTOR'S EGO

Don't be afraid to admit you've made a mistake. Even the legendary director Tyrone Guthrie, in reference to an offstage cry he had asked for while directing *Hamlet,* said, "Gordon, Duse couldn't have done it better, but it was a silly idea of mine. Forget it."* The rehearsal process is a give and take; a direction may work one day and fail in the next three rehearsals; don't be afraid to revise.

GIVING NOTES

Some directors give verbal notes immediately after a run-through; other directors may type them up and give them out at the next rehearsal. Verbal notes take up more cast time, but typed notes take up more director time. Find your own style.

SPLITTING REHEARSALS

Directors cannot afford to waste anyone's time. To have extras sitting around waiting for the first act crowd scene while you give specific attention to the leading actor's monologue is time wasting. Divide up rehearsal time so that you get maximum use of each actor.

OTHER KINDS OF REHEARSAL

Pace rehearsal   Pace rehearsals are fun and can be very helpful to an actor. After you have reached the run-through stage, have your company rehearse a few scenes speaking very quickly but staying in character; then have them rehearse the same scenes very slowly. You will discover what scenes would benefit from a change of pace.

Line rehearsal   Actors can do a line rehearsal while making up or waiting between scenes. They simply say the lines by rote, just to make sure they have them securely memorized.

*Alfred Rossi, *Minneapolis Rehearsals* (Berkeley: University of California Press, 1970).

Rehearsal falls into two areas: the process of helping the actor by a creative atmosphere, by advice and discussion, by helping him to relate his work to others, and the business of shaping the play as a whole.
Hugh Morrison,
Directing in the Theatre

Following are two pages from the prompt book for *Susan B.!* The first is a song; the second is a spoken scene. In each case the stage manager's notes are on the right-hand page, and the director's notes are on the left-hand page. Performing Arts Repertory Theatre, New York. Director: John Henry Davis. Stage manager: Dan Kirsch.

Nostalgic – not sentimental

objective - to find inner
    strength through father

Exit quickly for jump - cut
      – with purpose

Great satisfaction
  "Their" turf – comfort,
Relaxation – "Politics is a friendly game

          Playful
      Stuffy patriotism
          Joy!

Mounting anger
(Getting back at
him for previous wrongs)

Rhythmic moves

Everything's OK -
argument is fun among
    men

Subtext : "The most natural
      thing in the world"
Women's attitude cheerful - with
    slight touch of steel

         Primal shock

      Strength and
        resolve

SUSAN

Don't worry, Guelma. I want to be arrested.   *S. looks up; G. opens her parasol*

SUSAN: WHAT A BEAUTIFUL DAY FOR AN ELECTION.
          THAT WAS ALWAYS WHAT FATHER USED TO SAY.
          AS HE SPRUCED HIS SUNDAY SUIT UP,
          HE'D SAY IT WITH SUCH PRIDE
          ESPECIALLY WHEN THE WEATHER
          WAS AWFUL OUTSIDE

Ladies exit DL, Men unfreeze Trotter sits C stool, Marsh puts bib on him. Williams lathers Trotter's face, Marsh sits right stool

3 MEN: WHAT A BEAUTIFUL DAY FOR AN ELECTION
          WHEN THE CITIZENS HAVE THE FINAL SAY.
          POLITICIANS GET ELECTED
          OR KNOCKED RIGHT OFF THEIR STOOLS
          IT'S EITHER MERRY CHRISTMAS

Williams puts razor to T.'s throat

TROTTER: OR APRIL FOOLS.
ALL: WHAT A BEAUTIFUL DAY FOR AN ELECTION
          IN THE BEAUTIFUL U.S. OF A.

All stand
hands over hearts, salute

TROTTER: THIS IS THE DAY THE VOTERS GLOW WITH PRIDE AND SELF-ESTEEM.
MR. & W.: PATRIOTISM SWELLS EACH MAN'S CHEST.
ALL: IT'S A BEAUTIFUL DAY
          AND DEMOCRACY'S LOOKING ITS BEST.

Sway R
Sway L

TROTTER: LET ME SAY A WORD FOR HORACE GREELEY
WILLIAMS: (Threatens TROTTER with razor, sits him on stool)
          GREELEY IS A MEALY-MOUTHED OLD SKUNK.

          (The WOMEN enter; watch scene from doorway.)

MARSH: GRANT HAS RAISED THE SPIRIT OF THE COUNTRY

TROTTER: WHAT SPIRIT IS HE RAISING WHEN HE'S DRUNK?

ALL MEN: WHAT A WONDERFUL WAY TO RUN A COUNTRY
          WHEN EACH CANDIDATE FACES JUDGMENT DAY.
          BUT IN CASE YOU RUN FOR OFFICE
          AND DON'T RECEIVE A VOTE
add S&E: THERE'S A WONDERFUL OLD SAYING
          YOU STILL OUGHT TO NOTE

Men fade up R, notice Ladies, and stop singing

SUS. &E.: IT'S A BEAUTIFUL DAY FOR AN ELECTION
          IN THE BEAUTIFUL U.S. OF A.

SUSAN: (spoken) Good morning, Gentlemen. We're here to vote for
          the President of the United States.

ALL MEN: VOTING TODAY? SHE THINKS SHE'S VOTING TODAY!
          SHE JUST GOT CARRIED AWAY
          SHE POPPED HER CORK (SHE POPPED HER CORK)!
          LADY, YOU MUST BE LIVING IN A DREAMLAND
          AND NOT IN THE STATE OF NEW YORK.

Men walk R in tempo

Final poses around ballot box, table

Williams
Trotter — [box] Marsh

Grand pause

Deal with all other men

Subtext: "Which of you guys is gonna do it, I'm
scared!"

Retreat R quickly

False bravado, unable to look her in the eye

Visceral, unthinking reaction

By "voice" realizes
what she has done   Looks at Susan, S. looks back

S. - "First time since our childhood - we're together"

Surprise, excitement "a victory"
speech informed by relationships

This is the first time men
have thought of it!

Outrage! New confidence

E. - Calm dignity: "I can deal with this
childish behavior"

Men ___ - tiger protecting her cubs - look a
precious child

Delay Guelma's X slightly for focus

Trotter surprised by being bumped

S. - Gently, "I'm a friend"

MR. WILLIAMS

Because under New York State Law, men are the voters, Woman.
Throw'em out, Marsh!

*Takes Guelma's arm,
starts women counter L
up R a few steps*

MR. MARSH

Miss, you'll have to leave my barbershop.

GUELMA

(All) right! You do not have to address us in that tone of (voice.)
(EVERYONE reacts in surprise.)

S. x's to Guelma

SUSAN

(We) are here to vote under the Constitution, a higher law than the New York
State (law.) The 14th Amendment - No state shall make any law which takes
away the rights of citizens. Read it. (SHE hands paper to MARSH.)

MR. MARSH

But this has nothing to do . . .

*S. pulls paper
from bodice*

ELIZABETH

Aren't we (citizens?)

*Marsh, Trotter look at paper,
then at each other*

GUELMA

(Can) you believe this?! How can you hesitate? Of course she's a citizen.

MR. WILLIAMS

All right, so what?

SUSAN

Voting's the right of a citizen.

ELIZABETH

(Where) do we sign the registration book? *Xing R to front of table*

MR. TROTTER

(You) can't sign this.

*Hands, arms around book; Marsh protects
it on table*

ELIZABETH

We will not move from this spot until you let us vote.

(SUSAN joins ELIZ., GUELMA runs over, sits.) *S. joins E, sitting
left side
of table*

SUSAN

(Guelma,) we're in for some trouble here. You'd better go home.

Marsh | Ballot Box | Trotter

Williams

*G. sits left side of
table, knocking Trotter
off stool*

Eliz. Su. Gu.

Polishing rehearsal   This is a run-through in which the director evaluates all the small touches, stopping to fix something if it isn't just right.

EVERYTHING IN MODERATION

The director's job is highly creative during the rehearsal stage, and there is no easy solution to many rehearsal problems. But we would advise that a way to proceed daily through the rehearsal process is with *moderation*—give enough notes to make your points, but don't give so many that the actors turn off; work on a difficult moment with high energy, but back off if the actor or technician doesn't get it today—he or she may get it tomorrow, or may never get it. As actress Jessica Tandy said, "It's a play, not the end of the world, so enjoy it, have fun with it. If it fails, well, it's a *play*."*

EVALUATING THE REHEARSAL PROCESS

We include a checklist here so that you may evaluate your production. The German playwright and poet Johann von Goethe used the following three questions to evaluate artistic work:

1. What was the artist trying to do?
2. How well did he/she do it?
3. Was it worth doing?

REHEARSAL PROCESS CHECKLIST

1. Is the directorial concept clear?
2. If there is a dramatic metaphor, is it used clearly throughout?
3. Have the following elements been used creatively?
   composition _____   emphasis _____
   stability _____   sequence _____
   picturization _____   balance _____
4. Is the blocking organic and interesting?
5. Are the actors in control? (no ad libs, for example)
6. Is there consistency—e.g., all props real, or all props mimed, not some of both?
7. Is there theatrical sensibility at work? (Don't let actors get into bed in pajamas but with their shoes left on.)
8. Do important scenes happen offstage? (e.g., "Oh, look! She can spin straw into gold," and it is offstage. If so, fix it).
9. Does this production respect the child audience?
10. How is the pace?
11. What needs fixing?

*Rossi, *Minneapolis Rehearsals*.

The playwright who creates a complex character as part of a sophisticated script must have a certain level of skill and maturity. An example of such a character is Blackhawk, Jim Thorpe's ancestor who narrates Thorpe's life in Saul Levitt's *Jim Thorpe, All-American*. A script like this requires equally sophisticated direction. Actors (clockwise from top): Stephen Guntli as Blackhawk, John Canary as Thorpe, David Froman as Hiram Thorpe, Jim's father. Performing Arts Repertory Theatre. Commissioned by the Alliance for Arts Education, Imagination Celebration of the John F. Kennedy Center for the Performing Arts, 1977. Directed by John Henry Davis. Music by Harrison Fisher.

As the opening nears, much of the final process revolves around the technical aspects of production. As director, you may feel you have lost some control. However, if you and your staffs have worked carefully, all aspects will come together.

FINAL TECHNICAL STAGES OF PRODUCTION

RUNNING A PRODUCTION MEETING WITH DESIGN TEAMS AND TECHNICAL STAFF

Production meetings function as progress reports. They can happen informally or be built into the master schedule. All designers report on where they are in the process; the technical staffs report on any problems they may be having. If you have production meetings fairly frequently, all opinions can be dealt with and most problems solved before they escalate into disasters.

RUNNING A DRY TECH OF THE SHOW

A dry tech is a rehearsal with all technical equipment and scene changes, but no actors. Dry techs are invariably *long* rehearsals, as it is the first time you are coordinating all the aspects of production and design into the show. There will be many starts and stops, as you'll open a scene, skip the actual dialogue, and proceed to the next sound, scenery, or light cue.

RUNNING A CUE-TO-CUE TECH WITH ACTORS

The cue-to-cue tech prepares the actor for the next rehearsal, the full technical rehearsal, in which you mix all the elements. In this tech, you skip the dialogue and move from cue to cue to familiarize the actors with the technical processes.

TECHNICAL REHEARSAL

The technical rehearsal is a tech with actors. Try to stay with a run-through schedule as much as possible. Your only objective in the technical rehearsal is to put the show together. Keeping the technical staff waiting while you ask an actor for a different meaning on a specific moment is unacceptable. Let the actors walk through the tech; remain calm in the face of technical problems. Techs are the most trying and least enjoyable rehearsal to get through, or "stagger through," as Tyrone Guthrie liked to say. Civility and courtesy and good leadership are particularly needed at this time.

AS PRODUCER I'M "ULTIMATELY RESPONSIBLE, YET WITHOUT CONTROL ONCE THE..." STOP THE CURTAIN!

COSTUME PARADE

One week before dress rehearsal ask the costumer and actors to have a costume parade on stage. This gives you a chance to see all the costumes and to make any last-minute suggestions or changes.

DRESS REHEARSAL

The dress rehearsal combines all the actors' work with the technical work into one production. Inevitably there will be missed cues and fluffed lines; your job is to keep the rehearsal running smoothly, so that everybody can do his or her job in the best possible way. Let your actors know that you do not expect an emotionally full performance while they are getting used to costumes, scenery, and the space itself. Also, let the technical staff know that you're on their side, too; you want them to proceed comfortably. In the dress rehearsal try not to make any major changes in dialogue, behavior, or blocking. Everyone is struggling to pull it together; changes will interfere with that process. If the schedule permits, run several dress rehearsals in the week before opening. At this stage, if the actors are unfamiliar with performing for the child audience, discuss with them again what to expect.

Now you're ready to bring the audience back into the process. These last stages involve the groups of young people for whom the entire production has been readied.

THE PREVIEW

Performing for young people is different from performing for adults in that young people will let you know when they are bored. So that your actors and technicians get to "try out" for their audience, invite some groups of young people to an open rehearsal. Let them know that this is a very special event, but don't tell them you are watching their reactions. Your actors will learn where the laughs are in the production and can begin to practice holding for them. You will see where the pace may be too slow, if the audience appears restless at that point. Your "out-of-town tryout" with children can give you a lot of practical information.

OPENING THE PLAY

Your cast and crew need open-ended warmth, excitement, and support from you on opening day. You have made a long and hard journey together; opening is the beginning of the public life of the play and the ending of your involvement. Ask the cast and crew to arrive one or two hours before curtain, but once the stage manager has called "half-hour," your job is done. There will be time during the run of the play to watch actors grow in their roles and to observe how the ensemble works together. This performance time can provide an excellent opportunity for learning and developing together as a director and company.

RUNNING THE PLAY

If you can be at every performance, your cast will work better as an ensemble. If you cannot be at every performance, the stage manager must be competent to run the show alone. Sir John Gielgud writes in *Stage Direction*, "I feel it is never too late to improve and alter—and especially to simplify—even when a play has been running for many weeks."

PERFORMANCES

....

Recently a young director had gone backstage on the opening night of a high school play under his direction and then had gone to the lobby to assist the play's start. There, a startled student usher confronted him and asked, "Aren't you the director of this play?" When the director admitted he was, the student, staring at him in bewilderment asked, "Then why aren't you back there directing it?"
Stephen Archer,
How Theatre Happens
....

*A good production is not
script plus performance; the
audience should not even be
aware of script and
performance as separate
things. A good production is
script-into-performance, an
intimate, point-to-point
transformation that moves us
only in its wholeness.*
Richard Hornby,
Script into Performance

**20-STEP PRODUCER'S
CHECKLIST AND
COUNTDOWN
PRODUCTION
CALENDAR**

CLOSING THE PLAY

No moment, except perhaps bringing up the curtain on the play, is as charged with electricity as the moment the final curtain falls. The entire staff, cast, and crew have participated in a creative event. Depending on a thousand and one factors, the event may have been, on the one hand, deeply satisfying, and on the other hand, terribly traumatic. All creative artists may perceive the event differently, and their lives may be changed to a greater or lesser degree. Closing the play is poignant because it marks the end of a very special journey—the private creative process made public and given willingly to your audience, whose lives you have certainly touched.

The producer's checklist and countdown calendar are not prescriptions. All productions differ, and their differences change the schedule. Some professional theatre companies that perform for young people have only one to two weeks of rehearsal time, but they work nine hours a day. On the other hand, some university companies take six to ten weeks to rehearse, but they work only two or three hours a night a few times each week. The total number of work hours may be very similar for the professional company and the university company, but the distribution varies.

The checklist and calendar thus suggest the logical sequence of work. You will be concerned with every step in the checklist, as each step is standard procedure in theatre. You'll modify the calendar to suit your needs.

A 20-STEP PRODUCER'S CHECKLIST

Step 1   Initial considerations in choosing a play
  Step 1a   Assuming the director's job or hiring a director
  Step 1b   The audience
  Step 1c   The place of performance
  Step 1d   The budget
  Step 1e   The potential cast available
Step 2   Analyzing and selecting the play (use script analysis checklist)
Step 3   Interpreting the play and choosing its style
Step 4   Acquiring the design teams
Step 5   Hiring the stage manager
Step 6   Planning the countdown production calendar (see sample, pages 242–243)
Step 7   The audition process (use actor audition checklist)
  Step 7a   Casting the play
Step 8   The first production/design team meetings
  Step 8a   Organizing the technical staff
Step 9   Management staff meetings
Step 10   First reading of the play
Step 11   Rehearsing the play

Step 12   Evaluating the rehearsal process (use rehearsal process checklist)

Step 13   Running a production meeting with design teams and technical staff

Step 14   Running a dry tech of the show

Step 15   Running a cue-to-cue tech with actors

Step 16   Technical rehearsal

Step 17   Costume parade

Step 18   Dress rehearsal

Step 19   The preview

Step 20   Opening the play

  Step 20a   Running the play, either in person or through the stage manager

  Step 20b   Closing the play

Countdown Production Calendar

DIRECTOR / ACTORS	TECH	MANAGEMENT TEAM

WEEK 6

DIRECTOR / ACTORS

Actors audition.
Director casts.

TECH

By audition time the designers and technicians should have met with the director and made some basic design decisions about *style, ground plan of set, costume* ideas, and materials. In this production schedule the point is to go from the drawing board into the workroom.

MANAGEMENT TEAM

The management team (MT) can help run auditions by handing out sign-in sheets; reading with auditioners; making call-back appointments, scheduling them; typing up the casting notice and posting it. If not yet done by director, MT arranges for the facility and the dates it is available.

MT reads the script thoroughly, engages a graphic artist, and, with the approval of the director, decides on logo; marketing slogan; colors and type face.

MT also figures the budget, allocating percentage amounts for designer; printing; mailing; etc.*

WEEK 5

DIRECTOR / ACTORS

Read entire play with entire cast and crew present.
Explain director's concept and style.
Ask each actor to make a log of his/her character in each scene and answer these questions: "What do I say? do?" "What do others say, do about me?" "What do I want?" "How might I try to get what I want?"
Ask each actor to divide each scene into his/her beats and assign an action verb to each beat—e.g., "to woo Wendy."
Read entire play again, stopping to discuss beats and ways to do them.
Begin to block first half by having actors improvise the scenes. Stage manager and actors record movement in script.
If play is a musical, have stage manager (SM) schedule musical rehearsals with musical director around scene rehearsals. If director is also musical director, insist actors learn music on their own, so that rehearsal time is for interpretive, not remedial, work.

TECH

Technical director (TD) works with stage manager to tape out set on floor of rehearsal room, including entrances, exits, doors, hallways. TD puts facsimiles of set units in place, e.g., a stair unit.
At first read-through and at first blocking rehearsal, designers and technicians are present to orient actors to the design.
TD schedules actors to meet with wardrobe and costume-building staff to take measurements.
Technical staff commences construction in all four design areas.

MANAGEMENT TEAM

MT sets ticket price and ticket distribution: where and when box office(s) is(are) open, e.g., in schools?
MT plans whole marketing campaign: those promotional elements that cost—newspaper ads (how many? how big?), direct mail campaign ("how many brochures can we afford to print and mail?")—and those publicity elements that do not cost: news releases, feature stories, radio talk show(s) appearances.
MT writes brochure/flyer copy; poster copy; newspaper ad copy, ticket copy, five *different* press releases with five *different* angles, public service announcement (PSA) copy for radio/TV of 10-, 30-, and 60-second durations. Graphic artist prepares boards for printer. MT decides on number needed of each item above and takes all items to printer.

WEEK 4

DIRECTOR / ACTORS

Run first half of play. Change anything from first rehearsals that no longer works. Have stage manager follow rehearsal with his/her book to check actors' movements with director's decisions previously recorded.
Discuss each actor's beats and actions, to keep actor on right exploratory track.
Insist all actors be off book by beginning of Week 3. *No exceptions.*
Begin to block second half of play, with actors improvising scenes.
Run second half of play, omitting musical numbers if musical. They will be added in Week 2.

TECH

Director may ask designers, TD, and technicians to attend rehearsal at end of week, when director runs the whole show. Tech staff views rehearsal to see if adaptations or changes in design and execution of design are needed.
TD delivers any finished set pieces to rehearsal area.
Costumers give actors facsimiles to wear of pieces that may affect behavior, e.g., a long skirt, a period shoe. (*No hand-held costumes or props since actors are still on book.*)
Costumers see actors for fittings.

MANAGEMENT TEAM

Get materials back from printer. Launch direct mail campaign: envelopes stuffed, labeled, mailed.
Open box office(s) to prepare for distribution campaign. Launch print material distribution: posters and flyers in schools, stores, restaurants, hotels, chamber of commerce offices, "Welcome Wagon" offices, tourist bureaus, medical offices, senior citizen centers, and places where people gather: bus and train stations, airports, athletic events, banks, churches, synagogues.
Begin telephone group-sales campaign. Sell Boy Scouts, senior citizens, etc. Require payment *now.*
Begin paid print (newspaper) ad(s) campaign.
Begin paid media (radio, TV) campaign.
Begin publicity print (No. 1 press release) campaign.
Begin publicity media (No. 1 radio and TV PSA) campaign.
Begin public campaign, speaking at lunches, etc.

WEEK 3

DIRECTOR / ACTORS

Run whole play *on book*, paying careful attention to all blocking and beat details, to exits and entrances; begin to use real properties.
Run whole play *off book*, with stage manager paying close attention to physical and movement details.
Have actors call "Line!" when they need help. *Do not allow actors to break character when calling for line.*
Run-throughs need a particular focus; e.g., in one run-through the director focuses on pace of scenes,

TECH

TD needs to watch rehearsal to see how show is progressing, so that TD can continue to inject into the rehearsal process any set pieces that will affect an actor's behavior.
First run-through *without* book should be run the same as last run-through with book. TD and tech staff do not add any technical elements to this run-through, the purpose of which is to see if actors know their lines. TD injects
After actors are comfortably off book, TD injects hand-held props and facsimile costume pieces.

MANAGEMENT TEAM

Continue distribution of printed material. (Bulletin boards, parking lots, car windshields, etc.)
Buy and run next set of newspaper and media ads.
Place No. 2 press release.
Place No. 2 PSAs.
Continue public presentation, working on new exposures, such as radio/TV show interviews; classroom visits in all schools to discuss program and how to buy tickets (no direct ticket selling in classes unless approved by principal); 10-minute visits to

	Rehearsal / Director	Technical & Design	Publicity & Business
WEEK 2	working. Run through play in each rehearsal, with as few interruptions as possible, and time it. If musical, begin to run through with musical numbers in place. Spend some time at each rehearsal this week (1) fixing and changing actor's choices if a moment isn't working, (2) looking at pace, (3) looking at a character's relationship to another character.	TD and staff put up as much set as they have finished. Designers are present at rehearsal to see what works, what doesn't. Purpose of this week is to get actors comfortable with technical elements of production. Actors are now responsible for care of props on stage and safe removal to prop table. TD or stage manager may assign scenery changes to actors. They may also assign set changes to stage crew. Makeup designer meets with actors to form design plan: will actor use own hair? or a wig? etc. Makeup designer also assesses whether or not actor can do own makeup. Costumers see actors again for fittings.	community leaders, to inform them of this good work in their community. Interview actors and technicians for program copy. Take copy to graphic artist. Take program copy and artist's boards to printer. Keep coordinated campaign look by using same colors. Continue distribution of material and/or check that it is still posted. Continue public appearances. Lengthen box office hours if possible. Follow up direct mail campaign with telephone campaign. ("Did you receive our material on *Peter Pan?* Will you be coming? May I reserve some seats for you once we receive your check? What day would you like to come?") Buy and run next set of paid print and media ads, stressing event is "coming soon." Place No. 3 news release. Place No. 3 PSAs. Arrange front-of-house activities for performances: recruit ushers, ticket takers, concession people; arrange parking for buses; arrange police/fire permits. Watch rehearsals for more promo ideas.
WEEK 1	First *technical rehearsal* with actors, cue to cue. Do not do whole play; this is to familiarize actors with lighting and sound changes. First *full technical rehearsal* with actors—the "stagger-through." Actors do not need to be at full value. Actors do *costume parade.* First *dress rehearsal:* tech, costumes, makeup. Actors are only in one of the following four places: (1) onstage, (2) in wings, ready to go on, (3) in green room, (4) in dressing room. No actors in front of house. Second *dress rehearsal.* No stopping except for emergency. Final *dress rehearsal* before audience of young people.	Lighting crew hangs, focuses, and gels lights. First lighting dry tech; no actors. First *technical rehearsal* with actors, cue to cue only. Do not do entire play; this is to familiarize actors with lighting, sound cues, and set changes. First *full technical rehearsal* with actors: *No* costumes or makeup. Do entire play, including all musical numbers, scene shifts, light cues, special effects. First *costume parade:* no makeup, no full lights. Actors wear full costumes and make costume changes in sequence, to show costume progression. First *dress rehearsal:* first complete tech with all elements, including makeup, faces only. All designers watch rehearsal, looking for balance. SM runs rehearsal from backstage as a performance. Second *dress rehearsal. No stopping* except for emergency. Final *dress rehearsal* in front of young people. Performance conditions apply. TD replaces facsimile props, costume pieces, and set pieces with as many real pieces as possible, unless props are expensive (food) or fragile (glass ornaments). Then facsimile props may be used up to first technical rehearsal. TD and set crew paint set. TD or SM must schedule cast and crew at different times, as they both need access to the set. Crews begin to put backstage area into shape for production week. This includes (1) clean-up, (2) installing backstage walk lights for actors, SM, (3) intercom set-up between light booth, SM, backstage, green room, dressing room, and front of house.	Continue telephone campaign. Buy next set of paid print and media ads, stressing a "new" angle, e.g., "meet the cast" or "win a prize at the raffle drawing." Place No. 4 news release. Place No. 4 PSAs. Assess your marketing and its rate of success with volume of ticket sales. Do you need any last-minute publicity stunts, such as dropping complimentary or half-price tickets from a hot air balloon? Watch final dress rehearsal.
PERFORMANCE WEEK(S)	Open and run the show.	Operate show. Technical staff runs it backstage, management staff runs it front of house, actors run it on stage.	Pick up programs from printer. Buy last set of paid print and media ads. Place No. 5 news release. Place No. 5 PSAs. Check front-of-house staff and discuss procedures for opening, including any emergency procedures. Do any last-minute promo, such as posting arrow signs pointing to theatre.

*If you have no money, you will need to raise it *fast.* One way is by selling advertising space in your program to local merchants and arranging to be prepaid.

Is there a difference between producing a play for young people and producing a play for adults?

I don't think so, but let's examine it. I've produced both on Broadway and for kids. On Broadway I found a script I liked; I optioned it, which means I bought the rights for a period of time. Once I had the rights, I had to raise the money, and I got three other coproducers to put up some money. The first person I hired was the director, and we began to shape the vision of the play. Then I planned the budget and found a theatre. It seems to me the processes, so far, are identical.

What is the next consideration?

The design process. You decide what you want to allocate for the set, costumes, etc. Then you meet with designers, look at their work, and hire them. The better designers have a pretty good sense of what things cost for what they want to do. This process is similar in children's theatre. With Performing Arts Repertory Theatre we say to our designers, "This is the script. This is what we want, and this is our budget for the design. Now, go design it for us. If you have an idea for something which will be just marvelous but will not fit within the budget, let us know, and we will make a decision as to whether we want to include that."

Then what is next? Casting?

Well, hiring the stage manager is very critical.

Why do you say that?

Stage managers govern so much of the logistics of the proceedings. If they are skillful, they can save so much time and money and effort and agony in bringing these elements together on a schedule that makes sense. The phone calls, the coordination, the set load-in and load-out, all of these things can get very complicated, and suddenly you can find, if you are not careful, that events are running your life. A good stage manager is worth his or her weight in gold.

Then what's next?

Working with the playwright is a continuous process, but a very important one here. If you go ahead and start planning your show, and your script is not really completed, you can find, particularly on Broadway, that the costs are so high that a treadmill has started going that is very hard to stop. Each season plays open that just

INTERVIEW

with Jay Harnick,
Producer and Artistic Director,
Performing Arts Repertory Theatre,
New York

have no right to be there; they get started and people don't stop them. It's very hard for the producer to suddenly say, "No, let's stop, let's stop. We've raised half a million dollars, but the play will fail." It takes a lot of courage to do that. The producer must pay close attention to the basic story in the script. There are a lot of children's plays that are really slender and intimate little stories that get tricked up, when they don't need it. What's appropriate is appropriate. Part of the fun in producing or directing is making decisions that you believe are appropriate for the story that you are presenting.

In your career you've interviewed thousands of actors. What do you look for?

Well, it usually has to do with energy for me. There's something radiating from that actor. The actor can be silent, but still some force of personality comes across the stage to me. Frequently, if given a choice between an actor who has a wonderful singing voice but not much real energy, and another actor who doesn't have such a good voice but has enormous appeal, I may frequently go with the latter actor.

Let's proceed to the rehearsal process. Is it any different in young people's theatre?

Not really. You expect the same discipline, the same craft, the same attention to detail, the same interchange between actor and actor, and the same exploration and growth.

Do you ever think about the audience, performing for five-year-olds rather than for adults?

Not really. That has more to do with the script than with the actors. I think that kids of any age are perfectly capable of understanding nuance and subtlety.

Why are we plagued in this country with so many companies producing uninteresting work for children?

Since it all begins with the script, I think it has to do with getting the authors. With our profit-oriented society and our communications industry, many wonderful writers are simply not available to write for the young people's theatre field. Or if they do write for children and are really gifted, they are quickly snapped up by television or film, where they can make a lot of money. Writing a show for children is not so different from writing a show for adults in terms of the amount of time necessary to do it. To write a play for children could take anywhere from three months to two years, if it's a good show. The difficulty in getting good plays has to do with the availability of money to get the playwrights to write them. At Performing Arts Repertory Theatre, among our most successful scripts is *Jim Thorpe, All American,* written by Saul Levitt, a distinguished Broadway playwright who wrote *The Trial of the Catonsville Nine* and *The Andersonville Trial.* A Kennedy Center grant provided Saul with several thousand dollars so that he could clear his desk and dedicate himself to our play. The same was true for Ossie Davis, who wrote *Escape to Freedom,* which was commissioned by the New York State Council on the Arts when they initiated a program for established playwrights to write for children's theatre. Sometimes we have to grab a playwright and convince him to write for this field. Tom Babe, for instance, who did our *Daniel Boone,* felt he wanted to write for an audience of children because it meant something to him and to his daughter, who was then seven.

What is the most exciting aspect of producing theatre for young audiences for you?

Well, I like plays that make a statement, that have something to do with the human condition. To be creating new plays with these statements is always very exciting.

What is the director's responsibility once the show has gone through the rehearsal process and it is opening night?

Many directors have a great deal of difficulty in cutting themselves off from a production. At a certain point it is no longer the director's production but the actors' production. But, normally, you watch the show from time to time to make sure that the work continues to represent what you want it to represent. The show will change. The show is different in its twentieth performance from what it was on its opening day. It's evolving. The actors are discovering more about their characters. In the beginning of the rehearsal process the director knows more about the characters than the actors do. The actors, if they are doing their jobs, will come to know more about the characters than the director does. It's always fascinating to see a company that's gone off on the road for a couple of months when they come back in town. The actors have discovered so much about those characters that the play is enormously enriched.

What would you do if you didn't work in the theatre?

Starve!! I would starve if I didn't work in the theatre. I love working in a realm of ideas and of projects that continually change, and the theatre provides me with that excitement.

8 MANAGING THEATRE FOR YOUNG PEOPLE

Managing a theatre is as creative in its own way as is directing a play. I think filling a house of 500 seats night after night is highly creative; it demands imagination, insight, and taste, if you're going to do it right.

Frederic Vogel, *executive director, Foundation for the Extension and Development of the American Professional Theatre*

Dollars and sense, and knowing how to use both, form the basis of this chapter. Many times the director must make both artistic and management decisions. The purpose of this chapter is to acquaint you with the structure, components, and philosophy of strong management in the theatre.

THE NEED FOR GOOD BUSINESS MANAGEMENT IN THE THEATRE

One way to think of management is as the art of measuring. A successful manager is one who knows, among other things, which yardsticks to use in his or her job, and how to use them appropriately.
The Editors,
"On Management," Harvard Business Review

Management's main purpose is to sell the art form. Good business management means creating a demand for your product, persuading the audience to come to your theatre, making money, and managing people. In essence it frees the artistic work to develop. Directors are primarily concerned with the creation of the artistic product; managers are primarily concerned with the development of the audience.

246

Often directors of theatre for young people are so deeply involved in the rehearsal process that they overlook managerial considerations until the last minute. Then there is a mad dash to get advertisements in the newspapers and handmade posters up in store windows. Planning a marketing campaign or approaching corporations for grants may seem too sophisticated for a director producing a play for young people once a season. But in reality these management practices will allow a young people's theatre to survive in a difficult economy. Managerial work must take place simultaneously with the artistic work of producing a play. If there is little or no budget to hire a managerial staff, one management solution is to recruit volunteers. Dedicated volunteers can execute all the practices as described in this chapter at the same time the director rehearses the play.

Managing the arts is a business. American artistic directors and administrators began to take this viewpoint seriously in the 1960s; the theatre business changed dramatically with the creation of the National Endowment for the Arts in 1965 and the fifty state arts councils. Professional theatres of a not-for-profit nature were born "overnight." Not-for-profit (NPO) means that an organization is not in business to make profits; it is in business to provide services. Not-for-profit organizations, such as theatres, hospitals, and universities, are not taxed by the government, and they are eligible to receive grants. Many young people's theatre companies operate as NPOs because they are affiliated with a university or because they cannot survive without corporate, governmental, or foundation support. NPO economic survival is based on a balance between earned (box office or touring fees) and contributed (grants) income.

It took just as many actors to perform *Macbeth* in the seventeenth century as it does in the twentieth, but with the addition of new technology and production/design staffs, the costs of producing theatre have escalated. One way to beat the automatic increases in cost is to manage a theatre operation more efficiently. Some basic business principles apply to theatre management; the following eight steps give you the beginning of an approach to running a theatre or producing a play from the management point of view.

THE EIGHT STEPS OF GOOD MANAGEMENT

STEP 1. ANALYSIS

Take inventory of yourself, your assets, and the world you are dealing with by analyzing the following factors:

You: you must develop the artistic vision Clarify what type of plays you wish to produce for young people: classics, contemporary, original scripts, or a combination. Once you define your artistic mission, you can begin to define the management counterpart that will support this artistic mission.

Your resources   Analyze your strengths and weaknesses in terms of you, your staff, your facility, and your inventory, i.e., what you own. This analysis will tell you about the kind of work you can do and the type of market you can reach.

Your competition   Analyze how your vision for your theatre stacks up against the other theatre companies in your community. If your visions are similar, you will be competing with them directly for the same time, money, and commitment from the various markets. If you can embody an artistic vision that is distinctive and marketable, you will have a greater chance for survival.

Your customers   All businesses selling a product or service need customers. Analyze who your customers might be, where they live, what need you could fill for them, and why they might become involved with you. Need must exist in order for the *general* public to become *your* audience.

Your universe   Analyze your community, state, government, economy, and the current technology. Local and national trends will affect your theatre. The most obvious trend in the 1980s is the severe cutback in government funding of the arts. Also, inflation and recession affect your markets and how they choose to spend their money: Does society feel theatre for young people is a necessity or a luxury? Technology also affects your organization. Video hardware, software, and cable TV will affect children's entertainment in the next decades.

STEP 2. PLANNING

In the planning stage you develop goals and objectives and the form of your organization. The choices are to be a profit-making business venture, to incorporate into a not-for-profit organization, or to work under another NPO structure, such as a local arts council or the local chapter of the Alliance for Arts Education (AAE). Your state arts council and state department of education can tell you where those councils and chapters are located within your state.

The advantages of working as a not-for-profit are: (1) you are not taxed by the government, (2) you are eligible to apply for and to receive grants, (3) you can mail letters and brochures under a bulk mailing permit at a very inexpensive rate, (4) you assume instant credibility when a respected agency such as the National Endowment for the Arts funds you, (5) businesses and individuals may support you, as their gifts to you are tax-deductible. The disadvantages of working as an NPO are: (1) you can't make a commercial killing and get rich, (2) you must have a board of trustees with whom you work, thereby giving up some autonomy. However, if you manage the board of trustees prop-

HMM... N.P.O. SEEMS THE WAY TO GO - TILL THE DOUBLOONS START POURING IN!

Only rarely are business failures or poor decisions the result of too much planning; almost universally they can be traced to management ego— the temptation to say, "I don't need a plan; I'm sure I can handle whatever develops."
Richard S. Sloma,
No-Nonsense Management

erly, it should act in an advisory capacity and have little to do with artistic decisions.

In this planning stage you also establish short-term goals—one year—and long-range goals—five years—and a beginning strategy on the means to reach these goals. A short-term goal might be to produce one play in the first year and to tour it to nearby schools. Some of the elements of a long-range plan might be the exploration of other products, of other places to perform, and a commitment to a large-scale fund drive, if the theatre is not-for-profit.

The three succinct questions that strategic planners ask are:

1. Where am I going?
2. How will I get there?
3. What obstacles might I encounter along the way?

STEP 3. FINANCIAL STRUCTURE AND BUDGETING

Your most important management task is setting up a financial structure. As in all financial considerations, professional help, such as hiring an accountant, is required. Now you can formulate a budget.

If you are operating as a profit-making business, you need to sell your product for more than it costs you to produce and distribute it. If you are operating as an NPO, a good strategy is to project a break-even line between your expenses and your income, then to try to stay in the black.

STEP 4. PUTTING IDEAS INTO ACTION

Once you have formulated your statement of purpose, your objectives, your structure, and your plan, you are ready for your first real step. One logical choice is to select a play you wish to produce and set up a timeline for producing it. Another choice would be to raise money from funding sources or advanced ticket sales and then produce a play. Either choice could be successful.

STEP 5. KEEPING ACCOUNTS

All businesses have records. Good business practice requires you to keep precise records, since they will tell you a lot about how you are doing. If you are unclear as to a simple and easy system of record-keeping, seek the advice of a professional accountant.

STEP 6. BUILDING YOUR INSTITUTION

Once you have produced many different plays that have been artistically successful, and you have begun to develop your audience, you are on your way to becoming an institution. To "institutionalize"

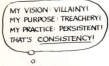

means that your theatre's presence improves the quality of life in your community, and the community can count on you to continue to make this excellent contribution. Institutionalizing also means continuity. Staff members may come and go, but the institutions and their artistic and managerial practices and philosophy remain. Peter Culman, managing director of Center Stage in Baltimore, suggests, "If you are selling your theatre as an entity, and not just selling a play or two a year, you have a better chance of winning the public to your support."

STEP 7. EVALUATION

In this step, ask yourself some very hard questions, such as: Is the plan working? Am I making more money than I have spent? What can I do better next season, both managerially and artistically?

STEP 8. MAINTAINING
CONSISTENCY AND CONTINUITY

Once you know what you are doing, the last step is to continue to produce your plays with a consistency of vision, purpose, and practice.

By following these eight steps, you are acting in a managerially competent way. Without a plan you simply react to circumstances: to rising or falling population, to changes in the marketplace, to changes in your staff, to changes in society's priorities. Allowing your theatre to be only a reactive organization robs it of the chance to be truly original in its vision and practice.

FOUR KEY JOBS IN MANAGING A THEATRE
FOR YOUNG PEOPLE

Now that you have a sense of why good business practice is important in the theatre, we will deal with four specific areas of theatre management. These four jobs are particularly important in young people's theatre. Many fine artistic companies have folded for lack of understanding of, and attention to, these matters.

We define these four jobs as follows:

1. The financial job: managing your dollars
2. The people, place, and thing job: managing your resources
3. The marketing job: selling yourself and your product
4. The fund-raising job: applying for grants and soliciting contributed income

These four jobs contain many different responsibilities. A competent theatre manager needs to be familiar with all these responsibilities, to be expert in some of them, to delegate some, and to be willing to rely on professional help for others. All of these tasks also overlap in some way, very much the way the roles of acting coach and interpretive artist overlap for the artistic director. A good theatre manager can balance all of these jobs, giving attention to each.

Ideally, a theatre producing work for young people has the budget to hire a professional manager. Professional business managers, in conjunction with the artistic and managing directors of a theatre company, assume all fiscal responsibilities.

In the university system the director can call upon the financial planners and business managers of the university itself to try to enlist their advice and aid for the young people's theatre. In a not-for-profit organization the director might look to the business community for advice and put a talented attorney and bright accountant on the theatre's board.

However, the director needs a working knowledge of the responsibilities that belong to the business manager: (1) running the box office; (2) accounting and record-keeping of all revenues and expenses; (3) long-range fiscal planning; (4) budgeting, both annual and long-range; (5) purchasing and invoice payments; (6) banking—deposits and investments; (7) payroll (if not handled by parent institution); (8) contracts, both union and nonunion; (9) insurance coverage—policies and claims.

THE FINANCIAL JOB: MANAGING YOUR DOLLARS

HOW TO PREPARE A SIMPLE BUDGET

Stephen Langley, author of *Theatre Management in America*, suggests that a manager ask these two questions: (1) What does my theatre earn? and (2) What does it cost to run? The two figures you come up with must in some way balance each other. Jim Rye, managing director of the Birmingham Children's Theatre, says, "In my budget, I propose my income for a play conservatively and my expenses liberally. That way, in the middle of the season, when unexpected expenses develop, I can cover them."

Budgets are made up of two kinds of items, flexible and inflexible. Inflexible items are those like postage that you will always have to buy, regardless of cost. Flexible items are those that you can control somewhat—for example, deciding to make costumes out of silk or cotton.

The following section outlines a simple procedure for budgeting.

Step 1 Pick the play you wish to produce.

Step 2 Obtain the rights and get the scripts, or if you are creating a new play with a playwright or actors, begin your work.

Step 3 Select the facility you intend to use and make an educated

The $5 million loss to dance companies that the [National Endowment for the Arts] budget reduction entails would be a calamity. With nuclear submarines costing approximately $1 million a foot, wouldn't it be in the national interest to build slightly shorter submarines, and give the savings to dance? Eliot Feld, dancer and artistic director, Eliot Feld Ballet, The New York Times

guess as to the number of seats you can sell; line up the dates for the performances.

Step 4 Add up the number of actors, designers, technicians, and managers you need to produce the play.

Step 5 Prepare a working budget. Estimate your potential income: Take the number of seats in the theatre (for example, 1,000) times the number of performances (for example, 10) times the ticket price (for example, $5). If you sold every seat, you'd have 10,000 seats to sell, and you'd have $50,000 potential income. However, project a conservative 50 percent capacity, or 5,000 seats, and $25,000 potential income. (An excellent tactic is to presell blocks of seats to organizations, such as the Girl Scouts of America. Group sales help solidify your income base.)

Step 6 Project other income, such as selling space for advertisements in the playbill ($1,000), concessions ($100 per performance, $1,000), or fees for touring performances ($500 × 4, $2,000). Add this figure, $4,000, to $25,000, for $29,000 potential income.

Step 7 Now list your expenses. Total these costs to see how your projected spending compares with your projected income.

The budget below is an actual one as prepared by Jim Rye for the Birmingham Children's Theatre. These figures represent a full season of producing theatre and consequently are higher than the figures for producing just one play. However, this budget works as a model and can be applied to producing one or two plays for young people in a season.

Budget for Birmingham Children's Theatre, Birmingham, Alabama July 1981–June 1982

	PROPOSED BUDGET	YEAR END 6/30/82
INCOME		
1. Earned income		
a. Subscription sales	$150,000	$158,000
b. Touring fees	20,000	20,500
c. Rental fees	400	575
d. Interest on CDs (certificates of deposit)	8,100	17,320
e. Ticket sales, young adult services	15,000	15,007
f. Other earned income	200	200
Total earned income	193,700	211,602
2. Contributed income		
a. Individual donations	6,000	7,500
b. Corporate contributions	8,500	8,200
c. Governmental (state arts council)	4,000	4,000
d. Women's committee (benefit)	7,000	8,755
Total contributed income	25,500	28,455
Total income, earned and contributed	219,200	240,057

	PROPOSED BUDGET	YEAR END 6/30/82
EXPENSES		
1. Administrative salaries/fees, including managing director, marketing director, public relations director, etc.		
2. Production salaries/fees, including actors, directors, designers, choreographers, composers, etc.	45,500	45,500
3. Administrative expenses, such as civic center rental, office supplies, telephone, entertaining, dues, travel, marketing campaign, etc.	53,900	56,400
4. Production expenses, such as costumes, sets, lighting, repairs, dry cleaning	48,560	49,750
5. Touring expenses	26,061	24,540
6. Young-adult services	14,850	14,650
Total expenses	10,000	10,019
	198,871	200,859

FISCAL CONSIDERATIONS FOR A HOUSE THEATRE: RUNNING THE BOX OFFICE

There are five major considerations in setting up a responsible, well-run box office: ticket policy; ticket pricing; seating policy; box office staff; physical location of box office.

Ticket policy   Ticket policies vary from theatre to theatre. Whether to sell individual and/or group tickets, to have tickets, or not to have tickets at all, the size and type of tickets are decisions you will have to make. In Appendix 3 we have listed two very good ticket houses from which you can receive advice on the best type of ticket for your situation.

Ticket pricing   One of the most important decisions you will make is choosing your ticket price and/or scale. Factors to think about are: (1) what the market will bear for young people's entertainment, (2) how your price competes with the other organizations in your community bidding for young people's time, (3) how many seats you are selling, per performance, per production, and per season, (4) the percentage of your total budget that is represented in the revenues from your ticket sales.

Ticket pricing is a tricky thing. In considering your options, assess your community. Your theatre may serve a middle-class to wealthy community in which families pay $5 per person to go to the movies, or take children to the theatre at $15-$50 a ticket. If you offer your

I'm a Baptist who hates to gamble, and this business is just like Las Vegas. It's a roll of the dice. Because of this, the most important management function is sound financial planning. Without that, you can do nothing.
Carol Jeschke,
arts administrator, Civic Center of Onondaga County, Syracuse, N.Y.; chairperson, CTAA Producer and Presenter Committee

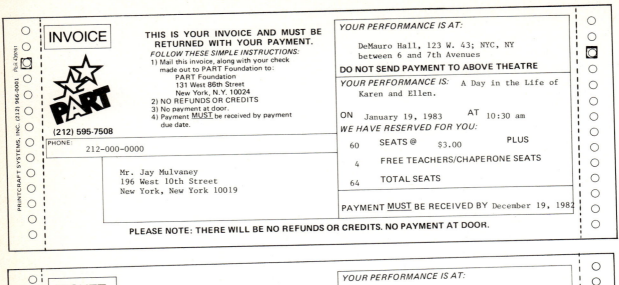

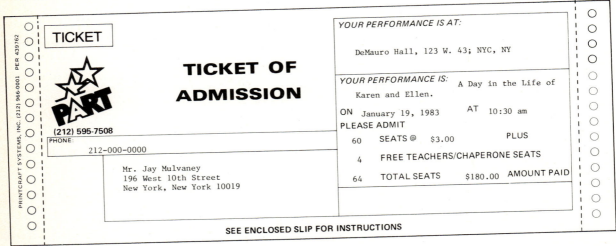

top: Sample invoice for an in-school-time field trip group ticket. The total amount is left blank so the buyer can change the number of tickets if necessary and insert the correct total.

below: Sample group ticket for an in-school-time field trip. Both invoice and ticket are on a computerized system; however, from 1970, when Performing Arts Repertory Theatre began this series of field trips, until the 1980–1981 season, all invoices and tickets were handwritten.

product at $3, you are underselling yourself. The community reaction might be, "If it's that *cheap,* it can't be very good." On the other hand, you may service a poor community, in which $3 would be the top price to get your audience in to know you.

Seating policy   In figuring out a seating policy, consider these two factors: (1) general admission: a first-come, first-seated basis? or (2) numbered and lettered seats by section, with a large seating chart visible in the lobby?

General admission is a much easier system with large groups of young people than individual tickets. This policy works very well for in-school-time field trips. The number-and-letter system works well for individual ticket buyers or small groups (families and birthday parties) and for public performances on weekends. If you run both school-time and public performances, it is possible, though confusing, to follow both policies.

The babes-in-arms question. The problem of small babies does not often come up in the adult theatre, since parents get babysitters at night. However, it does often occur in young people's theatre. You need to make a policy decision. If you decide not to admit any babes in arms, be prepared to lose some ticket sales to single parents who do not have sitters. One compromise is to permit babes in arms but post a notice saying that if an infant cries, the parent must remove it immediately. Other solutions are to offer a "cry room," where parents and infants can go during the performance, or to offer a babysitting service.

The box office staff Hire or designate one person as the box office treasurer. He or she may have a staff of assistants, but you as manager need one person to assume the responsibility. We do not recommend that you, the director, also assume this job.

The person you choose as treasurer must obviously be trustworthy. The treasurer is responsible for all tickets, sold and unsold. Impress on your treasurer the fact that tickets are a contract with the public; they are as valuable as the cash they represent. For example, if a ticket is unaccounted for, you cannot replace it, as it might actually have been sold. Accounting and record-keeping skills, as well as a friendly personal demeanor, are the keys to an effective box office treasurer.*

Physical location of the box office The box office needs to be easily accessible to the public as well as secure, comfortable, and well lit for the staff. It needs telephones with roll-over lines. Nothing will turn away a prospective ticket buyer more than a consistently busy phone line. Your box office is your public image; it reflects how you run your organization.

ALTERNATIVES TO A STAFFED PUBLIC BOX OFFICE

Take telephone orders or mail orders *only.* Mail tickets out from your central office and have a policy of no tickets at door, or you may sell tickets at the door, but only one hour before curtain. This is an easier, less expensive way to run ticket sales; what you have to evaluate is what sales you lose by not having a personal conduit to the public open at certain times.

*A clear A–Z treatment of box office policy and procedure is in Stephen Langley's *Theatre Management in America: Principles and Practice,* chapter XI (New York: Drama Book Specialists, 1980).

Never institute a practice that you can't put on the front page of the newspaper.
Richard Stickel,
professional fund-raiser

FISCAL CONSIDERATIONS FOR
A TOURING THEATRE

Consider your analysis of your marketplace and your competition before you determine what fees to charge.

A good rule to follow in order to break even is to charge the full amount of that performance's cost (housing, meals, fuel, vehicle rental, amortized actors' salaries, publicity, scenery, costumes—etc.) *plus* 33 percent to return to your overhead. Overhead comprises those budget items referred to earlier: rent, administrative salaries, telephone, materials, etc. This 33 percent figure is the lowest you should consider. However, if you wish to offer a lower fee to your community and can subsidize the tour with a grant, make sure the money "is in the bank" or at least guaranteed before you announce the subsidized fee. Otherwise you will run an automatic deficit.

LANGLEY'S THREE IMPORTANT
FINANCIAL DON'TS

Stephen Langley describes three unforgettable principles of fiscal management in *Theatre Management in America*. They are summarized here:

1. *Don't spend your income before you earn it.* Few producers or organizations make plans for a production unless they believe that it will do well at the box office. Optimism about ticket revenue, therefore, is likely to run high before opening night. Most ongoing theatres, whether they are profit or nonprofit, should be able to realize at least 50-60 percent of their total potential box office gross. Of course, everyone hopes that more income will actually be earned. Theatres that offer a season or series of different productions should think in terms of *average* box office income and *average* costs, so that the sell-out shows "carry" the less successful ones and expensive productions are balanced by inexpensive ones.

2. *Don't spend or budget the same dollar twice.* There is always a need to "stretch" the dollar as far as possible, but there is a limit as to how much this can be done. Optimism or inexperience sometimes leads people into the illusion that the same dollar can be spent twice. Most theatres generate income in advance of opening night through pre-opening or season ticket sales. If for any reason the production does not occur as advertised, the ticket money may have to be returned to the customer. There have been a number of unfortunate cases in which ticket revenue has been exhausted before production and operating costs have been paid, forcing the organization into bankruptcy.

3. *Don't get into the boat unless you can afford to sink.* If a project is initiated and financial commitments are made before there is good assurance that the necessary capital will be forthcoming, a lot of money is likely to be lost and a lot of reputations ruined. Because theatre is so highly speculative as a business, and because so many unexpected

There is a feeling afloat in our land that in children's opera there are little musicians who play little instruments and it doesn't cost very much. This simply isn't so. Programs for children cost as much as programs for adults.
Sarah Caldwell,
director, Boston Opera Company

things can happen to increase expenses or prevent productions from taking place as planned, producing organizations must always keep the possibility of financial disaster in the back of their minds and protect themselves, their investors, and the ticket buyers accordingly.

THE PEOPLE

Just as the director gets the best actors, a manager needs to get the best people for management jobs. A committed and articulate staff and volunteers are invaluable. These people bring to you their ideas, their plans, and their initiative to carry out the expressed goal of the theatre. Tapping them is a delicate job; egos are involved, after all. You might want to refer to the Myers-Briggs personality profile in Chapter 4, on pages 106–109, and apply it to your staff. Finding a unity of spirit among the people you work with will energize your theatre.

An excellent business practice is to *hire* a professional staff. When you hire a pro, you hire training, experience, and a fair exchange: work for pay. However, the financial realities in young people's theatre often make it impossible to afford a professional. So, if you compose your staff of students and volunteers, be prepared that some members may be inexperienced. However, if you have chosen dedicated people, you should receive excellent work in return for your good management.

One of your responsibilities to your staff is to delegate authority: who does what when. One way to be sure something gets done is to entrust one job to one person, from start to finish.

THE PLACES OF PERFORMANCE

The home theatre   The management considerations in relation to the performance space are (1) the number of seats available; (2) the amount of time the space is available to you for performance and possible rehearsal; and (3) whether the space serves your art form well. If your mission is to produce a big musical such as *Cinderella* for a large audience at a low ticket price, an intimate 200-seat laboratory space will not serve you well. A large auditorium of at least 1,000 seats, with a proscenium or thrust stage, will better suit your needs artistically and financially.

Your management options with regard to space are to rent, borrow, buy, or build. Many young people's theatre companies start out performing in whatever space is available to them for no or very little money—in libraries, schools, museums, parks, and even shopping centers. Creative exchange can also work. For years Performing Arts Repertory Theatre rehearsed its new plays in the auditorium of a kindergarten–sixth-grade school for three weeks per play, rent free. At the end of the three weeks the company gave a free performance to the school and community to which the PTA sold tickets and made money.

THE PEOPLE, PLACE, AND THING JOB: MANAGING YOUR RESOURCES

Business performance requires that each job be directed toward the objective of the whole business.
Peter Drucker,
The Practice of Management

above left: The courtyard of the Elizabethan and Bowmer Theatres of the Oregon Shakespearean Festival in Ashland. The size and style of a production determine which theatre it plays in.
Photo by Hank Kranzler

above right: The Performing Arts Center of the Governor Nelson A. Rockefeller Empire State Plaza in Albany, New York, home of the Empire State Youth Theatre. This performance space, which was designed for child audiences, is affectionately called "The Egg."
Photo by Donald Doremus

Aside from economics, the other important considerations are location and personal comfort. The theatre should be in a safe area of the community, with easy access by car or public transportation. The seats need to be placed in such a way that all of the child audience can see the stage, particularly the stage floor. The seats also need to work comfortably for children's bodies.

As society's sensitivity to the needs of handicapped people deepens, theatre managers must make every effort to give them access to the theatre-going experience. The handicapped are a great untapped market as well as a special audience; by providing them with equal and courteous treatment you may recruit them as supporters to your theatre.

Touring The one big consideration is the unknown. You may wish to be a company that won't perform unless certain space standards are met for artistic reasons. This is an unrealistic approach in touring young people's theatre. You cannot require fully equipped stages all the time because you simply can't get them.

What you can get is a *look* at the unknown. The best way to do this is to send a tour manager out on the road in advance of performance. The tour manager evaluates the space, draws a diagram, and alerts you to any problems. However, your budget may not allow for a tour manager. If this is true, have the company arrive at least two hours before the performance in order to deal with the space.

THE THINGS

The things are what you own, such as costumes and hammers. One way to save money is to take inventory, so that you know what you own. This helps to prevent you from buying the same roll of electrical tape *twice*.

OTHER RESOURCES: YOUR COMMUNITY, REGION, STATE, COUNTRY

Make the adults and young people of your community your partners. Provide them with a vested interest in whether you succeed or fail. You can do this by making them a part of you, by inviting them to dress rehearsals and to tours of your facility, by setting up seminars with actors after performances, by running a healthy volunteer organization headed by a vivacious community volunteer, by having community leaders make up your board, by thanking them through letters, free performances, lots of publicity, and by rewarding them with the ultimate return—a well-run theatre for young audiences.

According to marketing expert Philip Kotler, in order to survive in the world, all organizations, from the smallest business to a giant corporation such as A.T.&T., must perform three activities: (1) attract sufficient resources, (2) convert these resources into products, services, and ideas, (3) distribute these outputs to various consuming publics.* The organizations offer these activities in exchange for goods, services, or money from the public. They neither give their goods and services away free, nor do they force people to accept their offerings. Organizations work on the exchange system.

A BRIEF OVERVIEW OF MARKETING

The principle of exchange

The central concept of marketing is exchange. Exchange is the offering of value to someone in exchange for another value and requires two conditions: (1) two parties are involved; (2) each has something that is valued by the other. If one of the parties has nothing of value for the other party, exchange cannot happen. Value comes from what we want and need; if we feel a want for something, then that "something" has value. If someone else can find a product to meet our need, then that product can be marketed to us in exchange for goods, services, or money. For example, if parents believe children deserve to see the best in young people's theatre, and the Lafe Theatre Company tells all the parents in the community that it offers the best, those parents may exchange their money for the Lafe product for their children.

*Philip Kotler, *Marketing for Nonprofit Organizations* (Englewood Cliffs, NJ: Prentice-Hall, 1975), p. 5.

National movements are made up of people who have had to dig down deep into themselves, ask some important questions about what is important for our children, and decide to fight for it.
Ted Berger, *executive director, New York Foundation of the Arts.*

THE MARKETING JOB: SELLING YOURSELF AND YOUR PRODUCT

All business organizations perform two basic operating functions—they produce a good or a service and they market it. . . . Production and marketing are the very essence of economic life in any society.
Louis E. Boone and David L. Kurtz, *Contemporary Marketing*

What is marketing?

A professional marketer, then, is someone who is very good at "understanding, planning, and managing exchanges." Kotler defines marketing as: ". . . the analysis, planning, implementation and control of carefully formulated programs designed to bring about voluntary exchanges of values with target markets with the purpose of achieving organizational objectives. It relies heavily on designing the organization's offering in terms of the target market's needs and desires, and on using effective pricing, communication, and distribution to inform, motivate, and service the markets."*

You cannot create a need with marketing; the need must already exist. What the marketer can create is the demand for a product. Also, your marketing must be honest and not promise more than you and your theatre can deliver. What marketing can accomplish is to induce a consumer to try your product. If you have created unrealistic expectations that are not fulfilled, the consumer will not repurchase.

What is a market?

A market may be any cross section of the public at large. When you begin to target what section of the public might fill their need by your organization's goods and services, you are beginning to view that public as a market.

What is the job of the marketer?

The prime responsibility of every marketer is to know his or her product. The second responsibility is to know the marketplace: the needs of the buying public, the economic demographics, the education and business community's attitude toward your theatre, and the different potential markets. For example, Junior Programs in Olympia, Washington, presents excellent theatre for young people during school time downtown at a beautiful renovated theatre. The Junior Programs volunteers market in the schools; they also market to Olympia's senior citizens. The quality of the performances, the place, and particularly the time of day appeal to the senior citizen market.

Marketing plays for young people is like selling baby food: the buyer is not the consumer   The fact that the buyer is not the consumer poses an interesting problem for the marketers of young people's theatre. Essentially, if your product is *Cinderella*, and the target audience is four to ten years old, you are marketing to the child through the medium of the parent or teacher. If your product is *Teddy Roosevelt*, your target market is ten- through fifteen-year-olds and their families: You are marketing to both the young person and adult. The following principles of marketing apply, but you must keep this twist in mind when you target your audience.

*Kotler, *Marketing*, pp. 5, 182–184.

THE MARKETING MIX: THE FOUR P'S:
PRODUCT, PRICE, PLACE, PROMOTION

The Four P's are the four basic elements associated with marketing.

1. Product In terms of young people's theatre the product is the plays, the seminars, the workshops and residencies—whatever the artistic director chooses to offer. Take a look at the advantages and disadvantages of your product. Producing *Cinderella* puts you at an advantage. *Cinderella* is familiar to all consumers, both children and adults; they feel comfortable with it; it sells tickets. Producing opera for young people puts you at a disadvantage because it is harder to sell. You will need to find clever ways to promote it. If you choose to produce a season of plays without one or two surefire titles that will guarantee sales, you are starting out at a considerable disadvantage.

2. Price Profit-making businesses set their prices to increase profit dramatically. Not-for-profit theatres cannot always pass along the full cost of their products and distribution to their audiences because the cost becomes prohibitive. When making the price decision, the first step is to determine your objective. Do you want to (1) maximize profit? (2) just cover costs? or (3) lower the price to increase use? Once you decide on your objective, price setting is oriented to three considerations: cost, demand, and competition.

Cost-oriented pricing. You determine the price of a product by what it costs you to produce it, and then you add a fixed percentage on top to return to overhead.

Demand-oriented pricing. You vary the price of a product depending upon the demand; when the demand is heavy, the price is high; when the demand is less, the price is low. Demand-pricing works in the profit-making sector of society, but it would be a poor choice in the theatre. With the lower price you would be advertising that no market values this particular product. However, you could separate your series into "plays" and "musicals," and as musicals are more costly to produce and have a bigger audience draw than plays, you could price the musicals higher. Broadway constantly does this.

Competition-oriented pricing. You set the price of a performance based on what your competition charges for their performances. This pricing scheme does not take cost or demand into account; price reflects the competition only. If you are competing with a lot of events for young people in your community, it makes good sense to be within the same range as your competitors. You should not underprice or undervalue yourself, or overprice yourself out of business.

3. Place or distribution How and when your organization chooses to make goods and services available to customers determines distribution. The first decision to make regarding distribution is the level and quality of service you are going to offer to the consumer. If you were to market a play every hour in a family's living room, you could solve the distribution problem of their coming to you, but that is an obviously impractical solution for live theatre. You must decide the best place to give the performance and the best times for your target market. You can increase your distribution possibilities by providing mass transit or parking near your theatre, or by touring your theatre to the consumer, in schools, colleges, community centers.

Note: Theatre poses an interesting marketing problem. Unlike a commodity—shoes, for example—which can sit on a shelf indefinitely if no one buys them, a theatre seat, another commodity, exists only in time and space. Once the performance happens, that commodity is gone, never to be retrieved. Once you have lost that opportunity to sell that seat for that performance, you have lost that income forever. This is one reason why theatre marketers must be so aggressive and creative.

4. Promotion   Promotion is "persuasive communication"* about your product, price, and distribution. The key elements of promotion are personal selling, advertising, direct mail campaigns (including subscriptions), incentives, atmospherics, and publicity. These will be discussed as part of the marketing strategy.†

A BRIEF LOOK AT A MARKETING STRATEGY

A marketing strategy, whether it is to sell one play or a series of plays, has six steps: (1) Picking objectives, (2) analyzing the market (your customers), (3) targeting the market, (4) establishing a timetable and writing the marketing plan, (5) executing the program, involving the Four P's, (6) evaluation.

1. Picking objectives   Your objectives are what you hope to achieve by your marketing. One objective might be increased ticket sales. Another objective might be increased visibility in the community, so that you can attract more funding sources to your cause.

---

*Kotler, *Marketing*, p. 221.

†Business terms such as "promotion," "publicity," and "public relations" are often confusing because they are sometimes misused and misunderstood. An easy way to remember the differences between these terms is:

Promotion is any selling of your product that you pay for, as in buying newspaper advertising.

Publicity is any selling of your product that you do not specifically pay for, as the printing of a press release in a newspaper. Publicity is technically "free" in that the item being publicized is newsworthy. But keep in mind that publicity has indirect costs, in terms of staff time and materials. We include publicity as a component of promotion; it has its own special tools, such as the press release, discussed later in the chapter.

Public relations is the coordination of the entire image—the image you buy through promotions and the image you attain through free publicity.

"Just keep your marketing smarts to yourself.
You grow it and I'll push it."

Drawing by Donald Reilly; © 1980 The New Yorker Magazine, Inc.

2. Market analysis   In The Eight Steps of Good Management in the first part of this chapter, we discussed analysis. Analysis means to come to know your market; you may also be involved in "educating" your market about yourself, if you are a complete unknown to it. One way to assess your market is by an audience survey. (An excellent survey has been developed by Dr. Richard Semenik, chair of the marketing department at the University of Utah, Salt Lake City.)

3. Target marketing   Based on your analysis, you can pick the most attractive market segment for your organization to pursue. This is called target marketing. In 1978 Douglas Eichten, marketing director of the Guthrie Theatre, presented a marketing plan to the participants at the annual FEDAPT conference in New York City. Eichten's description of target marketing was similar to the rings of a tree, as shown on the next page. Once you decide on your target audience, you focus your entire promotional campaign on them.

If 400 people come to see a play in a 350-seat house, it's a sell-out. If 400 people come to a 2,000-seat house, it's a disaster. Don't measure success this way. Target the audience that is right for you; agree on that definition with everyone in your organization. This allows you to stop wasting energy seeking that audience whom you have not targeted.
Charles Ziff,
marketing consultant,
Ford Foundation

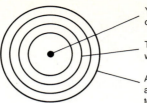

Your target audience, for example, 6 – 10-year-olds from your neighborhood, neighborhood X

The next audience, from neighborhood Y, within walking distance

An audience from another part of town, who attend the theatre there; you can work your way toward getting this audience, but it will take time

4. Establishing a timetable   Assign deadlines for various stages of the marketing process. A realistic timetable is an invaluable aid in converting your strategy into action. (Refer back to the management section of the Countdown Production Calendar, pages 242–243, for a suggested promotion timetable.)

5. Executing the program   You coordinate decisions on the marketing mix, the Four P's:

- Product—you decide what you are producing
- Price—you fix the price and set a policy
- Place (or Distribution)—you schedule the performances and services where you want them to happen
- Promotion—you begin to promote the total concept through your promotional strategies, and through your publicity campaign

6. Evaluation   Once the show has opened, you can begin to make judgments about effectiveness—i.e., did you reach your goal?—and about efficiency—i.e, how well did the marketing tools, such as the lists, work?

One way to reach your target audience and solve the distribution problem is to take your product—whether performance, workshop, or residency—right into the classroom. Performing Arts Repertory Theatre's Tom Hull is shown with students in a workshop in Irvington, New York, following a performance of *Young Tom Edison and the Magic Why.*

Economic goods and services	Marketing strategy	Performing arts
Customer-oriented	Product development	Artist-inspired
Below cost unacceptable	Pricing	Below cost acceptable
Location chosen to serve customer	Distribution	Location chosen to support arts companies
Large or moderate budget is typical	Promotion	Little or no budget is typical

Differences between marketing economic goods and services and marketing the performing arts.

Gene R. Laczniak and Patrick E. Murphy, "Marketing the Arts," Atlanta Economic Review, November-December 1977

TWO ASPECTS OF A MARKETING STRATEGY IN DETAIL: TARGET MARKETING AND PROMOTION

Target marketing and promotion are often overlooked in connection with theatre for young people. We emphasize them here because we believe excellent marketing can help further economic survival in the 1980s.

Target marketing

Target marketing is the most efficient way to market. It saves you dollars and sanity. The following chart, adapted from Michalann Hobson's Audience Development Guidelines, is published by FEDAPT. She advises marketers to adapt the guide for use in their own communities and not use it as a "blueprint."*

*The complete chart may be purchased from FEDAPT, 165 West 46th Street, New York, NY 10036.

TARGET AUDIENCE(S)	SOURCE(S)	ACCESS	POSSIBLE SALES PLANS

• Current attendees
• Past attendees
• Friends and family of current and past attendees
	• Your own mailing list (track *all* subscribers and single-ticket buyers to *all* events)	• Direct mail (personalized when possible)
		  —letter packs
		  —brochures
		  —newsletters
		  —telegram reminders
		• Lobby displays
		• Program stuffers
		• Tours
		• Seminars
		• Parties and other special events
			• Season tickets
			• Single tickets
			• Special discounts for family and friends (Prime groups to receive additional information via newsletters, seminars, etc.)

• High school teachers with families • College faculty with families	• Unions (residence addresses) • Schools (campus addresses) • School publications • Discipline associations • Book fairs	• Direct mail • Mail drops to teachers' boxes • Ads and feature stories • Personal contact • Displays	• Special discounts on season tickets for union members only given to union members in exchange for list • Imprint brochure with union tie-in • Group discounts to individual productions

• Students
  —Grades K–6
  —Grades 7–9
  —High school
	• School, drama, music, and arts clubs
	• PTA
		• Workshops in school
		• Speakers
		• Personal contacts
			• Group discounts (1 chaperone free for every 15 students)
			• Special prices/special times (Matinees must be scheduled to accommodate bus needs of area.)
			• Tours, study guides, seminars, and post-performance discussions

• Senior citizens	• Senior citizen centers • State agencies • Retirement associations	• Mail drops • Personal contact • Direct mail • Displays • Through grandchildren gimmick: one free grandparent for X number paid grandchildren	• Single ticket discounts • Group discounts • Passes (in exchange for volunteer services) • Tours, seminars, study guides, etc. • Special flyer describing senior citizen discounts or a paragraph in brochure
• Disadvantaged	• HAI (Hospital Audiences Inc.) • Half-way houses • State agencies • Local arts council • Schools	• Personal contact	• Free or very low prices (50¢) to previews or more difficult performances to sell • Set up with agency for short-notice as well as advance-notice patrons • Patron can be given opportunity to make advance reservations and then check day of performance for final availability • Add to the experience of groups brought through agencies by tours, prop demos, meet the cast, etc.

TARGET AUDIENCE(S)	SOURCE(S)	ACCESS	POSSIBLE SALES PLANS
• Women, parents, teachers, group leaders ("They buy the tickets.")	• Dept. stores • Boutiques • Food stores	• Displays • Piggy-back ads • Direct mail (bill stuffers) • Shopping bag stuffers	• Season tickets • Single tickets with special discount offers • Costume/fashion show combinations using actors as models • Craft shows, making props, etc. • $5.00 gift certificate from store with each subscription purchased—theatre pays store for each certificate issued • Food stores: special discount offer in bag stuffer, limited to a period of time that coincides with something store itself may be offering (e.g., a special on peanuts and peanut butter when your production is *Charlie Brown*)
	• Clubs, civic, social, religious	• Personal contact • Speakers at meetings	• Season tickets • Rebate to club for each subscription sold by club • Group discounts
	• Beauty parlors • Doctors' offices (any other waiting room situations)	• Scrapbooks of newspaper clippings • Brochures about the theatre: place brochures in pocket at back of scrapbook; convert to single-ticket flyers after subscription campaign is over, after first show opens	• Season tickets • Single tickets
• Children	• Schools • Youth centers • Churches, temples • Fast-food places • Ice cream and candy stores • Saturday-morning TV • Libraries	• Bulk distribution • PSAs (public service announcements) • Displays • Billboards	• Special matinee programs, workshops, tours, games • Let kids sell to their parents—gimmicks that require each to participate: balloons with free giveaway chits inside; lobby displays of children's art; contests; banners made by an art class, etc.

TARGET AUDIENCE(S)	SOURCE(S)	ACCESS	POSSIBLE SALES PLANS
• Tourists	• Information Bureaus • Chamber of Commerce • State Department of Commerce/Tourism • Hotel associations • Restaurant associations	• Displays • Personal contact • Special tie-ins with restaurants and hotels • Scrapbooks	• Single tickets • Special flyer with *maps,* schedule, prices, charge information, large phone number, emphasis on ease of ordering
• Newcomers	• Real estate agents • Newcomers clubs	• Bulk distribution through outlets	• Single tickets with introductory discount offer (Some newcomers clubs will allow a letter to be included with flyer or brochure.)
• Corporate and business employees and families	• Directors of personnel or recreation • Small business owners • Chamber of Commerce • Local business association	• Personal contact • Minipreviews at offices, plants, or malls (lunchtime) • Displays • Speakers at meetings (Note: All corporate materials should be simple, easy to follow, with clear explanation of benefits and uncomplicated price structures.)	• Corporate coupon plan: discount coupons sold in minimum of 25 to business to be resold to employees or given as gifts from business to clients; prime benefit is to get them and their children there at least once, with the best experience possible before and after! • Group sales discount on single tickets • Discount or free passes in return for poster displays • Tours, parties, meet the cast, corporate picnics, etc.
• Patrons of sports events	• On site at games	• Announcement at half time • Acting company in parades • Pennants with campaign slogan • Program stuffer • Combination promotions with teams—gimmick heaven! (Get team members to come to a production—announce to audience that they are there, etc.)	• Season tickets • Single tickets • Institutional image-building (Special discount chits, to be redeemed on either season or single tickets, given in return for permission to hand out at game)

Promotion: an analysis of its six components: personal selling, advertising, direct mail, incentives, atmospherics, publicity

The six components of promotion are: (1) personal selling; (2) advertising; (3) direct-mail campaign (including subscription); (4) incentives; (5) atmospherics; (6) publicity (including press releases, photo releases, feature stories, stunts).

The first task in your promotion campaign is to select a graphic look, including an attractive logo of your name, and a look for the particular show you are producing. Have a professional design the logo and look; make sure you are comfortable with it, as you will be living with it on a daily basis. Does it convey what you want it to convey?

The second task is to find a creative, catchy slogan that will focus the market's attention on you. In 1981 Performing Arts Repertory Theatre (PART), in its New York City season of performances for the theatregoing public, chose as its slogan "For the PART of you that will always be young." The campaign was coordinated by the Great Scott agency, and the design colors were bright green, black, and white. This slogan appeared on every brochure, letter, poster, and advertisement (see page 296).

Once you have your slogan, you can use it again and again to reinforce your image in each of the following elements of promotion.

Promotion: personal selling   Personal selling is the most effective type of marketing. People buy from people. Personal selling should happen any place you can set it up: door to door, at parties, at luncheons such as Rotary Club meetings, at schools, churches, temples, and on the telephone. Wherever a piece of your targeted market might gather is the place to do personal selling. The approach can be the hard sell or the soft sell, can be lighthearted (at a Rotary lunch) or a serious discussion (in front of the school board). The important thing is to be specific and clear about what you have to offer.

Promotion: advertising   Eric Hamburger, marketing director for the American Conservatory Theatre (ACT) in San Francisco, wrote a radio ad for *Romeo and Juliet*. The listener hears a soft but strong male voice speaking over the sound of birds and romantic piano music in the background: "Verona . . . a summer night . . . eyes meet . . . and love blooms . . ." Hamburger tells the story of a messenger who came to the theatre to pick up this ad copy for the radio station. He read it and said, "Wow, is this like TV?" Hamburger replied, "No, it's a little different; it's a live production." The young man said, "I sure would like to see that," and Hamburger filled in his ticket order form then and there. "This is a person who never would have been attracted to ACT's classical image, but that ad made *Romeo and Juliet* accessible to him."

You must believe your theatre is doing something terribly important. This belief will translate into drive, energy and a commitment which will show up in bigger ticket sales, better grantsmanship, and smart politics.
Joseph Melillo,
professional marketer, fundraiser, and consultant

Different logotypes, or logos, for eight very different organizations. Your logo identifies *you*—be sure it reflects the qualities you wish to project.

THE ACTING COMPANY 10th Anniversary Year

420 West 42nd Street
Times Square Station
P.O. Box 898
New York, New York 10108
Telephone: (212) 564-3510
Cable Address: ACTINGCO, NEW YORK

John Houseman, Producing Artistic Director
Michael Kahn, Artistic Director
Alan Schneider, Artistic Director
Margot Harley, Executive Producer

Mary Beth Carroll, General Manager

Incorporated as Group I Acting Co. Inc., a Not-For-Profit National Touring Company

THE CHILDREN'S THEATRE FESTIVAL

A professional project produced by the Department of Drama, University of Houston Central Campus
Houston, Texas 77004 (713-749-1427)

LONG WHARF THEATRE

222 Sargent Dr., New Haven, Conn. 06511 Exit 46 Conn. Tpke.

PROGRAMS FOR CHILDREN AND YOUTH

Children's Programs
Alliance for Arts Education
John F. Kennedy Center
Washington, D.C. 20566

Yellow Brick Road Shows

CHILDREN'S THEATRE COMPANY AND SCHOOL

The Two Penny Circus
R.R.#1, Barre
Vermont 05641
(802) 476-7873

Williamstown Theatre Festival

Williamstown Theatre Festival
1979
The 25th Year

P.O. BOX 517 WILLIAMSTOWN, MASS. 01267

The advertising campaign may be the most expensive item in your promotional budget. If you were advertising in New York City in 1981, for example, a one-quarter-page ad in the Sunday *New York Times* cost $5,000. Because advertising is so expensive, you must consider several points, based on the survey and analysis of your market:

- Which media does my targeted market use the most? TV, radio, newspapers, magazines, or others, such as billboards?
- How frequently should I place the ads, and with how much lead time before the event?
- How far will my advertising budget stretch?

You will create your own advertising plan, but here are a few ideas that work:

- Print media: If you are on a limited budget, approach a large corporation that buys a lot of newspaper ads to donate some of their ad space to you. At the bottom of your printed ad you give them gracious and thankful credit.
- Radio ads: It is better to buy less of more expensive time during "drive time"—7 to 9 A.M. and 4 to 7 P.M.—than more time at less desirable hours. If you have a star or local celebrity who will tape the ad for you, this will enhance your image.
- Television: Television time is *very* expensive but a huge image booster. Your approach here might be to do a slide and script public service announcement (PSA, which technically comes under publicity, because it is free). As a public service, radio and television stations will do brief commercials at no charge to the not-for-profit organization, if you supply them with the script and, in the case of TV, slides or a videotape. The PSA needs to be brief, to the point, and with all the pertinent information: name of play, date, time, place of performance, price of ticket, where to buy tickets, and some idea about the event that makes it irresistible. The following is an example of a 30-second PSA:

Performing Arts Repertory Theatre presents *The Midnight Ride of Paul Revere*, a rousing musical for the entire family, at the Martin Theatre, 108 East 89th Street in Manhattan, starting Thursday, March 19, at 7:30, Friday at 7:30, Saturday at 2 and 7:30 and Sunday at 1 and 3. All tickets $5. For information, call 595-7500. *The Midnight Ride of Paul Revere*. Don't miss it. Call 595-7500.

Promotion: direct mail   The two components of the direct mail drive are: (1) your mailing piece, either a self-mailer or a package, and (2) your lists.

A *self-mailer* is a brochure that folds and can be mailed without an envelope. All the necessary information is included in it.

A *package* consists of the following:

1. Outside envelope, with: (a) your slogan or list of benefits of why the customer should buy your product; (b) return address and logo; (c) stamp or postage meter (but statistics prove that stamps solicit better). With the outside envelope your first job is to get the customer to open it.
2. The brochure, which creates excitement about the theatre, with professional photographs and appealing colors. Inside the brochure must be your tag headline again, list of benefits, description of events, prices, and how to order.
3. Cover letter, two pages at the most, written by the artistic director or a celebrity, to reinforce the brochure. One-sentence paragraphs

A front cover is the first graphic a prospective buyer sees. The cover must persuade the prospect to *open* the self-mailer and start reading, so that you can sell the product. The Children's Theatre, Minneapolis.

UNLOCK THE DOORS TO WONDERLAND

The Children's Theatre
1981-82 Season

KIDNAPPED IN LONDON
PUSS IN BOOTS
THE LITTLE MATCH GIRL
THE COOKIE JAR
PHANTOM OF THE OPERA
ALICE IN WONDERLAND

1979-1980 Season

Mud Weavings
written and directed by Phyllis Weil

Mud Weavings, MTC's newest production, is based on the poetry of artistic director Phyllis Weil. Through verbal and visual metaphor, **Mud Weavings** takes a wide-eyed view of the ever changing world, a world where everyday phenomena, a sunrise or an ocean wave, are seen as magical to the child in all of us. **Mud Weavings** evokes the unexpected: a mountain inside a paper bag, a sonnet in a strawberry. This colorful production leaps with boundless imagination from mud puddles to freckles, dandelions to waltzes, feathers to infinity. Accompanied by a variety of live and electronic sound sources including piano, guitar, banjo, flute, and synthesizer, the company members sing, dance, juggle, mime and act their way through this joyous and unique presentation.

Musical Score by Steven Radecke
Production Supervised by Jacobina Caro
Costume and Scenic Design by Branislav Tomich and
Nickolas Kryah

Arm In Arm
from the book by Remy Charlip

Metro Theater Circus again presents, **Arm In Arm,** its highly acclaimed adaptation of the book* by noted author and artist, Remy Charlip. **Arm In Arm** is a fantasy, evoking images of wonder and delight in kaleidoscopic succession. The performance is about the connections between words and rhythms, movement and pictures, sounds and colors. Using silk banners, bright scarves, puppets, mobiles, confetti, and other strong visual elements, the company transforms the drawings, sayings, and stories from the book into theater, dance and music. Arm In Arm is at once humorous and tender, energetic and fanciful; thoroughly engaging to children and adults on a variety of levels.

Music by Steven Radecke
Adapted from the book by members of The Metro Theater Circus under the Co-direction of Jane Ekman and Phyllis Weil.

* 1968 By Remy Charlip. Published by Parents' Magazine Press.
Performances presented through special arrangement with
Arthur D. Zinberg, 11 E. 44 Street, New York, New York 10017.

The M... Progr...

Performance
The six memb...
gives a perfor...
by stimulatin...
for young pe...
and College. T...
approach to ...

Classroom
Each of the ...
session follo...
is to encour...
or her own ...
dramatics...

Study M...
Metro The...
through th...
school pri...
summarie...
other info...
in the Me...

Teache...
The Circ...
music to ...
carry-o...
educati...
creativi...

Res...
The M...
two w...
progr...
organ...
teach...
Since...
expo...
curri...
The ...
thro...
Arts

are effective; the colors of the printing should match your overall color scheme.
4. Coded order form, which states the "What's in it for me" idea—e.g., "Yes, I am ordering now for my whole family and saving 32 percent." The order form needs to be crystal clear so as not to be confusing. This form is the one traditionally most referred to, read and reread.
5. Return envelope. If you can afford a BRE, a business reply envelope, use it.

Statistics have shown that packages pull better in direct mail than brochures.

The second component of your direct mail campaign is your lists. The following are suggestions on how to build your lists:

• Personal contacts; the name and address of everyone you know who is a potential ticket buyer; borrow their Christmas card lists

An example of a season brochure for a company that *tours*. The focus is general because the purpose is to get a prospective sponsor interested enough to call or write the producer for more information.

Three handbills; the chief function of each is to promote and sell productions. Theatre Beyond Words in Toronto had its handbill designed by the art department of the University of Toronto. The Paper Bag handbill is in the form of a mask, with eyes and mouth cut out. Although "The Imagination Celebration" is free to the public, the Festival must sell itself in order to attract audiences.

for a mailing to "the whole family," if you are holding public performances.

- Approach local groups and service clubs, civic organizations, other theatres with youth programs, museums, symphony youth concerts, PTAs, AAUW's, Junior Leagues, and ask to borrow their lists. If, for a competitive reason, a group does not want you to see or to keep their list, they can do a mailing for you, at your cost.
- Collect programs of other events that are similar to yours. The programs may list contributors, patrons, donors, interested people. This can become a list with the help of the telephone book.
- Collect names of your single-ticket buyers (adults or teenagers) by having cards for them to fill out in the theatre before the curtain goes up.
- Leave space on your order form to say, "I have a friend(s) who would like more information about you. The name is _____."
- Run a raffle with coupons that request name, address, and telephone, and give away a prize at the opening performance. The community thinks it is entering a raffle, which it is, but you are collecting names for your mailing list.
- Piggyback mailing: interest the local department store, children's bookstore, or whatever business has a good targeted list, and ask the business to include your coded order form in a billing or promotional mailing. "Sell" mailings are statistically better than billings, in that billings produce a "psychological low," and your piece may get ignored in that moment.
- School directories: names and addresses of all students.
- You can buy mailing lists of faculty, administrators, etc., by name from several reputable list houses. We have included the names and addresses of two of these in Appendix 3.

No direct-mail campaign should be run without *coding.* Coding tells you what lists work and what lists do not work. A code must appear in a corner of the reply form. The designer designs the brochure with the reply form on the back of the mailing-label space.

Say you are printing a total of 10,000 brochures and you have five lists you want to use:

List source	Size	Code	Printer prints
High school teachers	3,000	E	ABCDE
Local arts council list of "sponsors interested in theatre for young people"	2,000	D	ABCD
List of patrons, borrowed from local dance company	1,000	C	ABC
List of patrons, borrowed from local museum	1,500	B	AB
House list, previous customers, etc.	2,500	A	A

right and opposite page: The two inside panels of a subscription brochure for The Children's Theatre, Minneapolis. It is an excellent example of an attractive, simple, easy-to-understand subscription brochure. This is a subscription campaign selling a company's own productions at its own theatre.

Subscribe!
Discover where Imagination leads.

This year buy a season ticket to The Children's Theatre Company and Discover where Imagination leads. On the wings of fantasy your family and friends will soar through time—transported into the magical, delightful world of young people's literature.

Discover Savings!

Purchase a subscription to the 1980-81 season and see **6 Shows for the Price of 4**, a **30% Savings** equivalent to **2 Free Shows** and up to **$12.75 Off the Single Ticket Price per Subscription.** Dare to Adventure—Share exhilarating, wondrous, touching experiences with a medley of mythical and true-to-life characters. The Children's Theatre Company's fabulous 1980-81 season is **Just a Subscription Away!**

Discover Extras too...

Subscriber **Newsletters** describe upcoming CTC events, outline additional benefits/discounts, and prepare your family for each visit to the Theatre.

This past season, subscribers greeted such luminaries as Dr. Seuss and children's book illustrator Nancy Ekholm Burkert at **Open Houses** and **Lecture/Symposiums.**

Thought-provoking, insightful **Discussion/Demonstrations** moderated by the Theatre's professional staff enhance performances.

Unable to make your season ticket performance? We'll gladly **Exchange Your Tickets** up to 24 hours prior to curtain time for another performance of the same show.

If season tickets are lost, stolen or forgotten, **Subscriber's Insurance** arranges for you to attend your performance.

Subscribers have the first opportunity to purchase **Extra Tickets** to the season's holiday favorite and traditional sell-out **Cinderella.**

1980-81 Season Poster.

Lifetime Renewal privileges assure subscribers that they may retain the same seats, performance date and time from year to year.

A Free 1980-81 Season Poster, created by resident artist Steven Rydberg, is CTC's gift to you.

6 Shows for the Price of 4. You Save Up to $12.75 on Single Ticket Price. A 30% Discount.

By ordering now you save:

	Single Tickets		Cinderella		All 6 Shows	Season Ticket Price	You Save
Adults	5 x $6.95	+	$7.50	=	$42.25	$29.50	$12.75
Children	5 x $4.95	+	$5.95	=	$30.70	$22.00	$ 8.70
Students	5 x $4.95	+	$5.95	=	$30.70	$22.00	$ 8.70
Senior Citizens	5 x $4.95	+	$5.95	=	$30.70	$22.00	$ 8.70

Tell the printer to print ABCDE on the first 3,000 brochures and then strike off the E; print ABCD on the next 2,000 and then strike off the D, and so on. You then mail the first 3,000 brochures to the high school teachers, the next 2,000 to the arts council list, and so on. When you receive an order form with ABCDE on it, you know that the order came from someone on the high school teachers list, etc.

Promotion: the subscription campaign The subscription campaign is executed six to eight months before the start of the season in order to sell a series of plays at a subscription rate. A good subscription base

The Children's Theatre Company 1980-81 Season Preview

THE ADVENTURES OF HUCKLEBERRY FINN *Mark Twain*

On a raft, summer days are hot as smoke and sweet as magnolia, but there is always human-kind to reckon with. Huck, with the runaway slave Jim, sets off down the Mississippi late one night—but what they escape *from* sometimes seems a might better than what they get *into*. Join us for Mark Twain's classic American adventure.

Sept. 20—Nov. 16

THE STORY OF BABAR, THE LITTLE ELEPHANT *Jean de Brunhoff*

Jean de Brunhoff—courtesy of Random House Books

Babar ventures away from the great forest and is befriended by a kind and generous Old Lady "always fond of little elephants." To the delight of his cousins Celeste and Arthur, Babar discovers refined city pleasures: elegant clothes, French pastries, and flashy motorcars. A beloved, charming musical tale.

(rights pending)

Oct. 18—Feb. 15

CINDERELLA *Charles Perrault*

Aboard a swiftly moving pumpkin carriage, the once forlorn and soot-covered Cinderella is trans-formed into a resplendent beauty through the magic of her fairy godmother. The traditional English panto comes to life with outrageous humor, glittering spectacle and Victorian carolers celebrating the return of this rags-to-riches favorite. "...a genuine not-to-be-missed holiday treat." Minneapolis Tribune.

Nov. 29—Dec. 28

THE THREE MUSKETEERS *Alexandre Dumas*

"En Garde!" A swashbuckling trio of quick-witted, keen-bladed musketeers, joined by the hot-blooded D'Artagnan embroil themselves in intrigue, romance and the deadly machinations of the sinister Cardinal Richelieu. A glorious adventure set in the international court of Louis XIII.

Jan. 23—April 3

THE CLOWN OF GOD *Tomie de Paola*

Tomie de Paola

A poor little juggler grows up in Renaissance Italy clowning first on dusty peasant streets and later in the marble courts of royalty. With age Giovanni's fame dwindles. Sneered at and abandoned by faces he'd once made laugh, the old man finds peace in the simplicity of a child's smile.

Feb. 28—April 5

Pick Your Favorite Time:

1980-81 Series	Huckleberry Finn	Babar	Cinderella	Three Musketeers	Clown of God	Land of Oz
A Friday 7:30	Sept. 26	Jan. 9	Dec. 5	Feb. 20	March 27	May 1
B Friday 7:30	Oct. 3	Feb. 13	Dec. 12	April 3	March 13	May 8
C Saturday 11:00	Oct. 4	Oct. 25	Dec. 6	Jan. 31	March 28	May 2
D Saturday 11:00	Oct. 11	Nov. 8	Dec. 20	Feb. 14	April 4	May 9
E Saturday 2:00	Sept. 20	Oct. 18	Nov. 29	Jan. 24	Feb. 28	April 18
F Saturday 2:00	Sept. 27	Oct. 25	Dec. 6	Jan. 31	March 14	April 25
G Saturday 2:00	Oct. 4	Nov. 8	Dec. 13	Feb. 14	March 28	May 2
H Saturday 2:00	Oct. 11	Jan. 10	Dec. 20	March 7	April 4	May 9
I Saturday 7:30	Sept. 20	Oct. 18	Nov. 29	Jan. 24	Feb. 28	April 18
J Sunday 2:00	Sept. 21	Oct. 19	Nov. 30	Jan. 25	March 1	April 26
K Sunday 2:00	Sept. 28	Nov. 2	Dec. 7	Feb. 8	March 8	May 3
L Sunday 2:00	Oct. 5	Jan. 11	Dec. 14	March 15	April 5	May 17
M Sunday 5:00	Sept. 28	Oct. 19	Nov. 30	Feb. 8	March 8	April 26
N Sunday 5:00	Oct. 26	Feb. 1	Dec. 7	March 15	April 5	May 3

Graphic Design/Evans & Smith

Pick Your Favorite Location:

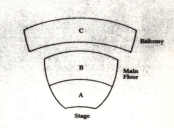

C — Balcony

B — Main Floor

A

Stage

To Order: Fill in Season Renewal Ticket Order Form.
Mail order form, payment, self-addressed stamped envelope to:

The Children's Theatre Company
2400 Third Avenue South
Minneapolis, MN. 55404
(612) 874-0400

The Childre[n]
1980-81 Seas[on]

Name _____
Address _____
City _____
Phone (Home) _____
☐ I am a new Subs[criber]
1. Series

1st choice   2nd choice

Current Subscribe[r]
To reserve the same seats you h[ave]
from the back of your season ti[cket]
3. Number of Seaso[n]

Adults
Children (17 and under)
*Student
Senior
Total Season Tickets

*Students must enclose copy of [ ]

4. Payment by:
☐ Check   ☐ Mas[ter]
Make checks payabl[e]
Card # _____
Expiration Date _____
Cardholder Signatu[re]
Season tickets will be [ ]

---

can be the backbone of a theatre's budget. Danny Newman, a genius at subscription, has written the definitive book, *Subscribe Now!* We recommend it in its entirety, as it is the complete blueprint on "How to do it."*

The success of any direct mail campaign is in how carefully and skillfully you select the lists and how specific and exciting your printed message is.

Promotion: incentives   The incentive most often used in theatre promotion is in the subscription campaign: "Subscribe Now and Save 32%!" or "Five plays for the price of three!" In a fund-raising campaign

*Subscribe Now! Building Arts Audiences Through Dynamic Subscription Promotion (New York: Theatre Communications Group, 1977).

it is: "Give $50 and get this designer tote bag free!" You need to decide the form of the incentive, the amount of the incentive, and the timing—when the customer receives the incentive.

Promotion: atmospherics   The warmth of your lobby, the cleanliness of the restrooms, the acoustics of the theatre, even the clothes the box office staff wears, all promote or detract from your theatre. These elements are promotional atmospherics. The more you can do to create an inviting, fun, nonthreatening, easy-to-enjoy atmosphere, the better you are promoting your total image.

Promotion: publicity and its four useful tools: press release, photo release, feature story, stunts   Publicity plays a very important function for the theatre. According to Richard O'Brien, well-known Broadway press agent, "To publicize well, you must touch all the bases; you must make every effort to reach every possible press outlet available to you. . . . The basic principles of publicity are to (1) become thoroughly familiar with whatever it is you wish to publicize—the more you know about something, the more potential news there is in it. (2) Decide where to publicize this news. (3) Do it."*

But one of the disadvantages publicity has as it relates to young people's theatre in the United States is the general reluctance of the press to cover theatre for young audiences. When PART's *Daniel Boone* by playwright Thomas Babe opened at Town Hall in New York for school-age children, the producers believed they had an excellent news item: Famous playwright writes play for children, produced by a prominent young people's theatre company. The New York press was singularly uninterested. Three weeks later, when Babe's adult play *Salt Lake City Skyline* opened at Joseph Papp's Public Theatre, all the papers covered it. This is one of the frustrations that managers of young people's theatre have in dealing with the press. However, the press is very important to a theatre's future; a manager always needs to be optimistic and to persevere.

Publicity: the press release. The press release is short, usually no more than a page. The reason for this is that no one wants to read more than a page, and the newspaper editor will not want to print more than that. In writing the press release, remember the five W's: who, what, when, where, and why.

Ellen Rodman, a former reporter for the *New York Times,* said in a 1981 interview, "You must send the press release to the right person. Call the newspaper and find out the name of the person to send it to— and spell the name right. If you don't spell it right, the reporter will think, 'Well! They don't read my byline' and may throw your release in the waste basket. You're dealing with egos, remember. Another

following page: Sections of two subscription brochures, one from the Detroit Youtheatre, the other from the Emelin Theatre, Mamaroneck, New York. The Wiggle Club is a very successful component of the Detroit theatre's marketing plan. Both these brochures advertise many different productions presented during a season. These are subscription campaigns by performing arts centers selling other theatre companies' productions.

*Publicity: How to Get It (New York: Barnes & Noble, 1977).

Thought you were too young to join a club? Not if it's

The Wiggle Club

...An introduction to "theatre-going" for boys and girls ages 3 to 8 years. Five specially selected shows designed for pre-schoolers PLUS • Your own Membership Pass Card • An Official Wiggle Club Button AND...a special "Graduation Certificate" (when you turn at least 5 years of age) which is also a ticket to you first Big Kids Show—as our guest!

WIGGLE CLUB MEMBERSHIPS: $10.00

These programs have been carefully selected for our "first-timers" to ensure a positive and fun experience in the performing arts. Although an hour in length, each show is composed of three or four 10-20 minute segments designed to hold the attention and excitement of our younger guests. In addition, the theatre is never totally darkened. For further show description, see the listings inside.

1981-1982 WIGGLE CLUB SHOWS

October 31 — CASPER & JASPER
Not Jest Jugglers, Specials Series
December 12, 1981 — CHRISTMAS ALL OVER THE PLACE
The Paper Bag Players, Musical/Play Series
January 23, 1982 — TOM GLAZER—LIVE!
Folk Sing-along, Specials Series
April 10, 1982 — BUNNY BUSINESS
Bob Brown Puppet Productions, Puppet Series
May 8, 1982 — BO-DINO
The "Dean" of Clowns, Specials Series

DETROIT YOUTHEATRE

The Detroit Institute of Arts
5200 Woodward Avenue
Detroit, Michigan 48202

Youtheatre '81-'82:
More Fun than a Three-Ring Circus!

SUPER STUFF FOR KIDS

The No Elephant Circus

Dinosaurs, Puppets and Picasso

Your choice of any seven (7) performances for only $17. Buy a SUPER PASS FOR A SUPER KID. Also good for SUPER PARENTS. You can't beat the price and proximity to home!

THE NO ELEPHANT CIRCUS   Oct. 11
Juggling clowns, magic, havoc and fun (11 a.m. and 2 p.m.)

DINOSAURS, PUPPETS AND PICASSO   Oct. 16
Music, art, theatre (11 a.m. and 2 p.m.)

THE CORNER STORE   Oct. 30
A variety show. Music, song and dance (2 p.m.)

MR. JIGGS   Nov. 27
Champ of the Chimpanzees (11 a.m. and 1 p.m.)

SPAGHETTI   Dec. 4
A fantasy-filled adventure (2 p.m.)

BEAUTY AND THE BEAST   Jan. 2
Nicolo Marionettes (11 a.m. 1 p.m. and 3 p.m.)

THE MAGICAL IMAGINATION SHOW   Jan. 22
Comedy sketches with outrageous characters (11 a.m. and 2 p.m.)

JACK AND THE BEANSTALK   Feb. 21-22
Nicolo Marionettes (11 a.m. 1 p.m. and 3 p.m.)

Note: While all pass holders are guaranteed seats, it is suggested that you call 24 hours in advance to confirm reservations.

(The Emelin asks your cooperation in limiting food and beverages to the lobby area only.)

FILL OUT AND MAIL TODAY!
SUBSCRIBE NOW!!

Because our seating capacity is limited, reservations will be honored in the order they are received.

Please send me the following subscriptions:

CABARET (3)
Subscriptions
(Circle 7 p.m. or 10 p.m. for Brubeck)   @ $36 each $ TOTAL
CHAMBER MUSIC (6)
Orchestra subscriptions
Mezzanine subscriptions   @ $60 each $
DANCE (5)   @ $56 each $
Subscriptions
THEATRE (3)
Subscriptions   for   Oct. 8, Jan. 7, April 28   @ $45 each $
                              Oct. 9, Jan. 8, April 29
FRIDAY NIGHT FILMS (7)
Picture passes   @ $36 each $
JAZZ AND STUFF (4)
Subscriptions   @ $15 each $
ORPHEUS CHAMBER ORCHESTRA (3)
Subscriptions   @ $36 each $
SUPER STUFF FOR KIDS (7)
Super Stuff passes   @ $30 each $
LIGHT OPERA (3)
Adult subscriptions   @ $17 each $
Children subscriptions
Circle Series: 8:30 or 2:30 p.m.   @ $25 each $
PAPER BAG PLAYERS (10)   @ $18 each $
December 27, 28, 29 30, 31 (Circle date)
        11 a.m. and 2 p.m. (Circle time)
Single tickets   @ $5.50 each $

TOTAL REMITTANCE $

Enclosed find my check for $ _____ made payable to the Emelin Theatre. Library Lane, Mamaroneck, New York 10543. I have enclosed a business size, stamped, self-addressed envelope for return of tickets. I understand that my cancelled check is my receipt, there are no refunds, and that all programs are subject to change.

NAME

ADDRESS

CITY, STATE, ZIP

PHONE (Day)

(Evening)

These performances have received assistance in part by the Westchester Arts Fund of the Council for the Arts in Westchester, supported by corporate contributions and the County of Westchester.
These performances have also been made possible with assistance from the New York State Council on the Arts.
The Chamber Music and Dance series are supported by a grant from the National Endowment For The Arts.

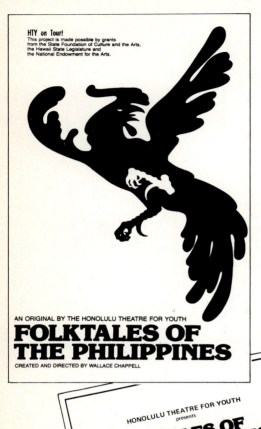

HTY on Tour!
This project is made possible by grants
from the State Foundation of Culture and the Arts,
the Hawaii State Legislature and
the National Endowment for the Arts.

AN ORIGINAL BY THE HONOLULU THEATRE FOR YOUTH
FOLKTALES OF THE PHILIPPINES
CREATED AND DIRECTED BY WALLACE CHAPPELL

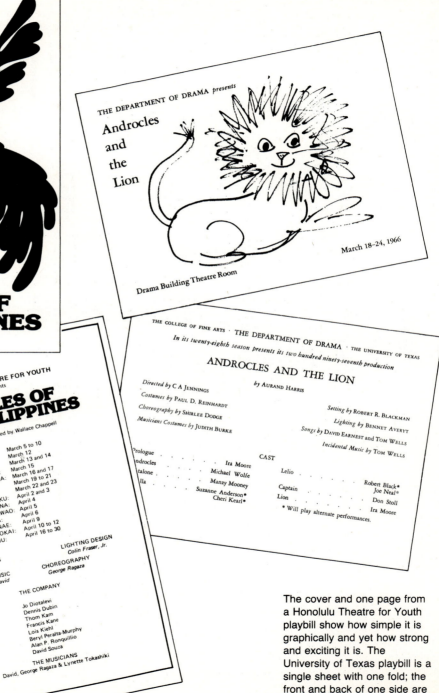

THE DEPARTMENT OF DRAMA *presents*
Androcles
and
the
Lion

March 18–24, 1966

Drama Building Theatre Room

THE COLLEGE OF FINE ARTS · THE DEPARTMENT OF DRAMA · THE UNIVERSITY OF TEXAS
In its twenty-eighth season presents its two hundred ninety-seventh production

ANDROCLES AND THE LION
by AURAND HARRIS

Directed by C A JENNINGS
Costumes by PAUL D. REINHARDT
Choreography by SHIRLEE DODGE
Musicians Costumes by JUDITH BURKE

Setting by ROBERT R. BLACKMAN
Lighting by BENNET AVERYT
Songs by DAVID EARNEST *and* TOM WELLS
Incidental Music by TOM WELLS

CAST

Prologue
Androcles . . . . Ira Moore   Lelio
Catalone . . . . Michael Wolfe
Illa . . . . Manzy Mooney   Captain . . . . . Robert Black*
                          Suzanne Anderson*   Joe Neal*
                          Cheri Kearl*   Lion . . . . Don Stoll
                                                                   Ira Moore
                                   * *Will play alternate performances.*

HONOLULU THEATRE FOR YOUTH
presents
FOLKTALES OF THE PHILIPPINES

created and directed by Wallace Chappell

HILO:	March 5 to 10
KA'U:	March 12
KONA:	March 13 and 14
KOHALA:	March 15
KAMUELA:	March 16 and 17
KAUAI:	March 19 to 21
LANAI:	March 22 and 23
WAILUKU:	April 2 and 3
LAHAINA:	April 4
MAKAWAO:	April 5
HANA:	April 6
KEANAE:	April 9
MOLOKAI:	April 10 to 12
OAHU:	April 16 to 30

LIGHTING DESIGN
Colin Fraser, Jr.

SET & COSTUMES
Joseph Dodd

CHOREOGRAPHY
George Ragaza

MUSIC
David

THE COMPANY

Jo Diotalevi
Dennis Dubin
Thom Kam
Francis Kane
Lois Kiehl
Beryl Peralta-Murphy
Alan P. Ronquillio
David Souza

THE MUSICIANS
David, George Ragaza & Lynette Tokashiki

3

The cover and one page from a Honolulu Theatre for Youth playbill show how simple it is graphically and yet how strong and exciting it is. The University of Texas playbill is a single sheet with one fold; the front and back of one side are shown. Even if the budget is low, a simple but elegant design can be effective.

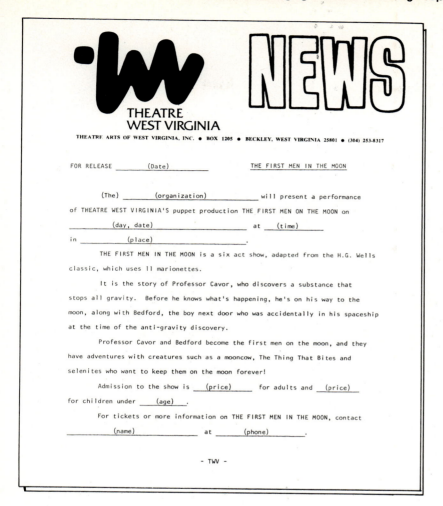

The press release must answer the five W's: who, what, when, where, and why.

....

Newspapers cannot really devote space to children's theatre because 1) children do not buy newspapers; 2) children's groups do not take costly ads; 3) not every person who buys a newspaper has children or an interest in children's events. Space is at a premium. A reporter might review a play for children and the review might never appear because it gets bumped for a "more important" piece that comes up or a piece of "hard news." That is a fact of American life, and you have to learn to deal with the system if you want to deal professionally with the American press.
Ellen Rodman,
director, Children's Informational Services, National Broadcasting Company, Inc.

....

point about press releases: Get them in on *time.* The day before is not 'on time.' Send the release at least two weeks before the event with a note; call the next week. If the reporter comes to a performance, make sure (1) tickets are at the box office in the right name, (2) give the reporter the best seat in the house, but on the aisle, not in the middle of a bunch of kids. And most importantly: never, never, never sit behind the reporter during the performance and say 'How did you like it?' Never put a reporter on the spot. The simple approach is best; the key to good press/theatre relations is maturity and professionalism."

Publicity: the photo release. The most important thing to remember about photographs is that if they are taken by a professional, they will help your work to look professional. If they are taken by an amateur, your work may look shoddy. One picture is indeed worth a thousand

The press photograph must make the reader *want* to share in the fun or the excitement shown. These two photos illustrate very different kinds of productions.

above left: Performing Arts Repertory Theatre: *Noah and the Whale, Jonah and the Ark.* Actors (clockwise from top): Marsha Kramer, Richard Culler, Cheryl Bayer, Henry Winkler (before his *Happy Days* television success), Don Potter. Created and directed by Rhoda Levine.

above right: Actors Theatre of Louisville: *A Full-Length Portrait of America* by Paul D'Andrea. Actors (stage right to left): Dierk Toporzysek, Susan Kingsley.

Photo by David S. Talbott

words, but newspaper editors are reluctant to use an unprofessional, badly lit, low-contrast photograph. Before you send a photograph to an editor, caption it, with the name of person(s) appearing in the photograph, the event, the photographer's name, your name and telephone number. Without a caption the photograph is worthless.

Publicity: the feature story. When you place a feature story, you have done a good day's work. The feature story covers some aspect of your theatre—an opening, a new play, a new tour—and usually includes photographs with the article. The publicist does not write the feature story; a newspaper reporter writes it, based on an interview with the theatre's director or staff. When Theatre Calgary wanted to call attention to their production of *Dracula*, they designed a promotion with the local bloodmobile, and this promotion became a feature story. The *Dracula* actors were on hand at the bloodmobile and donated blood; the bloodmobile nurses were at the performances of *Dracula* in uniform. In fact, several people fainted at the performances; the nurses treated them, and the theatre got terrific publicity.

Publicity: stunts. When Betty Lee Hunt was the press agent for *Grease*, before *Grease* had caught on and become the longest running play on Broadway, the producers begged her to come up with a publicity stunt. One of the many ideas she had was the "Sneaker Matinee." Anyone wearing sneakers to a matinee got a 50-percent discount on the ticket price. The gimmick mushroomed; soon hundreds of teenagers were standing on the ticket line in 1950s costumes, wearing their sneakers. Word of mouth spread about how much fun *Grease* was, and the show caught on.

This is just one example of a stunt. Stunts can be as wild or as exciting as you care to make them. However, keep your overall objective in mind: getting warm bodies in the seats of the theatre. If a stunt doesn't directly or indirectly sell tickets, it isn't working.

Your value as a theatre is tied up in your product. How you promote your image through paid promotions and free publicity determines the health of your public relations, which is the coordination of the entire image of your theatre.

This photograph and the events connected with it would make an appealing and effective feature story. Vilma Bufman, producer of Story Theatre at the Parker Playhouse in Fort Lauderdale, is handing a ticket to the first subscriber, Lee Feldman, who is accompanied by his mother, Lois.

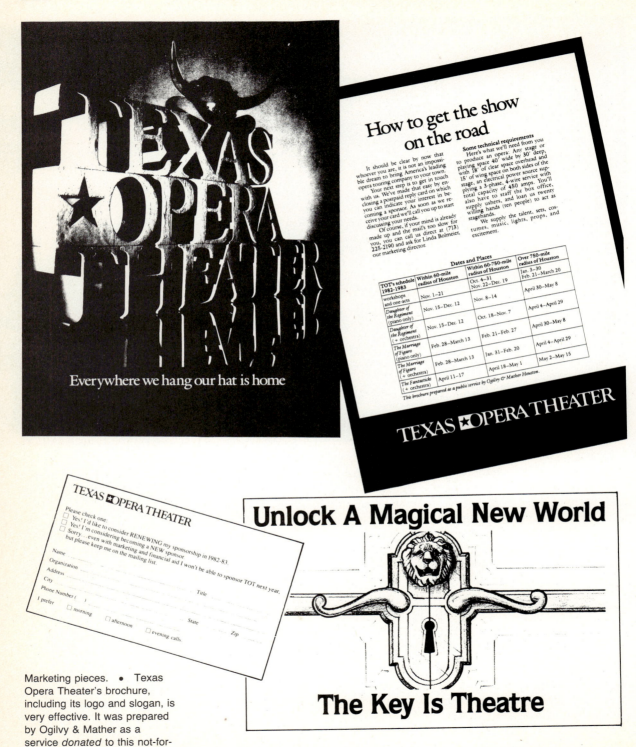

Marketing pieces. • Texas Opera Theater's brochure, including its logo and slogan, is very effective. It was prepared by Ogilvy & Mather as a service *donated* to this not-for-profit theatre. • A strong

Yes, I would like to order Guthrie Gift Certificates.

NAME _____
ADDRESS _____
CITY _____ STATE _____ ZIP _____
PHONE NO. _____
Qty _____ Gift Certificates at $9.45 / $7.45 / $4.95 (circle price desired)
TOTAL ENCLOSED _____ Check payable to The Guthrie Theater OR charge to:
_____ American Express _____ Diners Club _____ Master Charge
_____ BankAmericard _____ AMOCO Torch Club _____ Shoppers Charge
My Account # _____ Expiration Date _____
Authorizing Signature _____
☐ Mail to the above address
☐ Mail to the enclosed list (with card we'll sign from you)

GIVE THE GUTHRIE

HOW ABOUT THE **Guthrie** TONIGHT?
612 377-2224

Peel off this convenient reminder
Place it on your phone
or
on your phone book cover.

Omaha Junior Theater
3504 Center Street
Omaha, Nebraska 68105

Address Correction Requested

NON-PROFIT ORG.
U.S. POSTAGE
PAID
PERMIT NO. 750
OMAHA, NEBR.

Every DAD accompanied by a paying child gets in FREE on DAD'S DAY, Sun., July 27th.

Join us for our Summer Production — **THE GREAT CROSS COUNTRY RACE, or THE TORTOISE AND THE HARE.** Tickets for Non-members are $3.00 for adults, $2.00 for students, $1.50 for students 12 and under, and $1.50 for Senior Citizens. Tickets for Members are $2.50 for adults, $1.50 for students, $1.00 for students 12 and under, and $1.00 for Senior Citizens.

Become a Member of OJT. Family memberships cost $25.00 and allow your family to see all of our 1980-81 productions:

WIND IN THE WILLOWS • SLEEPING BEAUTY • THE MIRACLE WORKER • THE HOUSE AT POOH CORNER • DANCE/THEATER '76 (fall and spring concert)

Members also receive a reduced rate for our classes and our summer show!

Call 345-4849 for reservations.

THIS SEASON IS MADE POSSIBLE WITH THE SUPPORT OF THE NEBRASKA ARTS COUNCIL, A STATE AGENCY AND THE NATIONAL ENDOWMENT FOR THE ARTS, A FEDERAL AGENCY.

Third National Bank presents four works of art.

FREEDOM TRAIN

Young Abe Lincoln
Wednesday, March 24th, 7:30 PM at Symphony Hall. A relaxing look at life on the former. This fabulously successful musical on the road for 12 years, might be called "How to get ahead in politics without really trying." Young Abe was a failure in business, unhappily in love, a militia officer and led his men into battle only to find himself late for the war. He turned down a medal for bravery, so they finally gave him a medal for honesty.

The Midnight Ride Of Paul Revere
Wednesday, May 19th, 7:30 PM at Symphony Hall. A British spy lurks in the Sons of Liberty. Everybody knows that Paul Revere was a free don rider. But after you see this exciting musical you'll know why he rode so fast. Paul Revere gave away the most important secrets of his revolutionary group, the Sons of Liberty. But he didn't realize what he had done until the very last minute. See the mystery unravel in this extraordinary musical production.

Sunday, April 11th, 3:30 Symphony Hall. The story of Harriet Tubman and the underground Railway. Harriet was 25 when she made her escape route through the plantation. Pursued by slave catchers, she lay down in cellars, and returned again and more than 300 slaves never run my the sad... and I never the passenger

Three terrific plays.

This spring, Third National Bank is taking you back to see part of America's past with some marvelous musicals produced by the Performing Arts Repertory Theatre in New York. The plays have been acclaimed all across the country so bring the whole family to Symphony Hall to enjoy them!

How to get tickets: The supply of tickets is limited and there will only be one performance of each play, so don't miss out by waiting until the last minute. Tickets are available at any Third National Bank office. The regular ticket price is $3.00. But, when you make a $50 deposit to a

And a unique opportunity to buy
The Spirit of '76

This famous sculpture expresses the defiant spirit of the colonies in 1776. Third National Bank is proud to offer this bronze-finished commemorative sculpture at special prices for our depositors. $15.50 when you deposit $100 to $499 or $11.50 when you deposit $500 or more.

And a revolutionary piece of sculpture.

We are making available only to our depositors a unique bronze-finished casting of "The Spirit of '76" at a very special price. It stands over 16" tall and will make a very impressive addition to any home. The sculpture may be purchased for $11.50 if you deposit $500 or more or for $15.50 if you deposit $100 up to $500.

Third National Bank savings account, you may purchase as many play tickets as you need for only a dollar a ticket.

slogan is important, as shown on brochure for the Center for Puppetry Arts, Atlanta. • Gift certificates are an effective merchandising idea borrowed from retail stores. The Guthrie also distributes stickers for people to place near their phones. • Omaha Junior Theater has found a clever way to ensure an audience.
• The liaison between the Third National Bank of Springfield, Massachusetts, and Performing Arts Repertory Theatre during the Bicentennial year benefited both.

THE FUND-RAISING JOB: APPLYING FOR GRANTS AND SOLICITING CONTRIBUTED INCOME

Theatre companies that perform for young people have limited sources of income. Very often the income that a theatre generates is not sufficient to support its artistic vision and practice. To make up this income gap, or simply to increase its options, the theatre may turn to fund-raising. The need to raise money does not mean failure of the product or marketer.

According to professional fund raiser Richard Trenbeth, "Effective money raising is a business." Because it is a business, you need to approach all fund raising—from a single phone call to your wealthy relative to a major corporate appeal—in a systematic way.

W. Grant Brownrigg explains that one of the most important components in your fund-raising campaign is a written statement about you and your institution; it should include the following sections:

1. definition: general description in a few paragraphs
2. history and current events: summary of major accomplishments, in a few pages
3. long-range goals: four or five major accomplishments you hope to achieve over the next five years
4. plan of action: specific projects to be accomplished in the next year in order to achieve the long-range goals

If you've never done any fund raising, don't panic. Just use your instincts, as I did. I developed three types of approaches: 1) Cold. No personal contact; I wrote a concise two-page letter to the grants officer. 2) Warm. Have somebody's name, but nothing else; "I'm writing to you at the suggestion of my friend Peter." 3) Hot. "Dear Exxon. I enjoyed playing golf with you last week. How about giving me a million bucks?!"
Karen Hopkins,
vice president, development and planning, Brooklyn Academy of Music, Brooklyn, New York

TEXAS ★ OPERA THEATER
1980-81 Fund Drive: $480,000
(July 1, 1980 - June 30, 1981)

○ Curtain Raiser: $10 – 99   ○ Young Artist Patron: $1000 – 4999
○ Concert Master: $100 – 499   ○ Production Partner: $5000 and above
○ Conductor's Circle: $500 – 999

All gifts are tax deductible and will help maintain the artistic excellence and educational programs of the Texas Opera Theater.

Each gift may have very special meaning as it may be used to match a major National Endowment for the Arts Challenge Grant for which Texas Opera Theater has applied.

I will support the Texas Opera Theater with a contribution in the amount of $_____

○ Payment enclosed or
○ Pledge to be paid on or before June 30, 1981 for 1980-81 Fund Drive.
   Please send me a reminder of my pledge □ December 1980, □ February 1981,
   □ May 1981.
   Please make your check payable to Texas Opera Theater.

Signature_____Date_____

(Please print clearly)
Donor _____

Address _____

City, State, Zip _____

Telephone (s)_____
            Area Code   Day   Evening

A sample fund-raising envelope from the Texas Opera Theater.

5. reasons for support: summarize why money should be given to
   your institution*

   In order to prove how valuable they were to a community, an up-
state New York opera company paid its staff, actors, and technicians
one week in silver dollars. The community was astounded to see
where those "dollars" ended up—in the restaurant, at the grocery
store, at the laundromat. Because of this very graphic illustration, community support for that company dramatically increased.

DOING THE RESEARCH

The first step is to learn about all your potential funding sources and
make a list of them. Funding sources are divided into four broad categories:

1. **Government**
   Federal, with agencies such as The National Endowment for the
   Arts, the National Endowment for the Humanities, the Office
   of Education.
   State, such as your state arts agency or arts council, most often
   located in the state capital, as well as state departments of education.
   Local, such as county or municipal programs.
2. **Foundations**
   Family foundations, such as the John D. Rockefeller III Fund and
   the Heinz Endowment. These foundations give to organizations that reflect their own family interests. The personal approach works well with a small family foundation; a formal
   proposal is necessary for a large foundation. Well-connected
   business people in your community may know of foundations
   that have a particular interest in young people's theatre.
   Company-sponsored foundations, such as Mobil Oil and some
   of the tobacco companies. These foundations often support
   programs in the same geographical region in which they have
   offices and plants; the rationale is that you are servicing their
   employees and their community.
   Community foundations: these foundations tend to be small and
   to support only those activities that actively improve the quality of life in their home communities.
   Professionally managed foundations, such as Ford, which give
   large grants to a select few over a period of time.
3. **Corporations**
   Many businesses support the arts. It is a tax deduction for them
   and it is excellent public relations. The important aspect of
   dealing with corporations is to find the right match—your
   needs fill their needs—because with the cutbacks in government sponsorship of the arts in the 1980s corporations are getting hit hard with requests for money.

Corporate Fund Raising: A Practical Plan of Action (New York: American Council of the
Arts, 1978), p. 16.

4. Individuals

Wealthy patrons of the arts do indeed exist in the twentieth century in the United States. Whether they can be persuaded to part with their money for your theatre is your and your board's responsibility to investigate.

I tell my board that we follow the three G's in fund raising: Give it, Get it, or Get off.
Ronee Holmes,
sponsor and fund raiser

Polly Brown, director of development at the Guthrie Theatre in Minneapolis, has a personal rule that she applies to fund raising: (1) Be practical: how much does it *cost* you to raise every dollar? (2) Be persistent. (3) Be patient: eventually you'll get more givers as they warm to your cause.

From each of the four categories above there are basically two types of funding: (1) General, or operating support; (2) project support. General support is difficult to get; these grants are usually given on a matching basis for capital improvements or building campaigns. Project support is easier to get, and this is the type of support generally given. According to Stephen Langley, "There are a number of standard factors that most performing arts granting agencies use as criteria in selecting beneficiaries. These generally include:

1. The applicant's seriousness of purpose
2. The ability of the applicant to prove merit, to show a record of honest accomplishment and a realistic potential of development
3. The ability of the applicant to demonstrate responsibility of management and administration
4. Evidence that the applicant can be self-sustaining in future years if grant money is withdrawn."*

The late Robert Kingsley, corporate funding officer at Exxon for many years, claimed he looked at two factors when he was considering making a grant to a performing company: (1) the quality of the work: how it would reflect on Exxon, and (2) fiscal responsibility. "I hate the words 'innovative' and 'unique.' In your two-page letter to me tell me concisely how you are distinct from other theatres vying for the same money. And a little humor wouldn't hurt, either. Most letters and proposals are terribly dull." Kingsley related that 95 percent of the theatres he had to turn down never approached him again. "This is silly. I may have turned them down for a technical reason, such as the end of the funding cycle. I prefer those groups who keep me informed of their activities, who invite me to openings and receptions and benefits. They are trying to establish human contact. I like that. I should also tell you that one of the biggest weaknesses I've noticed in artists asking Exxon for money is when I ask them, 'What's in it for Exxon?' I get blank stares. Yet they are very articulate in describing their *own* needs."

Theatre Management in America: Principles and Practice (New York: Drama Book Specialists, 1981), p. 293.

If you find yourself in that situation and need to answer such a question, the following four points are good reasons for corporations to make grants to a young people's theatre: (1) funding a theatre for children is a wonderful way for a corporation to show its involvement in the community; (2) the corporation associates itself with quality by association with your theatre; (3) the corporation builds employee pride and morale by sponsoring an employee/family discount package and focusing on the family unit; (4) contributing to a young people's theatre will generate goodwill and may positively affect the corporation's sales.

HOW THE FUNDING PROCESS CAN WORK

The following describes an example of successful fund raising for a not-for-profit young people's theatre company.

Performing Arts Repertory Theatre's (PART) director of development, Barbara Miller, proposed in December, 1980, to hold a corporate luncheon in June, 1981, to introduce PART to many important funding sources in the New York City area. The luncheon would have an appealing angle in that it was to be held at the Theodore Roosevelt Birthplace in New York City, where PART's musical, *Teddy Roosevelt,* had been performed in the fall of 1980. The luncheon, which would be catered by a New York delicatessen, was to feature a half-hour presentation of excerpts from *Teddy Roosevelt.*

The stages of this particular funding process were as follows:

1. All PART board members were asked to invite peers from various corporations. For a desired audience of fifty PART invited 250 people. A general rule is that acceptances to such an event run at roughly 10–20 percent. *(Example 1, page 292)*

2. Barbara Miller followed up on the board members' invitations: she and board member Karen Westman called all 250 people to invite them personally.

3. The luncheon was held on June 4, 1981. Thirty-one corporations were represented; total attendance with PART staff and board was sixty people. PART's sales staff had compiled a list of the hundreds of communities PART companies had played in forty-six states over twenty years, along with a corresponding map that had pins indicating those communities. Many of the luncheon guests were fascinated by the scope of PART's touring and looked up their hometowns in the listing. The luncheon was a tremendous success, in that PART's work was new and very exciting to the corporate people. They personally experienced the excitement of excellent live theatre for young audiences and began to think of ways to help PART financially. Specifically, Barbara met (and happened to sit next to) Mary McCarthy of Warner Communications at the luncheon, and this is the case study we will follow.

4. Barbara Miller sent two letters after the luncheon. One was a thank you for attending; one was a friendly follow-up to those who did not attend.

5. Ms. McCarthy passed along her good opinion and PART's material within her organization to Virginia Brieant, Director, Contributions to the Arts.

6. Barbara Miller then called Virginia Brieant to make an appointment to talk about PART's dreams and financial needs in the immediate future. They met, with Managing Director Charles Hull and Artistic Director Jay Harnick. The meeting was positive, and Barbara followed up with a letter inviting Warner to a dress rehearsal. She also submitted a proposal for a series of public performances in New York City. (*Examples 2 and 3, pages 293–295*)

7. Based on the meetings, proposal, and dress rehearsals, which impressed them, Warner decided to give PART a grant of $15,000 to cover the advertising costs for the New York City series. Ms. Brieant called Barbara, informed her of the good news, and invited PART's staff to meet with Roger Smith, Warner's vice-president of corporate affairs. Mr. Smith offered to host a corporate luncheon for PART in November, 1981, to kick off the series, to introduce PART to other corporate funding officers, and to create favorable public relations for Warner. Smith offered PART public relations assistance through their staff member Jonas Halperin, and PART was put in touch with Great Scott, a highly creative ad agency to create the direct mail piece to market the series. PART also acquired the services of Richard Frankel, a freelance consultant, a specialist in direct mail, and Director of Marketing of Circle Repertory Company. An artistic and marketing decision was then made to present other performances than those originally proposed to Warner. The decision was discussed with Warner and approved.

The creation of the direct mail piece, letter, and the advertisement for the *New York Times* happened rapidly, and PART's staff began the promotion activities to develop the audience for the series. (*Example 4, page 296*)

8. The series opened with *Susan B.!* in November to 70 percent filled houses, which, given the newness of the event and the competitiveness of the New York market, was encouraging.

9. Warner gave a press conference on February 18, 1982, to announce all their grants in the arts.

10. Warner forwarded the $15,000 to PART, and Barbara set up a subsequent meeting with Roger Smith to discuss the 1982–1983 public series.

MANAGEMENT'S FINAL REPORT

The need for strong business management in the theatre will continue to increase as our society grows and changes. Managing a company so that the artistic product flourishes can be one of the most creative and satisfying jobs in the theatre. Creating brochures and budgets may not be glamorous, but when you do them well, you permit the sense of occasion to happen. Your audiences don't see the rigors of your board and budget meetings, but they do know you have what they want: theatre for young audiences produced and presented in a professional way. They have this knowledge because you communicated that image clearly, in both the artistic and business management of your theatre.

(On the ups and downs of managing a theatre:)
Some days you get the bear; some days the bear gets you.
Peter Culman,
managing director, Center Stage, Baltimore

**TWENTIETH
CENTURY-FOX**
FILM CORPORATION

HENRY GUETTEL
SENIOR VICE PRESIDENT
EAST COAST PRODUCTION

May 11, 1981

I'd like to invite you to a brief noontime interlude on Thursday,
June 4, for luncheon and a presentation of excerpts from Performing Arts
Repertory Theatre's hit musical, TEDDY ROOSEVELT.

I have been on the Board of Directors of this fine organization for a
number of years and can tell you (if you don't already know) that it is
America's best, as well as largest, theatre for young audiences. Since 1967,
PART has performed for seven million people in schools, civic centers, and
theatres in 46 states across the country. In addition three quarters of a
million school children have enjoyed our performances at Town Hall, PART's
New York home.

TEDDY ROOSEVELT is a superb representation of PART's biographical
musicals -- great fun for adults as well as young people. Don Nelsen wrote
in his Daily News review, "A bearhug for this Teddy," and Sy Syna of Spotlight Magazine deemed the show a "musical of the highest Broadway calibre."

The June 4 presentation will be at the historic Theodore Roosevelt
Birthplace, through the gracious cooperation of the National Park Service.
The birthplace is located at 28 East 20th Street, between Broadway and Park
Avenue South. Cocktails will be served at noon, a buffet smorgasbord at
12:30, and the half hour performance will begin at 1:00.

I do hope you can join me on this very entertaining occasion. I feel
that PART is an organization with which you will want to become acquainted.
Please return the enclosed card to Barbara Miller by May 25. Thank you.

Sincerely,

Henry Guettel

40 WEST 57th STREET, NEW YORK, NEW YORK 10019 • PHONE: (212) 977-5500 • CABLE ADDRESS: TCFNYKA, NEW YORK-TELEX 125395

Example 1 Each letter as sent out was personalized with a typed name and address
and signed by PART board member Henry Guettel.

Performing Arts Repertory Theatre
Foundation Inc.

131 West 86th Street
New York, N.Y. 10024
(212) 595-7500

September 2, 1981

Ms. Virginia Brieant, Executive Assistant
Warner Communications Inc.
75 Rockefeller Plaza - 19th Floor
New York, New York 10019

Dear Ms. Brieant:

It was lovely meeting with you today, and we were glad for the opportunity to learn more about the funding picture at Warner Communications and to tell you more about PART.

On behalf of Performing Arts Repertory Theatre, I am sending you the enclosed proposal for PART's Family Theatre Series in New York, with the hope that Warner will see the terrific cultural contribution that it could make to New Yorkers by sponsoring the series, which is the first of its kind. The series is for 1981-82, and your allocation of the funds could be scheduled to suit your needs with respect to your fiscal year; i.e. if the funding could not officially take place till '82, you would still be credited as the sponsor for the entire series (which begins the last week in November, '81).

The sponsorship requested is just for the cost of advertising (basically, a campaign in the Times), and if Warner were to pick up this expense, we would, of course, put your name on the series and the ads in whatever form you would designate.

Please be in touch with me as soon as possible about the possibilities. We would like you to see our work, which is uniquely professional and superb theatre for family viewing, at reasonable prices.

To this end, I cordially invite you to attend a dress rehearsal of either TEDDY ROOSEVELT, or SUSAN B!, our wonderful new musical about Susan B. Anthony. The rehearsals will take place in September as follows:

TEDDY ROOSEVELT   September 9   11:00 and 3:00
SUSAN B!   September 23   11:00 and 4:00

They will be held at PART's loft at 106 West 43rd Street (second floor). Wine and cheese will be served afterwards. I do hope you will attend.

Thank you again for a most pleasant meeting. I look forward to hearing from you soon.

Sincerely,

Barbara Miller

Barbara Miller
Director of Development

BM/ej
encls.

BOARD OF DIRECTORS

Jay Harnick
Artistic Director

Charles Hull
Managing Director

Emanuel Azenberg
David Dretzin
Henry Guettel
Jane Hewes
William E. Hickman
Stan Kovics
Judith O'Reilly Mack
Dr. Bonnie Maslin
Janice Morgan
Anne Navasky
George M. Nicholson
Dr. Lee Salk
Richard B. Smith
Beatrice Straight
Leigh Welles
Karen Corrigan Westman
Joan Javits Zeeman

ADVISORY COMMITTEE

Pat Carroll
Dixie Carter
Jean Dalrymple
Alfred Drake
Gary William Friedman
Dr. Audley Grossman
Sheldon Harnick
Helen Hayes
Milton Lyon
Julia Meade
Betsy Palmer
Mary Rodgers
Michael Schultz
Paula Silberstein
Stephen Sondheim
Marlo Thomas
Gwen Verdon
Henry Winkler

Example 2

PERFORMING ARTS REPERTORY THEATRE
131 West 86th Street
New York, New York 10024

212-595-7500

REQUEST FOR GRANT

General Summary of Proposal

Performing Arts Repertory Theatre (PART) is America's foremost producer of theatre for young people.

A vast national touring program brings PART's biographical plays and musicals to hundreds of thousands of school children, as well as family audiences across the country, each season.

With a unique blend of first-class professional entertainment, wholesome cultural enrichment, and proven educational value, PART's works present dynamic theatre of originality and distinction to our young audiences.

PART's resident Town Hall program draws an audience of approximately 100,000 young people annually. However, because this program is presented in school time only, a huge number of New Yorkers do not have access to PART's exceptional work. It is time, after fourteen years of growing success across the nation, to bring our highly professional, entertaining, and educational theatre to *family* audiences in New York. For though we are, indeed, creating superb theatre for young people, we always have taken pride in the fact that our work is equally enjoyable, and even edifying, for adults. Therefore we aim to create a cultural experience that can be thoroughly satisfying for a family to share.

To this end, PART will begin its new Family Theatre series for 1981–82 in New York in November, at the Martin Theatre in The Dalton School.

We are seeking funding for this series from Warner Communications in the amount of $15,000, which is the minimum required for an effective advertising campaign. We feel that the 1981–82 series (and the ads) should thus bear your name, in whatever form deemed desirable.

Organizational Background

PART's origins go back to 1961, when *Young Abe Lincoln* became the first young people's theatre to play Broadway, opening to praise such as that of critic Judith Crist: "At last. A company that gave the age-old promise of producing 'original works of professional standards for young audiences' has delivered the goods, a bright tasteful musical . . . presented with a self-confident professionalism. . . ."

Since incorporating as a nonprofit organization in 1967, PART has drawn on the abundance of musical and theatrical talents of New York City to provide lively, historically authentic theatre for young people in New York and all over America.

PART has, in fact, contributed an *extensive* literature to the theatre, attaining a singular excellence in our sphere by attracting such major writers, composers and lyricists as Ossie Davis, Thomas Babe, Mary Rodgers, Saul Levitt, Alice Childress, Albert Hague, Gary William Friedman, and Joe Raposo. These, as well as talented newcomers, have created a repertory of over thirty original works for PART.

Thus, in an article about theatre for young people, *New York Times* critic Dan Sullivan wrote that in PART's work he saw "good acting and good scripts combined" and asked, "What can be done to encourage this kind of children's theatre . . .?"

National and Resident Companies

PART now has become a major cultural institution across the nation and in New York. We are, indeed, the largest producer of theatre for young people in America: since 1967, with our vast touring program, we have presented close to 9,000 performances to nearly 7 million children in forty-six of the forty-eight continental states.

PART's resident program at Town Hall presents not only PART's own biographical musicals and dramas, but also the works of noted colleagues such as Alvin Ailey, New York City Ballet, Metropolitan Opera, Ballet Hispanico, National Theatre Company, and the Prince Street Players, among others. The youngsters who attend our regular Town Hall program pay $1.90 to $2.25 a ticket and, accompanied by their teachers, are bussed to Town Hall during school hours. As the primary tenant of Town Hall, we are the greatest source of its vitality.

Moreover, PART's Early Stages program brings to this same Town Hall series *free of charge* those impoverished youngsters from our inner-city schools who cannot afford even our low ticket price.

Philosophical Thrust

In an era when positive role models have virtually disappeared and even *the idea of being an American*, itself, has lost much of its power to produce a sense of pride in the country's citizens, many of PART's works offer portrayals of America's outstanding legendary figures and heroes. Often focusing on crucial turning points in these famous Americans' lives, PART's biographical plays provide today's young people with inspiring role models, a sustainable pride in the American heritage, and increased confidence in their own potential.

"Give them more heroes, and fewer villians, on whom they can pattern their lives. Encourage them to identify with persons, imaginary or real, whom they

Example 3

can love and admire," are the words of Dr. Martha M. Eliot, former Chief of the Children's Bureau of the Department of Health, Education and Welfare.

To this end PART has produced biographical dramas and musicals about such famous Americans as Tom Jefferson, Ben Franklin, Tom Edison, Elizabeth Blackwell, Jim Thorpe, Harriet Tubman, Teddy Roosevelt, and Susan B. Anthony, among many others.

PART productions also aim to instill hope, motivation, and stimulation for further study in our young audiences by inspiring them in the early stages of their development to take charge of their own lives in productive ways.

Often where nothing else can succeed, the mystery, excitement, and immediacy of the live performance can cut through youngsters' defenses and both touch the emotions and awaken the intellect, giving a fine tuning to the sensibilities and affording the opportunity to *learn* in a non-pressured situation.

Commendations and Funding Support

PART has been commended for excellence by the American Theatre Association, endorsed by the New York City Department of Cultural Affairs, and awarded the Special Recognition Citation by the Children's Theatre Association of America. PART productions have been recommended as curriculum-oriented by the New York State Education Department. The general reception with which PART's work has been met is illustrated in Appendix A.

PART is funded annually by the National Endowment for the Arts and the New York State Council on the Arts. Over the years we have received additional support from corporations such as U.S. Steel and Exxon and from the Helena Rubinstein, Shubert, and Richard Rodgers Foundations, as well as from the John F. Kennedy Center for the Performing Arts. Our current major supporters are listed on an enclosed sheet.

Specifics of Project

The 1981–82 Series will present three PART productions for family viewing: *Susan B.!,* a musical about Susan B. Anthony, "the woman on the dollar"; *The Sorcerer's Apprentice and Other Magical Tales,* a multi-media presentation by concert pianist, artist,

and puppeteer all-in-one (and two-time Emmy award-winner) Marshall Izen; and *The Man Who Hated Spring,* a musical about a dastardly villian who is bent on ruining the city's parks and the daffy team that stops him.

As stated in the proposal summary, we are requesting $15,000 from Warner Communications to fund the ad campaign for the series. The other costs involved—theatre rental, cast, production expenses, etc.—would come out of PART's budget.

Whatever other promotion Warner would undertake on behalf of the series would, of course, be welcomed. As an example: an insert in The Sunday *Times* could be targeted for the upper Manhattan residents only.

The price structure for the series would be as follows:

1. The basic ticket price *per show* would be $6.00 a seat; the cost of the entire series thus would be $18.00, if purchased by individual show; however,
2. A *subscription* for the entire series would cost $12.00 (a 33% discount).
3. Warner Communications *employees* would be entitled to a special rate—$10.00 for the series, or $4.00 for a single ticket.

We believe that an association between PART and Warner Communications in this Family Theatre series will be of benefit to each organization by providing both valuable visibility via a new and unique cultural experience for New Yorkers and *quality* theatre that is terrific for the whole family to share and is available at reasonable prices.

PART
Performing Arts Repertory Theatre

FOR THE PART OF YOU THAT WILL ALWAYS BE YOUNG

1. **2.** **3.**

NEW YORK'S FIRST THEATRE SERIES FOR FAMILIES

"**H**IGH QUALITY THEATRE WITH PROFESSIONALISM, PRIDE, POIGNANCY AND PUNCH."
— NEW YORK TIMES

For 20 years this outstanding New York company has been America's most successful touring theatre for family audiences.

PERFECT FOR AGES 8 AND UP

1. THANKSGIVING
SUSAN B! A lively musical based on Susan B. Anthony's spirited fight for women's rights.
book: Jules Tasca • lyrics: Ted Drachman • music: Thomas Tierney

2. CHRISTMAS
DINOSAURS, PUPPETS AND PICASSO
Multimedia magic by the Emmy award-winning Marshall Izen, blending puppetry, visual arts, and the music of Chopin, Stravinsky, Beethoven and Bach.

3. SPRING
TEDDY ROOSEVELT An exuberant musical about the early life of one of America's most colorful presidents.
book: Jonathan Bolt • lyrics: John Forster • music: Thomas Tierney

SUBSCRIBE & SAVE / 3 PLAYS
(Individual tickets $6) / FOR $15!

THE MARTIN THEATRE 108 E 89th ST. (bet. Park & Lex.) 595-7500 • PARKING NEARBY

• *This series is made possible through the support of Warner Communications Inc.* •

Pictures from left to right: Marshall Izen, Julianne Ross, Kay Walbye, Jill André, George Oliva

---

CLIP and MAIL

Complete coupon with credit card number, or check payable to:
PART
131 West 86th Street
New York, N.Y. 10024

NAME _____
ADDRESS _____
CITY _____
STATE _____ ZIP _____
PHONE: (day) _____ (eve.) _____
Charge to my: American Express, MasterCard, VISA
Account No. _____ Exp. Date _____
Interbank No. (MC only) _____
Signature _____

___Please send me _____ subscriptions for the dates and times checked below. My check for $_____ ($15 per subscription) is enclosed.
___Please send me individual show tickets for the dates and times checked below. My check for $_____ (@ $6 per ticket) is enclosed.

Susan B!	Dinosaurs, Puppets and Picasso	Teddy Roosevelt
☐ Tues. Nov. 24 7:30	☐ Sat. Dec. 26 1:00 & 7:30	☐ Tues. May 11 7:30
☐ Wed. Nov. 25 7:30	☐ Sun. Dec. 27 1:00 & 3:00	☐ Wed. May 12 7:30
☐ Fri. Nov. 27 1:00 & 7:30	☐ Tues. Dec. 29 1:00 & 3:00	☐ Fri. May 14 7:30
☐ Sat. Nov. 28 1:00 & 3:00	☐ Wed. Dec. 30 1:00 & 7:30	☐ Sat. May 15 1:00 & 3:00
☐ Sun. Nov. 29 1:00 & 3:00	☐ Sat. Jan. 2 1:00 & 3:00	☐ Sun. May 16 1:00 & 3:00
	☐ Sun. Jan. 3 1:00 & 3:00	C

Example 4

Can you define arts management for me?

I'd have to say the purpose of arts management is to create the atmosphere—which means structure and form and systems and procedures and techniques—in which the artist can reach his potential, is comfortable and can really grow and develop. He must be free of outside pressure, meaning the pressures of survival. The purpose of audience development or ticket sales is to be able to have the budget to build the scenery. The purpose of fund-raising is to allow for the rehearsal to happen. All management tasks are in support of the artist.

Do you have a theory about the basic principles of good theatre management?

I think the manager's or administrator's success and the project's success depends on his or her ability in human relationships. We work in a field where the product is totally a human product, developed by artists, who are unique. I think that the successful administrator must have the ability to guide, motivate, direct, stimulate, and energize other human beings. Let me be very clear: I'm not at all negating the need for fiscal procedures and cash flow projections, for cost effectiveness. But all of that without the ability to relate the gift of the artist to audience is totally meaningless.

I think that too much of arts-management and funding decisions are being made by people who have never worked in the arts. My concern is that management does not become the end in itself. There was a statement made at a meeting of the National Endowment for the Arts that we may be moving in the arts from a group of pioneers to managers to auditors! I worry that we are going to lose sight of the product. And that's what it's all about! Theatre is all about artists, it's not about managers. But never for a moment discount the need for what the manager does.

What are your criteria for judging young people's theatre?

Personally, I judge good theatre by whether or not it affects me and if I enjoy it. As a professional manager, I judge the excellence of the theatre by how many seats are filled, how many dead tickets are on the rack, how busy the phone is, how hard or easy it is to get the money raised—all of which speak to the authority of the product. If the seats aren't filled, something is wrong with the product.

What do you see as the working relationship in

INTERVIEW

with George Thorn, arts management consultant and director of the graduate program in Arts Administration, Virginia Tech, Blacksburg, Virginia

a theatre between artistic considerations and management considerations?

I think that is one of the things that I find most interesting about arts management, and the thing that's the hardest. I said that the purpose of management is to create the atmosphere in which the artist can work. The only thing that is as important in all of this is the product. All management must be there to support this product. But in today's world, whoever controls the money has the ultimate control. Therefore, no matter what the artist wants to do, he has to come ask the manager, "May I do it?" Now, that's going to be threatening to a lot of artists. So the manager must have the ability to make the ultimate evaluation so that the artist will have the resources to do what he wants to do. Hopefully, the manager and artistic director are mature adults and are able to have an aggressive, positive partnership. For example, I don't think anything should come out of the theatre without the artistic director's approval of the look of it, whether that's letterhead or ad copy. He doesn't have to approve every single item, but the concept, the campaign, and the look should be stimulated and approved by the artistic director. In the same way I don't think an artistic director would really put together that season without fully discussing it with the management and the audience-development people.

Many patrons and corporations and foundation people have looked upon artists as irresponsible in business management. How do you feel about this?

I don't think that it is a case of mistrust, but misunderstanding. I think it's good for the artistic director to have a good sense of management, of priorities, of moving that project forward. But he or she should never be asked to be responsible in a management sense. Nor should the management ever be asked to become artists. Management and artistic direction take two different kinds of people. I can work very comfortably in management; I cannot direct a play.

Let's talk about the concept of building an institution. You have stated that it's important because an institution transcends personalities. Are there other advantages?

An institutional base allows you to withstand change in the environment. If you're a summer operation and you're dependent on tourists to a certain degree, and there's a gas crisis, and your earned income falls off twenty percent (if you don't have an institutional base), it may mean you don't open the next season. Building an institution makes for a secure base for audience development, for fund-raising, for personalities coming and going, and allows you to withstand a bad production.

How does one build an institution?

I believe that the basis of the not-for-profit institution is in the board of trustees. The board stems from a very clearly defined purpose and artistic mission. This mission is usually conceived by the artistic director. People often say the board sets policy, but in a way the board looks to the artistic and managerial staff to develop and build the direction of the theatre. Then the board accepts and embraces those ideas.

Do you feel institution building is possible in young people's theatre?

Not only is it possible, but it is essential. There are wonderful institutions of children's theatre in this country and around the world. There's no reason why they all can't be institutions.

In university theatre there is often one person—the director—who must do many different jobs. What do you believe this director should know about theatre management?

The basic stuff. How to do a budget, how to market effectively, what promotion costs. We have a rare quality in the arts which is that ninety-nine out of one hundred people will answer any question you ask them. I guess my best advice is: Read a lot of books, use your common sense,

and pick up the phone to ask for help when you need it.

How do you perceive theatre in America has changed in the last twenty years?

Theatre in America has really changed since 1962, with the development of the not-for-profit theatre movement. I think it's fantastic in its size: it's a major growth industry, not just theatre, but not-for-profit performing arts.

In 1962 private foundations like Ford and Rockefeller began to make seed grants to major theatres in the country. Before 1962 there were maybe five or six not-for-profit theatres such as the Barter, the Arena, and the Alley. Now there are maybe a thousand not-for-profit professional theatres. I think that is incredible, but the next several years will be a serious test.

Why?

Economics, the nature of the country. I think people who are well-structured, have a good foundation, and anticipate what I think could be severe financial conditions, will survive and in the end will be greatly strengthened. We work in a highly sophisticated and competitive field, what with federal and state and individual funding, private corporations, private foundations, and new techniques of audience development.

Are we talking about survival of the fittest?

Yes, in a way. Survival of the artists who do their jobs well. And managers and administrators who are anticipating and responding to the changes in the environment will survive. Business cannot be business as usual. Certainly youth theatre is going to feel it as hard if not harder than other theatres because of the school budget cuts. Theatres may have to make cuts in their operations in the 1980s, but they can't cut the taxes, they can't cut insurances, they can't cut utilities. So, whenever they have to cut their operation, they must always cut in the area of the product, which is the *last* place they should cut!

What is the alternative?

To try to raise or earn more money, to rethink or change our way of working. You don't change the quality of the product, but you may change your way of producing it.

I would think, given hard times, quality would be even much more important.

Yes. I think it's important every day.

SPONSORING THEATRE FOR YOUNG PEOPLE

A good sponsor is something of an artistic director, choosing kinds of programming that will build a coherent program over a period of time, teaching and developing an audience—its taste, its standards, its ability to discriminate, its adventuresomeness, and certainly its knowledge—over years with great care.

Janet Oetinger, *"Performing Arts Touring and Sponsorship," Discussion Paper, National Endowment for the Arts*

THE BASICS OF SPONSORSHIP

Chapter 9 deals with finding and hiring theatre companies and bringing them into your community. A sponsor is the person or organization that takes on the financial and/or administrative responsibility for these tasks. Sponsorship is an art in itself, just as creative as producing is. The sponsor may be professional or nonprofessional, an individual patron, a state arts council, a large corporation, a PTA, or any community group. There are circumstances in which you as director can act as sponsor.

Good sponsorship requires talent, patience, and a willingness to put

....
Adult reactions to our sometimes motley band of traveling players are always interesting. A principal last year on the South Shore responded to our news that one of our vehicles had broken down and two of the performers would be about 20 minutes late with "Why don't you go ahead and start as planned at 9:00 a.m. and then when the other two get here they can join in."
Georgia Leigh Bills,
*musical director/tour manager,
New England Theatre Guild*
....

the interests of the community and the audience first. Though far from thankless, the job is often unsung because of its low profile—the hours of planning, telephone calls, meetings, and paperwork do not show. But sponsors are as invaluable to the arts as artists themselves. Without their dedicated commitment, many arts events in America would never happen. In the first part of this chapter we discuss basic principles of sponsorship and good reasons to be a sponsor. In the second part we factor out the procedures that are most appropriate for sponsoring theatre for young people.

FOUR BENEFITS OF SPONSORING

1. Your production season You can think of your total season as a *package*—part production, part presentation. It can be rounded out by presenting a play that you do not wish to produce yourself but that meets the needs of your audience.

2. Your actors By your arranging performances, they can observe professionals at work onstage. Workshops may enable your actors to work directly with the professional.

3. Your audience However brilliant your own work may be, variety challenges and stimulates your audience.

4. You Meeting other professional artists will enlighten, enliven, perhaps even infuriate, but definitely will also stimulate you. What you learn from them you can use in your own productions.

BRIEF OVERVIEW OF THE SPONSORSHIP JOB

Sponsoring the arts is a serious business that requires careful planning, community cooperation, and real money resources. Sponsoring requires strong fiscal management and intelligent planning. No real sponsoring can be achieved by spending $200 once a season.

Sponsors, like managers, serve the art and the artists. They hire companies, negotiate fees, sign contracts, obtain space, market a product, and generate promotion; in short, they must be as professional in their role as the artists are in theirs. Part of the role is for a sponsor to accurately assess his or her community and its markets, as discussed in Chapter 8. A sponsor needs to figure out what the community wants, then develop an enticing marketing strategy to deliver the product. This assessment is the "outer" focus of sponsoring.

Just as important is the "inner" focus, which is made up of a sponsor's artistic and administrative goals, dreams, and preferences. Goals act as a reminder as to who you are and what is your organizational purpose. Part of the fun of presenting performers is that you can be both realistic and adventuresome, with dreams tempered by intelligent assessment of real resources.

Sponsoring is a learning process; "practice makes perfect" in one

....

For sponsors, the most important thing is that they must believe and persevere. It is not easy, and it is not fun, but the rewards after the battle are substantial. When you're looking for money, be prepared for 99 "no's" before you get the one "maybe." But keep going.
Henry Dembowski,
National Arts consultant for the Kennedy Center, Washington, D.C.
....

sense does apply, since the more performances you sponsor, the more you'll learn about what to do and what not to do. Part of the job is to learn about the available resources and the restrictions under which companies may work. This understanding includes unions and their contracts.

DEALING WITH THE PRACTICAL ASPECTS OF SPONSORING THEATRE FOR YOUNG PEOPLE

Once you have considered philosophically why you wish to sponsor, the next step is dealing with the practical realities.

Just as you carefully decide the place and time of the performances of your own productions, deciding the right where and when to sponsor the professional company will contribute to your success or failure as a sponsor.

ASSESSING THE OPTIONS OF PLACE AND TIME: THE WHERE AND WHEN

The variables are *place* and *time*. **Place** can be:

- in the school
- at an arts center
- at a theatre
- in another facility, such as a university gymnasium or church basement
- outdoors, in a park, street, or amphitheatre

Time can be:

- during school time, 8 A.M.–3 P.M.
- not during school time: right after school, in the evening, or on the weekend

The time and place variables can work in many different successful combinations. The important point is to choose a place and time that make it as easy as possible for your audience to attend your event. The following quiz may help you identify your preferences.

SELF-DETERMINATION SPONSOR POLL

Directions: Circle the letter (or letters) in each question that best applies to you. Try to be as specific as possible. If you do not have an existing situation as a sponsor, make up your answers as you would like your situation to be. There are no "right" or "wrong" answers. *Your* opinion is the answer to mark. Analysis follows on pages 303–304.

1. I want to sponsor programs for
   a. kindergarten–6 grades.

Everything comes together when young people are absorbed in a performance. This is the Detroit Youtheatre, a major sponsor of productions for young audiences. In this theatre, which has a capacity of 1,200, Mickey Miners and staff present about 400 performances a year during their October to May season.

    b. families with young children.

    c. grades 7–9.

    d. grades 9–12.

2. Philosophically, I believe that
    a. theatre is an event you go to—it doesn't come to you.
    b. being able to go to the theatre is an important thing for the entire community to do.
    c. theatre is for all the people.
    d. theatre should be free.

3. I have
    a. a college auditorium at my disposal.
    b. a terrific facility with 800+ seats at my disposal.
    c. a terrific facility with 300+ seats at my disposal.
    d. no terrific facility—an adequate high school gym or a school auditorium.

4. My schools and their populations are
    a. within walking distance of my facility.
    b. within easy transportation of my facility.
    c. spread out all over my town/city.
    d. spread out all over my county.

5. From the local school authorities I have gotten
    a. resistance to my ideas if it concerns them in any detailed way.

    b. a willingness to help me as long as the arts "do not interfere with education."

    c. serious cooperation from the board of education.

    d. indifference, but no real resistance.

6. I want to

    a. make some money for my organization by sponsoring.

    b. make a killing financially and go on to more expensive events.

    c. break even financially.

    d. bring arts to all kids, even if I have to raise funds to do it.

7. I want to sponsor productions

    a. with familiar titles that I am comfortable with, like *Cinderella.*

    b. from companies who are famous.

    c. with excellent content; I don't care about the title.

    d. with content that is new to me and will be new and challenging to the kids.

8. I am a sponsor

    a. with some sponsoring and marketing experience.

    b. who is a veteran sponsor and a marketing whiz.

    c. who has never sponsored but has observed how it is done.

    d. who is brand new to *all* of this.

9. I am a sponsor

    a. working with the support, both emotional and financial, of an institution.

    b. working within the restrictions of an indifferent institution.

    c. working with a loosely formed committee.

    d. working alone.

10. My annual budget for sponsoring young people's theatre is

    a. whatever I wish to spend.

    b. whatever I made through previous ticket sales.

    c. $200–$1,000, mostly PTA money.

    d. $1,000–$10,000, including some school budget money.

ANALYSIS OF SELF-DETERMINATION SPONSOR POLL

Add up the number of a's, b's, c's, and d's. Answers a and b indicate an interest in sponsoring performances for the public, not in school time. Answers c and d indicate an interest and preference for sponsoring programs during school time, either in the school itself or in a facility to which the young people are bussed.

Question 1. Grades K–6 and families will come on Saturdays. Teenagers usually won't, unless you are presenting a name performer. Teenagers traditionally avoid children's theatre events because they are striving for their own independence. Anything that smacks of "children" usually turns them off. If you want to reach grades 7–12, provide the service during school time, at least until you are established.

Question 2. Answers a and b indicate a preference for public performances; answers c and d indicate a preference for assemblies during the school day.

Question 3. a and b: Most college auditoriums have a good number of seats; if you fill them all, and you have been conservative with your budget, you may break even or make some money. c: You can't break even generally with only 300 seats to sell, unless you're sponsoring a *very* inexpensive program. d: It's better to sponsor in school time with a poor facility—the students have to go. The public won't come to be uncomfortable, usually.

Question 4. a and b: The easier it is for the public to come, the easier it is to get them there *on their own time.* c and d: If they live far away from your facility, better to play to them when they are a captive audience, in school time.

Question 5. a: They won't help much, but they won't hurt your public series. b: Self-explanatory—they don't want you in the schools on their time. c: They *want* you in the schools, and so they'll help. d: They won't help much, but they won't interfere with your scheduling in the schools.

Question 6. a and b: You can only do this with good ticket sales. c and d: You probably will *not* charge for tickets, if it takes place in school time, as so many school boards are opposed to this practice. You'll have to raise the money from other sources. *Note:* If you can charge for in-school performances, this is a practical way to sponsor. You have a captive audience who pays.

Question 7. a and b: Familiar titles and famous companies are always marketable and will draw in the audience. c and d: Unfamiliar titles or avant-garde material are difficult to market until the community so thoroughly trusts you and your organization that they will take the risk and attend.

Question 8. a and b: You need marketing experience to sponsor a public performance, because the audience doesn't have to come. c and d: If you are inexperienced, you can still have a tremendously successful experience with a good company and a "captive" audience.

Question 9. Self-explanatory.

Question 10. a: You're lucky, and very atypical. b: If your only revenue is ticket sales, you're stuck in that rut. You'll have to make it work for you and really develop a paying audience. c and d: If your budget is limited—no money for advertising, etc.—and the money came from school groups, your responsibility is to put the program in the schools for all students.

ORGANIZING YOURSELF

Once you've decided the kind of sponsoring you wish to pursue, consider the following three possible ways for you to organize:

1. You can be a volunteer organization, with no legal entity. However, this means that *you* or whoever signs the contract is personally liable, if for any reason you default and cannot pay. You may also be liable if an actor trips and breaks a leg in a facility that you are using but which does not have adequate insurance. Being a nonlegal volunteer organization means you cannot receive grants, as you are not tax-exempt. If you do not need to fund-raise, and you want to keep your sponsorship on a philanthropic basis—that is, your *own* philanthropy—to cover any emergency or crisis, then you can remain a volunteer organization with no incorporation.

2. You can ally yourself with a tax-exempt, not-for-profit organiza-

tion, such as a church, temple, arts council, university, or already existing theatre company that does not sponsor events for young people. Since budgets need to be kept separate, you can set up a separate bank account. All proceeds are paid to that account and all checks drawn against it. Since you are under the umbrella structure of your parent organization, you benefit from its tax-exempt status. However, with the benefits come the responsibility of adhering to its bylaws, mandates, philosophies, and practices. In certain situations this arrangement may be fine. In other situations the parent/child relationship may be constricting. Before establishing a liaison such as this, investigate some key issues. For example, will the parent organization have artistic or administrative control of the events you sponsor? Will its board of trustees tell you what to book? More subtly, will they "advise"? And if you do not "take" the advice, will that attitude cause problems? Obviously, any parent organization that is willing to have you work with it is interested in having a smooth relationship. But differences in philosophy and taste can hamper your creative processes and growth. This is an important issue to mull over as you decide how to form your organization.

3. The third possibility is for you to form your own 501C3 tax-exempt, not-for-profit, sponsoring organization, with your own board of trustees, volunteer committees, bylaws, bank accounts, insurance, and autonomy. This task is not nearly as awesome as it sounds. If you wish to incorporate, Thomas Wolf's book *Presenting Performances: A Handbook for Sponsors* can assist you. Or, contact an attorney. The one most important job in incorporating is the selection of the board of trustees.

The board is ultimately responsible for all facets of the organization's health: Its financial credibility and liabilities rest with these people. Staff or volunteer help can be dismissed, but the board *is* the organization. We refer to the board as "a board of *trustees*," rather than "a board of *directors*." The distinction between them is the major definition of a board. A board advises an organization; it guides; it carries out the bylaws; it holds *in trust* the organization's integrity to the community. A board supports the administration of the organization in artistic and administrative policy, but it does not *direct* such policy.

SELECTING THE FACILITY

The important factors to consider in selecting a site for sponsorship purposes are its availability, its audience capacity, its accessibility to the community and to the artists, its onstage suitability to the production, and its offstage and outdoors facilities. You may not have a choice of several facilities in your community, but if you do, match the facility to your administrative needs (numbers of seats, for example) and the technical needs of any company you might consider hiring.

A business organization's results are directly traceable to the individuals who make up that organization. . . . So one of your top-priority activities must be to constantly assess individuals in your organization and outside it, to seek out those rare individuals who are genuinely committed to success, and then—(and this is the crux of the matter) to build around them.
Richard S. Sloma,
No-Nonsense Management

"CANDY, T-SHIRTS, AND PENCILS": YES, BUT WHAT IS YOUR REAL BUDGET?

The 1980s will require sponsors to work in fiscally smart ways. Good business practice fosters good business; bad business practice can ruin the most promising venture. As Chapter 8 illustrates, good business practice means a real understanding of money and its management: where to get it, how to raise it, how best to spend it.

First, examine your fiscal thinking as it relates to spending.

Do not let budgets and contracts intimidate you. They are pieces of paper with an important purpose, but they are a road map, a guide only. Make up a simple budget based on what you must spend of what you have and can earn; show it to an accountant. Study all contracts carefully before you sign them, and show them to an attorney.

You cannot move into the real world of sponsoring young people's theatre if you are only committed to the $200 event. You can raise $200 by bake sales, pizza sales, pencil sales, and car washes—but can you raise $2000? That's the issue. The car wash profit of $200 is a strong start for sponsoring young people's theatre, but only a start. Some young-audience sponsors in the United States appear to have a streak of helplessness when considering budgets. "The PTA gave us $200 a school for the year. That's it." University-audience sponsors spend thousands of dollars for the national tour of a current Broadway hit. Universities pass on the cost to the parent through student activities funds and to the student through ticket sales. Granted, tickets for theatre for young audiences cannot be priced at $25, but sponsors *can* charge what the market will bear, which is often a fee comparable to a movie fee. Sponsors *can* attempt to raise money through the school board; they *can* attempt a policy of asking each child to contribute toward in-school-time performance costs. With the cuts in arts subsidies in the 1980s, the one place left to go for money to support theatre for young audiences is into the pockets of individuals.

LIST OF POSSIBLE RESOURCES

Tom Wolf, director of the New England Foundation for the Arts, has said that managing arts money is "creative parsimony." Managing arts money involves the searching out of all kinds of resources.

1. The school budget   Some enlightened school districts budget a line item annually for arts programming that ensures that their students will have some arts events every year. In a series of meetings, convince the school board to create such a line item, and volunteer to administer this program. Your sponsoring need not be limited to performances only. Many excellent young people's theatre companies that tour run workshops and residencies of one to many days.

You can then begin to explore additional funding sources that are available for schools. Locate a grant; help write the proposal. If through your skillful grantsmanship you bring money and successful programs into the school district, the district's cooperation will increase.

Henry Dembowski, a school principal and arts consultant in Marblehead, Massachusetts, wanted to run an arts program in the early 1970s but there was no money for it. The school board's attitude was traditional: "Arts are a frill." The board and the town, however, had an enormous financial and emotional commitment to its student football team. Dembowski discovered that it cost the school district $3,786 annually to *launder* the football uniforms. Dembowski approached the school board and said, "Give me the same amount of money that you spend annually to launder the football uniforms, and I'll run an arts program in this town." In the 1980s Dembowski's arts program is a leader in its field in Massachusetts. The arts program is now a line item in the budget, and a complete arts department grew from this beginning.

2. In-school-time field trips   Because the audience contributes part or all of the money, and because the audience is guaranteed, in-school field trips are an option. These trips usually take the students to a concert in busses. However, some school districts are choosing to save the bussing money and allowing students to pay toward a program that happens right in the school. The school sends a letter to the parents, requesting money for the event. If a student cannot pay, a discretionary fund may contribute.

3. Community organizations   Create a liaison with the local PTA, a local cultural group such as a local arts council, or a service organization such as Rotary. Instead of their bringing in one event a year, you might suggest you work together to bring in several events.

4. Community businesses   Just as you may have approached your local business community for funding of your own theatre, you can approach them for support of your sponsoring efforts, as long as you can answer their question, "What's in it for me and my business?"

5. Fund-raising   If you have incorporated and are tax-exempt, you are eligible for grants. Find out if your state arts council and your state department of education have grants for which your organization can apply. If possible, visit someone at the two departments and acquaint them with your ideas and plans. Get your name on their mailing lists; you'll receive newsletters in which grant deadlines and eligibility are often announced.

6. Public performances   Your resource here is your population. Your revenue is in your ticket sales. Just as you weighed all factors that contribute toward good ticket sales in your own theatre as outlined in

Chapter 8, you need to weigh these same factors again for sponsoring events.

Once you have planned the budget and begun to raise the money, it is time to hire the company.

FINDING AND HIRING THE ARTISTS

When you begin the process of considering companies to sponsor, there are seven factors to consider:

1. Quality of the performance: The artistic and business reputation of the company must be excellent.
2. Appeal of the company: The company must excite you in order for you to be fully committed.
3. Suitability to your audience: The production must be geared to your audience age group, and the material appropriate.
4. Marketability of the company: There should be a marketing "hook" such as a famous name, a play with a sell title, or content particularly appealing to your community.
5. Accessibility of the company: Their tour schedules and your needs have to mesh properly.
6. Technical requirements of the production: The company needs to be able to perform safely in your space, their sets must fit, and the lighting requirements must be met either by your facility or by the company.
7. The fee of the company.

The most important thing to remember about performers is that their behavior cannot be predicted simply by their profession. A creative person may be responsible or irresponsible, organized or disorganized, sensitive or insensitive. For this reason, sponsors must assess the personalities of performers on an individual basis and adjust their behavior accordingly.
Thomas Wolf,
Presenting Performances: A Handbook for Sponsors

The most important factor is the quality of the company's work. Be very careful when you book; protect your interests by booking only the best. You can determine what is the best work available by previewing the company yourself and analyzing their craft. If you cannot preview, ask the company to give you references. You must be able to afford the company without depending solely on the revenue from the sale of this performance(s). What happens if their fee is $1,000 and you only sell $200 worth of tickets? You will be required to make up the balance in some way, because you will have signed a contract which is a legal and binding agreement.

YOUR RESOURCES: WHERE TO LOOK FOR COMPANIES

1. There are two showcases in the United States annually. One is the Producers Association of Children's Theatre (PACT) Showcase. Several New York City Actors' Equity Association producers present this showcase each year, generally in March, in New York City. The producers invite presenters to preview, in three days, eighteen to twenty-six selections of productions that will tour the following season. There is a registration fee that covers lunches, a cocktail party, and sponsor-development seminars in addition to the previewing. To receive a bro-

chure, write in January to: Performing Arts Repertory Theatre Foundation, Inc., 131 West 86th Street, New York, NY 10024. Telephone: (212)595-7500.

The other showcase is the National Showcase of the Performing Arts for Young People. In two days this showcase presents selections by sixteen companies from all over the United States and Canada. The site of the showcase changes from year to year, in order to be accessible to various companies and sponsors. It is generally in March and features different companies every year. Theatre companies who tour are encouraged to apply to the showcase board, which consists of theatre professionals. There is a fee to the companies that showcase. There is also a registration fee for sponsors who attend; this fee covers a banquet, parties, seminars, and the preview itself. For company applications or for a sponsor brochure detailing time and place of the National Showcase, contact Cultural Resources Council, 411 Montgomery Street, Syracuse, NY 13202. Telephone: (315)425-2155.

2. The National Endowment for the Arts compiled a directory of excellent companies for the Artists-in-Schools program in 1979. Each state arts agency received this directory, and will share this information.

3. Organizations such as your state arts agency, state department of education, or the American Theatre Association, particularly the Children's Theatre Association (CTAA) branch, will know of companies. They will not endorse any company, but they may recommend one for further investigation. Occasionally a state arts agency will run a showcase; the Southern Arts Federation has a regional meeting annually the first weekend in October in Atlanta, Georgia, with roughly six to ten companies performing for preview.

4. Theatre Communications Group publishes an annual directory, "Theatre Profiles," which lists many of the excellent professional theatre companies in the United States. Those that tour productions for

above left: At the 1982 PACT (Producers Association of Children's Theatre) Showcase at Kaufmann Auditorium in New York City, eight producers presented twenty-four different productions. One of PART's presentations, *First Lady*, is shown here. Actors (stage right to left): Christina Denziger, Lee Welch, Marcia Savella, Richard Kind.

Photo by Gerry Goodstein

above right: At the 1980 National Showcase of the Performing Arts for Young People at the Civic Center of Onondaga County in Syracuse, New York, sixteen theatre companies presented sixteen different productions. One of the companies was a Canadian one, Theatre sans Fil of Montreal, shown here.

young people list themselves that way in the directory. There is a modest fee. Contact Theatre Communications Group, 355 Lexington Avenue, New York, NY 10017. Telephone: (212)697-5230.

5. Word of Mouth. School districts, service organizations, and local arts councils can tell you whom they have booked and who has been a success. You might also ask them who was not successful, but accept this opinion carefully. There are many reasons for failure, including a sponsor failing to provide the proper services, which can make the company look bad. Be fair to the companies you are considering; gather many opinions and judge for yourself.

MAKING THE CONTACT

Once you have the names, addresses, and telephone numbers of several companies that interest you, contact them. Your goal in the first telephone call is to establish a relationship. The company cares about you because they want your business; you care about the company because you may want to have them in your community. Be as specific as you can about the number of performances and services you want, time of year, and budget. Some fees are negotiable. If you cannot meet the fee, say so. You may be able to fill a "hole" (an empty date) for the producer; in turn, the producer may be able to give you a price break.

Block booking, the pulling together of multiple dates by a sponsor, allows a producer to reduce the fee for each service—bulk buying, as it were. Since the sponsor arranges the block booking, the producer saves marketing and sales cost and passes this saving along to the sponsor.

Once you have received the materials from several companies, checked out references, and cleared several dates with your facility, you're ready to make a decision.

NEGOTIATING THE CONTRACT

A contract is an instrument created to minimize, if not altogether eliminate, the ordinary human impulses to forget, to overlook, to misunderstand.
Joseph Golden,
On The Dotted Line: The Anatomy of a Contract

Good faith between a sponsor and producer is absolutely necessary. Begin the process of contracting for services only if you are organized and you have enough money to pay the company and your expenses. A contract is a legal agreement between two parties: You each agree to certain conditions. Following is a sample contract between Performing Arts Repertory Theatre and a sponsor. Notice the initialed alteration of number 4c. This indicates a compromise between the buyer and seller; they have negotiated the contract. Who provides what is clear.

If, once you receive the contract, you decide to cancel, you must (1) call the producer and (2) return the contract, unsigned, marked "canceled." Canceling for "personal" reasons—"we didn't sell any tickets" or "we never should have booked a Friday night, that's a home basketball game"—is not acceptable. It is the sponsor's responsibility to check dates for all conflicts before signing the contract. Companies by necessity book compact tours; your cancelation may leave them stranded that day. They must continue to pay their expenses and overhead but they earn no income.

Preparing for this day is identical to preparing for the day of your own company's performances. The same meticulous attention to detail, personnel management, promotion, and publicity is required.

PREPARING FOR THE DAY OF THE PERFORMANCE

GETTING THE PUBLICITY MATERIALS

Producers are notorious for being irresponsible about getting adequate materials on time to sponsors. It you don't receive materials with the contract, find out when you can expect to receive them; if you do not receive them by the date, ask again. You should receive a complete press kit if you are running public performances, or study guides if the performances are in schools.

SUCCESSFUL MARKETING IS 99% PERSONAL SELLING!

EXECUTING A MARKETING PLAN

Sponsors can follow the same plan as outlined in Chapter 8, modifying it to fit any unusual characteristics of the sponsored company. The key to successful marketing is personal selling; the sponsor's presence at schools, at school board meetings, and at various leader organizations will help persuade the community to support the project.

Covering the media thoroughly is part of the marketing strategy. Cover television, radio, newspapers; pay for advertising as well as solicit feature articles in newspapers or interviews on TV and radio. All of these activities will alert your potential audience.

COVERING THE SCHOOLS

Approach the schools and their personnel warmly and professionally. If you are sponsoring an in-school-time performance, you will be coordinating the school's schedule with the company's; you're the "middleman." If you are sponsoring public performances, you still need the school's cooperation, in that your audience base is located there. Since one of your tasks is to make the theatregoing experience as easy as possible, running a ticket booth in school during the day is an excellent opportunity to increase ticket sales. For example, Shirley Trusty Corey runs a large and successful artists-in-schools program in New Orleans. Ms. Corey claims one of the main reasons for her success is the volunteer she has in each school. The coordinator is the trouble-shooter.

Following are both pages of a sample contract between Performing Arts Repertory Theatre (producer) and the fictitious Pizza Man Productions (sponsor). A contract is a necessary part of doing business in a professional way. It represents good faith between the two parties.

TO: Mr. Alvin Railey
Pizza Man Productions
16 Quail Path
East Orleans, MA 02643
617-555-1212(w)

Performing Arts Repertory Theatre
131 West 86th Street
New York, New York 10024
212-595-7500

Dear Sponsor:

When signed by you and us, this letter shall constitute an agreement between you (the "Sponsor") and us ("PART") relating to Sponsor's presentation of ___two___ performance(s) [or _____ residency] of PART's production entitled

_____SUSAN B!_____
Name of Show

at ___Peter Louis High School Auditorium_____ ___ _____
Name of Theatre(s) or Auditorium(s) or School(s)

located at ___Country Side Drive_____
Street Address

in ___East Orleans_____ , ___MA_____
City   State

on the following schedule:

Date(s)	Times(s)	Theatre(s) (if different from above)
February 25, 1983	10:30 am	
	12:30 pm	

1. PART shall at its sole expense provide the production at the time(s), date(s) and place(s) specified above.

2. Sponsor shall pay to PART:

$ _1,500.00_ as performance [or residency] fee

$ _--------_ as fee for _____workshop(s)

$ _--------_ as travel expense

$ _1,500.00_ . TOTAL

3. The total amount due under Paragraph 2 above shall be paid as follows:

$ ___300.00___ to accompany signed contract

$ _1,200.00___ on day of first performance

$ _1,500.00___ TOTAL

All payments shall be made to PART Foundation and mailed to the address set forth above, and any payments shall be deemed made only when received.

(CONTINUED ON BACK)

312

4. Sponsor shall provide at its expense:

   a. The theatre or auditorium referred to above (with stage cleared and complete with adequate stage lighting) made available to PART exclusively one and one-half (1½) hours prior to the performance(s);

   b. Two (2) dressing rooms (with mirrors) and with windows and doors masked to insure privacy, sufficient to accommodate six actors;

   c. ~~Four~~ Three people to help unload and load scenery before and after performance(s) and to run the lights during the performance(s).

5. It is further agreed as follows:

   a. There shall be no audio or visual broadcast or recording of the performance(s) permitted;

   b. There shall be no discrimination or segregation in admission or seating based on race, sex, national origin or religion;

   c. PART shall be under no liability for failure to appear or perform in the event that such failure is caused by or due to the physical inability of any of PART's personnel to perform, or acts or regulations of public authorities, labor difficulties, civil tumult, strike, epidemic, interruption or delay of transportation services, or any other cause beyond PART's control; but any payment due PART from Sponsor allocable to such cancelled performance(s) need not be made and, if already made, shall be refunded;

   d. In the event sponsor cancels any performance(s) for any reason, the sponsor shall remain liable to PART for the full agreed upon amount set forth in Paragraph 2.

   If the foregoing accurately sets forth your understanding with us, kindly sign and return to us the enclosed copy of this letter, together with your check, at which time it shall constitute a binding agreement between you and us.

SPONSOR: PLEASE FILL IN ALL BLANKS, KEEP ONE COPY, AND RETURN ONE SIGNED COPY TO PART. THANK YOU.

ACCEPTED AND AGREED TO:

Pizza Man Productions
Sponsoring Organization

By _Alvin Railey_
   Alvin Railey

Date ____6/28/82____

Phones at which sponsor can be reached:

Work phone: 617-444-0000

Home phone: 617-000-4440

Very truly yours,

PERFORMING ARTS REPERTORY THEATRE FOUNDATION, INC. (PART)

By _Christine Bourgeas_

Date ____6/18/82____

PLEASE ADVISE: Contact person at site of performance.

Name: Heather Caroline Hill

Address: 279 Stanley Drive

City: North Truro, MA 02651

Work phone: 617-555-1212

Home phone: 617-555-2121

COVERING ADMINISTRATIVE ODDS
AND ENDS: BUSSES, POLICE, FIRE SAFETY

If your audience is arriving by school busses, where will the busses park? Will they drop off and pick up? If they park, invite the bus drivers to the performance. You're responsible for these arrangements.

Check out all regulations concerning the fire department and your space. Do you need to hire police? Who pays? What is the fire code for your facility?

COVERING THE TECHNICAL
REQUIREMENTS OF THE COMPANY

The company may ask you to fill out a technical questionnaire so that they will know what to expect backstage. If the company does not ask you to fill in a tech sheet, they may be fairly casual about their requirements. However, you can avoid last-minute panic by speaking directly with the company about their technical requirements or having your tech person speak with their tech person. You don't want any technical surprises on the day of the performance. A company that does not have complex technical requirements may send you a more general fact sheet, such as the one shown here.

THE DAY OF THE PERFORMANCE

Your chief job as sponsor on the day of the performance is to provide a calm center for everyone involved. Certain amenities, such as coffee in the morning, will earn you a special place in the artists' memories. Touring is hard work, and your extra efforts can make the difference between "just one more stop" and "a special place."

THEIR SHOW ON YOUR ROAD WRAP-UP

Following is a sample performance preparation fact sheet. The producer sends it to the sponsor about three weeks before the performance. The fact sheet (1) reminds the performance space people when the company will arrive; (2) assures successful arrangements by repeating some of the contract provisions, e.g., the need for two dressing rooms.

The sponsor's job is complex because many things have to be done simultaneously. You can simplify the task by asking, "What if the situation were reversed, and I were in a touring company? Professionally and personally, how would I wish to be treated?"

Your final responsibility to the company is to pay them promptly according to the terms in the contract. If you enjoyed the performance, an unsolicited endorsement letter that the company could use publicly is a professional courtesy. If you did not enjoy the performance, let the company know.

Presenting the performing arts is not an exact science. If you are (1) prepared for anything, (2) don't make any assumptions, and (3) ground your decisions in practical realities, sponsoring theatre for young people can be an exciting and rewarding experience.

FACT SHEET

Dear Sponsor:

     Our production of _____SUSAN B!_____ is scheduled to be performed for you on __February 25, 1983_____ at ___10:30 and 12:30_____ . In order to insure that all goes as smoothly as possible, please pass a copy of this sheet on to the principal and the maintenance chief (janitor, superintendent, etc.) of the building where the performance will take place.

    *** Please send us right away: _____ a signed copy of the contract
                                                 _____ the time(s) of the performance(s)
                                                 _____ the place and address of the performance(s)

    *** Please mail us a map (may be hand drawn) showing the location of the auditorium within your community.

A. PLEASE BE SURE THAT

1. The stage has been cleared of all band equipment, desks, etc. and that it has been swept clean; and that the lighting board/equipment is unlocked.
2. One person familiar with the lighting board be available during set up and to help work lights during the show.
3. One room; unlocked, providing privacy and close to the stage; is set aside for a dressing room.
4. For WORLD MYTH & MUSIC there are two microphones on stands -- one of which can be removed and carried -- and two stools or chairs on stage.
5. For WHEN THE SPIRIT SAYS SING there is on stage a piano, preferably in tune and unlocked; a piano bench; two microphones -- one for the piano and one on a stand which can be removed and carried.
6. FOR ALL PERFORMANCES, if they are to take place in an open space such as a gymnasium, there are two units which can be used for privacy on either side of the area -- tables set on end, or platforms, or sliding screens would all be suitable.

B. YOU SHOULD KNOW THAT

1. Our group will arrive approximately one hour to one half hour before the time of the performance.
2. The performance lasts approximately 45 minutes to one hour.
3. For optimum enjoyment of the performance:
   a. Students should be prepared by use of teacher study guides.
   b. Bells and buzzers should be shut off in auditorium during the performance.
   c. Shades on auditorium windows should be drawn and doors shut during the performance.
4. The taking of pictures and/or making of visual or sound recordings during the performance is expressly forbidden.

    * We thank you for your cooperation and look forward to playing for you. *

If you have any questions please call or write us at: PART FOUNDATION
                                                        131 West 86 Street
                                                        New York, New York 10024
                                                        212-595-7500

Sponsoring theatre for young people is worthwhile and exciting. It can bring about spontaneous and mutual delight such as this during an audience participation session after a performance. Actor William Wesbrooks is shown with a volunteer. Periwinkle Productions: *The Magic Word.*

COMPREHENSIVE SPONSOR CHECKLIST

(One sheet per performance if performance site information varies)

Title of performance(s): _____
Name of producing company: _____
Address: _____
Telephone: _____
Contact at producing company: _____
Union: _____
Total number of performances: _____ Total number of sites: _____
Rehearsals scheduled: _____ Where: _____ When: _____
Date contract received: _____ Date contract sent back: _____
Date contract rider received: _____ Date contract rider sent back: _____
Deposit: _____ Date sent: _____
Date light plot rec'd: _____
Date publicity materials rec'd: _____

The magic of excellent theatre at work. This child is in a Detroit Youtheatre audience.

Date publicity materials placed in newspaper: _____ On radio/TV: _____
Date study guides rec'd: _____
Date study guides duplicated, if nec.: _____ Date distributed: _____
Distributed to: _____ Rechecked on: _____

Site Information
Date of performance: _____ Place: _____ Time: _____
Site contact: _____ Telephone: _____
Show title, if different from above: _____
Date principal or house manager notified in writing of performance: _____
                                        Date reminded: _____
Date custodian/maintenance staff notified in writing of performance: _____
_____ Reminded: _____
How many seats available: _____ Audience: grades _____
                                                public _____
Stage area to be cleared & swept clean? ___ When? ___ Date checked: _____
Sound system working? _____ Date checked: _____
Lighting system working? _____ Date checked: _____

Day of Performance Information
Date and time company/performer due to arrive in town: _____
Where staying: _____ Telephone: _____
Stage manager/tour manager name: _____
Time company due to arrive at performance site: _____
Building door unlocked? _____ Dressing rooms unlocked? _____
Crew assigned backstage:
Names: _____ Tel.: _____ When to report: _____ Time in: _____
_____ Tel.: _____ When to report: _____ Time in: _____
_____ Tel.: _____ When to report: _____ Time in: _____
_____ Tel.: _____ When to report: _____ Time in: _____
Crew assigned front of house: Ushers, refreshments, etc.:
Names: _____ Tel.: _____ When to report: _____ Time in: _____
_____ Tel.: _____ When to report: _____ Time in: _____
_____ Tel.: _____ When to report: _____ Time in: _____
_____ Tel.: _____ When to report: _____ Time in: _____
Chaperones in house for performance:
Names: _____ Tel.: _____ When to report: _____ Time in: _____
_____ Tel.: _____ When to report: _____ Time in: _____
_____ Tel.: _____ When to report: _____ Time in: _____
_____ Tel.: _____ When to report: _____ Time in: _____
Stage area cleared and clean? _____
Sound system plugged in? _____
Lighting system unlocked, plugged in, lights focused on stage? _____
Dressing room keys distributed? ___ How many? ___ Deposit rec'd _____
                                        Deposit returned _____
Reread contract:
Has *everything* covered in contract and *everything* company has requested
been provided? _____
_____
What is missing? _____Who will fix it? _____

. . . .
*All I remember is how excited
some kids were and how
boring touring can be and
how cold Idaho and Montana
are in the winter.*
Steve Wing,
*managing director, Montana
Repertory Theatre, 1980*
. . . .

When? _____

If problems arise, call the producer immediately.

During the Performance

Crew backstage? _____

Front-of-house crew seated or in lobby? _____

Doors shut to auditorium? _____

Back-and-forth walking not encouraged? _____

Brief curtain speech from sponsor/head usher? _____

After the Performance(s)

Date payment mailed to producing co.: _____ (should be day of perf.)

Date written report of event mailed to funding sources, school personnel, etc.:

_____(should be *immediately*)

Clean-up crew for: Front of house: _____ Tel.: _____

                                                         _____ Tel.: _____

                         Backstage: _____ Tel.: _____

                                                       _____ Tel.: _____

                       Auditorium: _____ Tel.: _____

                                                        _____ Tel.: _____

                 Dressing rooms: _____ Tel.: _____

                                                           _____ Tel.: _____

Evaluation forms: Date rec'd from co.: _____ (or wrote up own)

Date distributed: _____ Date collected: _____

Date mailed copy to company: _____

Follow up on media coverage: Who? _____ Date done: _____

Any reviews to clip and file _____ What? _____ Which paper? _____

Date reviews mailed to company: _____

Follow up on school coverage: Use of study guides, etc. Who? _____

Date done: _____

Planning for next event: Date to begin: _____

Date to recontact company or find a new one:

_____

Options

(Use this list if any of these options apply to you)

How many seats available this performance? _____

How many performances? _____

Total number of seats available: _____

How many tickets printed _____ Printer: _____ Tel: _____

How many tickets sold one week before performance: _____

Plan for selling more tickets: _____

_____

Programs? _____ Date to printer: _____ Back from printer: _____

Date brought to house: _____

Press invited?

_____ Who? _____ Tel.: _____ Attending: _____ Date rechecked: _____

_____ Who? _____ Tel.: _____ Attending: _____ Date rechecked: _____

TV critics invited?

_____ Who? _____ Tel.: _____ Attending: _____ Date rechecked: _____

_____ Who? _____ Tel.: _____ Attending: _____ Date rechecked: _____

Radio critics invited?

_____ Who? _____ Tel.: _____ Attending: _____ Date rechecked: _____

_____ Who? _____ Tel.: _____ Attending: _____ Date rechecked: _____

Funding sources invited?

_____ Who? _____ Tel.: _____ Attending: _____ Date rechecked: _____

_____ Who? _____ Tel.: _____ Attending: _____ Date rechecked: _____

School personnel invited? (superintendent, board, principals, supervisors)

_____ Who? _____ Tel.: _____ Attending: _____ Date rechecked: _____

_____ Who? _____ Tel.: _____ Attending: _____ Date rechecked: _____

We want our children to love what many of us have come to love, the theatre, and to be able to grow, spiritually and emotionally, and to have some lively entertainment. Our mission statement, "To bring the best theatre available to our children," to all our children, is still what we want. And I don't think you can put it more simply than that.

Anita Wesson,
sponsor, Children's Theatre Board of Winston-Salem, N.C.

What do you think are the principles of good sponsorship?

A good sponsor is first and foremost a host. We are, in a sense, hiring a group of artists to work with us on a common goal within our community. We want the artists we hire to enjoy their stay in Michigan, and we want to get their best performance. So, we're going to do everything possible to make their stay comfortable. They can concentrate on their art, and we'll concentrate on the problems. We bend over backward to make the artists feel welcome. We have a party for the company. We want them to have a chance to relax for an evening in a private home and have a good meal and some fun. We also do a welcome packet, listing things to do in Detroit. We try for courtesy transportation if they don't have their own. We have available, whenever possible, theatre tickets, if they choose to use them. We don't push them, but we make many options available.

Professionally, we do everything to make sure that we're ready for the production. We have the theatre ready, the house staff ready, the stagehands ready, everybody ready. We provide lunches for the company between shows. These are little things, and they're just common courtesies that should be done in the profession.

Those touches can make all the difference in the world.

Well, it's amazing the horror stories that we get from some companies arriving in a town. The sponsor calls and says, "I left a map at the hotel. Your first school is such and such. I'll try to get in to see you. I put the check in the mail." That's it. The company is staying in some awful motel and traveling with a map in the morning. They arrive at the location, and there's nobody to greet them, no coffee, no nothing. Half the time the school doesn't even know they're arriving. And then heaven help them if the performance isn't good! The sponsor's screaming bloody murder because fourth-grade teacher Mr. Jones didn't like the performance. What they do not realize is that it is all the actor can do to keep his brains unscrambled under those poor conditions.

How do you work good sponsorship on the road?

We have a road manager who travels with the company and works for the company. Our man

INTERVIEW

with Mickey Miners, Director, Detroit Youtheatre, Detroit Institute of Arts, Detroit, Michigan

calls ahead to make sure the school knows about the performance. He calls to make sure the janitors are notified. Then, instead of the stage manager, who's trying to work with the performers to get unpacked and get things into dressing rooms, our man gets the stage ready.

Do you feel there is a difference between sponsoring theatre for young people and sponsoring theatre for adults?

Yes. Sponsoring theatre for young people is more difficult. It's more difficult because of conditions. If we sponsored only in our own theatre, sponsorship would be easy because we maintain control. But in young people's theatre, we must reach out to the entire state of Michigan, and sometimes they're not ready for us. And sometimes we're not ready for them, either. Also, in young people's theatre, we're not selling directly to our audience. With adult theatre you advertise a show, but ultimately it is the audience's decision whether or not to come. This is not the case with young people's theatre. The teacher, the parent, the Brownie leader, or somebody else ultimately makes the decision.

Let's talk about some of your marketing strategies.

We do everything possible to give people a reason to come. So we have a birthday party package, complete with party invitations and favors. We have a "Happy Birthday" sign in the lobby. The child gets a gift "from the cast." It's all included in the package. We have Salute Days for the Scouts; organizations are always looking for things to do. We work with holidays. We take advantage of Black History Month. We can also collaborate with the cultural center during special exhibits. We have celebrity parties for the youngsters to meet the performers after the shows.

Do you market programs differently for your Monday through Friday performances at the theatre than you do for your Saturday schedule?

Yes, because Monday through Friday we're working with schools, and schools are easier to advertise to than the public is. We go to the school, we talk to the PTA, we go to curriculum-coordinating meetings, and do all sorts of things to get large groups of children all at one time, and you can provide teaching materials that relate the programs to the curriculum. This is the kind of marketing we do in the schools; we make ourselves very visible and accessible.

How do you compare the Detroit Youtheatre when you started to work there in 1964 with what it is now?

It's completely different. We started with sporadic puppet shows and a film series. Now we're programming at a constant level for a much wider age range. We're far more professional now. The industry's different now. When we started out, there were cute shows and a few gutsy shows. And everybody talked about the puppets! Now the other series outdraws the puppet shows, because the entire industry deals with not only delightful things but gutsy things as well. But I would never want to do a season without a *Cinderella,* a *Sleeping Beauty,* a *Pinocchio.* That's fun and an important part of childhood—plus those stories are good. I also want to do stories about famous people and about

situations, and I want to explore poetry, and I want dance. I love mime. We have had a mime on our series for the last fourteen years. Marcel Marceau can now come to Detroit and play a week to full houses. That's exciting. And we're going to take a part of that praise, because some of those people paying to see it were *kids* who saw it free in schools fourteen years ago when we put our first mime on tour.

What do you hope for young people's theatre in the future?

First and foremost, I want to fill all the seats that are currently vacant. I want to see major stars like Carol Channing do a kids' show. She's a natural. I mean, that lady can communicate with a three-year-old and a ninety-three-year-old with the same technique. And that's what theatre's all about. I'd love to get some well-known performers to do theatre for young people. I'd love to have the economics to do that. I would love to charge the same for a live theatre performance that movie owners charge for the movie *The Wiz.* As sponsors, we have also got to do our work better. For example, Henry Winkler used to work for PART. If we could pay artists like Henry Winkler to keep them working in the field and get teachers and principals and the volunteers to treat them as artists, we could make young people's theatre even better in the future. The people who are going to do this are the talented people in the country. Professional sponsoring is happening more and more, but it's going to take us a few more generations. But we'll get there.

10·THE DIRECTOR AS EDUCATOR

*For of course when the theatre is fine, it will
teach, in the profound way it always has . . .
simply by being; which of course is what our
rapt child deserves—the re-presentation of strong
human experience, clarified and intensified, like
sunlight through a burning glass.*

Jonathan Levy, *"A Theatre of the Imagination"*

The concept of "total theatre" is new to the theatre. Shakespeare didn't develop study guides; Molière didn't hold seminars; David Belasco didn't conduct backstage tours of the theatre. Only since the 1960s have theatres added education people to their staffs to promote liaison with schools and communities. Even more recently have numbers of theatres held seminars for adult ticket-holders. In many theatres directors still frown on any educational accouterments, making grand statements like, "The production must stand on its own."

Certainly the production must first and foremost have artistic merit. No study guide can rescue a bad theatre piece. Particularly for young audiences, no seminar will ever clarify the convoluted, overintellectualized intentions of a director. Nor can visits from the actors enliven a tired production, at least not for long. The intrinsic difference between young people's theatre and theatre for adults is the child audience, with its particular emotional, cognitive, and social needs. Con-

322

sequently, as a director of theatre for young people, you must understand the special needs of this child audience. Because theatre is often new to them, children need adequate preparation to know what is happening.

Given the limited number of performances young people attend, you are being unrealistic if you hope that one production will immediately stimulate a full aesthetic experience. In your role as educator you must ensure that a theatre experience—before, during, and after—is an optimum one. Remember, if you don't take the lead in presenting total theatre, someone who knows little about your production can usurp your job as educator and may do more harm than good.

Theatre is not a traditional component in elementary classrooms. Children must learn about the theatre before they fully appreciate it. You must prepare each child to become a theatre gourmet. Just as reading about a country before you travel there increases rather than spoils its impact, so can preparation and follow-up increase the effectiveness of a production.

You may have heard stories, mostly from parents who have a particular interest in professional theatre, of their five-year-olds being mesmerized for four hours by a particularly dense production of *Hamlet*. Or the three seven-year-olds who staged the entire first act of *Waiting for Godot* the day after the production. Or a child who "discovered" the theatre while walking down Broadway, paid the $40 ticket price, entered the building, and became an avid theatregoer. These children are unusual and live in places where the theatre is readily accessible.

Not all children are as lucky as the drama critic Clive Barnes, who once stated in his review of a children's play:

"Frankly, I suspect what is known as Children's Theatre will always be a mystery to me. As a child, fortunately, I was never exposed to its childish excesses. I had the good fortune to grow up on adult—or what is laughingly known as adult—theatre. At least my raw and callow brain was never patronized. The first play I happened to see was *King Lear*. Gielgud was Lear and he never gave me the occasion to look back." Few children have the "good fortune" to see John Gielgud in *Lear*. In fact, most children wouldn't even understand *King Lear* on the first viewing. You must try to prepare them to understand and appreciate the theatre as much as any privileged child who lives in London or New York.

Your task as educator is not to develop pieces that teach about the hazards of drugs or the development of the metric system. Lectures by experts and slide shows accomplish these educational goals in a more appropriate manner. Your job is to develop materials, train actors, and assist teachers in presenting a total package that is first and foremost entertaining, as well as being instructive. Remember, the production does not itself change because of what you do in your job as educator. What you are working on is extra-production materials and experiences

We know that children hardly have any artistic criteria to be able to assess the value of a work of art. That is why they are so easily led astray and satisfied with the shallow and trivial—and that is why our responsibility is so great.
Ilse Rodenberg,
president, ASSITEJ

I wish children's theatre would rethink its self-perception of having to be educational. I know why it reached this point: its market was the schools, and the schools said, "It better be educational!" Children go to the theatre to be entertained. If they are enlightened too, that is truly good theatre.
Ellen Rodman,
director, Children's Information Services, National Broadcasting Company

to help prepare the kids for the play and assist the parent or teacher to follow up what occurred.

This role may seem new to you. Most directors, undervaluing their function as educators, make the development of performance preparation and follow-up a low priority. Well-intentioned but unsophisticated in the field of education, they distribute poorly conceived study materials or present boring seminars on the theatre. We will attempt to answer all your questions and alleviate your fears by delineating the best and most expedient way to become a fine educator.

PREPARING THE TOTAL THEATRE PACKAGE

This chapter is not concerned with how theatre educates, but rather with how the director should relate to education on a practical level: developing a *total theatre* event for young people and beginning to accomplish this *total theatre experience*. You will notice that, unlike most of the previous chapters, this text is not divided into general principles and those specific to young people's theatre. The two main areas of this chapter are: (1) developing performance-based materials, (2) evaluating the production.

AN ARGUMENT FOR TOTAL THEATRE

You may have to justify the total theatre package to your cast, crew, board of directors, and even your funding agencies. Here are your three best surefire arguments:

1. Many experiences require preparation   Let's liken the theatre experience to the art experience. Few children go to a museum for the first time without someone to explain what they are seeing. Whether a teacher, a parent, or a tour guide, someone usually points out various aspects of the art. If left unattended, most children would be bored quickly or would probably laugh at the statues of "naked people." A museum is different from a theatre, however, in that people can generally spend as much or as little time as they want in viewing a single painting. The painting remains; theatre keeps moving.

Let's also compare the theatre with a sporting event. Suppose you take your English cousins to a baseball game. These cousins have never seen baseball; they are confused; they spend three hours trying to figure out what is going on. If you had prepared them by explaining the rules and objectives, they would know what to look for, become involved in the action, and actually enjoy the game. Theatre is not baseball, of course, but it is similar in one important respect: Knowing what to look for increases one's enjoyment.

A first theatrical experience can be equally confusing and unenjoyable. The complexity of the experience may be overwhelming: all those

If a class is to have a common experience when viewing theatre, then they should have some common expectations or points of departure. Since children's theatre is most frequently a group experience, it would probably be beneficial to conceive of that activity as containing pre-viewing, viewing, and post-viewing components.
Helane S. Rosenberg and Jeffrey K. Smith,
CTR Research Issue

lights and noise! Children get bored, or laugh. Some children with an instinct for the theatre may focus on the event. Most of today's children who watch television, where the camera's eye does all the focusing for them, need help in zeroing in on the theatrical event. You need to prepare your audience for the theatre event.

2. Leading researchers in education, psychology, and arts education stress preparation for education experiences Much documentation exists in related disciplines (in such publications as *Journal of Educational Psychology* and *Review of Educational Research*) that justifies and advocates the use of written and personal preparation for educational experiences. Behavioral scientists, experts in testing and measurement, and designers of curricula have conducted research in the area of *advance organizers* (as psychologists refer to information that describes or suggests what is to follow). You're not alone in wanting to provide the optimum experience for young people. Take your cue from educational researchers.

3. A total theatre package will help sell your production The materials that you develop for the production will first be shown to adults.

The Kingdom of the Root Vegetables is a play developed by the Looking Glass Theatre, Providence, Rhode Island, in the Nutrition Education Through the Arts Program. Children are shown taking parts as vegetables in the play, which teaches good eating habits *and* entertains—a necessary combination. Directed by Karen De Mauro.

If well developed, these advance organizers can be one of the best ways of advertising your product. Not only are good production-related materials educational for the children, but they also can effectively sell the production to adults, who make the booking decisions.

METHODS AND MATERIALS: THE TOTAL THEATRE PACKAGE

Your primary decision is choosing the kind of presentation you want to develop. Your choices are: (1) television videotape, (2) slide and tape package, (3) seminars and/or arts workshops, (4) study guides, (5) any combination of the first four. Your choices depend, of course, on the amount of money, personnel, and time you have available as well as the location of the performance (school or theatre). Ideally, you could use all of the above choices, but you have to be realistic and work within your limitations. In fact, the most effective package might be preperformance videotape, actors visiting the classroom immediately after the performance, and classroom teachers using the study guides during the weeks following the performance. You will have to choose the preparations and follow-ups that best fit your situation, but a thorough understanding of your options can help you make the best artistic and educational choices.

TELEVISION VIDEOTAPE

For the director/educator the greatest boon of the eighties is the television videotape. Exciting artistic possibilities, unlimited educational potential, and current growth in television-equipped classrooms make the videotape one of the best ways to prepare a class of young people for a theatre event. Instead of attempting to compete with television, you can harness its power and popularity for use in conjunction with the theatre production. Although the initial preparation is time-consuming and costly, once the tape is completed, you have a packaged artistic product that can be duplicated and distributed relatively easily and with little expense.

There are three main arguments in favor of producing your own videotape as a preproduction advance organizer: star power, scope, uniformity.

Star power Children love celebrities. After one of your actors appears on video, this readily recognizable performer can often have as much charisma for the children as Mr. Rogers. The young people, particularly those below third grade, who see the tape rarely distinguish between this television performance and a national broadcast. Even if they know the show was locally made, they still love to see this taped actor suddenly appear live in their school or on the stage. Remember, knowing that actors can have such strong impact means you must take care in not abusing this power. After the first impact has worn off, the actors must of course keep the audience interested by their talent as performers. But the initial wooing task may be made easier by the videotape.

The host of a show, maybe you, can elicit a powerful response as well. One director of a university production who appeared in the preperformance videotape was constantly recognized throughout the community. As she greeted the school bus on the day of the performance, she (and her production) commanded great respect.

Scope The scope of the videotape is almost limitless. Any location where a camera has access can be shown; on tape, any number of actors and crew members can enter the classroom; any technical effect, prop, or costume can be shown. The scope of this tape is as vast as your imagination.

One of the most commonly used formats is the talk show/magazine interview format, based loosely on such popular shows as *The Tonight Show* or *PM Magazine.* In this type of program you or someone else with a winning personality and a pleasant voice presents various demonstrations, interviews, rehearsals, and technical segments based on the play. You can interview actors about their characters, show various stages of the same scene throughout the rehearsal process, or take the audience on a backstage tour of the theatre. You can add a segment with one actor teaching the audience a song from the play. You can even show costumes being developed from sketch to actual garment. You can demonstrate how a flashpot works. You can focus on a scale model of a stage set, and then show the completed setting. The magic of television compresses time and space. You can make television tapes that are magical as well as educational.

Uniformity By choosing to produce a videotape as a preperformance advance organizer, you are assuring that each class' preparation is relatively uniform. You develop an artistically sound, well-presented product. All the teacher has to do is put the tape onto the monitor.

A recent study investigated the consequences of providing various videotaped advance organizers to children before their viewing of live theatre.* Three hundred fourth, fifth, and sixth graders were assigned to four groups. Each group viewed a different tape, of the same length and produced by the same crew, but with differing emphasis. The researchers concluded that significant differences existed in the children's responses. The children who viewed the tapes about the technical aspects of the play seemed to be able to focus on the various technical aspects without their emotional response to the story being affected. The study also suggests that the balance between empathy and aesthetic distance may be tilted toward aesthetic appreciation through the use of a videotape that tells the children something about the story before they see the play.

*Helane S. Rosenberg and Jeffrey K. Smith, "The Effects of Advance Organizers on Children's Responses to Theatre Viewing," *Children's Theatre Review,* 30, No. 2 (Spring 1981).

SLIDE-AND-TAPE PACKAGE

The preparation of photographic slides and accompanying audio cassette tape is another approach for implementing a production. A slide-and-tape package is really a "poor man's videotape" and has been utilized in classrooms for the last decade. All you need to do to prepare a slide-and-tape package is to take photographs of what you want to show, put them together in logical sequence, and add a voice-over (yours or someone else who has a pleasant voice) onto the cassette. The slides are numbered, and the tape has a "beep" sound to signal when to change the slide. Although slides are not really novel, they are extremely practical, since almost every school has a cassette tape recorder and slide projector with carousel.

The contents of the photographs may include a series on the development of rehearsals, a day in the life of an actor, or the progressions from prop sketch to actual prop. The tape can include songs and music from the production as background music. The best subjects deal with the magic of theatre: transformations of spaces, faces, and bodies. In the manner of a travelogue, you can take your future audience where they've never been: backstage to see the entire production process.

SEMINARS AND/OR ARTS WORKSHOPS

Certainly the most personal way to complement a production is by sending real live people to visit the classroom before or after the play, or by conducting such visits at the theatre. Whether the person is an actor or a staff member, the personal effect of direct, human contact often outweighs the logistical difficulties of scheduling classroom visits and the length of time spent in developing the materials and manner of presentation.

The content of these pre- and postperformance sessions should be related, of course, to the person's specialty and training. Actors can conduct arts activities: music, drama, dance, and integrated arts workshops. Also, single-subject sessions related to the story or major concepts of the play in such areas as social studies, science, or math can be presented by actors. Because many actors don't have classroom teaching experience or training, make sure they are interested in this type of activity before you insist they visit the school. Most actors, particularly those performing for young people, find they derive great benefit from direct confrontation with the kids. Instead of being exhausted after performing and then leading activities in the classroom, actors find they are exhilarated by such contact.

Metro Theatre Circus, a seven-person St. Louis-based company, presents workshops in the schools directly after each performance. The performer, each with a particular specialty, enters the classroom and conducts a workshop and a question-and-answer session. The Circus states: "The actors may work to create a spontaneous dramatic scene,

I think it's very hard to ask actors to come into schools and to ask them to make these very necessary subtle relationships. But actors can do it with children if they know their stuff.
Peter Slade,
interview in Birmingham, England

develop a movement sequence, explore rhythmic patterns, or perhaps compose a group poem or story. The goal in these workshops is to guide the child to explore his or her own imaginative resources. It is hoped that this process will be both challenging and joyous."

Designers and technical staff often feel they are the forgotten members of the staff of a theatre for young people. Yet the technical staff can add an often missing element: an exploration of the behind-the-scenes creative process. Some of the designers can explain how and why the technical elements were constructed; they can even lead the class through the making of simple props or costumes.

STUDY GUIDES

American theatres use study guides more than any other performance-related material. Relative ease of development and distribution, teachers' familiarity with written lesson plans, and limited expense make study guides a good choice for preparing a class to view a production. The study guide should be easy to read, pleasing to the eye, and concise. Study guides that try to prove just how brilliant you are end up in the trash can.

Having requested study guides from over 200 professional, community, and university companies that perform for young people, we began to draw some conclusions about the current state of the art of

The company members of Metro Theatre Circus, St. Louis, have training and experience both in performing for children and in facilitating arts activities in the classroom. *Mud Weavings.* Written and directed by Zaro Weil.

....

The child without access to a stimulating arts program is being systematically cut off from most of the ways in which he can perceive the world. His brain is being systematically damaged. In many ways he is being de-educated.
Dr. Jean Huston,
"Why Children Should Draw," Saturday Review, September 1977
....

the study guide. The following list represents what is most commonly included in the contents:

1. **Theatre philosophy and policy.** The artistic or education director states the overall goals of the company, the artistic objectives of this production, and the expectations for the audience's enjoyment.
2. **Information about the cast and production staff.** Often included are biographies and past theatre credits.
3. **Plot summary and other script-related material.** The study guide summarizes the story and presents important background information about the period or people depicted in the script, as well as about the author.
4. **General theatre procedures.** The study guide explains to the teacher what to expect from the production and how to help during the performance.
5. **Evaluation form.** Often included is a short response form to be filled in by the teacher or sponsor.
6. **Request for materials.** Frequently the company requests production-related letters, essays, stories, and pictures that the audience created following the performance. These materials are often analyzed or displayed by the theatre.
7. **Activities for classroom.** Types of activities include drama, movement, visual art, music, creative writing, language arts, imagination, creative problem-solving, and discussion questions.
8. **Bibliography.** Two kinds of bibliographies are included: one lists books that are production-related; the other lists books that deal with general arts activities.

Many of the study guides surveyed were excellent, but others were not. The most effective ones were:

- aesthetically pleasing
- written in clear, concise language
- aimed at teacher, not at student (often the activities were age-ranged, so that teacher could choose activities appropriate for class development)
- not overwhelming in content or sophistication level, particularly for a teacher with no arts experience
- easily recognizable as belonging to a particular company; each study guide from a company looks like the previous study guide from that company
- thematically consistent, including such aids as treasure map, crossword puzzles, cutouts

Walt Whitman said, "To have great poets, we must have great audiences." The children of today will be the audience of tomorrow. To have great drama we must have great audiences. Train the dramatic instinct of the children of today and the drama of tomorrow will be great drama because its audiences will demand it.
Constance Mackay,
How to Produce Children's Plays, 1915

Opposite is a study guide from Yellow Brick Road Shows, Huntington Beach, California.

IMAGINATION MAP

Yellow Brick Road Shows

Dear Friend:

To increase the value of the live theatre experience, we suggest you "follow-up" "A Tale of Two Sisters" with some of these activities! They are designed as a springboard for your imagination. Many of the techniques employed here can be used again by you as vehicles for bringing other classroom subjects to life. (Look for special "classroom" notes.)

We hope the Yellow Brick Road Shows "Imagination Map" proves valuable and we welcome all correspondence from both you and your students. For further reading in Creative Drama please consult the bibliography. Additional "Imagination Maps" are available – see centerfold.

Rita Grossberg, Artistic Director

Dr. Ronald D. Wood, Education Advisor, CSUF

Possible Discussions

- After the show you and your class might discuss how - seeing theatre is different from watching television, or going to the movies.

- Other subjects to be discussed just after the show might be:

  Who was in the story?
  What happened to them?
  Where did they go?
  How did you help them?

- Later discussions might include sharing personal thoughts about:

  Dreams
  Seeing something that was really something else
  Emotions (like the wizards anger, the sister's fear etc.)

Classroom

Applying a personal approach to topical discussions by including questions like: How would you feel if ... What would you do if ... etc., will aid in stimulating creative discussion

Creative Writing

Many ideas included in the Creative Drama section can be used to stimulate writing projects. Here are a few more you might like to try:

- Write a story about:
  The Magic Berry Bush Bonnie saw
  The Black Cloud that turned into Ravens
  The Day the Wizard learned to Change His Form
  The Night Mary spent at the Wizard's Castle
  Where Bonnie and Mary's Parents Are

- Write a letter:
  From Bonnie and Mary to their parents telling them about the Wizard
  From Bonnie to Gamble thanking him for his help
  From Mary to Bonnie telling her that She's in trouble
  From the Wizard to Gamble telling him that he will share his magic with him

- Or make up new stories about Bonnie, Mary, Gamble and the Wizard.

Classroom

Let the class use their imaginations to write fictional stories based on factual topics you are studying. It will encourage the growth of versatile minds!

Creative Drama

Creative Drama uses the child's natural impulse for dramatic play as an instrument to encourage the development of his/her own creative resources. It does so without the pressure or embarrassment caused by performing in front of an audience. To use creative drama in the classroom you need not be trained in theatre. You need only to be conscious of the individual nature of self-expression.

Sensory Exercises

Listening

- With eyes closed listen to the sounds outside of the room, inside the room, inside yourself

- Take turns making a series of sounds. With eyes closed try to determine how the sounds were made. Quietly share ideas with your neighbor.

- In the play there were times when what you heard was not what it appeared to be. This time as you take turns making a series of sounds use your imagination to think of what magical things the person making the sounds might be doing.

Tasting and Smelling

- Bring to the classroom a variety of things to taste and smell. With blindfolds on try to determine what each thing is.

- Now without the actual object to taste or smell, imagine that you are tasting it, smelling it (pantomime the action).

Touching

- Bring to the classroom a large cloth or pillowcase "feely bag" filled with objects to touch. With blindfolds try to identify each one.

- Now imagine what they might be if you found each one hidden in Gamble Gold's Coat!

Seeing

- Look at the colors in the classroom, outside the window. How many colors do you see?

- Look at the faces of your friends. How do they look different from one another?

- Have someone stand in front of everyone. After you have all looked carefully, close your eyes as the person changes the way they look (button or unbutton something, stand the collar up on your shirt, etc.) Open your eyes and see who sees the change first. Take turns.

- In the play there were times when what you saw was not what it appeared to be. Take the class for a walk and take a look at the clouds. What might they be?

Classroom

Broaden the study of many topics by taking them into the sensory realm i.e. what might it feel like to walk on the moon, on the ocean floor, or snowy mountain top?

Storytelling

- As you tell a story ask the children to provide various sounds ("The Bremen Town Musicians" calls for various animal sounds)

- As you tell a "made up" story stop at various points and ask questions like:
  Then what did he do?
  Then where did She go?
  Then how did they feel?
  In this manner the class will join you in composing a story.

- Sit in a circle. Begin a story. Allow each person, in turn, to add on to the story. Remember the story must start with the first person in the circle and with the last.

- As you tell a story have the class pantomime the action. Later, small groups can create their own stories and appoint their own narrator who will tell the story as they pantomime it.

Classroom

The story telling games are an excellent aid in language development for younger children and in developing composition skills in your older children.

Creative Environment

It may be helpful in establishing and maintaining control to use a pre-arranged control device such as a tambourine or cymbal. The device should indicate the times when action is to "freeze" or certain rhythms are too be maintained.

Environments Created with Sound

- As you tell a story have the class provide sound at appropriate moments.
- In pairs take turns telling a story and having your partner make sound effects for you.
- With some sounds try to create together the mood of:
  The Wizard's Magical Forest
  The Wizard's Castle
  The Night that Mary went out to pick Chestnuts

Environments Created with Bodies

- As one half of the class makes sounds creating an environment, have the other half grow into the creatures that might inhabit those environments. Trade roles.
- Assign various environments to groups of about five children. See if the class can guess what type of environment each group has created!

Moving Through Environments

- In the play the characters moved differently when moving through a dream (slow motion). Ask the class to try various activities (bouncing ball, jumping rope, climbing a ladder, etc.) while moving through:
  A Dream
  A Cloud
  Jello
  Ice Water
- Ask half the class to create an environment through which the other half must pass.

Classroom Notes

Creating and moving through environments can be especially useful in studying geography, history, and science, i.e. Columbus and his men discovering America.

Creating Character

- Talk about the many changes the Wizard made with his body, i.e. he became a tree, a bird, a lion, etc ...
- Try changing your form as the Wizard did
- With a partner take turns teaching each other new form's as the Wizard did Mary (as if you were mirroring one another).

Classroom

To learn the shapes of letters, numbers or various geographic locations try using your bodies, individually, in pairs or in groups!

Visual Art

The technical simplicity of our show stimulates the child's visual imagination. You will discover this when you try some of these ideas.

- Ask your class to draw alone, in pairs, or in small groups:

  The Sisters (Bonnie and Mary)
  Gamble Gold and his Coat
  The Wizard Changing his Form
  The Wizard's snake
  The Raven's Stealing Bonnie's Berries
  The Sister's Cottage
  The Secret Passage to the Wizard's Castle
  The Wizard's "Magic Room"
  A Map of the Wizard's Land

- Or Build out of "found" objects – clay, paper mache, cardboard or styrofoam:

  The Wizard's Castle
  A Dream Machine
  A Wizard Mask or Dream Mask
  Puppets of the Sister's and Gamble Gold

Classroom

To enhance the study of people, places and things try creating them visually, i.e. a paper mache igloo in and around which two or three class members might dramatize a typical Eskimo day.

A Note About Music

Musical strengths may be developed in a variety of ways from ideas given in the Creative Drama material. A few examples are given here:

- When you are working on "listening" try using various types of recorded music to stimulate the imagination with regard to action.
- When you create environments with sound let the children try classroom instruments in a new way to create moods.

- When you are using your bodies in different ways, as the Wizard did try using different kinds of music to stimulate the changes.
- As you tell a story let the class make "sound effects" with found objects, i.e. erasers, pencils, book covers.

Classroom

Often the music of a certain time period or country you are studying will offer the class new suggestions about what the people were like!!

Bibliography

"Drama/Theatre Framework for California Public Schools." State Department of Education, Sacramento, California, 1972.

Heinig, Ruth Beall and Stillwell, Lyda. "Creative Dramatics for the Classroom Teacher." Englewood Cliffs, N.J.: Prentice - Hall, Inc., 1974.

McCaslin, Nellie. "Creative Dramatics in the Classroom." New York: David McKay Co., 1974.

Siks, Geraldine Brain. "Creative Dramatics: An Art for Children." New York: Harper and Brothers, 1958.

Way, Brian. "Development Through Drama." London: Longmans, 1967.

This rainbow is hand-tinted by members of the Yellow Brick Road Shows.

The Imagination Map was set on an Alpha Comp in American Typewriter Medium;   Paper Carnival Craft Groove – Sunshine;   Graphic Design – Dean Gerrie and David Sandstrom;   Printing – Detail Quality Printing, Santa Ana, California.

Reproduced on the preceding page is an excellent study guide developed by the Yellow Brick Road Shows in Huntington Beach, California. Its merits include brevity, visual appeal, simplicity, and, most of all, fun!

THEATRE IN EDUCATION: A CASE STUDY OF THE ULTIMATE THEATRE PACKAGE

....

The work in schools or the theatre should relate closely to the needs of the children. This is best achieved through a working liaison with the theatres. . . . In my view Theatre in Education should strike a balance between (1) drama as a teaching method, and (2) theatre as an enriching experience. In both types of work, it should relate closely to the schools it serves and the community.
Stuart Bennett,
former TIE leader, Belgrade Theatre, Coventry, England
....

Theatre in Education (TIE), the theatre movement that began in England in the mid-sixties, combines the best features of theatre for young people and drama in education. Its practitioners, called actor/teachers because they are trained and/or experienced in theatre and education, develop original theatre pieces tailored to their own artistic needs and the curricular needs of the young people in the community. These actor/teachers work closely with school administrators, teachers, and young people to develop pieces that are primarily theatrical but also have educational objectives. Involvement occurs in the planning stages through lecture/demonstrations, during the performance itself in the form of participation from the audience, and after the performance through evaluation sessions with teachers. In the two decades since the idea was developed, teams of actor/teachers have evolved ways of working within school systems that can be replicated in America.

The following discussion illustrates from beginning to end just how the British-based Belgrade TIE team approached the total theatre package of *Ice Station Zero*,* an original piece for seven- to eleven-year-olds on nuclear energy.

Several months before intense planning begins, leaders from the team meet initially with members of the Advisory Council, a group made up of head teachers from representative schools, to discuss long-range plans. At this meeting both artistic factors—theme, type of participation—and practical factors—bussing, cost—are discussed. After the ideas are approved at the meeting, class teachers, who have been informed months earlier that a program will take place, receive specific information concerning the play's major issues and theme. Many teachers use this four-month lead time to develop lessons on related topics such as hovercrafts, nuclear energy, or democratic voting process.

Back at the theatre the team is developing the piece. One member, usually the writer/researcher or the designer, begins to work on materials for this production. The team provides a packet of materials for the teacher containing information on a wide variety of production-related topics. The team also develops a letter from one of the characters in the play to be sent to each classroom. In order to be as realistic as possible, the letter is mailed from France, since it mentions that the character is currently vacationing there. During this phase the designer also constructs boarding passes, to be distributed to each child upon entering the theatre.

*Participation aspects of *Ice Station Zero* are presented in Chapter 5, "Creating a Play for Young People."

Just before opening, the team again meets with the Advisory Council to submit a script for approval. The team also holds lecture/demonstrations for teachers who wish to preview the production. Both attending teachers and Advisory Council members, who have known the team for many years, often give constructive suggestions.

The run begins. The classes who have been prepared and who have diligent teachers are easy to spot. They seem to understand every production and story aspect and participate eagerly.

After the production the team holds follow-up sessions with teachers to elicit feedback, which is carefully noted for future reference. Some team members attend follow-up sessions in various classrooms around Coventry. Other team members sift through the teachers' evaluation forms and read the catalogue materials sent from young people.

Of course, you may not have the ability to develop such complex programs, particularly if you serve a wide variety of locations, but you may get ideas from TIE about an ultimate theatre package.

PRODUCTION EVALUATION

Science almost seems to be the antithesis of art. The term "theatre research" makes many artists bristle. A systematic empirical process may on the surface seem to have little value for the theatre. In fact, the reverse holds true; many of the ways in which scientists view the world can be used to take a closer look at the artistic process and product. The way scientists measure changes in various behavioral, cognitive (learning), and affective (emotional) levels of children can help the artist understand the educational aspects of the theatre. The following section of this chapter deals with how scientific methods can serve artistic and educational objectives.

This section may at first seem to go against your grain. But take it for what it is: a minicourse in measurement methods that can help you become a better theatre artist. As you read these principles, fancy yourself more of a scientist than an artist. Take a systematic view of how theatre effects change, instead of just "feeling" that it does. Try to think of measuring response as well as understanding it instinctively. These principles are based on a discipline (just as the directing process is based on discipline), but it is the discipline of systematic replicability.

Research in the theatre represents the wave of the future. Don't resist too vigorously! If you don't want to become a full-fledged scientist, you may, of course, hire a research associate. As director, however, you must be aware of these principles to oversee the research operations. New procedures are constantly being developed in this rapidly growing field. The following section is only a beginning. If just one reader develops a superior evaluation technique, then this section will be more than worthwhile.

Research in children's drama shall be defined as the development of new or the validation of existing historical, theoretical, descriptive, or experimental knowledge in creative drama or children's theatre by means of scholarly and/or scientific investigation. . . . CTAA endorses and encourages an ongoing program in research in an effort to further develop theory, and validate and strengthen existing practices within the field.
CTAA Executive Committee, *April 1980*

EVALUATING THE PRODUCTION: AUDIENCE RESPONSE

Of course you want to know how the audience responded to the production. You can use three methods:*

- You can *observe* the audience during the production.
- You can *ask* the audience after the production.
- You can *analyze* the audience's *material* written after the production.

OBSERVING THE AUDIENCE

A good director watches the audience during a performance. Through experience the director learns what to look for: when the audience laughs; when they wiggle; when they are silent; when they lean forward. All these behaviors tell the director how the play is being received.

Certainly, you feel the vibrations of the audience. You can sense whether the audience likes the play or not. You have an instinctive way of knowing, but how can you measure this rapport? Which scenes were the most memorable? When exactly did the audience pay most attention? Which were the favorite technical effects?

A checklist of audience behavior can help you to combine your sensitive skills as an audience observer with the systematic observation

Children onstage with actors during an audience participation session of The Second City Children's Theatre. No evaluator of audience response could miss the expression of delight on the children's faces or fail to see their active body positions.

Photo by J. V. III

*Another way to investigate theatre's effectiveness is to compare it to something else in terms of teaching information. So, for example, you could compare the effectiveness of the play *Paul Revere* with a traditional lecture for the purpose of teaching about the American Revolution. This approach does not measure theatre's effectiveness as art, but rather as a teaching tool. The conduct of a study of this nature is beyond the scope of this chapter.

techniques of the scientist. What you are then looking at is how the theatre action affects the behavior of the audience.* By using a checklist, you can begin to make your response more objective and specify which moment affected which behavior. Ultimately, you can draw comparisons between different audiences' responses, between scenes of the same plays, and between plays.

An added plus for observing behaviors of young people is that their behavior is more overt. Unlike adult audiences, kids show you how they feel by moving around. The other types of measures we will discuss (questionnaire and interview) often prove more valid for the adult audience because adults can more easily *tell* you how they feel. Observing behaviors of children, however, can provide you with a reliable measure of what is occurring.

Following is a simplified observational checklist with explanations of overt behavior. This checklist represents just one way of classifying behaviors.† Although you will be asked to observe one individual child at a time, the instrument measures group change—the average or mean of the audience response. As a group measure the instrument has more scientific validity and is appropriate for the study of a group phenomenon: an audience.

Reliability—*the degree to which a given observation or measurement could be repeated by an independent observer with the same result.* Validity—*the extent to which researchers are able to observe or measure what they intend to observe or measure.*

AUDIENCE BEHAVIOR CHECKLIST

	Child 1	Child 2	Child 3	Child 4
Watching/listening onstage				
Watching offstage				
Sharing enjoyment				
Disrupting others				
Discussing relevant information				
Discussing irrelevant information				
Applauding, laughing, smiling				
Rising and moving				
Imitating actor				
Wiggling and yawning				
Keeping time to music/words				
Manipulating object not associated with action of play				

Note: The first behavior in each pair is classified as **positive**, the second as **negative**.

*You can only directly observe changes in what the audience is *doing*, their behavior. The changes in *affect*, how they feel, and *cognition*, what they think, are measured in other non-observational ways.

†The behaviors used in this audience behavior checklist were drawn from a content analysis of audience behaviors of similar subjects during seventy performances of a similar production. The behaviors were classified by the researchers as negative or positive. The instrument was then validated through a series of audience behavior observations of subjects not in the final study.

The core of the method remains the same, no matter what the nature of the observational study. One observer watches one child for 30 seconds and marks an X to note whatever behavior occurs for that child during the time period. The next 15 seconds are for taking a quick rest and finding the next child. (Children are randomly assigned to observers as the kids enter the auditorium.) The important factors in scoring are making a quick decision, marking the behavior, and moving on. The time intervals may be indicated by a flashing light placed unobtrusively, or by a sound tape that can be heard only by the observers through an earphone. The observer must be close enough to see and hear each child, or watch the audience through a one-way mirror. Many observers are needed to observe an entire audience or even a representative sample of the audience. Training sessions must be held before the experiment begins to ensure rater reliability and consistency among the raters—making sure each observer is viewing and classifying behaviors in the same way.

By keeping track of which scored behaviors are responses to which

Note the intense concentration on the faces of the audience members during a performance by Pennsylvania State Children's Theatre Ensemble. Directed by Helen A. Manfull.

specific moments, the director can discover which theatrical moments elicited which responses. In other results of the Rosenberg and Smith studies of responses to *Story Theatre* mentioned earlier in the chapter, the director found out that the audience, who had been prepared by a videotape, exhibited the same number of positive behaviors during the choreographed scene changes as they had during the regular action. An audience who had not been prepared by videotape before the performance and who probably did not know that the scene shift was "part" of the production, exhibited more negative behaviors during the scene shift.

In another Rosenberg and Smith study age differences were made specific. An audience of third and fourth graders viewing *Story Theatre*, for example, exhibited more positive behaviors in scenes with larger groups and in scenes in which the characters played animals. An audience of fifth and sixth graders, when viewing the same production of *Story Theatre*, exhibited more positive behaviors during two- to four-person scenes and during scenes when the rock band played. Knowledge of this nature can help a director age-range plays and draw conclusions about a particular audience's likes and dislikes prior to selecting or directing a production. A checklist is not foolproof, but it can help you to discern more about your audience.

INTERVIEWING THE AUDIENCE

Another way to determine how the audience responded is to interview each child after the production. The potential interviewer must be trained to understand the specifics of interviewing. The central task of an interview is to set up situations and a questioning approach that will increase the flow of valid, relevant information.

The tools for this task are:

- *strategy*, which includes the purpose and objectives, the time and place, and who interviews whom
- *techniques*, which are specific forms of verbal and nonverbal behaviors,
- *tactics*, which are ways in which techniques are varied to meet problems*

The advantages of the interview over the questionnaire include an opportunity to motivate and to guide the person being interviewed. Interviewing also allows flexibility in questioning, control over the interview situation, and opportunity to evaluate the validity of the information by observing the respondent's nonverbal behavior. Remember, an interview is more formal than a conversation, although

*A complete book on interviewing is: Raymond L. Gorden, *Interviewing: Strategy, Techniques, and Tactics*, 3rd ed. (Homewood, IL: Dorsey Press, 1980).

Because of their rapport with the children, actors often can easily determine audience reactions by questioning the children after a performance. Jack Tale Players, Ferrum College, Ferrum, Virginia. Directed by R. Rex Stephenson.

some of the same skills are used for each, such as talking and listening and positively reinforcing information through nonverbal means.

An interview may be *scheduled*—tightly structured with specific questions in a fixed sequence using specific words—or *non-scheduled*—very loose, guided only by a central purpose. Probably for your first experiments in interviewing young people you should use a moderately scheduled interview procedure. The specifics then include:

- contents of the questions
- exact wording of some questions
- sequence of the questions

The following is part of a sample interview schedule from the *Story Theatre* sequence. It was used with children in grades five and six and was geared to work well with novice interviewers.

SAMPLE INTERVIEW

INSTRUCTIONS: Your task is to discover as many specific responses to the production of *Story Theatre* as possible. The more concrete and detailed the account, the better. Although there are eight possible categories we want to explore, you should not mention any area until after you have asked the first questions in the order indicated.

The first question takes an indirect approach, giving you time to build up rapport with the respondent and to demonstrate a nonjudgmental attitude.

1. What sorts of responses did you have to *Story Theatre?* Possible probes: Do you remember any scene in which the actors played animals? Do you remember any costumes that the actors wore? Do you remember when the band played?

2. What (other) sorts of scenes do you remember most? Possible probes: Do you remember Henny Penny? Do you remember when the actors all stood on the highest platform? What was the first scene?
3. Tell me about another scene that you liked.
4. Tell me what happened in that scene.
5. Describe that part to me.
6. Why do you think that character did that?
7. Why do you think the director/designer did that?
8. Here is a photograph of a moment in the play. What's happening here?
   Possible probe: What is that actor doing?

The answers were recorded and their content analyzed to find out how the various audiences responded to the production.

Pat Goldberg, in her study of audience responses, developed a category system to examine the responses of school-age individuals (grades 4 through 12) to the theatre production.* A system of this specificity can enable you to classify interview responses.

CATEGORY SYSTEM

Knowledge. Statements in this category indicate the individual received information from the play.

Inference. Statements in this category indicate the individual made a mental leap from behavior on stage to some conclusion of meaning of behavior.

Evaluation. Statements in this category indicate the individual is making a judgment about experiencing the production. This category has four subcategories: general, production, content/script, sensory perception.

Enjoyment. Statements in this category indicate the individual liked or disliked the production as a whole or some part of it.

Preference. Statements in this category indicate the individual likes something "better than" or "less than" something else.

Empathy. Statements in this category indicate the individual was personally involved in the production through expression of an emotion or identification with a character and/or situation.

Sensory Perception. Statements in this category indicate the individual has noticed color, light, movement, sound, but does not refer to it as an intentional effect of the production as used by the designer or director.

Sensory Reaction. Statements in this category indicate the individual is describing a reaction to what he or she experienced during performance.

No Reaction. The student states he didn't have, or can't remember, a reaction to a particular part of the play.

Other. Statements that do not fit into the above categories are placed here.

---

*Pat D. Goldberg, "Development of a Category System for the Analysis of the Response of the Young Theatre Audience." Dissertation, Florida State University, 1977.

QUESTIONNAIRE

The questionnaire is not a separate method; it is an extension of the interview. The most essential difference between an interview and a questionnaire is that the interviewer asks the questions orally, while in a questionnaire the respondent reads the question. For this reason the questionnaire is not appropriate for young people below grade four. Nothing about the nature or the form of the questions or answers distinguishes the interview from the questionnaire. The plusses for using the questionnaire are economy—no paying and training of interviewers—and anonymity—no worry about questions being answered to please the interviewer.

SEMANTIC DIFFERENTIAL

A form of questionnaire that is more appropriate for young audiences, who may have a limited reading and writing ability, is the *semantic differential*. A semantic differential is made up of sets of adjective pairs that describe opposite attributes of the production. The semantic differential helps the respondents to clarify their responses and the researcher to classify and statistically utilize the responses. In a rough/smooth adjective pair, for example, the respondent can evaluate the production as:

rough   1   2   3   4   5   smooth

Here 1 means very rough, 2 means somewhat rough, 3 means a combination of rough and smooth, 4 means somewhat smooth, and 5 means very smooth. For children below grade four, the number of discriminations may be reduced from five to three:

rough   1   2   3   smooth

An added benefit of using the semantic differential is that it can be personally administered.

Following is a semantic differential used in a Rosenberg and Smith study.* Included are directions and adjective pairs.

SEMANTIC DIFFERENTIAL

This page contains lists of adjectives. These adjectives might be used to describe the play, *Story Theatre*. The adjectives directly across the page from each other are opposites. For example: hot—cold, old—young. Between each set of opposites are the numbers 1, 2, 3, 4, and 5.

---

*The adjective pairs used in the semantic differential were drawn from a content analysis of approximately 1,500 essays concerning the theatre experience written by elementary school children.

Read each set of opposites. Decide which word tells how you feel about *Story Theatre*. Circle the number that is closer to the way you feel. For example:

hot   1   2   3   4   5   cold

If hot describes the way you feel about *Story Theatre,* circle 1. If you think it was sort of hot, circle 2. If you think it was cold, circle 5. If it was sort of cold, circle 4. If it was not hot or cold or was a combination of hot/cold, circle 3.

hot	*1*	*2*	*3*	*4*	*5*	*cold*
hard	*1*	*2*	*3*	*4*	*5*	*soft*
good	*1*	*2*	*3*	*4*	*5*	*bad*
loud	*1*	*2*	*3*	*4*	*5*	*quiet*
full	*1*	*2*	*3*	*4*	*5*	*empty*
dry	*1*	*2*	*3*	*4*	*5*	*wet*
rough	*1*	*2*	*3*	*4*	*5*	*smooth*
old	*1*	*2*	*3*	*4*	*5*	*young*
little	*1*	*2*	*3*	*4*	*5*	*big*
high	*1*	*2*	*3*	*4*	*5*	*low*
light	*1*	*2*	*3*	*4*	*5*	*dark*
messy	*1*	*2*	*3*	*4*	*5*	*neat*
tame	*1*	*2*	*3*	*4*	*5*	*wild*
greedy	*1*	*2*	*3*	*4*	*5*	*generous*
pretty	*1*	*2*	*3*	*4*	*5*	*ugly*
fast	*1*	*2*	*3*	*4*	*5*	*slow*

CONTENT ANALYSIS OF WRITTEN MATERIAL AND ARTWORK

Often young people respond to the production by sending stories, letters, essays, and pictures to the actors and the technicians after the production. These works are wonderful pieces of creativity and can be treated as such. Or you can begin systematically to summarize and trace trends in responses through content analysis. Content analysis, a simple survey and cataloguing approach, can provide you with some helpful information: which scenes the children liked, what moments seemed special, which actors are most remembered. Content analysis helps you tally information and know what to look for as you read the essays. As you analyze, keep a list of:

- scenes mentioned
- actors mentioned
- technical aspects mentioned
- special moments (songs or chases, for example) mentioned

Once you have developed a method of cataloguing these four categories, begin to list the words—adjectives, adverbs, nouns—used in the

My all-time favorite letter arrived during our first season, when we were touring *The Taming of the Shrew.* . . . *After playing one particularly rural school I received the following note which made everything worth it. It was written on a half a piece of yellow legal paper with a ball point pen, no greeting, no capitals, no punctuation, many misspellings, but* what *sincerity. "When i heerd you was gonna do Shakespeare i tried to sneak out but i got caught and im glad i did."*
John S. Benjamin,
artistic director, Theatre Arts of West Virginia, Inc.

descriptions. The *scene* most mentioned in a survey of a large group of young people's essays about a production of *Story Theatre* was "The Robber Bridegroom." The children most typically described this scene as "spooky," "exciting," "scary," and "fun." Because this reaction was the intention of the director, she felt pleased that the children had responded in this way. From the same set of essays, the director found out that one particular *actor* was rarely mentioned or was described unfavorably as "boring," "dumb," or "too creepy." The director then spent some extra time working with this actor.

In a similar manner you can classify the artwork you receive. Pictures can provide a more detailed account of visual response to the production. As you conduct a simple content analysis, you will find out which actors, which scenes, which events, what props and costumes appear in the pictures. Children don't usually draw what is easiest to draw, as adults do, so you will get an idea of what children liked by what they choose to picture. In response to the same production of *Story Theatre,* the fact that many children drew both the onstage band and the actors in the same picture helped verify the director's decision to place the band onstage.

Be aware that many of the young people's work is colored by classroom discussion after the production. Of course, you want to encourage follow-ups of this nature. For the purpose of content analysis, however, you must try to discern and use responses uncolored by such group discussion.

EVALUATING THE PRODUCTION: PARENTS AND TEACHERS

Probably the kind of specific, systematic research we just described would be inappropriate for use with parents and teachers in an analysis of the immediate audience response. Parents and teachers are one person removed from being an audience member. They can tell you how they *perceived* the audience response or how they themselves responded—interesting, but not really what you're trying to discover. Where teachers and parents can be more helpful is in observing the long-term effects of a production. Parents and teachers know their children well. Although they are not "systematic" in their observations, they have a both deeper and broader view of their children and may be able to provide great insight into any lasting effects.

Both the interview and the questionnaire can be useful. Typically, about 40 percent of mailed questionnaires will be returned; so you will need a large sample of parents and teachers. Despite the long time commitment necessary, much valuable information can be gleaned from an interview sample. You may conduct the interviews by telephone, although this is somewhat more difficult. Proceed to develop your interview structure in the manner described in the previous section on interviews.

The last section of this chapter might have been titled "The Director as Researcher." We have tried to teach you how to evaluate your production's intended artistic and educational effect. The ultimate purpose of such an evaluation must always be to make theatre better. One of your goals as "Director as Educator" is to be educated yourself. In these days of accountability and computer technology, no longer can you merely be the "eccentric artiste," making great productions but unable to deal with society.

We cannot predict the future of young people's theatre. Yet we can see the future of educational aids: biofeedback, computer technology, videodiscs, the entire information explosion. You as director may continue to come up with brilliant, original artistic productions. But, if you don't become an active participant in the age of science, you are likely to become victimized by it.

A FINAL WORD

....

In the end I do not distinguish science and art, except as methods. Art is the representation, science the explanation—of the same reality.
Herbert Read,
Education Through Art

....

The Kennedy Center has one of the most respected programs of theatre for young people. How would you describe its relationship to education?

Well, we've always felt first of all that it's important for students to see the very best performances. But we've also felt that too often people take students to a performance without any preparation or without follow-up. Going to the theatre just becomes a field trip without any significance. I feel that if proper preperformance activities and postperformance activities are conducted, the performance will have a much greater impact on the student. Activities give them something to remember, some things to hang their thoughts on.

How should theatre fit into a school curriculum?

Theatre as a performance is more of a culminating activity. A class might discuss the aesthetics in general—you know, the visual and aural impressions. A class may study about the subject of a play they are going to see. The play might be the culmination of a study of Jim Thorpe, in the case of PART's production of *Jim Thorpe, All-American.* It shouldn't be an isolated event in the curriculum. It becomes something to get excited about, something to build toward.

I agree. If theatre can do so much for education, what does education do for theatre?

If you get kids turned on to theatre, you get a new theatregoer, a new subscriber to the theatre. That's the most obvious advantage for a theatre program in the school. There are so many obvious more-or-less commercial advantages. It provides employment for actors, and it provides an outlet for new scripts. It does provide you with an audience that becomes more critical. The more they see, the more critical they can be. You have to be even better in the future.

In "Performance: The Complete Experience," developed at the Kennedy Center, you talk about ways to implement a production. What do you like about the various approaches?

Of course, ideally, using all approaches will give you the best results. Unfortunately, the classroom teacher is not always comfortable with the arts. I suppose that's basically the reason we set up workshops here to help provide teachers with a comfort level. Possibly the least effective is

INTERVIEW

with Jack Kukuk, Director of Education, Kennedy Center

using a study guide with the classroom teacher, unless that teacher has had some experience and some training. I would say maybe the most effective might be to send one of the actors or someone from the production to visit the school. These people can give off an excitement level and an anticipation level to the students and something to key onto after the performance. There are obviously other things that can be used: audio aids, films about theatre, about costuming, any of the aspects of theatre. If their only experience as an audience has been at an athletic event or a Saturday movie, a place where whistling and stomping and cheering is the norm, the children don't know it's different when they go to the theatre. They should be given some indication as to what's expected of them.

What are the qualities of a person who you think should develop these materials?

You can say a person who understands children and basic education approaches and concepts would be best. Very often that person is not the director.

If not the director, who should write these materials? Who are the people who should be involved in this process?

In the performance guide we talk about three different kinds of people. We talk about the artist or director; we talk about the teacher; and we talk about the presenter or the person in between who bridges the gap. One, two, or all three of those people must be involved. There are both artistic and educational objectives.

What's your philosophy at the Kennedy Center about the educational objectives of the arts experience?

Well, number one and primarily, we believe that the quality of the production is the most important, not only the actors and the sets, but the material that's being presented. And one of the most important aspects of our program is the commissioning of new works: the development of new pieces. Over the past years we have developed at least a dozen new pieces for young people. We're interested in encouraging the better artists to perform for young people in a program specifically designed to work within the school situation. We do not want the plays to be isolated incidents in the students' lives. They should be a major activity that has educational value, but the value is enhanced by specific activities that orient and involve the children.

So "enhance" is the key?

Yes. The performance has to stand on its own. We can't say there's no value in taking them to the performance, because we believe the performances are of terrific value. But we feel if you're going to do that much, you might as well go the extra mile and provide activities and set up a situation to increase that value even more.

As director of education, what are some of your goals at the Kennedy Center?

We've established at the Center what we hope is going to be an annual Arts and Aesthetic Education Institute for teachers. And we're hoping that we'll get teachers more involved in aesthetic programs that will affect the students. I would just like to see an artistically literate population.

What can you do besides wait until this new generation of arts-educated kids grows up? I mean, how can you reach these principals and administrators?

The Kennedy Center and a number of other organizations are working on new development of aesthetic education programs through colleges and universities, through teacher in-service programs, teacher and administrator in-service programs. So we're not waiting. It's been happening, and we're finding changes. More and more school systems, even faced with budget cuts, are making across-the-board cuts, rather than just taking the arts and chopping there first. And again, it's because they are beginning to see the value that the arts can have for young people.

I'd like to know what you would like to see happen in the future for theatre for young people.

The obvious answer is I'd like to see more and better theatre for young people. This is the time in their life that they must have the very best. I'd like to see many more and better arts experiences for children in situations that provide the best atmosphere for that.

APPENDIX 1

SCRIPTS (MENTIONED IN THE TEXT) FOR PRODUCTION FOR YOUNG PEOPLE

As explained in the text, categorizing scripts is difficult. Many of the scripts fit in several categories. We have placed these scripts in the following categories more to assist in play selection than to make rigid classifications. Each title is followed by the author's name.

ADVENTURE OR ADVENTURE/JOURNEY

The Arkansaw Bear: Harris
The Blue Bird: Maeterlinck
The Golden Fleece: Cullen
The Great Cross Country Race: Broadhurst
The Haunted Maples: Schwarz
The Hide-and-Seek Odyssey of Madeline Gimple: Gagliano
Marco Polo: Levy
The Marvelous Adventures of Tyl: Levy
Merlin's Tale of King Arthur's Magic Sword: Engar
Noah and the Great Auk: Doughty
The Odyssey: Falls and Beattie
Special Class: Kral
Step on a Crack: Zeder
Wiley and the Hairy Man: Zeder

CLASSICS (WRITTEN ORIGINALLY AS NOVELS)

The authors of various adaptations are listed.

Alice in Wonderland (Carroll): Chorpenning, Gerstenberg, Jackson, Koste, Le Gallienne and Friebus, Manhattan Project, and Miller
A Christmas Carol (Dickens): King, Fields,* Way
Huckleberry Finn (Twain): Whiting
Little Women (Alcott): DeForest, Spencer
Peter Pan† (Barrie): Barrie
Robinson Crusoe (Defoe): Miller
Tom Sawyer (Twain): Adix,* Koste, Schlesinger, Schneider, Spencer
Treasure Island (Stevenson): Goodman, Mason, Way
The Wizard of Oz (Baum): Thane
A Wrinkle in Time (L'Engle): Falls*

There are many unpublished adaptations of classics, as well as the published scripts listed here. Script houses usually publish only one script each for each classic novel. The stars denote unpublished scripts.

†Barrie wrote the play first, then the novel.

347

FAIRY TALES

The authors of various adaptations are listed.

Aladdin: Glennon, Goldberg, Norris
Beauty and the Beast: Brill, Glennon, Gray
Cinderella: Chorpenning
Hansel and Gretel: Chorpenning, Goldberg, Miller
Jack and the Beanstalk: Chorpenning, Goldberg*
Pinocchio: Miller, Way
Sleeping Beauty: Chorpenning, Shaw, Way
The Snow Queen: Margito and Weil
Snow White: Miller, White, and others

There are many unpublished adaptations of fairy tales, as well as the published scripts listed here. As for classic scripts, script houses usually publish only one script each, for each fairy tale. The star denotes an unpublished script.

FANTASIES

The Beeple: Cullen
The Butterfly: Mofid
Five Minutes to Morning: Melwood
The Land of the Dragon: Miller
The Man Who Killed Time: Fauquez
Mooncusser's Daughter: Aiken
The Rabbit Who Wanted Red Wings: McCaslin
Reynard the Fox: Fauquez
The Tingalary Bird: Melwood
Winterthing: Aiken

HISTORY PLAYS

Abe Lincoln of Pigeon Creek: Wilson
Daniel Boone: Babe,* Baptist
Escape to Freedom (Frederick Douglass): Davis
*First Lady** (Eleanor Roosevelt): Bolt
Jim Thorpe, All-American: Levitt
Mean to Be Free (Harriet Tubman): Kraus
*Susan B.!** (Susan B. Anthony): Tasca
*Teddy Roosevelt**: Bolt

The stars denote unpublished scripts commissioned and produced by PART.

ORIGINAL PLAYS DEVELOPED BY THEATRE COMPANIES

Beans: Sheffield Ensemble Theatre (SET)
Car-Makers: Belgrade TIE
Commedia Cartoon: Metro Theatre Circus
Dandelion: Paper Bag Players

Do You Love Me Still?: Metro Theatre Circus
Folktales of the Philippines: Honolulu Theatre for Youth
Home Sweet Home: Belgrade TIE
Ice Station Zero One: Belgrade TIE
Metricks!: Looking Glass Theatre
Mud Weavings: Metro Theatre Circus
Raduz and the Three Clouds: Asolo Touring Theatre
Rare Earth: Belgrade TIE (Methuen, publisher)
Sweetie Pie: Leeds TIE (Methuen, publisher)
Story Theatre: Paul Sills and Company (French, publisher)

All of these scripts, except the three indicated, are unpublished. Some are available from the companies that originated them.

PLAYS BASED ON CLASSIC PLAYS AND LEGENDS

Androcles and the Lion: Harris
The Rude Mechanicals: Graczyk
Scapino: Dunlop and Dale
To Be: Graczyk

PLAYS BY MOLIÈRE

The Doctor in Spite of Himself
The Imaginary Invalid
The Miser
Scapin
Tartuffe

PLAYS BY SHAKESPEARE

As You Like It
The Comedy of Errors
Coriolanus
Hamlet
Julius Caesar
Macbeth
The Merry Wives of Windsor
Midsummer Night's Dream
Much Ado About Nothing
Romeo and Juliet
The Taming of the Shrew
Twelfth Night

PLAYS ORIGINALLY INTENDED FOR ADULT AUDIENCES BUT APPROPRIATE FOR HIGH SCHOOL AUDIENCES

Ah Wilderness!: O'Neill
Cyrano de Bergerac: Rostand

Dracula: Deane and Balderston
The Importance of Being Earnest: Wilde
The Member of the Wedding: McCullers
The Mousetrap: Christie
The Three Sisters: Chekhov
You Can't Take It with You: Kaufman and Hart

MUSICALS FOR FAMILY AUDIENCES

Annie: Charnin and Strouse
The Apple Tree: Bock and Harnick
Cinderella: Rodgers and Hammerstein
Peter Pan: Barrie, Charlap, Leigh
The Pirates of Penzance: Gilbert and Sullivan
Rags to Riches: Harris
The Robber Bridegroom: Uhry and Waldman
The Sound of Music: Rodgers and Hammerstein
Strider: Rozovsky, Kalfin and Brown
West Side Story: Laurents, Bernstein, Robbins
The Wizard of Oz: Gabrielson, Arlen, Harburg

APPENDIX 2

PUBLISHERS OF BOOKS AND PLAYS FOR THEATRE FOR YOUNG PEOPLE

Many of these publishers will send you a complete catalogue on your written request. Some of them sell scripts outright; to some you pay royalties; from some you rent the scripts and scores.

Anchorage Press
Box 8067
New Orleans, LA 70182
(504) 283-8868

Bakers Plays
100 Chauncy St.
Boston, MA 02111
(617) 482-1280

Coach House Press
53 West Jackson Blvd.
Chicago, IL 60604
(312) 922-8993

Contemporary Drama Service
Box 457-FS
Downers Grove, IL 60515
(312) 495-0300

Creative Book Company
8210 Varna Ave.
Van Nuys, CA 91402
(213) 989-2334
  "How-to" books

Drama Book Publishers
821 Broadway
New York, NY 10003
(212) 228-3400

Dramatic Publishing Company
4150 North Milwaukee Ave.
Chicago, IL 60641
(312) 545-2062

Dramatists Play Service, Inc.
440 Park Ave. South
New York, NY 10016
(212) 683-8960

Samuel French, Inc.
25 West 45th St.
New York, NY 10036
(212) 582-4700

Heinemann Educational Books
4 Front St.
Exeter, NH 03833
(603) 778-0534

Methuen, Inc.
733 Third Ave.
New York, NY 10017
(212) 922-3550

Music Theatre International
119 West 57th St.
New York, NY 10019
(212) 975-6841

New Plays, Inc.
Box 273
Rowayton, CT 06853

New Scripts Service
Ed Kessell
Department of Speech and Theatre
St. Louis Community College at Florissant Valley
3400 Pershall Rd.
St. Louis, MO 63135
    An unpublished-plays catalogue is available

On Stage
P.O. Box 25365
Chicago, IL 60625
(312) 275-6836

Pickwick Press
Box 4847
Midland, TX 79701

Pioneer Drama Service
2172 South Colorado Blvd.
P.O. Box 22555
Denver, CO 80222
(303) 759-4297

Players Press, Inc.
P.O. Box 1132
Studio City, CA 91604
(213) 789-4980

Plays, Inc., Publishers
8 Arlington St.
Boston, MA 02116
(617) 536-7420

Playwrights Coop
8 York St.
Toronto, Canada M5J1R2
(416) 363-1581

Rodgers & Hammerstein Library
598 Madison Ave.
New York, NY 10022
(212) 486-7378

Tams–Witmark Music Library
560 Lexington Ave.
New York, NY 10022
(212) 688-2525

Telos Press
Sociology Department
Washington University
St. Louis, MO 63130

APPENDIX 3

THEATRICAL SUPPLIERS

THEATRICAL GENERAL SUPPLIES

General Theatrical Supplies
Alcone Company
575 Eighth Ave.
New York, NY 10018
(212) 594-3980

Norcostco-Atlanta Costume
2089 Monroe Dr., N.E.
Atlanta, GA 30324
(404) 874-7511
Los Angeles: (213) 960-4711
Portland, OR: (503) 222-7368
Dallas: (214) 748-4581
Houston: (713) 734-2189
Minneapolis: (612) 533-2791
Detroit: (313) 961-1713
Fargo, ND: (701) 235-9071
Philadelphia: (215) 923-7737
   Costumes, posters, lighting, makeup, scenery
   hardware

Theatre Service and Supply Corp.
1792 Union Ave.
Baltimore, MD 21211
(301) 467-1225

THEATRICAL BUSINESS SUPPLIES

ATS Ticket Service
375 North Broadway
Jericho, NY 11753
(516) 433-7227

Ed Burnett
Consultants, Inc. (Direct Mail)
2 Park Ave.
New York, NY 10016
(212) 679-0630; (800) 223-7777
   Mailing lists for purchase

Footnotes
F. Randolph Associates, Inc.
1300 Arch St.
Philadelphia, PA 19107
(215) 567-0505
   Posters, books, T-shirts

Market Data Retrieval
Ketchum Pl.
Westport, CT
(203) 226-8941
   Mailing lists for purchase

Marketing Ideas Packet
Texas Opera Theatres, Houston
Jones Hall, 615 Louisiana
Houston, TX 77002
(713) 227-1287
   Excellent marketing suggestions and materials
   from this Texas opera company; ideas readily
   translate into actions for theatre for young
   people

Package Publicity Service
1501 Broadway
New York, NY 10036
(212) 354-1840
  Ready-made promotion for well-known
  productions

Promotion 'N Motion, Ltd.
1619 Broadway
New York, NY 10019
(212) 582-9334
  Ready-made promotional materials, including
  T-shirts

Ticket Craft
1925 Bellmore Ave.
Bellmore, NY 11710
(516) 826-1500; (800) 645-4944
  Advice and actual tickets

COSTUMES

To buy, to rent, or to construct

The Costume Collection
1501 Broadway, Suite 2110
New York, NY 10036
(212) 989-5855
  Available only to not-for-profit organizations

Eaves and Brooks Costume Co.
423 West 55th St.
New York, NY 10019
(212) 757-3730

Foam Crafters
1327 Levee St.
Dallas, TX 75207
(214) 748-2115

Rose Brand Textile Fabrics
517-27 West 35th St.
New York, NY 10001
(212) 594-7424; (800) 223-1624

Rubie's Costume Co.
One Rubie Plaza
Richmond Hill, NY 11418
(212) 846-1008

Universal Costumes
1540 Broadway
New York, NY 10036
(212) 575-8570

Wilshire Foam Products
1240 East 230th St.
Carson, CA 90745
(213) 241-4073

MAKEUP SUPPLIERS

Kabuki Make Up Supplies
Mitsuyoshi Co. Ltd.
3-6-14 Koishikawa Bunkyo
Tokyo 112, Japan

Mehron, Inc.
250 West 40th St.
New York, NY 10018
(212) 997-1011

Ben Nye Makeup
Ben Nye Company
11571 Santa Monica Blvd.
Los Angeles, CA 90025
(213) 477-0443

The M. Stein Cosmetic Co.
Stein's Theatrical Makeup
430 Broome St.
New York, NY 10013
(212) 226-2430

TECHNICAL EQUIPMENT: LIGHTING, SOUND, SCENERY

Berkey Colortran U.S.
1015 Chestnut St.
Burbank, CA 91502
(213) 843-1200

BML Stage Lighting Co., Inc.
P.O. Box 672
James Street Ind. Park
Somerville, NJ 08876
(201) 725-0810

Decor Electronic Products
Theatrical and Architectural Dimming Systems
P.O. Box 606
San Marcos, TX 78666
(512) 392-6041

International Theatre Concepts
13690 Elm Creek Rd.
Osseo, MN 53369
(612) 425-0646
    Portable scenery panels and lighting to convert open space to a theatre space

Olesen
1535 Ivar Ave.
Hollywood, CA 90028
(213) 461-4631

Kliegl Bros.
32-32 48th Ave.
Long Island City, NY 11101
(212) 786-7474

Rosco
36 Bush Ave.
Port Chester, NY 10573
(914) 937-1300
    or
1135 North Highland Ave.
Los Angeles, CA 90038
(213) 462-2233

Skirpan Lighting Control Corporation
61-03 32nd Ave.
Woodside, NY 11377
(212) 274-7222
    or
1155 North LaCienega Blvd.
Los Angeles, CA 90069
(213) 657-6383

Teatronics Incorporated
101-D Suburban Rd.
San Luis Obispo, CA 93401
(805) 544-3555

Tech Theatre Incorporated
4724 Main St.
Lisle, IL 60532
(312) 971-0855

APPENDIX 4
. . . .

SERVICE AGENCIES

Actors' Equity Association (AEA)
165 West 46th St.
New York, NY 10036
(212) 869-8530
    The union for professional actors; the contract under which professional companies for young people work is the TYA (Theatre for Young Audiences) contract; contact Barbara Colton, national first vice president and chairperson, Theatre for Young Audiences Committee

American Council for the Arts (ACA)
570 Seventh Ave.
New York, NY 10018
(212) 354-6655
    A publisher and membership organization and resource for arts information

American Theatre Association
Branch: Children's Theatre Association of
 America
1010 Wisconsin Ave., N.W.
Washington, DC 20007
(202) 342-7530
 A membership organization for students,
 teachers, artists, theatre companies; services
 available: a newsletter, job bank, annual
 August convention

ASSITEJ/USA, Inc.
Association Internationale du Théâtre pour
 l'Enfance et la Jeunesse
c/o Dr. Ann Shaw
42 Riverside Dr.
New York, NY 10024
 ASSITEJ/USA is an international children's
 theatre association; an international conference
 is held every four years; theatre companies
 from the host country and from other
 countries are invited to perform

Association of College,
 University and Community
 Arts Administrators (ACUCAA)
P.O. Box 2137
Madison, WI 53701
(608) 233-7400
 Service organization with excellent
 publications on the nuts and bolts of
 presenting and producing the performing arts

Clearinghouse for Arts Information, Inc.
625 Broadway
New York, NY 10012
(212) 677-7548
 An excellent storehouse of information on the
 arts, through their library and publications and
 through their staff, who can make suggestions
 concerning funding assistance and
 management-assistance organizations;
 newsletter is *For Your Information*

The Foundation Center
888 Seventh Ave.
New York, NY 10106
(212) 975-1120
 The center for research about foundations and
 their giving policies

Foundation for Extension and Development of
 the American Professional Theatre (FEDAPT)
165 West 46th St.
New York, NY 10036
(212) 869-9690
 Agency providing consulting services and
 seminars to not-for-profit professional theatre
 in the U.S.; excellent annual three-day
 conference in management techniques and
 philosophies, held in New York in November

The Grantsmanship Center
1031 South Grand Ave.
Los Angeles, CA 90015
 An excellent agency with published articles
 about fund-raising; very thorough and
 interesting materials

National Endowment for the Arts (NEA)
Washington, D.C. 20506
(202) 634-6313
 Founded in 1965, the federal agency that
 makes grants to deserving not-for-profit
 theatre companies; "theatre for youth" no
 longer exists as a separate category; theatres
 performing for young audiences compete with
 all other theatres; NEA helps to support the 50
 state arts councils, which in turn make grants
 on a local basis to artists, companies, and
 institutions; state arts councils are usually
 located in the state's capital city; a list can be
 purchased from ACA, American Council for
 the Arts

Opportunity Resources for the Arts, Inc. (OR)
1501 Broadway
New York, NY 10036
(212) 575-1688
 Placement service for arts employment for
 organizations and individuals

Theatre Communications Group (TCG)
355 Lexington Ave.
New York, NY 10017
(212) 697-5230
 Communications and service agency for not-
 for-profit professional theatre in the U.S.;
 extensive publications, including *Theatre
 Profiles*, national auditions, *ArtSearch*, a job
 bank, and mailing lists; some services are
 available to nonmembers

Theatre Development Fund (TDF)
1501 Broadway, Suite 2110
New York, NY 10036
(212) 221-0013
   Consultants in development of voucher ticket
   programs and other audience-development
   systems

Theatre Library Association (TLA)
111 Amsterdam Ave.
New York, NY 10023
   A national organization to "further the
   interests of gathering, preserving, and making
   available performing arts resources in all
   forms"

Volunteer Lawyers for the Arts
36 West 44th St., Suite 1110
New York, NY 10036
(212) 575-1150
   A first-class volunteer group designed to assist
   not-for-profit arts groups who cannot afford
   their own lawyers

BIBLIOGRAPHY

CHAPTER 1

Birner, Willam B. *Twenty Plays for Young People.* Anchorage, KY: Anchorage Press, 1967.

Brockett, Oscar G. *The Theatre: An Introduction*, 4th ed. New York: Holt, Rinehart and Winston, 1979.

Chorpenning, Charlotte. *Twenty-one Years with Children's Theatre.* Anchorage, KY: Anchorage Press, 1955.

Corey, Orlin. *Theatre For Children—Kid Stuff, or Theatre?* Anchorage, KY: Anchorage Press, 1974.

Davis, Jed H., and Mary Jane Evans. *Theatre, Children, and Youth.* New Orleans: Anchorage Press, 1982.

Goldberg, Moses. *Children's Theatre: A Philosophy and a Method.* Englewood Cliffs, NJ: Prentice-Hall, 1974.

Koste, Virginia Glasgow. *Dramatic Play in Childhood: Rehearsal for Life.* New Orleans: Anchorage Press, 1978.

Lifton, Betty Jean, ed. *Contemporary Children's Theater.* New York: Avon Books, 1974.

Mackay, Constance D. *How to Produce Children's Plays.* New York: Henry Holt, 1915.

McCaslin, Nellie. *Theatre for Children in the United States: A History.* Norman: University of Oklahoma Press, 1971.

_____, ed. *Theatre for Young Audiences.* New York: Longmans, 1978.

Saint-Denis, Michel. *Theatre: The Rediscovery of Style.* New York: Theatre Arts Books, 1960.

Swortzell, Lowell. *All the World's a Stage.* New York: Delacorte Press, 1972.

Wilson, Edwin. *The Theatre Experience,* 2nd ed. New York: McGraw-Hill, 1980.

CHAPTER 2

Bettelheim, Bruno. *The Uses of Enchantment: The Meaning and Importance of Fairy Tales.* New York: Alfred A. Knopf, 1976.

Clurman, Harold. *On Directing.* New York: Macmillan, 1972.

Cole, Toby, and Helen Krich Chinoy. *Directors on Directing.* New York: Bobbs-Merrill, 1963.

Craig, Edward Gordon. *On the Art of the Theatre.* New York: Theatre Arts Books, 1956.

Dean, Alexander, and Lawrence Carra. *Fundamentals of Play Directing,* 4th ed. New York: Holt, Rinehart and Winston, 1980.

Hodge, Francis. *Play Directing: Analysis, Communication and Style,* 2nd ed. Englewood Cliffs, NJ: Prentice-Hall, 1982.

Morrison, Hugh. *Directing in the Theatre.* London: Pitman and Sons, 1973.

Staub, August W. *Creating Theatre: The Art of Theatrical Directing.* New York: Harper & Row, 1973.

CHAPTER 3

Boleslavsky, Richard. *Acting: The First Six Lessons.* New York: Theatre Arts Books, 1949.

Chekhov, Michael. *To the Actor.* New York: Harper & Row, 1953.

Cohen, Robert. *Acting Power.* Palo Alto, CA: Mayfield, 1978.

Crawford, Jerry L., and Joan Snyder. *Acting in Person and in Style,* 2nd ed. Dubuque, IA: William C. Brown, 1980.

Hagen, Uta, and Haskel Frankel. *Respect for Acting.* New York: Macmillan, 1973.

McGaw, Charles. *Acting Is Believing*, 4th ed. New York: Holt, Rinehart and Winston, 1980.

357

Moore, Sonia. *The Stanislavski System.* New York: Viking Press, 1966.
Stanislavski, Constantin. *An Actor Prepares.* New York: Theatre Arts Books, 1936.
———. *Creating a Role.* New York: Theatre Arts Books, 1961.

CHAPTER 4

Biddle, Bruce J., and Edwin J. Thomas, eds. *Role Theory.* New York: John Wiley, 1966.
Goffman, Erving. *The Presentation of Self in Everyday Life.* Garden City, NY: Doubleday Anchor Books, 1959.
Grotowski, Jerzy. *Towards a Poor Theatre.* New York: Simon and Schuster, 1968.
Elkind, Samuel. *Improvisation Handbook.* Glenview, IL: Scott, Foresman, 1975.
Jung, Carl G. *The Portable Jung.* New York: Penguin Books, 1976.
Lazurus, Arnold. *In the Mind's Eye.* New York: Rawson Associates, 1977.
Linklater, Kristin. *Freeing the Natural Voice.* New York: Drama Book Specialists, 1976.
Machlin, Evangeline. *Speech for the Stage,* 2nd ed. New York: Theatre Arts Books, 1980.
Marowitz, Charles. *The Act of Being: Towards a Theory of Acting.* New York: Taplinger, 1978.
Masters, Robert, and Jean Huston. *Mind Games.* New York: Delta Books, 1979.
Parnes, Sidney J. *Creative Behavior Guidebook.* New York: Charles Scribner's, 1967.
Richardson, Alan. *Mental Imagery.* New York: Springer, 1969.
Spolin, Viola. *Improvisation for the Theatre.* Evanston, IL: Northwestern University Press, 1963.

CHAPTER 5

O'Connor, John, and Lorraine Brown, eds. *Free, Adult, Uncensored: The Living History of the Federal Theatre Project.* Washington: New Republic Books, 1978.
O'Toole, John. *Theatre in Education.* London: Hodder and Stoughton, 1976.
Roose-Evans, James. *Experimental Theatre.* New York: Universe Books, 1973.
Smiley, Sam. *Playwrighting: The Structure of Action.* Englewood Cliffs, NJ: Prentice-Hall, 1971.
Sweet, Jeffrey, ed. *Something Wonderful Right Away.* New York: Avon Books, 1978.
Whitton, Pat, ed. *Participation Theatre for Young Audiences: A Handbook for Directors.* New York: New Plays for Children, 1972.
Wills, J. Robert. *The Director in a Changing Theatre.* Palo Alto, CA: Mayfield, 1976.
Williams, Jay. *Stage Left.* New York: Charles Scribner's, 1974.

CHAPTER 6

Buchman, Herman. *Stage Makeup.* New York: Watson-Guptill, 1971.
Corey, Irene. *The Mask of Reality.* Anchorage, KY: Anchorage Press, 1968.
Corson, Richard. *Stage Makeup,* 5th ed. Englewood Cliffs, NJ: Prentice-Hall, 1975.
Gillette, A. S. *Stage Scenery: Its Construction and Rigging,* 2nd ed. New York: Harper & Row, 1981.
Hill, Margot Hamilton, and Peter A. Bucknell. *The Evolution of Fashion: Pattern and Cut from 1066 to 1930.* New York: Reinhold, 1967.
Ingham, Rosemary, and Elizabeth Covey. *The Costumer's Handbook.* Englewood Cliffs, NJ: Prentice-Hall, 1979.
Jones, Robert Edmond. *The Dramatic Imagination.* New York: Theatre Arts Books, 1941.
Parker, W. Oren, and Harvey K. Smith. *Scene Design and Stage Lighting,* 4th ed. New York: Holt, Rinehart and Winston, 1979.
Pecktal, Lynn. *Designing and Painting for the Theatre.* New York: Holt, Rinehart and Winston, 1975.
Pilbrow, Richard. *Stage Lighting.* New York: Drama Book Specialists, 1979.

Russell, Douglas A. *Stage Costume Design: Theory, Technique and Style.* Englewood Cliffs, NJ: Prentice-Hall, 1973.

———. *Theatrical Style: A Visual Approach to the Theatre.* Palo Alto, CA: Mayfield, 1976.

Welker, David. *Theatrical Set Design,* 2nd ed. Boston: Allyn and Bacon, 1979.

CHAPTER 7

Allensworth, Carl, with Dorothy Allensworth and Clayton Rawson. *The Complete Play Production Handbook.* New York: Thomas Y. Crowell, 1973.

Archer, Stephen M. *How Theatre Happens.* New York: Macmillan, 1978.

Brook, Peter. *The Empty Space: A Book About Theatre.* New York: Atheneum, 1968.

Dolman, John, Jr., and Richard K. Knaub. *The Art of Play Production.* New York: Harper & Row, 1973.

Gassner, John. *Producing the Play,* rev. ed. New York: Holt, Rinehart and Winston, 1953.

Gielgud, John. *Stage Direction.* New York: Theatre Arts Books, 1963, 1979.

Grotowski, Jerzy. *Towards a Poor Theatre.* New York: Simon & Schuster, 1968.

Gruver, Bert. *The Stage Manager's Handbook.* New York: Drama Book Specialists, 1972.

Joseph, Bertram. *A Shakespeare Workbook.* New York: Theatre Arts Books, 1980.

Langley, Stephen, ed. *Producers on Producing.* New York: Drama Book Specialists, 1976.

Marshall, Norman. *The Producers and the Play,* London: Davis Poynter, 1975.

Rossi, Alfred. *Minneapolis Rehearsals: Tyrone Guthrie Directs Hamlet.* Berkeley: University of California Press, 1970.

CHAPTER 8

See Appendix 4 for addresses of organizations.

Arts Advocacy: A Citizen's Action Manual. New York: American Council for the Arts, 1980.

The Foundation Directory. New York: The Foundation Center. Issued biennially.

The Foundation Grants Index. New York: The Foundation Center. Issued annually.

Get Me to the Printer: On Time, On or Under Budget and Looking Good. New York: Off Broadway Theatre Alliance, 1981.

Guide to Corporate Giving in the Arts, 3rd ed. New York: American Council for the Arts, 1983.

Hodgson, Richard S. *Direct Mail and Mail Order Handbook,* 2nd ed. Chicago: Dartnell Press, 1974.

Hummel, Joan. *Starting and Running a Non-Profit Organization.* Minneapolis: University of Minnesota Press, 1981.

Kotler, Philip. *Marketing for Non-Profit Organizations.* Englewood Cliffs, NJ: Prentice-Hall, 1975.

Langley, Stephen. *Theatre Management in America: Principle and Practice,* rev. ed. New York: Drama Book Specialists, 1980.

Morrison, Bradley G., and Kay Fliehr. *In Search of an Audience: How an Audience Was Found for the Tyrone Guthrie Theatre.* New York: Pitman Publishing, 1968.

Nelson, Charles A., and Fredrick J. Turk. *Financial Management for the Arts: A Guidebook for Arts Organizations.* New York: American Council for the Arts, 1975.

Newman, Danny. *Subscribe Now!: Building Arts Audiences Through Dynamic Subscription Promotion.* New York: Theatre Communications Group, 1977.

Raising Money for the Arts: A Conference Report. New York: American Council for the Arts, 1979.

Reiss, Alvin H. *The Arts Management Reader.* New York: Marcel Dekker, Inc., 1979.

Skjei, Eric, and Craig W. Smith. *Getting Grants.* New York: Harper & Row, 1981.

Sloma, Richard S. *No-Nonsense Management: A General Manager's Primer.* New York: Macmillan, 1977.

CHAPTER 9

Anderson, Douglas. *Hub City Touring: Seattle Repertory Theatre on the Road.* Denver: Western States Arts Foundation, 1977.

Barrell, M. Kay. *The Technical Production Hand Book.* Denver: Western States Arts Foundation, 1976.

Broadman, Muriel. *Understanding Your Child's Entertainment.* New York: Harper & Row, 1977.

Cornelison, Gayle, ed. *Directory of Children's Theatre in the United States.* Washington: American Theatre Association, 1980.

Golden, Joseph. *On the Dotted Line: The Anatomy of a Contract.* Edited by Carol T. Jeschke. Syracuse, NY: Cultural Resources Council of Syracuse and Onondaga County, Inc., 1979.

National Endowment for the Arts, Artists in the Schools Program. *Theatre Resources Handbook/Directory.* Washington: 1980.

Oetinger, Janet. Discussion Paper: *Performing Arts Touring and Sponsorship.* Washington: Program Coordinate Office, National Endowment for the Arts, 1979.

Presenting the Performing Arts. Madison, WI: Association of College, University and Community Arts Administrators, 1977.

Tour Organizer's Handbook. Touring Office of the Canadian Council, September, 1977.

Wolf, Thomas. *Presenting Performances.* New York: American Council for the Arts, 1977.

CHAPTER 10

American Council for the Arts in Education: Special Projects Panel. *Coming to Our Senses.* New York: McGraw-Hill, 1977.

Broadman, Muriel. *Understanding Your Child's Entertainment.* New York: Harper & Row, 1977.

Gardner. Howard. *The Arts and Human Development.* New York: John Wiley, 1973.

Gorden, Raymond L. *Interviewing: Strategy, Techniques, and Tactics,* 3rd ed. Homewood, IL: Dorsey, 1980.

Huck, Schuyler, William H. Cormier, and William G. Bounds, Jr. *Reading Statistics and Research.* New York: Harper & Row, 1974.

Ornstein, Robert E. *The Psychology of Consciousness,* 2nd ed. New York: Harcourt Brace Jovanovich, 1977.

Piaget, Jean. *Plays, Dreams, and Imitation in Childhood.* New York: W. W. Norton, 1962.

Redington, Christine. *Can Theatre Teach?* Elmsford, NY: Pergamon Press, 1982.

Spradley, James J. *The Ethnographic Interview.* New York: Holt, Rinehart and Winston, 1979.

INDEX

361

3151